MOSAIK 1

German Language and Culture

VISTA®
HIGHER LEARNING

Boston, Massachusetts

On the cover: Traditional frame houses, Freudenberg, Germany

Publisher: José A. Blanco
Professional Development Director: Norah Lulich Jones
Editorial Development: Brian Contreras, Sharla Zwirek
Project Management: Sally Giangrande
Rights Management: Ashley Dos Santos, Annie Pickert Fuller
Technology Production: Fabián Montoya, Paola Ríos Schaaf, Erica Solari
Design: Radoslav Mateev, Gabriel Noreña, Andrés Vanegas
Production: Manuela Arango, Oscar Díez, Adriana Jaramillo Ch.

Student Text ISBN: 978-1-68005-053-0
Library of Congress Control Number: 2016947899

1 2 3 4 5 6 7 8 9   WC   21 20 19 18 17 16

MOSAIK 1

German Language and Culture

		KONTEXT	FOTOROMAN

KULTUR

STRUKTUREN

WEITER GEHT'S

KONTEXT	FOTOROMAN

KAPITEL 3

Familie und Freunde

KAPITEL 4

Essen

KULTUR

STRUKTUREN

WEITER GEHT'S

The *Fotoroman* Episodes

Fully integrated with your textbook, the **Mosaik Fotoroman** contains 8 dramatic episodes—one for each lesson of the text. The episodes relate the adventures of four students who are studying in Berlin.

The **Fotoroman** dialogues in the printed textbook lesson are an abbreviated version of the dramatic episode featured in the video. Therefore, each **Fotoroman** section can be used as preparation before you view the corresponding video episode, as post-viewing reinforcement, or as a stand-alone section.

As you watch the video, you will see the characters interact using the vocabulary and grammar you are studying. Their conversations incorporate new vocabulary and grammar with previously taught language. At the conclusion of each episode, the **Zusammenfassung** segment summarizes the key language functions and grammar points used in the episode.

The Cast

Learn more about each of the characters you'll meet in **Mosaik Fotoroman**:

George
is from Milwaukee, Wisconsin.
He is studying Architecture.

Meline
is from Vienna.
She is studying Business.

Hans
is from Straubing, in Bavaria.
He studies Political Science and History.

Sabite
is from Berlin.
She studies Art.

About **Zapping TV Clips**

A TV clip from the German-speaking world appears in the first **Lektion** of each **Kapitel**. The purpose of this feature is to expose students to the language and culture contained in authentic media pieces. The following list of the television commercials is organized by **Kapitel.**

Kapitel 1
Deutsche Bahn
(29 seconds)

Kapitel 2
TU Berlin
(1 minute, 15 seconds)

Kapitel 3
Bauer Joghurt
(33 seconds)

Kapitel 4
Yello Strom
(39 seconds)

Ancillaries

- **Student Activities Manual (SAM)**

  The Student Activities Manual consists of three sections: the Workbook, the Video Manual, and the Lab Manual. The Workbook activities provide additional practice of the vocabulary and grammar for each textbook lesson. The Video Manual section includes activities for the **Mosaik Fotoroman**, and the Lab Manual activities focus on building your listening comprehension, speaking, and pronunciation skills in German.

- **Lab Audio MP3s**

  The Lab Audio MP3 files on the Supersite contain the recordings needed to complete the Lab Manual activities in the Student Activities Manual.

- **Textbook Audio MP3s**

  The Textbook Audio MP3 files contain the recordings needed to complete the listening activities in **Kontext**, **Aussprache und Rechtschreibung**, **Hören**, and **Wortschatz** sections. The files are available on the **Mosaik** Supersite.

- **Fotoroman Video**

  All episodes of the **Fotoroman** are available for streaming on the **Mosaik** Supersite.

- **Online Student Activities Manual (WebSAM)**

  Completely integrated with the **Mosaik** Supersite, the WebSAM provides online access to the SAM activities with instant feedback and grading. The complete audio program is online and features record-submit functionality for select activities.

- **Mosaik Supersite**

  The Supersite (**vhlcentral.com**) gives you access to a wide variety of interactive activities for each section of every lesson of the student text, including: auto-graded activities for extra practice with vocabulary, grammar, video, and cultural content; teacher-graded Partner Chat, Virtual Chat, and composition activities; reference tools; the **Zapping** TV commercials; the **Fotoroman** episodic videos; the Textbook Audio MP3 files, the Lab Program MP3 files, and more.

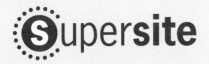

Each section of your textbook comes with activities on the **Mosaik** Supersite, many of which are auto-graded with immediate feedback. Plus, the Supersite is iPad®-friendly*, so it can be accessed on the go! Visit **vhlcentral.com** to explore the wealth of exciting resources.

KONTEXT
- Image-based vocabulary activities with audio
- Additional activities for extra practice
- **Aussprache und Rechtschreibung** presentation followed by record-compare activities
- Textbook activities
- Chat activities for conversational skill-building and oral practice

FOTOROMAN
- Streaming video for all episodes of the **Fotoroman** with teacher-controlled options for subtitles
- Textbook activities
- **Zusammenfassung** section with key vocabulary and grammar from the episode
- Additional activities for extra practice

KULTUR
- Culture reading
- Internet search activity
- Textbook activities
- Additional activities for extra practice

STRUKTUREN
- Grammar presentations
- Chat activities for conversational skill-building and oral practice
- Streaming video of **Zapping** TV clip
- Textbook activities
- Additional activities for extra practice

WEITER GEHT'S
Panorama
- Interactive map with statistics and cultural notes
- Additional activity for extra practice

Im Internet
- Internet search activity
- Textbook activity with auto-grading

Lesen
- Audio-sync reading
- Additional activities for extra practice
- Textbook activities

Hören
- Textbook activities
- Additional activities for extra practice

Schreiben
- Submit your writing assignment online

WORTSCHATZ
- Audio recordings of all vocabulary items
- My Vocabulary to create lists and flashcards

Plus! Also found on the Supersite:

- All textbook and lab audio MP3 files
- Communication center for teacher notifications and feedback
- A single gradebook for all Supersite activities
- WebSAM online Workbook/Video Manual and Lab Manual
- vText online, interactive student edition with access to Supersite activities, audio, and video

*Students must use a computer for audio-recording.

Icons

Familiarize yourself with these icons that appear throughout **Mosaik**.

Online Activities

The mouse icon indicates when an activity is also available on the Supersite.

Pair Activities

Two heads indicate a pair activity.

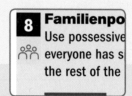

Group Activities

Three heads indicate a group activity.

Recycle

The recycling icon indicates that you will need to use vocabulary and grammar learned in previous lessons.

Partner and Virtual Chat Activities

Two heads with a speech bubble indicate that the activity may be assigned as a Partner Chat or a Virtual Chat activity on the Supersite.

Listening

The listening icon indicates that audio is available on the Supersite.

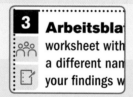

Worksheets

The activities marked with these icons require worksheets that your teacher will provide for you to complete the activity in a group.

Info Gap Activities

Two heads with a puzzle piece indicate an activity which will be done with a partner using a handout your teacher will provide.

Ressourcen

Ressourcen boxes tell you exactly what print and digital resources you can use to reinforce and expand on every section of the textbook lesson with page numbers where applicable.

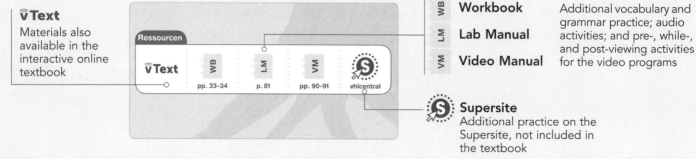

v̂Text

Materials also available in the interactive online textbook

WB Workbook

LM Lab Manual

VM Video Manual

Additional vocabulary and grammar practice; audio activities; and pre-, while-, and post-viewing activities for the video programs

⑤ Supersite

Additional practice on the Supersite, not included in the textbook

Why Learn German?

Explore Your Future

Are you already planning your future career? Employers in today's global economy look for workers who know different languages and understand other cultures. Your knowledge of German will make you a valuable job candidate, especially if you want to work abroad in the European Union.

In addition, studying a foreign language can improve your ability to analyze and interpret information and help you succeed in many other subject areas. When you first begin learning German, your studies will focus mainly on reading, writing, grammar, listening, and speaking skills. Many people who study a foreign language claim that they gained a better understanding of English. German can even help you understand the origins of many English words and expand your own vocabulary in English. Then, when you travel to a German-speaking country, you'll be able to converse freely with the people you meet. You'll find that speaking to people in their native language is the best way to bridge any culture gap.

The German-Speaking World

The German language is spoken primarily in Germany, Austria, and Switzerland and holds official status in Belgium, Liechtenstein, Luxembourg, and the European Union. The United States has the largest German-speaking population outside of Europe. After English and Spanish, German is the third most commonly spoken language in over a dozen states in the nation. After Hispanics, German descendants are the largest ethnic group in the U.S., making up about one third of the German diaspora worldwide.

German culture has a broad historical past dating back more than two thousand years. From Goethe to Mozart and from Gutenberg to Einstein, German language and culture has influenced the spheres of arts and sciences. Today, the German-speaking population has major economic and political importance in the European Union and beyond.

How to Learn German

Start with the Basics

As with anything you want to learn, start with the basics and remember that learning takes time! The basics are vocabulary, grammar, and culture.

Vocabulary | Every new word you learn in German will expand your vocabulary and ability to communicate. The more words you know, the better you can express yourself. Focus on sounds and think about ways to remember words. Use your knowledge of English and other languages to figure out the meaning of and memorize words like **Wasser, Apfel, Buch, Karte,** and **Fisch.**

Grammar | Grammar helps you put your new vocabulary together. By learning the rules of grammar, you can use new words correctly and speak in complete sentences. As you learn verbs and tenses, you will be able to speak about the past, present, or future, express yourself with clarity, and be able to persuade others with your opinions. Pay attention to structures and use your knowledge of English grammar to make connections with German grammar.

Culture | Culture provides you with a framework for what you may say or do. As you learn about the culture of German-speaking communities, you'll improve your knowledge of German. Think about a word like **Kindergarten**, and how it relates to the level of education and who attends it. Think about and explore customs like **die Sternsinger** ("Star Singers" who dress up in costume on Epiphany) and how they are similar to celebrations with which you're familiar. Observe customs—watch people greet each other or say good-bye. Listen for idioms and sayings that capture the spirit of what you want to communicate.

Die Sternsinger in traditional costumes.

Listen, Speak, Read, and Write

Listening | Listen for sounds and for words you can recognize. Listen for inflections and watch for key words that signal a question such as **wie** (*how*), **wo** (*where*), or **was** (*what*). Get used to the sound of German. Play German pop songs or watch German movies. Borrow audiobooks from your local library. Don't worry if you don't understand every single word. If you focus on key words and phrases, you'll get the main idea. The more you listen, the more you'll understand!

Speaking | Practice speaking German as often as you can. As you talk, work on your pronunciation, and read aloud texts so that words and sentences flow more easily. Don't worry if you don't sound like a native speaker, or if you make some mistakes. Time and practice will help you get there. Participate actively in German class. Try to speak German with classmates, especially native speakers (if you know any), as often as you can.

Reading | Read the lyrics of a song as you listen to it, or read books you've already read in English translated into German. Use reading strategies that you know to understand the meaning of a text that looks unfamiliar. Look for cognates, or words that are related in English and German, to guess the meaning of some words. Read as often as you can, and remember to read for fun.

Writing | German has standardized and largely phonetic rules for spelling. You'll need to learn how to interpret the sounds of the German language, but once you do, you can become a proficient speller. Write for fun—make up poems or songs, write e-mails or instant messages to friends, or start a journal or blog in German.

Tips for Learning German

- Listen to German radio shows. Write down words that you can't recognize or don't know and look up the meaning.

- Watch German TV shows or movies. Read subtitles to help you grasp the content.

- Read German-language newspapers, magazines, or blogs.

- Listen to German songs that you like —anything from contemporary pop music to traditional **Volksmusik**. Sing along and concentrate on your pronunciation.

Beatrice Egli, Swiss pop singer

- Seek out German speakers. Look for cultural centers where German might be spoken in your community. Order from a menu at a Viennese restaurant in German.

- Pursue language exchange opportunities (**Schüleraustausch**) in your school or community. Join language clubs or cultural societies, and explore opportunities for studying abroad or hosting a student from a German-speaking country in your home or school.

Practice, practice, practice!

Seize every opportunity you find to listen, speak, read, or write German. Think of it like a sport or learning a musical instrument—the more you practice, the more you will become comfortable with the language and how it works. You'll marvel at how quickly you can begin speaking German and how the world that it transports you to can change your life forever.

- Connect your learning to everyday experiences. Research naming the ingredients of your favorite dish in German. Research the origins of German place names in the U.S., like Anaheim, California and Bismarck, North Dakota, or of common English words like *pretzel, hamster, pumpernickel, rucksack, waltz, dachshund, glitz,* and *strudel.*

- Use mnemonics, or a memorizing device, to help you remember words. Make up a saying in English to remember the order of the days of the week in German by using their abbreviations (Mo, Di, Mi, Do, Fr, Sa, So).

- Visualize words. Try to associate words with images to help you remember meanings. For example, think of different sorts of **Wurst** as you learn the names of different types of meat. Visualize a national park and create mental pictures of the landscape as you learn names of animals, plants, and habitats.

- Enjoy yourself! Try to have as much fun as you can learning German. Take your knowledge beyond the classroom and find ways to make the learning experience your own.

Hallo! Wie geht's?

Communicative Goals

You will learn how to:

- greet people and say good-bye
- make introductions
- use polite expressions

Wie geht's?

MICHAEL Guten Tag, Herr Brenner, wie geht es Ihnen?
HERR BRENNER Hallo, Michael! Es geht mir ziemlich gut. Und dir?
MICHAEL Mir auch, danke.

PAUL Vielen Dank!
JOHANNES Bitte!

MARIA Bis später, Lukas!
LUKAS Tschüss, Maria. Bis bald!

CHRISTOPH Guten Tag, Herr Arnold. Das ist Christina Schöller.
HERR ARNOLD Guten Tag, Frau Schöller!
CHRISTINA Freut mich.

Vocabulary Tools

Wortschatz

Begrüßung und Abschied	*hellos and good-byes*
Guten Morgen.	*Good morning.*
Guten Abend.	*Good evening.*
Gute Nacht.	*Good night.*
Bis dann.	*See you later.*
Bis gleich.	*See you soon.*
Bis morgen.	*See you tomorrow.*
Auf Wiedersehen.	*Good-bye.*
Schönen Tag noch!	*Have a nice day!*
Prima.	*Great.*
Es geht.	*So-so.*
(Nicht) schlecht.	*(Not) bad.*
Mir geht's nicht (so) gut.	*I'm not (so) well.*
Höflichkeiten	***polite expressions***
Gern geschehen.	*My pleasure.*
Entschuldigung.	*Excuse me.*
Entschuldigen Sie.	*Excuse me. (form.)*
Es tut mir leid.	*I'm sorry.*
ja	*yes*
nein	*no*
sich vorstellen	***introducing oneself***
Wie heißen Sie?	*What is your name? (form.)*
Schön dich/Sie kennen zu lernen.	*Nice to meet you. (inf./form.)*
Personen	***people***
die Frau	*woman*
der Freund / die Freundin	*friend (m./f.)*
der Junge	*boy*
das Mädchen	*girl*
der Mann	*man*
Herr	*Mr.*
Frau	*Mrs.; Ms.*
wo?	***where?***
hier	*here*
da/dort	*there*

Ressourcen

 v̂Text
 WB pp. 1–2
 LM p. 61
 vhlcentral

Anwendung

ACHTUNG

There are formal and informal ways of saying *you* in German. Use **du** and its plural, **ihr**, in informal address; use **Sie** in formal situations.

MARKUS Guten Tag, ich heiße Markus. Und du? Wie heißt du?
ANNA Ich heiße Anna.
MARKUS Angenehm, Anna.

SOFIA Guten Tag, Katrin!
KATRIN Hallo, Sofia!
SOFIA Wie geht's?
KATRIN Mir geht's gut, danke! Und wie geht es dir? Alles klar?
SOFIA Sehr gut, danke!

---

1 **Was passt?** Put these expressions into the correct categories.

Bitte!	die Frau	der Mann
Danke.	der Freund	Tschüss!
Entschuldigung.	Guten Tag!	Wie geht's?

Polite expressions	People	Hellos and good-byes
_____	_____	_____
_____	_____	_____
_____	_____	_____

---

2 **Was fehlt?** Complete each conversation with the appropriate word.

1. —_____ Dank!
   —_____ geschehen!
2. —Guten Morgen. Ich _____ Daniel.
   —Guten _____, Daniel.
3. —Hallo, Lina! _____ geht's?
   —_____ gut.
4. —Auf _____, Frau Stein. Schönen Tag noch!
   —_____.
5. —Hallo, David! Das _____ Lara.
   —Hallo, Lara! Schön, dich _____ zu lernen!
6. —Guten Abend, Herr Klein. Wie geht es _____?
   —Hallo, Tom. Es geht _____ gut, danke. Und dir?

---

3 **Kurze Gespräche** Listen to the conversations and decide whether each conversation is **höflich** (*formal*) or **vertraulich** (*informal*).

	höflich	vertraulich
1.	☐	☐
2.	☐	☐
3.	☐	☐
4.	☐	☐
5.	☐	☐
6.	☐	☐

---

4 **Antworten Sie** Provide an appropriate response to each question or statement you hear.

1. _____
2. _____
3. _____
4. _____
5. _____
6. _____

 Practice more at **vhlcentral.com**.

Kommunikation

5 Minidialoge
With a partner, select the response that best completes each conversation, then role-play the mini-dialogues.

1. —Guten Tag, Frau Meier!
   a. —Hallo, Frau Schneider!   b. —Nicht schlecht.
2. —Danke, Sabine.
   a. —Bitte.   b. —Bis bald!
3. —Auf Wiedersehen!
   a. —Prima.   b. —Tschüss!
4. —Wie heißen Sie?
   a. —Ich heiße Paul.   b. —Vielen Dank.
5. —Wie geht es Ihnen, Herr Huber?
   a. —Bis dann.   b. —Danke, gut.
6. —Ich heiße Anka.
   a. —Freut mich.   b. —Entschuldigung.
7. —Gute Nacht, Lara. Bis morgen.
   a. —Ja, bis dann.   b. —Freut mich.
8. —Guten Tag, Herr Melchior. Das ist mein Freund.
   a. —Gern geschehen.   b. —Angenehm.

6 Begrüßungen
In small groups, look at the illustrations, then act out a short dialogue in which the people greet each other, ask each other's names, and ask each other how they are. Pay attention to the use of **du** and **Sie**.

1. Professor Fink

2. Frau Sperber

3. Anja

4. Franz

7 Diskutieren und kombinieren
Your instructor will give you and a partner worksheets with descriptions of five people. Use the information from your worksheet to introduce yourself and talk about how you are. Role-play each of the five people on your worksheet.

BEISPIEL

S1: Hallo, ich heiße Martin. Und du?
S2: Hallo, ich heiße Sandra. Wie geht's?
S1: Ziemlich gut. Und dir?

8 Kennen lernen
In groups of three, introduce yourself and ask your partners how they are. Then introduce your partners to the members of another group.

BEISPIEL

S1: Hallo, ich heiße Sina. Und wie heißt du?
S2: Ich heiße Katja. Hallo, Sina.
S1: Und wie geht's dir?
S2: Prima, danke. Und wie geht's dir?
S1: Ziemlich gut. Katja, das hier ist Thomas.
S3: Hallo, Katja. Schön dich kennen zu lernen.

Aussprache und Rechtschreibung

 Audio

The German alphabet

The German alphabet is made up of the same 26 letters as the English alphabet. Although the alphabet is the same, many of the letters (**Buchstaben**) are pronounced differently.

Buchstabe	Beispiel	Buchstabe	Beispiel	Buchstabe	Beispiel
a (ah)	**A**bend	i (ih)	**I**dee	r (err)	**R**egen
b (beh)	**B**utter	j (yot)	**j**a	s (ess)	**s**ingen
c (tseh)	**C**elsius, **C**afé	k (kah)	**K**atze	t (teh)	**t**anzen
		l (ell)	**l**esen	u (ooh)	**U**niversität
d (deh)	**d**anke	m (emm)	**M**utter	v (fau)	**V**ogel, **V**ase
e (eh)	**E**lefant	n (enn)	**N**ase	w (veh)	**W**asser
f (eff)	**f**inden	o (oh)	**O**per	x (iks)	**X**ylophon
g (geh)	**g**ut	p (peh)	**P**apier	y (üpsilon)	**Y**acht, T**y**p
h (hah)	**h**allo	q (koo)	**Q**uatsch	z (tset)	**Z**elt

The symbol **ß** (**Eszett** or **scharfes s**) is used instead of a double **s** in certain words. **Eszett** is never used at the beginning of a word. It is capitalized as **SS**.

ß (Eszett, scharfes S)   Stra**ß**e (*street*)

An **Umlaut** (¨) can be added to the vowels **a**, **o**, and **u**, changing their pronunciation.

a	**A**pfel	ä (a-Umlaut)	**Ä**pfel
o	**O**fen	ö (o-Umlaut)	**Ö**fen
u	**M**utter	ü (u-Umlaut)	**M**ütter

In German, all nouns are capitalized, no matter where they appear in a sentence. When spelling aloud, say **großes a** for *capital a*, or **kleines a** for *lowercase a*. To ask how a word is spelled, say: **Wie schreibt man das?** (lit. *How does one write this?*)

1 **Aussprechen** Practice saying the German alphabet and sample words aloud.

2 **Buchstabieren** Spell these words aloud in German.

1. hallo	4. Explosion	7. Bäcker	10. Frühling
2. Morgen	5. typisch	8. Straße	11. tanzen
3. studieren	6. Universität	9. Juwelen	12. Querflöte

3 **Sprichwörter** Practice reading these sayings aloud.

Wer A sagt, muss auch B sagen.[1]

Übung macht den Meister.[2]

[1] You have to finish what you've started. (lit. *Whoever says A must also say B.*)

[2] Practice makes perfect.

Willkommen in Berlin! Video

Meline und George kommen nach Berlin. Hier treffen sie Sabite und Hans.
Ist es eine freundliche Begrüßung (friendly welcome)?

MELINE (am Telefon) Lukas... ah, Kreuzberg, okay. Lukas...

SABITE Hallo?
GEORGE Hallo. Ich bin George. Wie heißt du?
SABITE Ich heiße Sabite. Nett dich kennen zu lernen.
GEORGE Nett dich kennen zu lernen, Sabite.

SABITE Alles in Ordnung?
GEORGE Hier sind die Schlüssel. Danke, vielen Dank.
SABITE Gern geschehen. Keine Ursache. Bis später.

GEORGE *Talk to you later.*
Auf Wiederhören.

HANS Entschuldigung. Was für ein Chaos! Hier ist die Bürste... und der Lippenstift. Und hier ist das Handy.
MELINE (am Telefon) Tschüss, Lukas.

HANS Ich heiße Hans. Schönen Tag!

---

1 **Richtig oder falsch?** Choose whether each statement is **richtig** (true) or **falsch** (false).

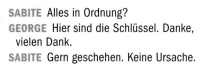 1. Sabite hilft (helps) Hans.

2. Meline ist am Flughafen (airport).

3. George hat (has) die Schlüssel.

4. Meline telefoniert mit (calls) Lukas.

5. George trifft (meets) Sabite.

6. Hans geht es ganz okay.

7. Meline geht nach (is going to) Kreuzberg.

8. Meline hat eine Bürste, einen Lippenstift und ein Handy.

9. Sabite geht es gut.

10. Hans sagt: „Willkommen in München."

7

MELINE Ich bin's, Meline.
SABITE Meline, hallo. Nett dich kennen zu lernen.
MELINE Freut mich. Wie geht es dir?
SABITE Mir geht es gut.

8

SABITE Oh, das ist George. Hallo, George. Das ist Meline. Meline, George.
GEORGE Hallo.
MELINE Nett dich kennen zu lernen.
GEORGE Freut mich.

9

HANS George?
GEORGE Ja!
HANS Hallo! Ich bin Hans. Willkommen in Deutschland. Nett dich kennen zu lernen. Wie geht's?
GEORGE Ganz okay.

10

GEORGE Das ist Sabite.
SABITE Hallo.
HANS Hi.

Nützliche Ausdrücke

- **Wie heißt du?**
  What's your name?
- **Nett dich kennen zu lernen.**
  Nice to meet you.
- **Ist jemand da?**
  Anyone there?
- **Keine Ursache.**
  Don't mention it.
- **Auf Wiederhören.**
  Talk to you later.
- **Was für ein Chaos!**
  What a mess!
- **der Lippenstift**
  lipstick
- **das Handy**
  cell phone
- **Freut mich.**
  It's a pleasure.
- **Willkommen in Deutschland.**
  Welcome to Germany.

1A.1
- **Hier ist die Bürste.**
  Here's the brush.

1A.2
- **Hier sind die Schlüssel.**
  Here are the keys.

1A.3
- **Ich bin George.**
  I'm George.

---

 2 **Zum Besprechen** Imagine that you and your partner are exchange students meeting for the first time. Greet each other, give your names, and be sure to include an appropriate goodbye. Be prepared to present your conversation to the class.

3 **Vertiefung** Germany's tallest structure is the television tower (**Fernsehturm**) in Berlin. Use the Internet to find its nicknames in German.

Hallo, Deutschland! Reading

SAYING "HELLO" CAN BE A COMPLEX social interaction. Should you shake hands? Kiss cheeks? Keep your distance? The answers depend on where you are, who you are, and who you're talking to.

In general, Germans shake hands more than Americans do, and eye contact is an important feature of this gesture. If you've just been introduced to someone, shake hands, look them in the eye, and say **Freut mich**. In a business setting, a handshake is more or less obligatory, but friends may or may not shake hands when greeting. As in North America, friends in Germany, Austria, and Switzerland can often be seen greeting each other with a hug or a kiss on the cheek.

Greetings vary depending on time of day, level of formality, and region. In formal situations, you can say **Guten Morgen** in the morning, **Guten Tag** from morning to late afternoon, and **Guten Abend** in the evening. In Bavaria or Austria, you are likely to hear **Grüß Gott°** at any time of day. **Hallo**, **Tag**, and **Grüß dich°** are all common informal greetings. In Bavaria, use **Servus°** to say hello or goodbye to friends.

Deciding between informal and polite forms of address requires some judgment. In general, use the familiar forms **du** and **ihr** with children, teenagers, family members, and fellow

students. Use the polite form **Sie** with anyone else until they invite you to call them **du**. Always use **Sie** with people with whom you are not on a first-name basis. Address men as **Herr** and women as **Frau**, regardless of their marital status.

Grüß Gott Hello. (lit. Greet God) **Grüß dich** Hello. (lit. Greet you (inf.)) **Servus** Hello; Good-bye (inf.)

---

1 **Richtig oder falsch?** Indicate whether each statement is **richtig** (*true*) or **falsch** (*false*). Correct any false statements.

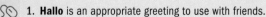

1. **Hallo** is an appropriate greeting to use with friends.
2. When meeting someone new, shake hands and say **Freut mich**.
3. You should always use **Sie** with other students.
4. You should shake hands to greet business partners.
5. German friends often greet each other with a hug.

6. **Guten Abend** is an appropriate way to greet your boss in the morning.
7. You are more likely to hear **Grüß Gott** in Austria than in Berlin.
8. **Du** is used to address adults you don't know.
9. It is appropriate to address children with **du**.
10. When you are not sure whether to use **Sie** or **du**, you should follow the lead of the other person.

 Practice more at **vhlcentral.com**.

Wie geht's?

Geht's dir gut?	*Are you all right? (inf.)*
Und dir?	*And you? (inf.)*
Geht es Ihnen gut?	*Are you all right? (form.)*
Und Ihnen?	*And you? (form.)*
So weit, so gut.	*So far, so good.*
Spitze!	*Great!*
Schön dich zu sehen.	*Nice to see you. (inf.)*
Schön Sie zu sehen.	*Nice to see you. (form.)*
Herzlich willkommen.	*Welcome.*
Was geht?	*What's up?*

Auf Wiedersehen, Goodbye

One characteristic feature of the German language is its wealth of regional differences. Many dialects have their own greetings, from **Moin Moin** along the North Sea Coast to Switzerland's **Grüezi mitenand**. But how do German speakers say good-bye?

- **Auf Wiedersehen** and **tschüss** are the most standard good-byes.
- The formal Swiss counterpart is **Uf Widerluege.**
- The informal **Mach's gut** is similar in meaning to *Take care.*
- In Baden-Württemberg and the Saarland, **Ade** is common.
- In Austria, **Pfiati** is often used among friends.

Das Brandenburger Tor°

On December 22, 1989, thousands cheered as West German Chancellor Helmut Kohl walked through the Brandenburg Gate to shake hands with East German Prime Minister Hans Modrow. It was the first time since the construction of the **Berliner Mauer°** in 1961 that East and West Germans had been permitted to pass through the gate.

Built in 1791, the **Brandenburger Tor** was one of fourteen toll gates that encircled the city. Over the next two centuries, the **Tor** withstood an invasion by Napoleon's soldiers, falling bombs in World War II, and the Cold War partition of East and West Germany. Today, the **Tor** is one of Berlin's most popular attractions, a symbol of German unity, and a monument to Berlin's tumultuous past.

Tor *Gate* **Berliner Mauer** *Berlin Wall*

🔗 IM INTERNET

Fashionably late isn't always fashionable. How do German and American manners differ when it comes to punctuality, greetings, and formality?

Find out more at **vhlcentral.com**.

---

2 **Was haben Sie gelernt?** Answer the questions.

1. How would you say good-bye to a friend or fellow student in a German-speaking country? List three options.
2. What did Germans celebrate at the Brandenburg Gate in 1989?
3. Name some historical events that occurred near the Brandenburg Gate.
4. What does the Brandenburg Gate now symbolize?

3 **Sie sind dran** In pairs, practice meeting and greeting people in these situations.

1. It's 10 a.m. and you run into your German professor at the grocery store. What do you say?
2. Now you're purchasing your groceries. How do you say "hello" and "good-bye" to the cashier?
3. Just as you're leaving the store, you run into an old friend. Say "hi" and ask how your friend is doing.

1A.1 Gender, articles, and nouns  Presentation

Startblock Like English nouns, German nouns can be either singular or plural and may be preceded by a definite or indefinite article. Unlike English nouns, all German nouns have a gender. German nouns are always capitalized, regardless of where they appear in a sentence.

Was für **ein Chaos**!

Hier ist **die Bürste**. Hier ist **das Handy**.

Gender

- All German nouns have a gender: masculine, feminine, or neuter. While most nouns referring to males are masculine and most nouns referring to females are feminine, the genders of nouns representing objects and ideas need to be memorized.

MASCULINE	FEMININE	NEUTER
der **Mann**	die **Frau**	das **Buch**
*the **man***	*the **woman***	*the **book***
der **Junge**	die **Blume**	das **Mädchen**
*the **boy***	*the **flower***	*the **girl***

ACHTUNG

Nouns ending with **-chen** are always neuter.

- Nouns ending with **-in** that refer to people are always feminine.

die Freund**in**	die Schüler**in**	die Professor**in**
*the (**female**) friend*	*the (**female**) student*	*the (**female**) professor*

- Other feminine noun endings include -**ei**, -**heit**, -**schaft**, -**ung**, and -**tät**.

die **Bäckerei**	die **Freundschaft**	die **Universität**
*the **bakery***	*the **friendship***	*the **university***

Definite and indefinite articles

- The definite article, equivalent to *the* in English, precedes a noun and indicates its gender. The masculine article is **der**, the feminine article is **die**, and the neuter article is **das**.

MASCULINE	FEMININE	NEUTER
der **Tisch**	die **Tür**	das **Fenster**
***the** table*	***the** door*	***the** window*

QUERVERWEIS

You will learn more about forming plurals in **1A.2**.

- The definite article **die** is used with all plural nouns, regardless of gender.

	SINGULAR		PLURAL	
MASCULINE	**der** Tisch		**die** Tische	*the tables*
FEMININE	**die** Tür		**die** Türen	*the doors*
NEUTER	**das** Fenster		**die** Fenster	*the windows*

- The indefinite article **ein(e)** corresponds to *a* or *an* in English. It precedes the noun and matches its gender. Note that both masculine and neuter nouns take the form **ein**, while feminine nouns take **eine**.

MASCULINE	FEMININE	NEUTER
ein Tisch	**eine** Tür	**ein** Fenster
a table	*a door*	*a window*
ein Mann	**eine** Frau	**ein** Mädchen
a man	*a woman*	*a girl*

- There is no plural form of the indefinite article.

Er ist **ein Mann**.   ▶   Sie sind **Männer**.
*He is **a man**.*   *They are **men**.*

Compound nouns

- Compound words are very common in German. As in English, two or more simple nouns can be combined to form a compound noun.

die Nacht   +   das Hemd   =   **das Nachthemd**
night   *shirt*   *nightshirt*

Hier ist **der Lippenstift**.

- The gender and number of a compound noun is determined by the last noun in the compound.

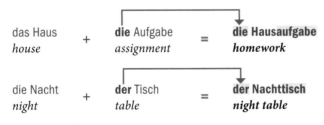

das Haus   +   **die** Aufgabe   =   **die Hausaufgabe**
house   *assignment*   *homework*

die Nacht   +   **der** Tisch   =   **der Nachttisch**
night   *table*   *night table*

Ressourcen

v̂ **Text**

WB
pp. 3–4

LM
p. 63

Ⓢ
vhlcentral

Jetzt sind Sie dran!   Indicate the gender of each noun: **Maskulinum**, **Femininum**, or **Neutrum**.

	Maskulinum	Femininum	Neutrum			Maskulinum	Femininum	Neutrum
1. der Mann	☑	☐	☐		7. eine Frau	☐	☐	☐
2. die Freundin	☐	☐	☐		8. ein Mädchen	☐	☐	☐
3. der Junge	☐	☐	☐		9. ein Tisch	☐	☐	☐
4. das Hemd	☐	☐	☐		10. eine Nacht	☐	☐	☐
5. die Aufgabe	☐	☐	☐		11. die Universität	☐	☐	☐
6. ein Freund	☐	☐	☐		12. ein Buch	☐	☐	☐

Anwendung

1 Was fehlt? Write the appropriate article.

der, die, das   **ein, eine**

1. _____ Fenster   5. _____ Frau
2. _____ Tisch   6. _____ Tür
3. _____ Student   7. _____ Mann
4. _____ Freundschaft   8. _____ Mädchen

2 Ergänzen Sie Write each noun in the appropriate column. Include the definite and indefinite article.

Bäckerei	Haus
Buch	Hemd
Freund	Junge
Freundin	Schülerin

Maskulinum	Femininum	Neutrum
der Mann; ein Mann		

3 Sätze Complete each sentence with the appropriate definite or indefinite article.

1. _____ Junge heißt Paul.   4. _____ Buch ist prima!
2. Wie heißt _____ Lehrerin?   5. _____ Türen sind hier.
3. Jasmin ist _____ Mädchen.   6. Lara ist _____ gute Studentin.

4 Bilden Sie Wörter Write the compound word with the appropriate definite article.

BEISPIEL

das Haus + die Aufgabe =
die Hausaufgabe

1. die Kinder + der Garten
= _____

2. der Schlaf (*sleep*) +
das Zimmer (*room*) =
_____

3. das Telefon +
die Nummer =
_____

4. der Computer +
das Spiel (*game*) =
_____

 Practice more at **vhlcentral.com**.

Kommunikation

5 **Was ist das?** In pairs, take turns identifying each person or object. Provide both the definite and indefinite articles.

▶ **BEISPIEL**
S1: der Junge
S2: ein Junge

1.

2.

3.

4.

5.

6.

6 **Was passt zusammen?** In pairs, take turns creating compound nouns using words from the list. Write down each compound noun with the appropriate article.

der Schlüssel

der Ring

▶ **BEISPIEL**
S1: der Schlüssel / der Ring
S2: der Schlüsselring

die Hand

der Schuh

die Nacht

der Bus

das Haus

die Katze

das Eis

der Bär

7 **Was zeichne ich?** In small groups, take turns drawing pictures of nouns you've learned so far, for your partners to guess. The person who guesses correctly is the next to draw. Don't forget the article!

8 **Gedächtnisspiel** Play a memory game. The first player says a noun with the appropriate definite or indefinite article, and the next player repeats the previous noun and says his or her own. Go around the class until someone forgets an item or uses the wrong article. That player starts the next round.

1A.2 Plurals  Presentation

Startblock Plurals in German follow several patterns. These patterns can help you remember the plural form of each noun you learn.

ACHTUNG

The best way to be sure of a noun's plural form is to memorize it when you learn the singular form. Being familiar with the patterns of plural formation can make this process easier.

- In German dictionaries and vocabulary lists, singular nouns are listed along with a notation that indicates how to form the plural. There are five main patterns for forming plural nouns.

notation	singular	plural
- ¨	das Fenster ⟶ die Mutter (*mother*) ⟶	die Fenster die Mütter
-e ¨e	der Freund ⟶ der Stuhl (*chair*) ⟶	die Freunde die Stühle
-er ¨er	das Kind (*child*) ⟶ der Mann ⟶	die Kinder die Männer
-n -en -nen	der Junge ⟶ die Frau ⟶ die Freundin ⟶	die Jungen die Frauen die Freundinnen
-s	der Park ⟶	die Parks

ACHTUNG

Two plurals that do not follow the standard pattern for feminine nouns are **die Mütter**, plural of **Mutter**, and **die Töchter** (*daughters*), plural of **Tochter**.

- Most masculine and neuter nouns form the plural by adding -e or -er. Plurals with the -er ending always add an **Umlaut** when the vowel in the singular form is **a**, **o**, or **u**.

  der Tag (*day*) ⟶ die Tage   das Buch ⟶ die Bücher

- If the singular form of a noun ends in -el, -en, or -er, there is no additional plural ending, but an **Umlaut** is added to the stem vowel **a**, **o**, or **u**.

  der Apf**el** (*apple*) ⟶ die Äpf**el**   das Zimm**er** (*room*) ⟶ die Zimm**er**

- For feminine nouns ending with -in, add -nen to form the plural.

  die Freund**in** ⟶ die Freund**innen**   die Schüler**in** ⟶ die Schüler**innen**

- For most other feminine nouns, add -n if the singular form ends in -e, -el, or -er. Add -en if it does not. Note that feminine plurals with these endings never add an **Umlaut**.

  die Blum**e** (*flower*) ⟶ die Blum**en**   die Frau ⟶ die Frau**en**

- The -s ending is added to most words borrowed from other languages and to most nouns ending with vowels other than e.

  das Sofa ⟶ die Sofa**s**   das Auto ⟶ die Auto**s**

Ressourcen

v̂Text

WB
pp. 5–6

LM
p. 64

vhlcentral

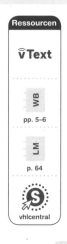

Jetzt sind Sie dran!

Write the plural form of each singular noun and vice versa.

Singular

1. das Café _die Cafés_
2. die Schülerin _____
3. der Stuhl _____
4. die Tochter _____

Plural

5. die Zimmer _das Zimmer_
6. die Universitäten _____
7. die Äpfel _____
8. die Schüler _____

Anwendung und Kommunikation

1 Schreiben Write the plural form.

1. das Buch _____
2. der Mann _____
3. der Tag _____
4. die Blume _____
5. die Mutter _____

6. das Auto _____
7. der Junge _____
8. die Tür _____
9. das Kind _____
10. der Park _____

2 Plural Complete each sentence with the plural form of the appropriate word.

BEISPIEL Holiday Inn und Marriott sind ____Hotels____.

Apfel	Buch	Freundin
Auto	Computer	Hotel
Blume	Freund	Tag

1. BMW und Volkswagen sind _____.
2. Rosen und Tulpen (*tulips*) sind _____.
3. Dell, HP und Acer sind _____.
4. Granny Smith und Macintosh sind _____.
5. Eine Woche (*week*) hat sieben (*seven*) _____.
6. Anna, Monika und Emma sind _____.
7. *Harry Potter* und *Sag mal* sind _____.
8. Lukas und Felix sind _____.

3 Was ist das? In pairs, take turns identifying each object, place, or person. Give both singular and plural forms.

▶ **BEISPIEL**
S1: *die Blume*
S2: *die Blumen*

1.

2.

3.

4.

5.

6.

7.

Practice more at **vhlcentral.com**.

1A.3 Subject pronouns, *sein*, and the nominative case

 Lukas, **du bist**...

 **Ich bin** George.

Subject pronouns

- In German, as in English, any noun can be replaced with an equivalent pronoun. A subject pronoun replaces a noun that functions as the subject of a sentence.

Maria ist nett.   **Sie** ist nett.   **Der Junge** ist groß.   **Er** ist groß.
Maria is nice.   *She is nice.*   *The boy is tall.*   *He is tall.*

subject pronouns		singular		plural	
1st person		ich	*I*	wir	*we*
2nd person		du	*you* (inf.)	ihr	*you* (inf.)
		Sie	*you* (form.)	Sie	*you* (form.)
3rd person		er	*he/it*	sie	*they*
		sie	*she/it*		
		es	*it*		

- The gender of a noun determines the gender of the pronoun that replaces it. German uses **er** for all masculine nouns, **sie** for all feminine nouns, and **es** for all neuter nouns.

Der Tisch ist klein. ▶ **Er** ist klein.   **Das Buch** ist neu. ▶ **Es** ist neu.
The table is small. *It's small.*   *The book is new.* *It's new.*

- The pronoun **Sie/sie** can mean *you, she, it,* or *they,* depending on context. Write **Sie** with a capital **S** to mean *you* in a formal context, and **sie** with a lowercase **s** to mean *she, it,* or *they.*

Das ist Frau Hansen. **Sie** ist Lehrerin.
*That's Mrs. Hansen. **She** is a teacher.*

Das sind Lara und Jonas. **Sie** sind Schüler.
*That's Lara and Jonas. **They're** students.*

Woher kommen **Sie**?
*Where are **you** from?*

QUERVERWEIS

German speakers often use the third-person singular pronoun **man** where English speakers would say *one* or *you.*

The verb *sein*

- **Sein** (*To be*) is an irregular verb: its conjugation does not follow a predictable pattern.

sein (*to be*)			
singular		**plural**	
ich **bin**	*I am*	wir **sind**	*we are*
du **bist**	*you are* (inf.)	ihr **seid**	*you are* (inf.)
Sie **sind**	*you are* (form.)	Sie **sind**	*you are* (form.)
er/sie/es **ist**	*he/she/it is*	sie **sind**	*they are*

Ich bin Amerikaner.
I'm American.

Sie ist Deutsche.
She's German.

Wir sind Freunde.
We are friends.

The nominative case

QUERVERWEIS

You will learn more about cases in **1B.1**, **3B.2**, **4B.1**, and **4B.2**.

- German has four *cases* that indicate the function of each noun in a sentence. The case of a noun determines the form of the definite or indefinite article that precedes the noun, the form of any adjectives that modify the noun, and the form of the pronoun that can replace the noun.

German cases		
Nominativ	**Der** Mann ist alt.	*The man is old.*
Akkusativ	Ich verstehe **den** Mann.	*I understand the man.*
Dativ	Der Assistent zeigt **dem** Mann den neuen Computer.	*The assistant is showing the man the new computer.*
Genitiv	Das ist der Assistent **des** Manns.	*This is the man's assistant.*

- The grammatical subject of a sentence is always in the nominative case (**der Nominativ**). Subject pronouns are, by definition, nominative pronouns. The nominative case is also used for nouns that follow a form of **sein**, **werden** (*to become*), or **bleiben** (*to stay, to remain*).

Das ist **eine gute Idee**.
*That's **a good idea**.*

Wir bleiben **Freunde**.
*We're still **friends**.*

- The definite and indefinite articles you learned in **1A.1** are the forms used with nouns in the nominative case.

nominative articles				
	masculine	**feminine**	**neuter**	**plural**
definite	der Junge	die Frau	das Mädchen	die Jungen
indefinite	ein Junge	eine Frau	ein Mädchen	– Jungen

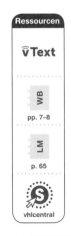

Ressourcen

v̂ Text

WB
pp. 7–8

LM
p. 65

vhlcentral

Jetzt sind Sie dran!
For each noun, write the correct subject pronoun. For each pronoun, write the appropriate form of **sein**.

1. der Apfel ___er___
2. das Haus _____
3. die Jungen _____

4. die Hausaufgabe _____
5. Brigitte und ich _____
6. die Schülerin und du _____

7. wir ___sind___
8. ihr _____
9. du _____

10. Sie _____
11. ich _____
12. er _____

Anwendung

1 **Was ist richtig?** Select the appropriate subject pronoun.

1. (Ihr / Wir) seid in Deutschland.
2. (Er / Ich) ist Katjas Freund.
3. (Du / Sie) sind nett!
4. (Ihr / Ich) seid Amerikaner.

5. (Wir / Ich) sind Deutsche.
6. (Ich / Du) bin Schülerin.
7. (Es / Du) bist prima!
8. (Ihr / Sie) ist intelligent.

2 **Was fehlt?** Write the correct form of **sein**.

1. Herr und Frau Schlüter _____ dort.
2. Lena und ich _____ hier.
3. Ich _____ Anna.
4. Du _____ Schüler.
5. Herr Doktor, Sie _____ Experte.
6. Das Buch _____ sehr interessant.
7. Ihr _____ Kinder.
8. Das Fenster und die Tür _____ offen (*open*).

3 **Sätze ergänzen** Write the pronoun and the appropriate form of **sein**.

> **BEISPIEL**
>
> _Sie sind_ im (*at the*) Restaurant.

1. _____ Freundinnen.

2. _____ Deutschlehrer.

3. Mia, Tim und ich, _____ Schüler.

4. Sara, _____ allein (*alone*).

5. _____ müde (*tired*).

6. Jan und du, _____ Freunde.

4 **Bilden Sie Sätze** Write complete sentences using **sein**. Then, replace the subjects with subject pronouns, where possible.

BEISPIEL Samuel / intelligent
Samuel ist intelligent. Er ist intelligent.

1. Lukas und ich / Schüler
2. du / nett
3. es / ein gutes (*good*) Buch
4. Michael und du / in Deutschland

5. Danielle und Johanna / Deutsche
6. ich / Amerikaner
7. Sie / unfair, Frau Henke
8. das Haus / gigantisch

Kommunikation

5 **Was sehen Sie?** These pictures have been mislabeled. In pairs, take turns reading and correcting the labels.

▶ **BEISPIEL** Kinder

S1: Das sind Kinder.
S2: Nein, das sind Lehrerinnen.

1. Stühle   2. ein Tisch   3. ein Lehrer

4. Autos   5. Männer   6. ein Fenster

6 **Beschreibungen** Tell your partner that you are like each of the people listed.

 BEISPIEL Paul / in Amerika (du)
Jan und Sara / tolerant (ihr)

S1: Paul ist in Amerika, und du?
S2: Ich bin auch in Amerika. Jan und Sara sind tolerant, und ihr?
S1: Wir sind auch tolerant.

1. die Lehrerin / intelligent (du)   3. Felix / romantisch (du)
2. Klara und Tim / Freunde (ihr)   4. Max und Lisa / Studenten (ihr)

7 **Freut mich!** In groups of three, role-play these situations. Each person should say something about him-/herself using a form of **sein**.

 BEISPIEL

S1: Hallo, ich bin Max.
S2: Hallo, Max! Schön dich kennen zu lernen.
    Ich bin Sara und das ist Julia. Wir sind Studentinnen.

1. You are meeting your classmates for the first time. Introduce yourself and ask how each person is doing.

2. You and your friend are invited to a birthday party. Exchange greetings and introduce yourselves to other guests.

Wiederholung

1 Memory-Spiel With a partner, create a set of cards to play Memory, featuring ten nouns you learned in this lesson. For each noun you draw, create a matching card showing the word with the definite article. Shuffle the cards and place them face down. Take turns matching pictures and words.

2 Freut mich! In pairs, practice introducing yourselves in formal and informal situations.

3 Schatzsuche With a partner, find one word or phrase from this lesson that corresponds to each description. Compete against other pairs to see which team can complete their list first. Remember: all words must be spelled correctly, nouns must be preceded by the appropriate definite article, and no word or phrase can be used more than once.

1. a feminine plural noun
2. a formal greeting
3. an informal way to say goodbye
4. a neuter noun that refers to a person
5. a response to the question "**Wie geht's?**"
6. a plural noun ending in -**s**
7. a sentence using a subject pronoun with **sein**
8. a noun that has identical singular and plural forms

4 Was ist das? In pairs, take turns identifying the objects and people.

> **BEISPIEL**
> **S1:** Was ist das?
> **S2:** Das ist ein Auto.

1. _____

2. _____

3. _____

4. _____

5. _____

6. _____

5 Diskutieren und kombinieren Your instructor will give you and a partner two worksheets with different images and labels. Work together to form the compound words.

6 Arbeitsblatt Your instructor will give you a worksheet (**das Arbeitsblatt**). Ask your classmates to say their names and spell them for you. Don't forget to greet them, ask how they are, and say thank you!

BEISPIEL

S1: Guten Morgen!
S2: Hallo!
S1: Wie geht's?
S2: Es geht mir gut.
S1: Wie heißt du?
S2: Ich heiße Nadia.
S1: Wie schreibt man das?
S2: N-A-D-I-A.
S1: Wie ist dein Nachname (*last name*)?
S2: Mueller. M-U-E-L-L-E-R.
S1: Danke!

Zapping
S· Video

Familien fahren° besser mit der Bahn

Deutsche Bahn (**DB**) is the German railway company, based in Berlin. The **Deutsche Bahn** offers a **Sparpreis** (*discount price*) for families. Children under age 15 ride free when accompanied by an adult and pay half-price fares when traveling alone. This advertisement presents the **Deutsche Bahn** as a convenient and comfortable transportation option for families, allowing parents and children to interact and enjoy themselves on the way to their destination.

Die Bahn macht mobil: www.bahn.de

Sag mal°, weißt du noch, wie die Beiden von vorne aussehen?°

Warum fragst du mich?° Du kennst die länger als ich.°

Jetzt mit Gratiseis° für Kinder.

---

fahren *ride* **Sag mal** *Say...* **weißt du..., wie die Beiden von vorne aussehen?** *do you know what those two look like from the front?* **Warum fragst du mich?** *Why are you asking me?* **Du kennst die länger als ich.** *You've known them longer than me.* **Gratiseis** *free popsicle*

 Verständnis Circle the correct answers.

1. How much does the **DB** family package cost?
   a. 49 euro   b. 60 euro   c. 39 euro   d. 55 euro

2. What do children riding the train receive?
   a. Bücher   b. Äpfel   c. Eis   d. Blumen

 Diskussion Discuss the following questions with a partner.

1. What is train service like in your country? How do you think it compares with the services offered by the **Deutsche Bahn**?

2. Does this commercial make you want to travel by train in Germany? Why or why not?

Communicative Goals

You will learn how to:
- talk about classes
- talk about schedules

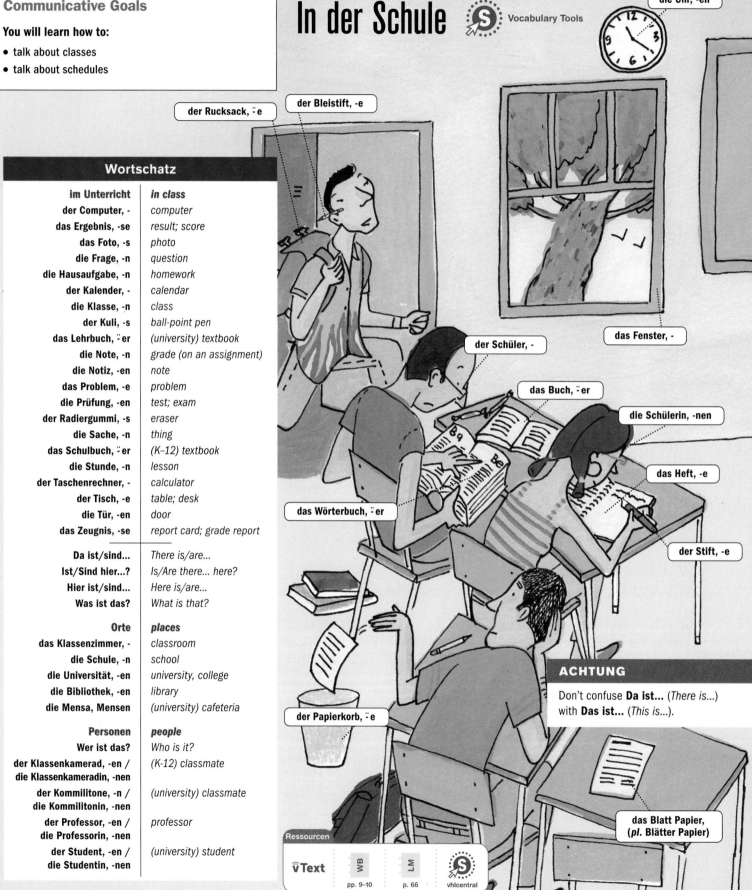

Vocabulary Tools

die Uhr, -en

der Rucksack, ̈e

der Bleistift, -e

das Fenster, -

der Schüler, -

das Buch, ̈er

die Schülerin, -nen

das Heft, -e

das Wörterbuch, ̈er

der Stift, -e

der Papierkorb, ̈e

das Blatt Papier, (pl. Blätter Papier)

Wortschatz

im Unterricht	*in class*
der Computer, -	*computer*
das Ergebnis, -se	*result; score*
das Foto, -s	*photo*
die Frage, -n	*question*
die Hausaufgabe, -n	*homework*
der Kalender, -	*calendar*
die Klasse, -n	*class*
der Kuli, -s	*ball-point pen*
das Lehrbuch, ̈er	*(university) textbook*
die Note, -n	*grade (on an assignment)*
die Notiz, -en	*note*
das Problem, -e	*problem*
die Prüfung, -en	*test; exam*
der Radiergummi, -s	*eraser*
die Sache, -n	*thing*
das Schulbuch, ̈er	*(K–12) textbook*
die Stunde, -n	*lesson*
der Taschenrechner, -	*calculator*
der Tisch, -e	*table; desk*
die Tür, -en	*door*
das Zeugnis, -se	*report card; grade report*
Da ist/sind...	*There is/are...*
Ist/Sind hier...?	*Is/Are there... here?*
Hier ist/sind...	*Here is/are...*
Was ist das?	*What is that?*
Orte	*places*
das Klassenzimmer, -	*classroom*
die Schule, -n	*school*
die Universität, -en	*university, college*
die Bibliothek, -en	*library*
die Mensa, Mensen	*(university) cafeteria*
Personen	*people*
Wer ist das?	*Who is it?*
der Klassenkamerad, -en / die Klassenkameradin, -nen	*(K-12) classmate*
der Kommilitone, -n / die Kommilitonin, -nen	*(university) classmate*
der Professor, -en / die Professorin, -nen	*professor*
der Student, -en / die Studentin, -nen	*(university) student*

ACHTUNG

Don't confuse **Da ist...** (*There is...*) with **Das ist...** (*This is...*).

Ressourcen

v̂Text · WB pp. 9–10 · LM p. 66 · vhlcentral

die Tafel, -n

die Karte, -n

der Lehrer, -
(die Lehrerin, -nen f.)

der Schreibtisch, -e

der Stuhl, ⸚e

Anwendung

1 Was passt nicht? Select the word that doesn't belong.

1. der Professor / das Problem / die Universität / die Studentin
2. das Fenster / das Schulbuch / die Notizen / das Heft
3. der Stift / der Bleistift / der Papierkorb / der Kuli
4. die Tafel / der Schreibtisch / der Stuhl / die Prüfung
5. die Tür / das Ergebnis / der Tisch / die Uhr
6. das Problem / der Radiergummi / die Frage / das Ergebnis

2 Ergänzen Sie Select the words that best complete each sentence.

1. Annika ist...
   a. der Stuhl.　　b. die Schülerin.　　c. die Stunde.
2. Wer ist das? Das ist...
   a. der Bleistift.　　b. der Taschenrechner.　　c. der Professor.
3. Wo sind die Bücher? Sie sind...
   a. in der Bibliothek.　　b. im Ergebnis.　　c. im Papierkorb.
4. Frau Meier ist...
   a. die Lehrerin.　　b. die Schülerin.　　c. die Schule.
5. Im Klassenzimmer sind...
   a. Tische.　　b. Noten.　　c. Universitäten.
6. Das Quiz und der Test sind...
   a. Hausaufgaben.　　b. Prüfungen.　　c. Ergebnisse.

3 Was ist das? Label each item.

 ▶ **BEISPIEL** *der Bleistift*

1. _____ 　　2. _____ 　　3. _____

4. _____ 　　5. _____ 　　6. _____

4 Zuordnungen Write each word you hear in the correct category.

Orte	Personen
1. _____	5. _____
2. _____	6. _____
3. _____	7. _____
4. _____	8. _____

Kommunikation

5 Was ist das?
 In pairs, take turns pointing at items and people in your classroom and asking each other to identify them.

BEISPIEL

S1: *Was ist das?*
S2: *Das ist ein Bleistift. Wer ist das?*
S1: *Das ist der Lehrer.*

6 Im Rucksack
List six items that are in your backpack. Then, work with a partner and compare lists.

In meinem (*my*) Rucksack ist/sind...

1. _____
2. _____
3. _____
4. _____
5. _____
6. _____

In _____s Rucksack ist/sind...

1. _____
2. _____
3. _____
4. _____
5. _____
6. _____

WERKZEUG

To say that something belongs to someone, add an **-s** to the person's name (**Marias Heft**; **Julians Buch**). Add an apostrophe if the name already ends in **-s** (**Niklas' Heft**; **Tobias' Buch**).

7 Ist da...?
In pairs, take turns asking each other questions about what you see in the illustration.

BEISPIEL

S1: *Ist da ein Papierkorb?*
S2: *Nein. Da ist ein Bleistift. Ist da...?*

8 Ratespiel
Play Pictionary as a class.

- Take turns going to the board and drawing images representing words from the lesson vocabulary.
- The person drawing may not write any letters or numbers.
- The person who correctly identifies the drawing in German gets to go next.

Aussprache und Rechtschreibung  Audio

The vowels *a*, *e*, *i*, *o*, and *u*

Each German vowel may be pronounced with either a long or a short sound. A vowel followed by **h** is always long. A double **oo**, **aa**, or **ee** also indicates a long vowel sound. In some words, long **i** is spelled **ie**.

Fahne	**wen**	**ihn**	**doof**	**Mut**	**diese**

A vowel followed by two or more consonant sounds is usually short.

Pfanne	**wenn**	**in**	**Sonne**	**Mutter**	**singst**

When the German letter **e** appears in the unstressed syllable at the end of a word, it is pronounced like the *e* in the English word *the*.

danke	**Schule**	**Frage**	**Klasse**	**Dinge**	**Vase**

In certain words, an **Umlaut** (¨) is added to the vowel **a**, **o**, or **u**, changing the pronunciation of the vowel.

Bank	**Bänke**	**schon**	**schön**	**Bruder**	**Brüder**

---

1 Aussprechen Practice saying these words aloud.

1. Kahn / kann
2. beten / Betten
3. Robe / Robbe
4. Buch / Butter
5. den / denn
6. Saat / satt
7. Rogen / Roggen
8. Sack / Säcke
9. Wort / Wörter
10. Stuhl / Stühle
11. Hefte
12. Tage

2 Nachsprechen Practice saying these sentences aloud.

1. Der Mann kam ohne Kamm.
2. Wir essen Bienenstich und trinken Kaffee.
3. Am Sonntag und am Montag scheint die Sonne.
4. Das U-Boot ist unter Wasser.
5. Ich habe viele Freunde in der Schule.
6. Der Mantel mit den fünf Knöpfen ist schöner als die Mäntel mit einem Knopf.

3 Sprichwörter Practice reading these sayings aloud.

Sag mir, mit wem du gehst, und ich sage dir, wer du bist.[1]

Der frühe Vogel fängt den Wurm.[2]

[1] Tell me who your friends are, and I will tell you who you are.
[2] The early bird catches the worm.

Oh, George! Video

George und Hans treffen (*meet*) Meline und Sabite im Biergarten.
Melines Handy klingelt...

> **SABITE** Wer ist es?
> **MELINE** Lukas.
> **SABITE** Oh, dein Freund?
> **MELINE** Ja. Nein. Ja.

> **MELINE** Wir haben Probleme.

> **MELINE** Hast du einen Freund?
> **SABITE** Ja. Torsten. Er ist Student.
> **MELINE** Hast du ein Bild?

> **GEORGE** Sabite? Sabite, hallo.
> **SABITE** Hallo.
> **HANS** Hallo.
> **SABITE** Was ist da drin?
> **GEORGE** Lehrbücher! Wörterbuch... Hefte...
>   Stifte... Kalender.
> **HANS** Hast du auch einen Computer?

> **KELLNERIN** Bitte schön?
> **HANS** Ein Wasser, bitte.
> **GEORGE** Einen Kaffee und ein
>   Stück Strudel.

> **MELINE** Ich habe keinen Freund mehr.
> **SABITE** Wie geht's dir?
> **MELINE** Mir geht es sehr gut.

ÜBUNGEN

1 Richtig oder falsch? Indicate whether each statement is richtig or falsch.

1. George hat ein Wörterbuch.
2. Sabite hat ein Bild von (*of*) Torsten.
3. George will (*wants*) das Brandenburger Tor sehen (*to see*).
4. Im Bauhaus-Museum gibt es viele Bücher.
5. Meline telefoniert mit Lukas.

6. Die Kellnerin hat einen Freund.
7. Torsten ist Student.
8. Hans hat einen Stadtplan.
9. Die Kellnerin heißt Laura.
10. George bestellt (*orders*) Kaffee und Steak.

PERSONEN George Hans Meline Sabite Kellnerin

GEORGE Ich habe eine Idee. Hast du einen Stadtplan?
HANS Ja!
GEORGE Was muss ich in Berlin sehen? Das Brandenburger Tor!
HANS Checkpoint Charlie!

SABITE Potsdamer Platz!
GEORGE Marlene-Dietrich-Platz!
KELLNERIN Das Bode-Museum. Und das Jüdische Museum!

HANS Wie viele Kurse hast du belegt?
SABITE Ah, vier.
MELINE Bauhaus-Museum.
HANS Ja!
MELINE Im Bauhaus-Museum gibt es viele...
SABITE Stühle! Viele Stühle. Und Tische.

GEORGE Wie heißt sie?
SABITE Ähm, Leyna? Oh, George.
HANS Sie hat einen Freund?
GEORGE Ja.

Nützliche Ausdrücke

- **Prost!**
  Cheers!
- **Wer ist es?**
  Who is it?
- **Hast du ein Bild?**
  Do you have a picture?
- **Was ist da drin?**
  What's in there?
- **Hast du auch einen Computer?**
  Do you have a computer, too?
- **die Kellnerin**
  waitress
- **Bitte schön?**
  May I take your order?; May I help you?
- **das Wasser**
  water
- **der Kaffee**
  coffee
- **das Stück Strudel**
  a piece of strudel
- **Ich habe keinen Freund mehr.**
  I don't have a boyfriend anymore.
- **die Idee**
  idea
- **der Stadtplan**
  city map
- **Was muss ich in Berlin sehen?**
  What do I have to see in Berlin?
- **Ist alles in Ordnung?**
  Is everything alright?
- **Wie heißt sie?**
  What's her name?

1B.1
- **Wir haben Probleme.**
  We have problems.

1B.2
- **Hast du einen Stadtplan?**
  Do you have a city map?

1B.3
- **—Wie viele Kurse hast du?**
  —How many classes are you taking?
- **—Vier.**
  —Four.

---

2 **Zum Besprechen** With a partner, role-play a scene where one of you plays the waiter (**Kellner**) or waitress at a **Biergarten** and the other plays a customer ordering food. Here are some common items to order.

eine Cola	ein Stück Strudel
einen Kaffee	einen Tee
einen Saft (*juice*)	ein Wasser

3 **Vertiefung** The characters mention several important sites and museums in Berlin. Research these and other monuments and plan a day of sightseeing in Berlin to present to the class. Mention at least three sites that interest you and include their names in German.

Die Schulzeit Reading

ALTHOUGH THE WORD AND THE concept were invented by **Friedrich Fröbel**, a teacher in 19th-century Germany, **Kindergarten** is called **Vorschule** in Germany. There are many privately-run **Kindergärten**, an equivalent of preschool.

Public school for German children starts at age six, with **Grundschule°**. For the first four years, all **Grundschüler** attend school together. But after age ten, students are streamed into three different kinds of schools, usually as recommended by their teacher.

The most academically rigorous option is **Gymnasium**. **Gymnasium** lasts eight years, and graduates need to pass difficult exit exams to earn their **Abitur°**. The "Abi" gives students access to competitive internships and a university education.

A more vocationally-oriented option is **Hauptschule**. Students typically finish **Hauptschule** at age 15 or 16. They may then attend **Berufsfachschule°**, where they can train for a variety of professions, from mechanics to physical therapy.

The third option is **Realschule**, which has stricter academic requirements than **Hauptschule**. After graduation, students may seek further schooling that will lead them into careers like banking, IT, or social work.

This three-track system has been in use for decades, but in recent years it has come under serious criticism. The **Abitur** is associated with higher social status, and more and more families push to have their children admitted into **Gymnasium**. **Realschule** still generally leads to solid employment opportunities, but there is now a stigma attached to **Hauptschule**, which makes the job search more difficult for its graduates.

In some states, there is a fourth option for secondary school students: the **Gesamtschule°**. These comprehensive schools have no entrance requirements. They offer college preparatory classes for students who perform well, general education classes for students with average performance, and remedial courses for those who need additional support. **Gesamtschulen** were introduced in 1969 with the hope of eliminating inequalities associated with the three-track system, but they have been slow to take root.

Grundschule *elementary school* **Abitur** *high school diploma* **Berufsfachschule** *vocational school* **Gesamtschule** *comprehensive school*

ÜBUNGEN

1 **Was fehlt?** Complete the statements.

1. _____ is not part of the German public school system.
2. _____ invented the word **Kindergarten**.
3. German elementary school is called _____.
4. Children normally begin school at age _____.
5. **Grundschule** lasts _____ years.
6. After age ten, students are streamed into three kinds of schools: **Gymnasium**, **Hauptschule**, and _____.
7. **Gymnasium** graduates receive a diploma called the _____.
8. Students who have earned their **Abitur** can attend _____.
9. After finishing _____, students may attend **Berufsfachschule**.
10. The _____ offers an alternative to the three-track system.

Die Schule

die Abschlussfeier, -n	graduation
die Pause, -n	recess
der Schulleiter, -	(male) principal
die Schulleiterin, -nen	(female) principal
bestehen	to pass a test
durchfallen	to flunk; to fail
schwänzen	to cut class
langweilig	boring

Ein süßer° Beginn

In German-speaking countries, the first day of school is a festive occasion. Excited **Erstklässler°** are presented with **Schultüten** by their parents on the morning of their first day of school. The **Schultüte** is a decorated paper cone, filled with candies, chocolates, school supplies, and other treats. With their unopened **Tüten** in hand, the **Erstklässler** set off for **Grundschule. Alles Gute für den ersten Schultag!°**

süßer *sweet* Erstklässler *first-graders* Alles Gute für den ersten Schultag! *Best wishes on your first day of school!*

Noten in Deutschland

Deutsche Noten:	1	2	3	4	5/6
US-Äquivalente:	A/A+	A-/B+	B/B-	C/D	D-/F

Der Schultag

The school day in Germany typically lasts from 7:30 or 8:00 in the morning until 1:00 in the afternoon, with a 15-20 minute mid-morning break, called the **Große Pause**. Many schools do not have cafeterias, since students go home at lunch time. They then have the afternoon to do homework and participate in extracurricular activities. Students have only 6 weeks of summer vacation, but they get longer breaks during the school year, with 2 weeks off in the fall, 2 weeks for Christmas, and 2 weeks in the spring.

TIPP

The German word for *one* is **eins**. A straight-A student is called **ein(e) Einserschüler(in)**.

🔗 IM INTERNET

Subjects: What subjects do students study at **Gymnasium**? What are **Pflichtfächer**? What are **Wahlfächer**?

Find out more at **vhlcentral.com**.

---

2 **Richtig oder falsch?** Indicate whether each statement is **richtig** or **falsch**. Correct the false statements.

1. Most German students eat lunch in their school cafeterias.

2. Students get a midmorning break called the **Große Pause**.

3. Students get 12 weeks of vacation every summer.

4. Children in their first year of school are called **Kindergärtner**.

5. The **Schultüte** is a test that elementary school students take on the first day.

3 **Die Schule: anders in Deutschland** In pairs, discuss the similarities and differences between school life in Germany or other German-speaking countries and in your country. What do you like best about each system? Why?

1B.1 | *Haben* and the accusative case  Presentation

Startblock To describe what someone or something has, use the irregular verb **haben** with the accusative case.

Haben

haben (*to have*)			
ich **habe**	*I have*	wir **haben**	*we have*
du **hast**	*you have* (inf.)	ihr **habt**	*you have* (inf.)
Sie **haben**	*you have* (form.)	Sie **haben**	*you have* (form.)
er/sie/es **hat**	*he/she/it has*	sie **haben**	*they have*

Ich **habe** ein Buch.
I have a book.

Greta **hat** eine Karte.
Greta has a map.

Wir **haben** eine Frage.
We have a question.

ACHTUNG

A direct object receives the action of a verb directly and answers the question *what?* or *whom?*

QUERVERWEIS

The accusative case is also used following certain prepositions. You will learn more about this usage in **3B.2**.

Ressourcen

v̂ **Text**

WB
pp. 11–12

LM
p. 68

S
vhlcentral

The accusative case

- In **1A.3**, you learned that the function of a noun in a sentence determines its case, as well as the case of any article or adjective that modifies it. A noun that functions as a direct object is in the accusative case (**der Akkusativ**).

definite articles				
	masculine	**feminine**	**neuter**	**plural**
nominative	der Stuhl	die Tür	das Fenster	die Notizen
accusative	de**n** Stuhl	die Tür	das Fenster	die Notizen

indefinite articles				
	masculine	**feminine**	**neuter**	**plural**
nominative	ein Stuhl	eine Tür	ein Fenster	– Notizen
accusative	ein**en** Stuhl	eine Tür	ein Fenster	– Notizen

Der Lehrer hat **den Stift**.
*The teacher has **the pen**.*

Ich kaufe **ein Bleistift**.
*I'm buying **a pencil**.*

Sie öffnet **die Tür**.
*She's opening **the door**.*

Wir haben hier **ein Problem**.
*We have **a problem** here.*

Jetzt sind Sie dran! In the first column, complete the sentences using **haben**. In the second column, indicate whether each underlined phrase is in the **Nominativ (N)** or **Akkusativ (A)** case.

1. Wir ___haben___ die Bücher.
2. Ich _____ Fotos.
3. Herr Müller _____ ein Haus.
4. Ihr _____ morgen Schule.
5. Max und Julia _____ viele Hausaufgaben.
6. Lena _____ eine Theorie.

___N___ 7. Sie ist <u>eine gute Schülerin</u>.
____ 8. David hat <u>eine Frage</u>.
____ 9. Ich habe <u>ein Problem</u>.
____ 10. Du hast <u>einen Stuhl</u>.
____ 11. Ihr seid <u>Schüler.</u>
____ 12. Herr Meier trinkt <u>ein Glas Wasser</u>.

Anwendung und Kommunikation

1 Bilden Sie Sätze Write complete sentences.

BEISPIEL ich / haben / ein Radiergummi

Ich habe einen Radiergummi.

1. du / haben / ein Computer
2. ihr / haben / ein Taschenrechner
3. der Lehrer / haben / ein Buch
4. wir / haben / ein Problem
5. ich / haben / eine Frage
6. das Mädchen / haben / ein Freund

2 Was haben wir? Rewrite each sentence using **haben** with the subject provided.

BEISPIEL Das ist ein Computer. (Inge)

Inge hat einen Computer.

1. Das ist ein Rucksack. (Peter)
2. Das ist ein Kuli. (ich)
3. Das ist ein Schulbuch. (ihr)
4. Das sind Fotos. (du)
5. Das ist ein Wörterbuch. (Erik und Nina)
6. Das ist eine Karte. (wir)

3 Was haben sie? With a partner, take turns saying what each person has.

 ▶ **BEISPIEL**

Patrick hat Fotos.

Patrick

1. du

2. die Schüler

3. Bettina

4. ich

5. du und Abdel

6. wir

4 Im Klassenzimmer In groups, take turns discussing what items are in your classroom and what each of you has brought to class.

BEISPIEL

S1: *Was haben wir hier?*
S2: *Wir haben Stühle und Bänke.*

S1: *Was hast du?*
S2: *Ich habe ein Heft.*

 Practice more at **vhlcentral.com**.

1B.2 Word order  Presentation

Startblock By changing the order of words in a sentence, you can shift emphasis or turn a statement into a yes-or-no question.

Statements

- In German, the verb is always the second element in a statement. The first element is often the subject, but it can also be a time expression or a prepositional phrase.

1ST	2ND	3RD
Ich	**habe**	heute Abend viele Hausaufgaben.

I have a lot of homework tonight.

1ST	2ND	3RD
Heute Abend	**habe**	ich viele Hausaufgaben.

Tonight I have a lot of homework.

- A direct or indirect object may be placed in first position, but this is a less common phrasing, used to place emphasis on the object. When the subject is not the first element in the sentence, it immediately follows the verb.

1ST	2ND	3RD
Viele Hausaufgaben	**habe**	ich heute Abend.

I have a lot of homework tonight.

- You can use the conjunctions **und** (*and*), **aber** (*but*), and **oder** (*or*) to combine two statements into one sentence, without affecting the word order of either statement.

Heute Abend haben wir viele
Hausaufgaben **und** morgen haben wir Unterricht.
*Tonight we have a lot of homework **and** tomorrow we have class.*

Yes-or-no questions

- To turn a statement into a yes-or-no question, move the verb to the first position. Move the subject to the second position, since it must immediately follow the verb. Use **ja** or **nein** to respond to this type of question.

STATEMENT	QUESTION
Die Lehrerin ist nett.	**Ist die Lehrerin** nett?
The teacher is nice.	*Is the teacher nice?*
Jetzt habt ihr einen Computer.	**Habt ihr jetzt** einen Computer?
Now you have a computer.	*Do you have a computer now?*

QUERVERWEIS

You will learn how to form negative statements in **2B.3**.

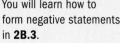

Ressourcen

v̂Text

WB
pp. 13–14

LM
p. 69

vhlcentral

 Jetzt sind Sie dran! Turn each statement into a yes-or-no question.

1. Ich habe ein Buch.
   _____

2. Ich bin Schülerin.
   _____

3. Das sind Mitschüler.
   _____

4. Der Apfel ist gut.
   _____

5. Wir haben viele Fotos.
   _____

6. Tobias und Jasmin haben Rucksäcke.
   _____

7. Lukas hat einen Taschenrechner.
   _____

8. Ich habe ein Problem.
   _____

Anwendung und Kommunikation

1 **Sätze** Combine each pair of sentences using **oder**, **aber**, or **und**, as indicated.

> **BEISPIEL** Ben hat gute Noten. David hat schlechte Noten. (aber)
> *Ben hat gute Noten, aber David hat schlechte Noten.*

1. Du hast ein Blatt Papier. Ich habe einen Bleistift. (und)
2. Ist das Buch gut? Ist es schlecht? (oder)
3. Es geht mir ziemlich gut. Ich habe ein Problem. (aber)
4. Ist Ela da? Ist sie im Unterricht? (oder)
5. Wir haben heute viele Hausaufgaben. Morgen haben wir eine Prüfung. (und)
6. Ich heiße Sophia. Das ist Mia. (und)

2 **Noch einmal** Rewrite each sentence twice, changing the order of the underlined elements.

> **BEISPIEL** Ich habe <u>heute</u> *(today)* <u>eine Prüfung</u>.
> *Heute habe ich eine Prüfung.*
> *Eine Prüfung habe ich heute.*

1. <u>Tim</u> hat <u>heute Abend</u> <u>Deutschhausaufgaben</u>.
2. <u>Max und Lisa</u> haben <u>ein Haus</u> <u>in Berlin</u>.
3. <u>Wir</u> sind <u>jetzt</u> <u>im Unterricht.</u>
4. <u>Ich</u> bin <u>jetzt</u> <u>in Berlin.</u>

3 **Wer hat was?** In pairs, take turns asking and answering questions.

> **BEISPIEL** Junge / Problem (nein / Frage)
> **S1:** *Hat der Professor ein Problem?*
> **S2:** *Nein, er hat eine Frage.*

1. Frau / Blatt Papier (nein / Foto)
2. Emil und ich / Bleistifte (ja)
3. Lehrerin / Kalender (ja)
4. Schüler / Buch (nein / Heft)

4 **Was ist los?** In groups, take turns asking and answering yes-or-no questions about the image.

> **BEISPIEL**
> **S1:** *Haben die Schüler Bücher?*
> **S2:** *Ja, sie haben Bücher.*

 Practice more at **vhlcentral.com**.

1B.3 Numbers  Presentation

Startblock As in English, numbers in German follow patterns. Memorizing the numbers from **1** to **20** will help you learn numbers **21** and above.

Sabite hat **vier** Kurse.

George ist **21** Jahre alt.

- Every number up to one million is written as a single word. Numbers from **13** to **19** follow a pattern similar to English, adding the ending **-zehn** to each single-digit number. Numbers from **21** to **99** repeat this pattern, adding **und** plus the number in the tens place to each single-digit number: [*ones*] + **und** + [*tens*].

25 = **fünf** + **und** + zwanzig ▶ **fünfund**zwanzig

ACHTUNG

Ask **Wie alt bist du?** when you want to know someone's age. Answer: **Ich bin [*number*]. / Ich bin [*number*] Jahre alt.**

numbers 0–99							
0	null	10	zehn	20	zwanzig	30	dreißig
1	eins	11	elf	21	einundzwanzig	31	einunddreißig
2	zwei	12	zwölf	22	zweiundzwanzig	40	vierzig
3	drei	13	dreizehn	23	dreiundzwanzig	45	fünfundvierzig
4	vier	14	vierzehn	24	vierundzwanzig	50	fünfzig
5	fünf	15	fünfzehn	25	fünfundzwanzig	60	sechzig
6	sechs	16	sechzehn	26	sechsundzwanzig	70	siebzig
7	sieben	17	siebzehn	27	siebenundzwanzig	80	achtzig
8	acht	18	achtzehn	28	achtundzwanzig	90	neunzig
9	neun	19	neunzehn	29	neunundzwanzig	99	neunundneunzig

- Note that the **s** in **eins** is dropped at the beginning of a compound word.

41 = ein**s** + vierzig ▶ **ein**undvierzig   81 = ein**s** + achtzig ▶ **ein**undachtzig

- Likewise, **sechs** and **sieben** are shortened when they precede the letter **z**.

16 = **sech**zehn   66 = sechsund**sech**zig
17 = **sieb**zehn   77 = siebenund**sieb**zig

- In German, decimals are indicated by a comma (**Komma**), not a period (**Punkt**). When giving a unit of measurement (length, currency, etc.), say the unit instead of **Komma**. Note that units of currency are usually written after the number.

25,4 = fünfundzwanzig **Komma** vier   0,5 = null **Komma** fünf
4,99 € = vier **Euro** neunundneunzig   10,18 m = zehn **Meter** achtzehn

QUERVERWEIS

You will learn more about interrogative words in **2A.2**.

- Use **Wie viel?** to ask *How much?* and **Wie viele?** to ask *How many?*

Wie viel kostet das Buch?   **Wie viele** Blätter Papier habt ihr?
How much does the book cost?   *How many* pieces of paper do you have?

numbers 100 and higher			
100	(ein)hundert	1.000	(ein)tausend
101	hunderteins	1.300	tausenddreihundert
128	hundertachtundzwanzig	5.000	fünftausend
200	zweihundert	10.000	zehntausend
300	dreihundert	50.000	fünfzigtausend
400	vierhundert	100.000	hunderttausend
500	fünfhundert	460.000	vierhundertsechzigtausend
600	sechshundert	1.000.000	eine Million
700	siebenhundert	1.050.000	eine Million fünfzigtausend
800	achthundert	7.000.000	sieben Millionen
900	neunhundert	1.000.000.000	eine Milliarde

- Note that German uses a period where English typically uses a comma to separate thousands, millions, etc.

2.320.000	1.999,99 €	5.225,00 $
2,320,000	*€1,999.99*	*$5,225.00*

- Numbers in the millions and higher are written as separate words.

2.016.000
zwei Millionen sechzehntausend

1.000.050.000
eine Milliarde fünfzigtausend

Mathematical expressions

- Use these expressions to talk about math.

mathematical expressions					
+	plus	×	mal	=	ist (gleich)
–	minus	÷	geteilt durch	%	Prozent

6 + 7 = 13 ▶ **Sechs plus sieben ist dreizehn.**
Six plus seven is thirteen.

8 – 2 = 6 ▶ **Acht minus zwei ist gleich sechs.**
Eight minus two equals six.

3 · 3 = 9 ▶ **Drei mal drei ist gleich neun.**
Three times three equals nine.

20 : 5 = 4 ▶ **Zwanzig geteilt durch fünf ist vier.**
Twenty divided by five is four.

ACHTUNG

Note that German speakers typically use the symbol · to indicate multiplication and the symbol : to indicate division.

Ressourcen

v̂ Text

WB
pp. 15–16

LM
p. 70

vhlcentral

Jetzt sind Sie dran! Write each number or equation in words.

1. 37
   siebenunddreißig

2. 212

3. 49

4. 368

5. 24

6. 75

7. 1991

8. 587

9. 16 + 15 = 31

10. 97 – 17 = 80

11. 18 : 9 = 2

12. 12 · 3 = 36

Anwendung

1 **Eins, zwei, drei...** Fill in the missing number, then write the number in words.

BEISPIEL   0, 5, 10, ___15___, 20; ____fünfzehn____

1. 2, 4, _____, 8, 10; _____
2. 0, 10, 20, _____, 40; _____
3. 670, 671, 672, 673, _____; _____
4. 3.456, 3.457, 3.458, _____, 3.460; _____
5. 35, 40, 45, 50, _____; _____
6. 1.899.996, 1.899.997, 1.899.998, 1.899.999, _____; _____

2 **Wie alt bist du?** With a partner, take turns asking and saying how old each person is.

BEISPIEL   Anna: 16
S1: Wie alt ist Anna?
S2: Sie ist sechzehn Jahre alt.

1. Tim: 19
2. Sara: 11
3. Herr Wolf: 73
4. Frau Öztürk: 101

5. Niklas: 5
6. Herr Braun: 42
7. Jasmin: 21
8. Frau Schröder: 67

3 **Was sehen Sie?** Write how many there are of each item.

► BEISPIEL

(860) Student
Da sind
achthundertsechzig
Studenten.

(5.937) Buch
1. _____

(16) Mädchen
2. _____

(217) Tisch
3. _____

(54) Auto
4. _____

(12) Stuhl
5. _____

(4) Studentin
6. _____

4 **Matheprofi** In pairs, take turns reading the equations out loud.

1. $67 + 4 = 71$
2. $16 + 28 = 44$
3. $91 - 6 = 85$
4. $45 - 7 = 38$

5. $24 : 4 = 6$
6. $989 : 43 = 23$
7. $58 \cdot 2 = 116$
8. $213 \cdot 3 = 639$

 Practice more at **vhlcentral.com**.

Kommunikation

5 **Wie viele Einwohner hat...?** In pairs, discuss the population of each city.

> **BEISPIEL** München: 1.330.440
>
> **S1:** Wie viele Einwohner (*inhabitants*) hat München?
> **S2:** München hat eine Million dreihundertdreißigtausendvierhundertvierzig Einwohner.

1. Berlin: 3.450.889
2. Gelsenkirchen: 259.744
3. Hamburg: 1.783.975
4. Dresden: 532.058
5. Stuttgart: 601.646

6 **Wie viel kostet...?** In pairs, take turns asking about and saying the cost of each item.

> **BEISPIEL**
>
> **S1:** Wie viel kostet ein Computer?
> **S2:** Er kostet eintausenddreihundertvierundzwanzig Euro siebzehn.

Auto	Apfel
Haus	Blume
Tisch	Heft
Computer	Stuhl

7 **Wie viel sind...?** In pairs, discuss these exchange rates.

> **BEISPIEL** $120 = 83,44 €
>
> **S1:** Wie viel sind hundertzwanzig Dollar in Euro?
> **S2:** Das sind dreiundachtzig Euro vierundvierzig.

1. $450 = 312,70 €
2. $573 = 452,08 CHF (Schweizer Franken)
3. 781,45 € = 86.074,17 ¥ (Yen)
4. $1.628,50 = £985,88 (Pfund Sterling)

5. 3.816 € = £3.321,67
6. 6.487,15 CHF = $8.222,89
7. $14.005,90 = 9.733,30 €
8. £251.029 = $414.884,04

8 **Ich habe mehr!** In small groups, take turns exaggerating the number of items you have at home.

> **BEISPIEL**
>
> **S1:** Ich habe sieben Kulis.
> **S2:** Ich habe dreihundertfünfundneunzig Taschenrechner!
> **S3:** Und ich habe neuntausendvierundzwanzig Stifte!

1.253.687

Wiederholung

1 Fragespiel

In pairs, play a question game (**Fragespiel**) using the lesson vocabulary. Choose a person or object in the classroom. Your partner will ask yes-or-no questions to figure out the word you've chosen.

BEISPIEL

S1: *Bist du eine Sache?*
S2: *Nein.*
S1: *Bist du eine Person?*
S2: *Ja.*
S1: *Hast du einen Schreibtisch?*
S2: *Ja.*
S1: *Bist du ein Lehrer?*
S2: *Genau (Exactly)!*

2 Mathe

Write two numbers between 1 and 100 on separate index cards. Then, in small groups, make a pile of everyone's cards, shuffle, and take turns drawing two cards from the pile. The person who draws must create a math problem using the numbers. The first person to answer the math problem correctly draws next.

BEISPIEL

S1: *(draws 55 and 5) Fünfundfünfzig geteilt durch fünf.*
S2: *Fünfundfünfzig geteilt durch fünf ist elf.*

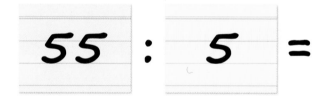

$$55 : 5 =$$

3 Ratespiel

In small groups, collect the items listed. One student leaves the group while the others distribute the items among themselves. The student then returns and tries to guess who has each item.

BEISPIEL

S1: *Hast du den Radiergummi?*
S2: *Nein.*
S1: *Hat Megan den Radiergummi?*
S2: *Nein, Simon hat den Radiergummi.*

der Bleistift	der Radiergummi
das Buch	der Rucksack
das Heft	der Taschenrechner
der Kuli	die Uhr

4 Im Schreibwarenladen

In groups of three, make a shopping list of school supplies. Then, role-play a trip to the store to buy the items you need. Present your scene to the class.

BEISPIEL

S1: *Guten Tag.*
S2: *Guten Tag. Haben Sie hier Hefte und Bleistifte?*
S1: *Ja, wir haben hier Hefte und Bleistifte.*
S3: *Wie viel kosten die Hefte?*
S1: *Sie kosten fünf Euro neunzig.*

5 Diskutieren und kombinieren

Your instructor will give you and your partner worksheets with different pictures of a classroom. Do not look at each other's pictures. Ask and answer questions to identify seven differences (**Unterschiede**) between the two pictures.

BEISPIEL

S1: *Ich habe zwei Türen. Hast du auch zwei Türen?*
S2: *Nein. Ich habe eine Tür. Hast du einen Lehrer?*
S1: *Ja, ich habe auch einen Lehrer. Hast du...?*

6 Arbeitsblatt

Your instructor will give you a game board. Play the game with your partners. Count the spaces aloud in German as you play.

7 Interview
Interview as many classmates as possible to find out if these statements (**Behauptungen**) apply to them. Write down their names.

BEISPIEL

S1: Hallo! Hast du einen Bleistift?
S2: Ja, ich habe einen Bleistift./
Nein, aber ich habe einen Kuli.

Behauptung	Name
1. Ich habe einen Bleistift.	Alexia
2. Ich bin 21 Jahre alt.	Markus
3. Ich habe ein Wörterbuch.	
4. Es geht mir gut.	
5. Ich bin Amerikaner(in).	
6. Ich bin Student(in).	
7. Ich habe ein Heft.	
8. Ich habe viele Hausaufgaben.	

8 Galgenmännchen
In small groups, play Hangman using the vocabulary you learned in **Lektion 1A** and **Lektion 1B**. For nouns, include the definite article. Give your partners a hint about each word.

BEISPIEL

S1: Es ist eine Person/eine Sache / ein Ort /
ein Ausdruck (*expression*).
S2: Hat das Wort ein S?
S1: Nein. / Ja, das Wort hat zwei S.

Mein Wör|ter|buch

Throughout this book, you will be encouraged to keep a personalized dictionary. By associating words with images, examples of usage (**Gebrauch**), synonyms, and antonyms, you will create entries that are relevant to you, and you will be better able to retain these new words.

Add five words to your personalized dictionary related to the themes **Begrüßung und Abschied** and **In der Schule**.

Sehr erfreut.

Übersetzung (*translation*)
Pleased to meet you.

Wortart (*part of speech*)
ein Ausdruck

Gebrauch
—Ich bin Herr Müller.
—Sehr erfreut.

Synonyme
Freut mich. / Angenehm. / Schön dich/Sie kennen zu lernen.

Antonyme
—

Vocabulary Tools

Panorama  Interactive Map

Die deutschsprachige Welt°

Länder° mit Deutsch als Amtssprache°

▶ Belgien
▶ Deutschland
▶ Italien (Region: Südtirol)
▶ Liechtenstein
▶ Luxemburg
▶ Österreich
▶ die Schweiz

Bevölkerung°

▶ **Belgien:** *10,4 Millionen Einwohner° (77.000 deutsche Muttersprachler°)*
▶ **Deutschland:** *81,1 Millionen Einwohner*
▶ **Italien:** *61,7 Millionen Einwohner (336.000 deutsche Muttersprachler)*
▶ **Liechtenstein:** *37.313 Einwohner*
▶ **Luxemburg:** *520.672 Einwohner (474.000 deutsche Muttersprachler)*
▶ **Österreich:** *8,2 Millionen Einwohner*
▶ **die Schweiz:** *8,1 Millionen Einwohner (4,8 Millionen deutsche Muttersprachler)*

QUELLE: das Haus der deutschen Sprache

Hauptstädte°

▶ **Belgien:** *Brüssel*
▶ **Deutschland:** *Berlin*
▶ **Liechtenstein:** *Vaduz*
▶ **Luxemburg:** *Luxemburg*
▶ **Österreich:** *Wien*
▶ **die Schweiz:** *Bern*

deutschsprachige Welt *German-speaking world* **Länder** *countries*
Amtssprache *official language* **Bevölkerung** *population*
Einwohner *inhabitants* **Muttersprachler** *native speakers*
Hauptstädte *capitals* **Sprachen** *languages* **Circa** *Approximately*
leben *live* **mindestens** *at least*

Legende:
— Landesgrenzen
• Stadt
◉ Landeshauptstadt
✪ Hauptstadt

Wien, Österreichs Hauptstadt

Bern, Hauptstadt der Schweiz

Unglaublich, aber wahr!

Belgien hat drei offizielle Sprachen°: Französisch, Niederländisch und Deutsch. Die deutschsprachige Region ist im Osten Belgiens. Circa° 76.000 Menschen leben° hier. Viele Belgier sprechen mindestens° zwei Sprachen.

Österreich
Die Alpen

Die Alpen sind das höchste Gebirge°
in Europa. Es ist circa 1.200 Kilometer
lang, und 29% sind in Österreich.
Deshalb heißt Österreich auch die
„Alpenrepublik". In Österreich leben
circa 4 Millionen Menschen° in den
Alpen. Das sind 50% aller Österreicher.
Der höchste Berg° in Österreich
ist der Großglockner. Er ist 3.798
Meter hoch.

Die Schweiz
Schokolade

Die Schweiz ist bekannt für Banken, Uhren,
Messer° und natürlich° Schokolade. Die
bekanntesten Schokoladenfirmen sind Lindt,
Tobler, Sprüngli und Suchard. Suchard
produziert Milka Schokolade. Vor allem
die Schweizer essen Schokolade gern°.
Pro Jahr isst° jeder Schweizer 11,7
Kilogramm Schokolade. Niemand° auf
der Welt isst mehr Schokolade als° die
Schweizer. In Deutschland isst man 11,4
Kilogramm Schokolade pro Person,
in Österreich 7,9, und in den USA nur
5,2 Kilogramm.

Geschichte
Die Hanse

Die Deutsche Hanse ist eine Union
von Kaufleuten°. Sie existiert zwischen Mitte
des 12. Jahrhunderts° und Mitte des 17.
Jahrhunderts. Bis zu 200 Städte im
nördlichen Europa sind in der Union, wie
zum Beispiel Zuidersee (heutiges° Holland),
Hamburg, Bremen und Lübeck (heutiges
Deutschland), Stockholm (heutiges
Schweden), Danzig (heutiges Polen) und Riga
(heutiges Lettland°). Diese Städte liegen°
vor allem an der Nordsee und der Ostsee°.

Deutschland
Die Berliner Mauer°

Vom 13. August 1961 bis 9. November
1989 ist die Berliner Mauer eine Grenze°
zwischen° Ost- und Westberlin. Die
Mauer umgibt° ganz Westberlin und
kreiert eine Insel°. Sie ist das Symbol des
Kalten Krieges°. Die Mauer ist 156,4
Kilometer lang. Sie ist zwischen 3,40 Meter
und 4,20 Meter hoch. Rund um Westberlin
stehen 302 Beobachtungstürme°.

⌖ IM INTERNET

1. Machen Sie eine Liste mit den
   wichtigsten (*most important*)
   Städten in Deutschland, Österreich
   und der Schweiz.
2. Der 9. November 1989 ist das Ende
   der Berliner Mauer. Suchen Sie (*Look
   for*) Informationen über diesen Tag.

Find out more at **vhlcentral.com**.

---

höchste Gebirge *highest mountain range* **Menschen** *people* **Berg** *mountain* **Mauer** *Wall* **Grenze** *border*
zwischen *between* **umgibt** *surrounds* **kreiert eine Insel** *creates an island* **des Kalten Krieges** *of the Cold War*
Beobachtungstürme *watchtowers* **Messer** *knives* **natürlich** *of course* **essen... gern** *like to eat* **isst** *eats*
Niemand *Nobody* **mehr... als** *more... than* **von Kaufleuten** *of merchants* **des 12. Jahrhunderts** *of the 12ᵗʰ century*
heutiges *present-day* **Lettland** *Latvia* **liegen** *are located* **Ostsee** *Baltic Sea*

⌖ Was haben Sie gelernt? Complete the statements.

1. Belgien hat _____ offizielle Sprachen.
2. Die deutschsprachige Region ist im _____ Belgiens.
3. Ein anderer (*other*) Name für Österreich ist die _____.
4. Der _____ ist der höchste Berg in Österreich.
5. Die Berliner Mauer existiert von 1961 bis _____.
6. Die Berliner Mauer ist 156,4 _____ lang.
7. Die Schweizer Firma Suchard produziert _____ Schokolade.
8. Jeder _____ isst 11,7 Kilogramm Schokolade pro Jahr.
9. Die Hanse existiert im _____ Europa.
10. Bis zu _____ Städte sind in der Hanse.

Lesen  Audio: Reading

Vor dem Lesen

Strategien

Recognizing cognates

Cognates are words in two or more languages that are similar in meaning and in spelling. Look for cognates to increase your comprehension when you read in German. However, watch out for false cognates. For example, you've already learned that in German, **Note** means *grade*, not *note*. Likewise, **bald** means *soon*, not *bald*, and **fast** means *almost*, not *fast*. Can you guess the meaning of these German words?

das Café	das Programm
der Doktor	das Restaurant
das Hotel	der Sommer
der Juli	das Telefon
das Museum	das Theater

Untersuchen Sie den Text

Look at this text. What kind of information does it present? Where do you usually find such information? Can you guess what this is?

Suchen Sie verwandte Wörter

Read the list of cognates in **Strategien** again. How many of them can you find in the reading? Do you see any additional cognates? Can you guess their English equivalents?

Raten Sie die Bedeutung

Besides using cognates and words you already know, you can also use context to guess the meaning of unfamiliar words. Find the following words in the reading and try to figure out what they mean. Compare your answers with a classmate's.

ägyptisch	Platz
Abakus	Straße

Adressbuch

Ägyptisches Museum

✉ **Residenzstraße 1**   📱 (089) 29 85 46
80333 München

Christian Hunner

✉ **Pfarrstraße 16**   📱 (089) 2 10 28 84
80667 München

Sparda-Bank

✉ **Arnulfstraße 15**   📱 (089) 5 51 42 – 4 00
80335 München

Heideck Apotheke°

✉ **Heideckstraße 31**   📱 (089) 1 57 52 52
80637 München

Il Galeone Ristorante Pizzeria

✉ **Hornsteinstraße 18**   📱 (089) 94 46 47 03
81679 München

Andreas Spitzauer

✉ **Appenzeller Straße 95**   📱 (089) 75 67 19
81475 München

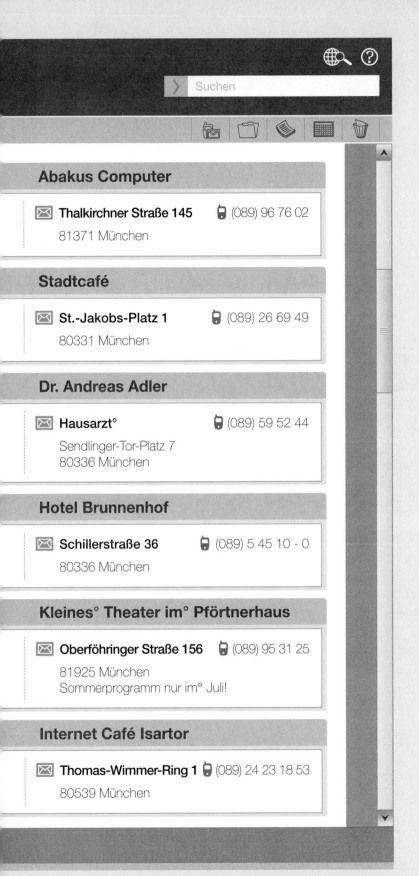

Abakus Computer

✉ **Thalkirchner Straße 145**　📱 (089) 96 76 02
81371 München

Stadtcafé

✉ **St.-Jakobs-Platz 1**　📱 (089) 26 69 49
80331 München

Dr. Andreas Adler

✉ **Hausarzt°**　📱 (089) 59 52 44
Sendlinger-Tor-Platz 7
80336 München

Hotel Brunnenhof

✉ **Schillerstraße 36**　📱 (089) 5 45 10 - 0
80336 München

Kleines° Theater im° Pförtnerhaus

✉ **Oberföhringer Straße 156**　📱 (089) 95 31 25
81925 München
Sommerprogramm nur im° Juli!

Internet Café Isartor

✉ **Thomas-Wimmer-Ring 1**　📱 (089) 24 23 18 53
80539 München

Nach dem Lesen

Wohin gehen sie? Say where each of these people should go, based on the clues.

BEISPIEL Lena loves to eat pasta but hates to cook.
Il Galeone Ristorante Pizzeria

1. Frau Scholz needs to reserve some hotel rooms.

_____

2. Christiane's computer is broken.

_____

3. Herr Meier thinks he has the flu.

_____

4. Nina would like to see some ancient Egyptian art.

_____

5. Herr and Frau Hansel want to go somewhere for coffee or tea.

_____

6. Andrea is meeting some friends for Italian food.

_____

7. Frau Müller needs to buy some aspirin for her daughter.

_____

8. Thomas wants to take his girlfriend to a play.

_____

9. Herr Trüb needs to deposit his paycheck.

_____

10. Sebastian's computer is broken, but he needs to send an e-mail.

_____

Unsere Einträge Select three listings from the reading and use them as models to create similar listings in German that advertise places or services in your area.

BEISPIEL

Stonydale Bank
Hunter Straße 206
50555 Stonydale
Tel. (555) 337-0665

Apotheke *pharmacy* **Hausarzt** *family physician* **Kleines** *Small* **im** *in (the)* **nur im** *only in (the)*

Hören

Strategien

Listening for words you know

You can get the gist of a conversation by listening for words and phrases you already know.

 To help you practice this strategy, listen to these statements and make a list of the words you have already learned.

_____   _____

_____   _____

Vorbereitung

Where are the people in the photograph? What are they doing? Do you think they know each other? Why or why not? What do you think they are talking about?

Zuhören

As you listen, check the words you associate with Tanja and those you associate with Rainer.

Tanja

— der Taschenrechner

— der Computer

— das Blatt Papier

— zwei Bleistifte

— die Prüfung

Rainer

— der Radiergummi

— die Hausaufgaben

— das Heft

— das Problem

— die Karte

Verständnis

Richtig oder falsch? Based on the conversation you heard, indicate whether each statement is **richtig** or **falsch**.

1. Rainer ist Deutschlehrer.

_____

2. Tanja geht es gut.

_____

3. Rainer braucht (*needs*) einen Taschenrechner.

_____

4. Tanja hat ein Problem mit den Hausaufgaben.

_____

5. Rainer hat einen Bleistift für Tanja.

_____

6. Tanja hat ein Blatt Papier für Rainer.

_____

7. Tanja hat zwei Bleistifte.

_____

8. Rainer hilft (*helps*) Tanja bei den Hausaufgaben.

_____

Stellen Sie sich vor! Introduce yourself in German to a classmate you do not know well.

- Greet your partner.
- Ask his or her name.
- Ask how he or she is doing.
- Introduce your partner to another student.
- Say good-bye.

Schreiben

Strategien

Writing in German

Writing can take many forms and serve many functions. You might write an e-mail to get in touch with someone, a blog entry to share your feelings or opinions, or an essay to persuade others to accept a point of view. Good writing requires time, thought, effort, and a lot of practice. Here are some tips to help you write more effectively in German.

DO

- Try to write your ideas in German.
- Decide what the purpose of your writing will be.
- Make an outline of your ideas.
- Use the grammar and vocabulary that you know.
- Use your textbook for examples of punctuation, style conventions, and expressions in German.
- Use your imagination and creativity to make your writing interesting.
- Put yourself in your reader's place to determine if your writing is interesting.

DON'T

- Don't translate your ideas from English to German.
- Don't simply repeat what is in the textbook or on a Web page.
- Don't use an online translator.
- Don't use a bilingual dictionary until you have learned how to use it effectively.

Thema

Machen Sie eine Liste

A group of German-speaking students will be spending a year at your school. Put together a list of people and places that might be useful or interesting to them. Your list should include:

- Your name, address, phone number(s), and e-mail address
- The names of two or three other students in your German class, their addresses, phone numbers, and e-mail addresses
- Your German instructor's name, office phone number, and e-mail address
- The names, addresses, and phone numbers of three places near your school where students like to go (a bookstore, a café or restaurant, a movie theater, etc.)

NAME: Prof. Reinhard (Deutschlehrer)
ADRESSE: Stonydale School
TELEFONNUMMER: (555) 654-3458 (Büro)
HANDY: (555) 919-0040
E-MAIL-ADRESSE: prof.reinhard@stonydale.edu
NOTIZEN: Ist aus Hamburg

NAME: Zest Coffee House
ADRESSE: 8970 McNeil Road
TELEFONNUMMER: (555) 654-0349
HANDY: —
E-MAIL-ADRESSE: info@zest.com
NOTIZEN: Hat sehr guten Kaffee und gute Musik

Lektion 1A

Begrüßung und Abschied

Hallo./Guten Tag. *Hello.*
Guten Morgen. *Good morning.*
Guten Abend. *Good evening.*
Gute Nacht. *Good night.*
Bis bald./Bis gleich. *See you soon.*
Bis dann./Bis später. *See you later.*
Bis morgen. *See you tomorrow.*
Auf Wiedersehen. *Good-bye.*
Schönen Tag noch! *Have a nice day!*
Tschüss. *Bye.*
Alles klar? *Is everything OK?*
Wie geht's (dir)? *How are you? (inf.)*
Wie geht es Ihnen? *How are you? (form.)*
Prima. *Great.*
Sehr gut. *Very well.*
Ziemlich gut. *Fine.*
Und dir/Ihnen? *And you?*
Mir auch. *Me, too.*
Es geht. *So-so.*
(Nicht) schlecht. *(Not) bad.*
Mir geht's (sehr) gut. *I'm (very) well.*
Mir geht's nicht (so) gut. *I'm not (so) well.*

sich vorstellen

Wie heißt du? *What is your name? (inf.)*
Wie heißen Sie? *What is your name? (form.)*
Und du/Sie? *And you? (inf./form.)*
Das ist.../Das sind... *This is.../These are...*
Ich heiße... *My name is...*
Freut mich./Angenehm. *Pleased to meet you.*
Schön dich/Sie kennen zu lernen. *Nice to meet you. (inf./form.)*

Personen

die Frau, -en *woman*
der Freund, -e / die Freundin, -nen *friend*
der Junge, -n *boy*
das Mädchen, - *girl*
der Mann, ⁻er *man*
Herr *Mr.*
Frau *Mrs.; Ms.*

Höflichkeiten

Danke. *Thank you.*
Vielen Dank. *Thank you very much.*
Bitte. *Please./You're welcome.*
Gern geschehen. *My pleasure.*
Entschuldigung. *Excuse me.*
Entschuldigen Sie. *Excuse me. (form.)*
Es tut mir leid. *I'm sorry.*
ja *yes*
nein *no*

Orte

wo? *where?*
hier *here*
da / dort *there*

- -

Nouns and articles *See pp. 10–11.*
Compound nouns *See p. 11.*
Plurals *See p. 14.*
Subject pronouns *See p. 16.*
sein *See p. 17.*
Nominative articles *See p. 17.*

Lektion 1B

im Unterricht

das Blatt Papier, (pl. Blätter Papier) *sheet of paper*
der Bleistift, -e *pencil*
das Buch, ⁻er *book*
der Computer, - *computer*
das Ergebnis, -se *result; score*
das Fenster, - *window*
das Foto, -s *photo*
die Frage, -n *question*
die Hausaufgabe, -n *homework*
das Heft, -e *notebook*
der Kalender, - *calendar*
die Karte, -n *map*
die Klasse, -n *class*
das Klassenzimmer, - *classroom*
der Kuli, -s *ball-point pen*
das Lehrbuch, ⁻er *(university) textbook*
die Note, -n *grade (on an assignment)*
die Notiz, -en *note*
der Papierkorb, ⁻e *wastebasket*
das Problem, -e *problem*
die Prüfung, -en *test; exam*
der Radiergummi, -s *eraser*
der Rucksack, ⁻e *backpack*
der Schreibtisch, -e *desk*
die Sache, -n *thing*
das Schulbuch, ⁻er *(K–12) textbook*
der Stift, -e *pen*
der Stuhl, ⁻e *chair*
die Stunde, -n *lesson*
die Tafel, -n *(black/white) board*
der Taschenrechner, - *calculator*
der Tisch, -e *table; desk*
die Tür, -en *door*
die Uhr, -en *clock*
das Wörterbuch, ⁻er *dictionary*
das Zeugnis, -se *report card; grade report*
Da ist/sind... *There is/are...*
Ist/Sind...hier? *Is/Are there... here?*
Hier ist/sind... *Here is/are...*
Was ist das? *What is that?*

Orte

die Schule, -n *school*
die Universität, -en *university, college*
die Bibliothek, -en *library*
die Mensa, Mensen *(university) cafeteria*

Personen

der Klassenkamerad, -en /die Klassenkameradin, -nen *(K–12) classmate*
der Kommilitone, -n / die Kommilitonin, -nen *(university) classmate*
der Lehrer, - / die Lehrerin, -nen *teacher*
der Professor, -en / die Professorin, -nen *professor*
der Schüler, - / die Schülerin, -nen *(K–12) student*
der Student, -en / die Studentin, -nen *(university) student*
Wer ist das? *Who is it?*

- -

haben *See p. 30.*
Accusative articles *See p. 30.*
Yes-or-no questions *See p. 32.*
Numbers and math expressions *See pp. 34–35*

Vocabulary Tools

Wortschatz

das Studium	*studies*
der Abschluss, ¨e / das Diplom, -e	*degree*
das Abschlusszeugnis, -se / das Diplom, -e	*diploma*
der Dozent, -en / die Dozentin, -nen	*college/university instructor*
das Fach, ¨er	*subject*
das Seminar, -e	*seminar*
das Stipendium, -en	*scholarship*
die Veranstaltung, -en	*class; course*
die Vorlesung, -en	*lecture*
belegen	*to take (a class)*
gehen	*to go*
lernen	*to study; to learn*
studieren	*to study; to major in*
Orte	***places***
das Café, -s	*café*
der Hörsaal, Hörsäle	*lecture hall*
der Seminarraum, -räume	*college classroom*
die Sporthalle, -n	*gym*
zum Beschreiben	***to describe***
einfach	*easy*
interessant	*interesting*
langweilig	*boring*
nützlich / nutzlos	*useful / useless*
schwierig	*difficult*
der Stundenplan	***schedule***
der Montag, -e	*Monday*
der Dienstag, -e	*Tuesday*
der Mittwoch, -e	*Wednesday*
der Donnerstag, -e	*Thursday*
der Freitag, -e	*Friday*
der Samstag, -e	*Saturday*
der Sonntag, -e	*Sunday*
die Stunde, -n	*hour*
die Woche, -n	*week*
das Wochenende, -n	*weekend*
die Zeit, -en	*time*
montags/dienstags/ mittwochs	*on Mondays/Tuesdays/ Wednesdays*
morgens	*in the morning*
nachmittags	*in the afternoon*
abends	*in the evening*

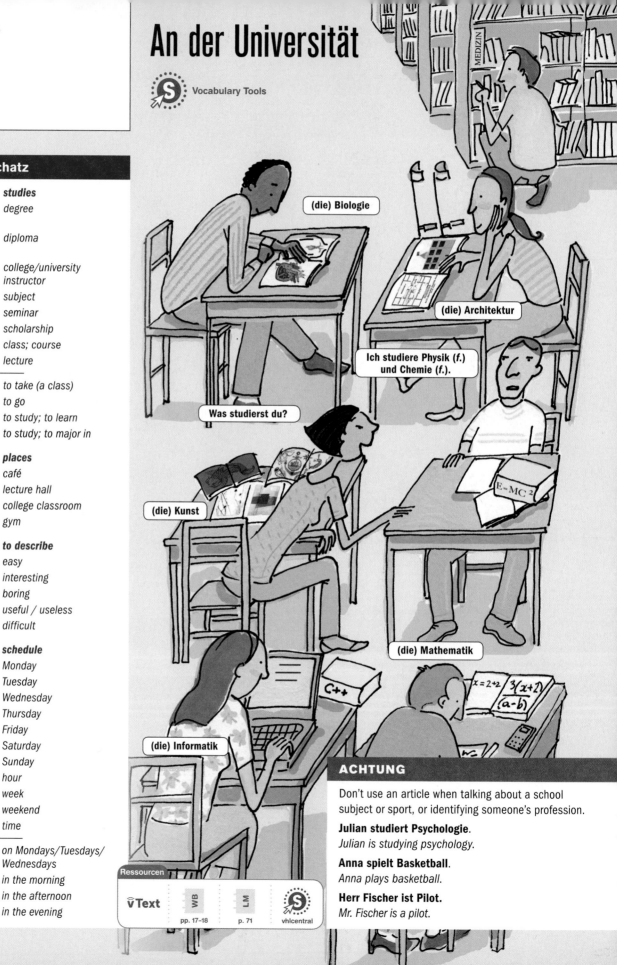

(die) Biologie

(die) Architektur

Ich studiere Physik (f.) und Chemie (f.).

Was studierst du?

(die) Kunst

$E = MC^2$

(die) Mathematik

(die) Informatik

$x = 2 + 2$ $\dfrac{3(x+2)}{(a-b)}$

ACHTUNG

Don't use an article when talking about a school subject or sport, or identifying someone's profession.

Julian studiert Psychologie.
Julian is studying psychology.

Anna spielt Basketball.
Anna plays basketball.

Herr Fischer ist Pilot.
Mr. Fischer is a pilot.

Ressourcen

vText | WB pp. 17–18 | LM p. 71 | vhlcentral

(die) Psychologie

(die) Fremdsprachen (f., pl.)

(die) Wirtschaft

(die) Geschichte

(die) Naturwissenschaften (f., pl.)

Anwendung

1 **Was passt zusammen?** Match related words in the two columns.

____ 1. der Computer	a. die Fremdsprache
____ 2. die Vorlesung	b. die Sporthalle
____ 3. die Biologie	c. der Hörsaal
____ 4. das Diplom	d. die Naturwissenschaft
____ 5. Montag, Dienstag, Mittwoch...	e. der Abschluss
____ 6. Deutsch	f. die Informatik
____ 7. Sigmund Freud	g. die Psychologie
____ 8. der Basketball	h. die Woche

2 **Das Unileben** Listen to the conversation between Hannah and Mehmet and indicate which classes each of them is taking this semester.

Veranstaltungen	Mehmet	Hannah
Mathematik		
Physik		
Chemie		
Geschichte		
Literatur		
Kunst		
Psychologie		
Medizin		
Informatik		

3 **Was fehlt?** Complete the sentences. Use each word once.

abends	Naturwissenschaften
Dozentin	Seminarraum
Fremdsprachen	Stipendium
Hörsaal	Wirtschaft

1. Die Vorlesung von Professor Huber ist im _____ C.
2. Chemie, Physik und Biologie sind _____.
3. Frau Klein ist _____ an der Uni.
4. Für ein Studium in _____ ist Mathematik nützlich.
5. Spanisch, Italienisch und Chinesisch sind _____.
6. Wir haben eine Veranstaltung in diesem (this) _____.
7. Eva hat ein _____ und studiert in England.
8. Morgens und nachmittags gehen die Studenten in Seminare und Vorlesungen, und _____ gehen sie in die Bibliothek.

Kommunikation

4 Auf dem Campus
Write a caption for each picture. Complete the sentences to say what each person is studying and add one sentence giving your opinion of each course. In pairs, take turns reading your sentences out of order. Your partner must decide which picture each sentence refers to.

▶ **BEISPIEL**

Max studiert __Informatik__.
__Informatik ist schwierig.__

1. Daniela studiert _____.
   _____

2. Björn studiert _____.
   _____

3. Anna studiert _____.
   _____

4. Mia und ich studieren _____.
   _____

5 Ihr Studium
Indicate whether each statement is **richtig** or **falsch**, in your opinion. Then, compare your answers with a classmate's.

BEISPIEL

S1: Chemie ist nützlich. Richtig oder falsch?
S2: Falsch. Chemie ist nutzlos.

	richtig	falsch
1. Mathematik ist schwierig.	☐	☐
2. Fremdsprachen sind nützlich.	☐	☐
3. Literatur ist interessant.	☐	☐
4. Ein Abschluss in Psychologie ist nutzlos.	☐	☐
5. Prüfungen in Geschichte sind einfach.	☐	☐
6. Ein Wirtschaftsstudium ist langweilig.	☐	☐

6 Arbeitsblatt
Your instructor will give you a worksheet. Keep a record of your classmates' answers to share with the class.

BEISPIEL

S1: Ist Mathematik einfach oder schwierig?
S2: Mathematik ist schwierig, aber nützlich.

7 Diskutieren und kombinieren
Your instructor will give you and a partner different worksheets. Each worksheet includes part of Sarah's weekly schedule. In pairs, take turns asking each other questions to fill in the missing information and complete the schedule.

BEISPIEL

S1: Hat Sarah montags Chemie?
S2: Nein, sie hat mittwochs Chemie.
S1: Hat sie montags Geschichte?
S2: Ja, sie hat montagnachmittags Geschichte.
S1: Hat sie...?

Aussprache und Rechtschreibung

 Audio

Consonant sounds

The German letter **g** has three different pronunciations. At the end of a syllable or before a **t**, it is pronounced like the *k* in the English word *keep*. In the suffix **-ig**, the **g** is pronounced like the German **ch**. Otherwise, **g** is pronounced like the *g* in the English word *garden*.

| Ta**g** | bele**g**t | schwieri**g** | **g**ehen | fra**g**en |

The German letter **j** is pronounced very similarly to the letter *y* in the English word *young*. However, in a small number of loanwords from other languages, **j** may be pronounced like the *j* in *job* or the *g* in *mirage*.

| **j**ung | **J**anuar | **j**a | **j**obben | **J**ournal |

The German letter **v** is pronounced like the *f* in the English word *fable*. In a few loanwords from other languages, **v** is pronounced like the *v* in the English word *vase*.

| **v**ier | **V**orlesung | **V**ase | Uni**v**ersität | **V**olleyball |

The German letter **w** is pronounced like the *v* in the English word *vote*.

| **w**issen | Mitt**w**och | **W**irtschaft | **W**ort | Sch**w**ester |

1 Aussprechen Practice saying these words aloud.

1. Garten
2. Essig
3. Weg
4. Jahr
5. Journalist
6. joggen
7. Vater
8. verstehen
9. Violine
10. Wasser
11. zwischen
12. weil

2 Nachsprechen Practice saying these sentences aloud.

1. Wir wollen wissen, wie wir das wissen sollen.
2. In vier Wochen wird Veronikas Vater wieder in seiner Villa wohnen.
3. Gestern war Gregors zwanzigster Geburtstag.
4. Jeden Tag soll ich Gemüse und Grünzeug wie Salat essen.
5. Meine Schwester studiert Jura an der Universität Jena.
6. Viele Studenten jobben, um das Studium zu finanzieren.

3 Sprichwörter Practice reading these sayings aloud.

Was ich nicht weiß, macht mich nicht heiß.[2]

Es ist nicht alles Gold, was glänzt.[1]

[1] All that glitters is not gold.

[2] Ignorance is bliss. (lit. *What I don't know, doesn't bother me.*)

Ressourcen

vText | LM p. 72 | vhlcentral

Checkpoint Charlie 🅢 Video

George und Hans reden über (*talk about*) das Studium und über
Meline und Sabite. Ist Hans in Sabite verliebt (*in love*)?

GEORGE Woher kommst du?
HANS Ich komme aus Straubing. Das ist
in Bayern.
GEORGE Wie viele Menschen leben dort?
HANS Hmm... etwa 100.000.

HANS Woher kommst du?
GEORGE Milwaukee, Wisconsin.
HANS Wie viel Uhr ist es dort?
GEORGE Wie viel Uhr ist es hier?
HANS Es ist Viertel vor zwei.
GEORGE Der Zeitunterschied ist sieben
Stunden. Also Viertel vor sieben morgens.

HANS Alles in Ordnung?
GEORGE Ich studiere Architektur, belege
Kurse in Städtebau, Physik, Mathematik
und Philosophie!

HANS Und du belegst einen Deutschkurs,
nicht wahr? Studieren ist nicht leicht.
George, du bist ein Mitbewohner und Freund.
Ich helfe dir.
GEORGE Wann?
HANS Morgens. Um 5.00 Uhr!

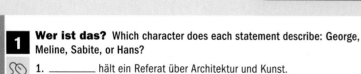

GEORGE Hey! Wir sind da!
HANS Check...
GEORGE ...point Charlie.

GEORGE Sabite kommt aus Prenzlauer
Berg. Und Meline?
HANS Was ist mit Meline?
GEORGE Woher kommt sie?
HANS Wien.

ÜBUNGEN

1 **Wer ist das?** Which character does each statement describe: George,
Meline, Sabite, or Hans?

1. _____ hält ein Referat über Architektur und Kunst.
2. _____ kommt aus Wien.
3. _____ belegt einen Deutschkurs.
4. _____ kommt aus Straubing.
5. _____ studiert Architektur.

6. _____ ist Hans' Mitbewohner und Freund.
7. _____ liest Bücher über Kunst und Mode.
8. _____ kommt aus Prenzlauer Berg.
9. _____ kommt aus Milwaukee.
10. _____ hilft (*helps*) George morgens um 5.00 Uhr.

7

HANS Sabite ist ganz anders. Sie liest Bücher über Kunst und Mode.

GEORGE Mode ist nutzlos. Ich halte am 20. Oktober ein Referat über Architektur und Kunst in Berlin. Sabite hilft mir.

HANS Was?

GEORGE Sabite studiert Kunst. Ich halte bald das Referat. Sie hilft mir.

8

GEORGE Alles in Ordnung, Hans?

HANS Ja, alles klar. Lernst du Philosophie mit Meline?

GEORGE Wo liegt das Problem?

HANS Was?

GEORGE Hans, findest du Sabite...

9

HANS Sabite ist nur eine Freundin.

GEORGE Okay.

HANS Also, ähm... hat Sabite einen Freund? Nein?

GEORGE Ich glaube nicht, dass sie einen hat.

10

HANS Du und Sabite, ihr seid nicht...?

GEORGE Nein!

HANS Okay.

GEORGE Okay.

Nützliche Ausdrücke

- **etwa**
  about

- **Wie viel Uhr ist es dort?**
  What time is it there?

- **der Zeitunterschied**
  time difference

- **Und du belegst einen Deutschkurs, nicht wahr?**
  And you're taking a German class, aren't you?

- **Ich helfe dir.**
  I'll help you.

- **Was ist mit Meline?**
  What's with Meline?

- **ein Referat halten**
  to give a presentation

- **Alles klar!**
  All right!

- **Wo liegt das Problem?**
  Where's the problem?

- **Sabite ist nur eine Freundin.**
  Sabite's just a friend.

- **Ich glaube nicht, dass sie einen hat.**
  I don't think she has one.

2A.1
- **Sabite studiert Kunst.**
  Sabite is studying art.

2A.2
- **Woher kommst du?**
  Where are you from?

2A.3
- **Es ist Viertel vor zwei.**
  It's a quarter to two.

2 **Zum Besprechen** In this episode, the characters talk about their classes. With a partner, discuss your classes and schedule. Mention what you are studying, how many courses you are taking, and which courses you have in the morning, afternoon, or evenings.

BEISPIEL

S1: Welche Faecher hast du?
S2: Ich habe Fremdsprachen und Geschichte. Und du?

3 **Vertiefung** George and Hans visit Checkpoint Charlie on their walk in Berlin. Find out more about this well-known landmark. What is its significance? What streets are nearby? What does "Charlie" refer to?

Uni-Zeit, Büffel-Zeit°

HISTORICALLY, UNIVERSITY EDUCATION in Germany has been government-funded and free for all students. In the past few decades, some states introduced modest tuition fees—usually 500 Euros per semester. However, the fees proved so unpopular that they have since been abolished. As of October 2014, all public universities are again tuition-free, even for foreign students.

Apart from cost, there are other significant differences between German and American university life. German universities typically offer only a limited amount of dormitory housing. Most students live off campus, either commuting from home or renting an apartment shared with other students. Unlike in most American Universities, students must decide on a major before they begin their studies, and there is little flexibility in the choice of courses.

In the past few decades, there has been an initiative to standardize degree requirements between countries. Part of this restructuring has included a push to transition from 4- to 6-year **Diplom** and **Magister**° degrees to 3-year **Bachelor** degrees. This change has met with resistance from students, including complaints that it simply compresses the original curriculum into a shorter time frame. Many students also object to the shift toward a heavier workload with more frequent testing.

The percentage of students studying at private universities remains very small, but it is gradually increasing. Whereas public universities have had problems with over-crowding, private institutions can offer smaller class sizes, giving students more contact with professors.

Statistische Informationen zum Thema Studium	
Neue Studenten pro Jahr°	ca. 1.000.000
Studenten, die nach dem° Bachelor weiter studieren°	78%
Bachelor-Studenten, die zum Studieren ins Ausland gehen°	15%
Bachelor-Absolventen°, die 1,5 Jahre nach dem Abschluss Arbeit° haben	ca. 97%

QUELLE: Der Tagesspiegel

Büffel-Zeit *cramming time* **Diplom, Magister** *degrees available before the education reform* **pro Jahr** *per year* **die nach dem** *who after the* **weiter studieren** *continue their studies* **ins Ausland gehen** *go abroad* **Absolventen** *graduates* **Arbeit** *work*

1 **Richtig oder falsch?** Indicate whether each statement is **richtig** or **falsch**. Correct the false statements.

1. The majority of universities in Germany are public.
2. German universities have always charged tuition fees.
3. Students in Germany have accepted reforms in education wholeheartedly.
4. It takes more time to earn a **Bachelor**'s degree than it did to earn the **Magister** or the **Diplom**.
5. Students now have a lighter workload with fewer tests.
6. A small percentage of students study at private universities.
7. Private and public universities charge the same tuition fees.
8. The majority of German students leave school after completing their Bachelor degree.
9. Most German students study abroad.
10. In Germany, most students live in dormitories.

Die Uni

der Besserwisser, -	know-it-all
der Mitbewohner, - / die Mitbewohnerin, -nen	roommate
das Referat, -e	presentation
das Schwarze Brett	bulletin board
das Studentenwohnheim, -e	dormitory
die Studiengebühr, -en	tuition fee
büffeln	to cram (for a test)

Der Bologna-Prozess

Die Bildungsminister° der Europäischen Union treffen sich erstmals° 1999 in Bologna in Italien. Das Ziel°: international einheitliche° Universitäts-Abschlüsse in ganz Europa und hohe° Mobilität für Studenten. In Europa müssen° Universitäten die Hochschulbildung° standardisieren. Bis zum° Jahre 2010 will man einen gemeinsamen° europäischen Hochschulraum° entwickeln°. Er wird im März 2010 in Budapest und Wien offiziell eröffnet°. 47 Mitgliedsländer° nehmen daran teil°.

Bildungsminister secretaries of education **treffen... erstmals** meet for the first time **Ziel** goal **einheitliche** standardized **hohe** high **müssen** must **Hochschulbildung** higher education **Bis zum** Until **gemeinsam** common **Hochschulraum** Higher Education Area **entwickeln** develop **eröffnet** opened **Mitgliedsländer** member countries **nehmen... teil** participate

Uni Basel

Universität Basel (gegründet° 1460): Viele brillante Wissenschaftler° belegen hier Vorlesungen und machen ihren° Abschluss in Medizin, Philosophie oder Psychologie. Der exzentrische Paracelsus (1493–1541) ist hier Professor für Medizin. Auch Holbein (1497–1543), Jung (1875–1961) und Hesse (1877–1962) leben° in Basel. Aber der berühmteste° Professor hier ist der Philosoph Friedrich Nietzsche (1844–1900).

Heute ist die Universität in Basel voller Leben° und sehr modern. Mehr als 13.000 Studenten sind hier. Viele studieren Biowissenschaften°. Andere° lernen Literatur, Wirtschaft oder Mathematik – für 850 Schweizer Franken pro Semester.

gegründet founded **Wissenschaftler** scientists **machen ihren** make their **leben** live **berühmteste** most famous **voller Leben** full of life **Biowissenschaften** life sciences **Andere** Others

🔗 IM INTERNET

Österreichische Universitäten. Wie ist das Studium in Österreich? Ist es mit dem (with the) deutschen System vergleichbar (comparable)?

Find out more at **vhlcentral.com**.

---

2 **Was fehlt?** Complete the sentences.

1. Nach der Bologna-Erklärung müssen viele Länder in Europa die Hochschulbildung _____.

2. Der Bologna-Prozess hat als Ziel international einheitliche _____.

3. Heute lernen Studenten in Basel _____, Literatur, Wirtschaft oder Mathematik.

4. Der berühmteste Professor der Universität Basel ist _____.

3 **Studentenleben** In pairs, discuss the similarities and differences between student life in German-speaking countries and in the United States. Would you like to study in a German-speaking country? Which system do you think is best? Give reasons for your answers.

2A.1 Regular verbs  Presentation

Startblock Most German verbs follow predictable conjugation patterns in which a set of endings is added to the verb stem.

Ich **studiere** Architektur.

Lernst du Philosophie mit Meline?

QUERVERWEIS

In **Kapitel 1**, you learned the irregular verbs **sein** and **haben**. You will learn more about irregular verbs in **2B.1**.

ACHTUNG

Depending on the context, **sie lernt** can be translated as *she studies, she is studying,* or *she does study.*

- To form the present tense of a regular verb, drop the **-en** or **-n** ending from the infinitive and add **-e**, **-st**, **-t**, or **-en/-n** to the stem.

	lernen (*to study*)		wandern (*to hike*)	
ich	lern**e**	*I study*	wander**e**	*I hike*
du	lern**st**	*you study*	wander**st**	*you hike*
Sie	lern**en**	*you study*	wander**n**	*you hike*
er/sie/es	lern**t**	*he/she studies*	wander**t**	*he/she hikes*
wir	lern**en**	*we study*	wander**n**	*we hike*
ihr	lern**t**	*you study*	wander**t**	*you hike*
Sie	lern**en**	*you study*	wander**n**	*you hike*
sie	lern**en**	*they study*	wander**n**	*they hike*

Lernst du Physik?
Are you studying physics?

Sie wandern im Sommer.
They go hiking in the summer.

- Regular verbs whose stems end in **-d** or **-t** add an **e** before the endings **-st** or **-t** for ease of pronunciation.

arbeiten (*to work*)			
ich arbeit**e**	*I work*	wir arbeit**en**	*we work*
du arbeit**est**	*you work*	ihr arbeit**et**	*you work*
Sie arbeit**en**	*you work*	Sie arbeit**en**	*you work*
er/sie/es arbeit**et**	*he/she/it works*	sie arbeit**en**	*they work*

Lena **arbeitet** in München.
*Lena **works** in Munich.*

Findest du Mathematik interessant?
Do you find math interesting?

QUERVERWEIS

As in English, the simple present can sometimes be used to talk about a future action. You will learn more about this usage in **2B.2**.

Wartet ihr auf eure Freunde?
Are you waiting for your friends?

Die Hefte **kosten** zu viel.
*The notebooks **cost** too much.*

- Verbs whose stems end in **-gn** or **-fn** also add an **-e** before the endings **-st** and **-t**.

Es regnet morgen.
It's going to rain tomorrow.

Öffnest du das Fenster?
Are you opening the window?

- If a verb stem ends in **-s**, **-ß**, **-x**, or **-z**, the **-s** is dropped from the second person singular ending.

heißen (*to be named*)			
ich heiße	*I am named*	wir heißen	*we are named*
du heißt	*you are named*	ihr heißt	*you are named*
Sie heißen	*you are named*	Sie heißen	*you are named*
er/sie/es heißt	*he/she/it is named*	sie heißen	*they are named*

Du heißt Jonas, nicht wahr?
Your name is Jonas, right?

Martin **reist** oft in die Schweiz.
Martin often travels to Switzerland.

Mein Hund **heißt** Fritz.
My dog's name is Fritz.

Ihr **grüßt** den Lehrer nicht?
You're not going to greet the teacher?

common regular verbs (present tense)			
antworten	*to answer*	leben	*to live*
bauen	*to build*	lernen	*to learn; to study*
bedeuten	*to mean*	lieben	*to love*
begrüßen	*to greet*	machen	*to do; to make*
belegen	*to take (a class)*	öffnen	*to open*
brauchen	*to need*	regnen	*to rain*
bringen	*to bring*	reisen	*to travel*
finden	*to find*	sagen	*to say*
fragen	*to ask*	schreiben	*to write*
gehen	*to go*	spielen	*to play*
hören	*to hear; to listen to*	suchen	*to look for*
kaufen	*to buy*	verstehen	*to understand*
kommen	*to come*	warten	*to wait*
korrigieren	*to correct*	wiederholen	*to repeat*
kosten	*to cost*	wohnen	*to live (somewhere)*

Kaufst du Kaffee im Supermarkt?
Do you buy coffee at the supermarket?

Ich **lerne** Deutsch.
I'm learning German.

Was **bedeutet** das auf Englisch?
What does that mean in English?

Wir **belegen** Biologie.
We're taking Biology.

ACHTUNG

Note that the **du**, **er/sie/es**, and **ihr** forms of **heißen** are identical.

QUERVERWEIS

Some verbs, including **bringen**, **finden**, **gehen**, and **schreiben** are regular in the present tense and irregular in the past tense.

Ressourcen

v̂Text

WB
pp. 19–20

LM
p. 73

S
vhlcentral

Jetzt sind Sie dran! Write the appropriate form of the verb.

1. Wir ___lernen___ (lernen) Deutsch.
2. Der Student _____ (wiederholen) den Satz (*sentence*).
3. Ich _____ (warten) auf den Bus.
4. Die Lehrerin _____ (korrigieren) die Prüfungen.
5. Du _____ (belegen) fünf Veranstaltungen.
6. Das Universitätsstudium _____ (kosten) sehr viel.
7. Ihr _____ (verstehen) Mathematik.
8. Wir _____ (brauchen) viel Papier und viele Bleistifte für den Unterricht.
9. Anja und Thomas _____ (begrüßen) den Dozenten.
10. Ich _____ (kaufen) eine Tasse Kaffee in der Mensa.
11. Wir _____ (machen) nachmittags Hausaufgaben.
12. Du _____ (öffnen) die Tür.

Anwendung

1 **Was ist richtig?** Select the verb that best completes each sentence.

1. Astrid und Jonas (wohnen / bedeuten) in Berlin.
2. Michaela (sucht / korrigiert) den Seminarraum.
3. Ich (baue / studiere) Informatik und Mathematik.
4. Wir (belegen / grüßen) sehr viele Vorlesungen.
5. (Belegst / Lebst) du in Deutschland oder in Österreich?
6. Ihr (macht / kauft) nachmittags Hausaufgaben.
7. (Warten / Kosten) Sie auf (*for*) den Bus, Professor Meier?
8. Du (sagst / reist) im Sommer nach (*to*) Spanien und Italien.

2 **Was fehlt?** Maria and Tim are meeting for lunch. Complete their conversation with the correct verb forms.

MARIA Hallo, Tim! Wie (1) _____ (gehen) es dir? Wie ist das Deutschseminar?

TIM Ach, es geht mir ziemlich gut. Im Seminar (2) _____ (schreiben) der Dozent viel an die Tafel, aber ich (3) _____ (verstehen) es gut. Und du? Wie (4) _____ (finden) du das Informatikseminar?

MARIA Ich (5) _____ (lieben) Informatik! Wir (6) _____ (bauen) heute einen Computer.

TIM Vielleicht (*Maybe*) (7) _____ (belegen) ich nächstes Semester auch Informatik. (8) _____ (Machen) du viele Hausaufgaben?

MARIA Ja! Samstags und sonntags (9) _____ (lernen) ich immer (*always*).

TIM Oje. Samstags und sonntags (10) _____ (spielen) Max und ich Computer.

3 **Schreiben** Write complete sentences using the cues.

1. ich / kaufen / einen Apfel
2. David / brauchen / das Wörterbuch
3. du / arbeiten / freitags und samstags
4. Lara / suchen / das Deutschbuch
5. Josef und ich / spielen / Basketball
6. lernen / ihr / Spanisch / ?
7. der Dozent / wiederholen / das Experiment
8. Hans und Jana / leben / in Irland
9. regnen / es / ?
10. öffnen / du / das Fenster / ?

 Practice more at **vhlcentral.com**.

Kommunikation

4 **Was fehlt?** Complete the sentences, and then, with a partner, take turns asking and explaining what each person is doing.

▶ **BEISPIEL**

Du ___hörst___ Musik.
S1: *Was mache ich?*
S2: *Du hörst Musik.*

1. Herr Becker _____.

2. Wir_____ Tennis.

3. Ihr_____ viel.

4. Ich_____ ein neues Fahrrad.

5. Heinrich_____ den Mann.

6. Hans_____ Emma.

5 **Bilden Sie Sätze** In pairs, use items from each column to create six sentences. You may use some items more than once.

BEISPIEL *Ich höre Musik.*

A	B	C
ich	hören	Deutsch
du	lernen	Hausaufgaben
Alena	lieben	Kunst
Anna und ich	machen	Musik
ihr	spielen	Naturwissenschaft
die Studenten	verstehen	Tennis

6 **Persönliche Fragen** In pairs, take turns asking and answering the questions.

1. Wie viele Kurse belegst du?
2. Lernst du Fremdsprachen?
3. Gehst du oft in die Sporthalle?

4. Was machst du morgens?
5. Was machst du nachmittags?
6. Was machst du abends?

7 **Gespräch** In pairs, fill in Student 2's half of the dialogue, then continue the conversation with your partner using at least four more regular verbs.

S1: Hallo! Studierst du hier an der Uni?
S2: …
S1: Ich auch! Was studierst du?
S2: …
S1: Ist Wirtschaft schwierig?
S2: …
S1: Montags und mittwochs habe ich Geschichte. Und du?
S2: …

2A.2 Interrogative words  Presentation

Startblock Use interrogative words to ask for information.

> **Wie viele** Menschen leben dort?

> **Was** ist mit Meline?

ACHTUNG

In **1B.3**, you learned to use **wie viel** with a singular noun and **wie viele** with a plural noun.

Wie viel Zeit haben wir?
Wie viele Bücher kauft er?

The word **viel(e)** by itself means *a lot (of)/many*.
Ich studiere viele Fächer.
Du arbeitest viel.

QUERVERWEIS

Answers to questions that ask **Wie...?** or **Wo...?** may require the dative case. You will learn about the dative in **4B.1** and **4B.2**.

interrogatives			
wann?	*when?*	**wie?**	*how?*
warum?	*why?*	**wie viel(e)?**	*how much/many?*
was?	*what?*	**wo?**	*where?*
welcher/welche/welches?	*which?*	**woher?**	*where (from)?*
wer/wen?	*who/whom?*	**wohin?**	*where (to)?*

- To ask an information question (one that cannot be answered with **ja** or **nein**), begin the question with an interrogative word.

Wann beginnen wir?	**Warum** machst du das?	**Wo** ist Frau Schultz?
When do we start?	*Why are you doing that?*	*Where is Mrs. Schultz?*

- Use **wer** when the person you're asking about is the grammatical subject of the verb and **wen** when the person is the direct object of the verb.

Wer begrüßt den Professor?	**Wen** begrüßt der Professor?
Who is greeting the professor?	*Who(m) is the professor greeting?*

- The form of **welcher** depends on the gender and number of the noun it modifies. Its three forms (**welcher/welche/welches**) have the same endings as the masculine, feminine/plural, and neuter forms of the definite article (**der/die/das**).

Welche Professorin lehrt Mathematik?	**Welcher Student** belegt Mathematik?
Which professor teaches mathematics?	*Which student is taking math?*

- Use **woher** to ask people where they are from and **wohin** to ask where they are going.

—**Woher** kommen Sie?	—**Wohin** geht ihr?
—Ich komme **aus Wien**.	—Wir gehen **in die Bibliothek**.
—Where are you from?	*—Where are you going?*
—I'm from Vienna.	*—We're going to the library.*

Ressourcen

v Text

WB
pp. 21–22

LM
p. 74

vhlcentral

Jetzt sind Sie dran! Select the appropriate interrogative for each question.

1. (Woher / Wer) kommst du?
2. (Wohin / Wann) haben wir Deutsch?
3. (Was / Wohin) reisen wir?
4. (Wer / Wo) braucht ein Blatt Papier?
5. (Welche / Woher) Seminare sind einfach?
6. (Wer / Wen) liebst du?

Anwendung und Kommunikation

1 **Was fehlt?** Complete each sentence with an appropriate interrogative word.

1. _____ spielen wir Tennis?
2. _____ kommt die Dozentin?
3. _____ kaufst du für das Studium?
4. _____ brauchst du einen Computer?
5. _____ lernst du?
6. _____ alt bist du?
7. _____ Kurse belegst du?
8. _____ Zeit haben wir abends?

2 **Schreiben** Write questions using the cues. Pay attention to word order.

> **BEISPIEL** Marie und Alex / woher / kommen
> *Woher kommen Marie und Alex?*

1. der Hörsaal / wo / ist
2. wie / die Deutschvorlesung / ist
3. gehen / wann / wir / in die Bibliothek
4. einen Kuli / wer / braucht
5. machst / was / du / samstags
6. wohin / gehen / nachmittags / die Studenten
7. welches / belegt / Seminar / ihr
8. lernt / warum / Paul / so viel

3 **Fragen** In pairs, write a question for each response.

> **BEISPIEL** Ich komme <u>aus Wien</u>.
> *Woher kommst du?*

1. Karl hat <u>montags, mittwochs und freitags</u> Vorlesungen.
2. Die Bibliothek hat <u>3.726</u> Bücher.
3. <u>Das Seminar</u> ist langweilig.
4. Das Heft kostet <u>3,50 €</u>.
5. Ich brauche das Buch *Siddhartha* für die Literaturvorlesung.
6. Ich wohne <u>in Berlin</u>.
7. <u>Der Dozent</u> wiederholt die Frage.
8. Anna liebt <u>Paul</u>.

4 **Interview** Prepare six questions about school life using interrogative words. Then, survey your classmates.

2A.3 Talking about time and dates  Presentation

Startblock Like English, German uses cardinal numbers (*one, two, three*) to tell time and ordinal numbers (*first, second, third*) to give dates.

Telling time

ACHTUNG

To specify the time of day, you can add **morgens**, **vormittags** (*before noon*), **nachmittags**, or **abends**. Use **vormittags** after 10 a.m. and **abends** after 6 p.m.

Es ist 9 Uhr morgens.
It's 9 a.m.

Es ist 11 Uhr vormittags.
It's 11 a.m.

- To ask *What time is it?*, say **Wie spät ist es?** or **Wie viel Uhr ist es?**. To answer, say **Es ist** + [*hour*] + **Uhr** + [*minutes*].

Es ist ein Uhr./
Es ist eins.

Es ist zwei Uhr./
Es ist zwei.

Es ist zwölf Uhr./
Es ist Mittag/Mitternacht.

- Use **vor** and **nach** to indicate minutes before and after the hour. Use **Viertel vor** for *quarter to* and **Viertel nach** for *quarter past*. In these constructions, omit the word **Uhr**.

Es ist **Viertel vor** elf./
Es ist zehn Uhr fünfundvierzig.

Es ist **zwanzig nach** vier./
Es ist vier Uhr zwanzig.

- Use **halb** to mean *half an hour before*. Note that it is not equivalent to the English phrase *half past*.

Es ist **halb zehn**.
Es ist neun Uhr dreißig.

Es ist **halb sieben**.
Es ist sechs Uhr dreißig.

- Use the 24-hour clock when talking about train schedules, movie listings, and official timetables. Do not use the expressions **Viertel vor**, **Viertel nach**, or **halb** with the 24-hour clock.

  20.30 Uhr = zwanzig Uhr dreißig
  8:30 p.m.

  18.45 Uhr = achtzehn Uhr fünfundvierzig
  6:45 p.m.

- To specify the time at which an event or activity will take place, use **um** + [*time*].

  —**Um wie viel Uhr** beginnt der Film?
  —*What time* does the movie start?

  —**Um** sechzehn Uhr zehn.
  —*At four-ten p.m.*

Ordinal numbers

QUERVERWEIS

See **1B.3** to review the cardinal numbers.

- The ordinal numbers (**die Ordinalzahlen**) from 1st to 19th are formed, with a few exceptions, by adding **-te** to the corresponding cardinal numbers. To form all other ordinals, add **-ste** to the cardinal forms. Use a period to indicate the abbreviated form of an ordinal number.

ordinal numbers								
1.	erste	*first*	7.	siebte	*seventh*	19.	neunzehnte	*nineteenth*
2.	zweite	*second*	8.	achte	*eighth*	20.	zwanzigste	*twentieth*
3.	dritte	*third*	9.	neunte	*ninth*	31.	einunddreißigste	*thirty-first*
4.	vierte	*fourth*	10.	zehnte	*tenth*	55.	fünfundfünfzigste	*fifty-fifth*
5.	fünfte	*fifth*	11.	elfte	*eleventh*	100.	hundertste	*hundredth*
6.	sechste	*sixth*	12.	zwölfte	*twelfth*	1000.	tausendste	*thousandth*

der **erste** Lehrer
the **first** instructor

die **zweite** Stunde
the **second** lecture

das **dritte** Fach
the **third** subject

Dates

die Monate (*months*)			
Januar	April	Juli	Oktober
Februar	Mai	August	November
März	Juni	September	Dezember

Januar ist der erste Monat.
January is the first month.

Dezember ist der zwölfte Monat.
December is the twelfth month.

- Answer the question **Der Wievielte ist heute?** (*What is the date today?*) with **Heute ist der** + [*ordinal number (+ month)*].

  Heute ist **der erste Mai**.
  *Today is **May first**.*

  Heute ist **der einunddreißigste**.
  *Today is **the thirty-first**.*

  23. März 2010 ⟶ **23.3.2010**
  March 23rd, 2010 ⟶ *3/23/2010*

  7. Oktober 2014 ⟶ **7.10.2014**
  October 7th, 2014 ⟶ *10/7/2014*

- To specify the day on which an event or activity takes place, use **am** before the date, and add **-n** to the ordinal number. Use the question **Wann hast du Geburtstag?** to ask someone when their birthday is.

  Ich habe **am 7. (siebten) Juli** Geburtstag.
  *My birthday is **on July 7th**.*

  Am 1. (ersten) Januar beginnt das neue Jahr.
  *The new year begins **on January 1st**.*

- The pattern **am** + [*time expression*] is also used with days of the week.

  am Montag
  on Monday

  am Dienstag
  on Tuesday

  am Wochenende
  on the weekend

- Like English, German uses cardinal numbers to refer to a particular year.

  1895 = achtzehnhundertfünfundneunzig

  2016 = zweitausendsechzehn

QUERVERWEIS

To form the accusative of ordinal numbers, add **-n** before masculine nouns. The feminine and neuter forms do not change.

Du trinkst deinen zweiten Kaffee.
You're having your second coffee.

Ich antworte auf die dritte Frage.
I'm answering the third question.

You will learn more about nominative and accusative adjective endings in **3A.2**

ACHTUNG

In writing, the day also comes before the month. Remember that an ordinal number is indicated by putting a period after the number.

Ressourcen

v̂Text

WB
pp. 23–24

LM
p. 75

vhlcentral

Jetzt sind Sie dran!

A. Select the correct time.

1. **7:15 a.m.** Es ist (Viertel nach / Viertel vor) sieben.
2. **2:00 p.m.** Es ist zwei Uhr (morgens / nachmittags).
3. **10:30 a.m.** Es ist (halb zehn / halb elf) vormittags.
4. **12:00 p.m.** Es ist (Mittag/Mitternacht).
5. **7:55 a.m.** Es ist (acht/sieben) Uhr fünfundfünfzig.
6. **8:37 p.m.** Es ist (zwanzig Uhr / achtzehn Uhr) siebenunddreißig.

B. Write the correct date.

7. **14. Februar** Heute ist der ___vierzehnte___ Februar.
8. **28. Dezember** Heute ist der _____ Dezember.
9. **3. Juli** Heute ist der _____ Juli.
10. **30. Mai** Heute ist der _____ Mai.
11. **11. Oktober** Heute ist der _____ Oktober.
12. **7. August** Heute ist der _____ August.

Anwendung

1 Was ist richtig? Select the sentence that refers to the time shown.

1. Es ist zwei Uhr. /
   Es ist drei Uhr.

2. Es ist Viertel
   vor eins. /
   Es ist zwölf
   Uhr vierzig.

3. Es ist fünf
   Uhr zwanzig. /
   Es ist zehn
   vor drei.

4. Es ist zwei Uhr
   fünfundvierzig. /
   Es ist Viertel
   vor zwei.

2 Wie spät ist es? Write a sentence indicating the time shown on each clock or watch.

▶ **BEISPIEL**

Es ist Viertel nach vier.

p.m.

1. _____ 2. _____

p.m.   p.m.   a.m.   a.m.

3. _____ 4. _____ 5. _____ 6. _____

a.m.   p.m.

7. _____ 8. _____ 9. _____ 10. _____

3 Wer hat Geburtstag? Write out the date indicated to say when each person's birthday is.

BEISPIEL Angela Merkel hat am (17.) *siebzehnten* Juli Geburtstag.

1. Arnold Schwarzenegger hat am (30.) _____ Juli Geburtstag.
2. Heidi Klum hat am (1.) _____ Juni Geburtstag.
3. Karl Lagerfeld hat am (10.) _____ September Geburtstag.
4. Michael Fassbender hat am (2.) _____ April Geburtstag.
5. Die Tennisspielerin Steffi Graf hat am (14.) _____ Juni Geburtstag.
6. Der Fußballspieler Mesut Özil hat am (15.) _____ Oktober Geburtstag.
7. Die Musikerin Nena hat am (24.) _____ März Geburtstag.
8. Der Musiker Herbert Grönemeyer hat am (12.) _____ April Geburtstag.
9. Der Schauspieler (*actor*) Christoph Waltz hat am (4.) _____ Oktober Geburtstag.
10. Die Schauspielerin Sibel Kekilli hat am (16.) _____ Juni Geburtstag.

 Practice more at **vhlcentral.com**.

Kommunikation

4 **Um wie viel Uhr...?** In pairs, look at the class schedule. Take turns
asking and answering questions about the start times of classes.

S1: Wann und um wie viel
Uhr ist Literatur?
S2: Literatur ist dienstags
und donnerstags um
halb neun.

	Montag	Dienstag	Mittwoch	Donnerstag	Freitag
8.30		Literatur		Literatur	Chemie
9.25	Biologie	Biologie	Biologie		Chemie
10.20		Kunst		Kunst	
11.15	Informatik		Informatik		Informatik
12.10	Mathematik	Deutsch	Deutsch	Deutsch	Mathematik

5 **Der Wievielte ist heute?** In pairs, take turns pointing at different
dates on the calendar and having your partner tell you the date.

S1: Der Wievielte ist heute?
S2: Heute ist der dritte Oktober.

Oktober

Montag	Dienstag	Mittwoch	Donnerstag	Freitag	Samstag	Sonntag
		1	2	3	4	5
6	7	8	9	10	11	12
13	14	15	16	17	18	19
20	21	22	23	24	25	26
27	28	29	30	31		

6 **Geburtstage** Ask your classmates when their birthdays are. Find out
whose birthday is closest to yours.

S1: Wann hast du Geburtstag?
S2: Ich habe am siebten Dezember Geburtstag.
Und wann hast du Geburtstag?
S1: Ich habe am neunten Oktober Geburtstag.

7 **Interview** In pairs, take turns asking and answering
the questions.

S1: Wann hast du Geschichte?
S2: Montags, mittwochs und freitags um
Viertel nach elf. Und du?

1. Welcher Tag ist heute?

2. Wann hast du Geburtstag?

3. Wann gehst du in die Sporthalle?

4. Wie spät ist es?

5. Um wie viel Uhr gehst du in die Mensa?

6. Wann hast du Unterricht?

Wiederholung

1 Graffiti
In small groups, take turns drawing items from the lesson vocabulary and guessing what they are.

S1: Ist das ein Diplom?
S2: Nein!
S3: Ist das ein Stipendium?
S2: Ja, richtig!

2 Verabredungen
Take turns asking and answering questions using the cues and the images.

▶

S1: Wohin reist du im Sommer?
S2: Ich reise nach Spanien.

reisen

1. gehen

2. lernen

3. kosten

4. kaufen

5. hören

6. begrüßen

3 Feste
Ask your classmates on what day these holidays fall. Add three additional holidays.

Weihnachten (*Christmas*)

S1: Wann ist Weihnachten?
S2: Weihnachten ist am 25. Dezember.

- Silvester (*New Year's Eve*)
- Neujahrstag (*New Year's Day*)
- Columbus-Tag
- Halloween
- Veteranentag
- Heiligabend (*Christmas Eve*)

4 Zeitzonen
In pairs, take turns telling your partner what time it is in each North American city and asking what time it is in a German-speaking country.

S1: In Pittsburgh ist es fünfzehn Uhr zwölf. Wie viel Uhr ist es in Österreich?
S2: In Österreich ist es einundzwanzig Uhr zwölf. In Calgary ist es halb vier. Wie viel Uhr ist es in Deutschland?

Uhrzeit in...	Uhrzeit in Deutschland / in Österreich / in der Schweiz
Pittsburgh, PA: 15.12	+ 6 Stunden
Calgary, AB: 3.30	+ 8 Stunden
Fairbanks, AK: 22.54	+ 11 Stunden
Ft. Stockton, TX: 11.45	+ 7 Stunden
Hope, BC: 15.28	+ 9 Stunden
London, ON: 3.09	+ 6 Stunden
Needles, CA: 12.30	+ 9 Stunden
Tifton, FL: 21.36	+ 6 Stunden
Winnipeg, MB: 20.15	+ 7 Stunden

5 Arbeitsblatt
Your instructor will give you a worksheet. Talk with your classmates to figure out the starting lineup of a race.

S1: Der Wievielte bist du?
S2: Ich bin der vierzehnte. Die wievielte bist du?
S1: Ich bin die achte.
S1 schreibt: Ben ist der vierzehnte.
S2 schreibt: Sarah ist die achte.

6 Diskutieren und kombinieren
You and your partner each have two schedules. One shows your activities. The other shows a partial list of your partner's activities, with one activity missing each day. Ask and answer questions to complete both schedules.

S1: Was machst du am Sonntag um neun Uhr morgens?
S2: Ich mache Hausaufgaben. Und was machst du am Freitag um vier Uhr nachmittags?
S1: Ich habe Yoga.

Zapping

 **S** Video

TU Berlin

The **Technische Universität Berlin**, or **TU Berlin**, is a modern-looking institution with a long and impressive history. Founded in 1879, the **TU** is one of the biggest technical universities in Germany, and the only one in Berlin to offer an engineering degree (**Ingenieur-Abschluss**). The TU also has a larger percentage of international students (**Studenten aus dem Ausland**) than any other German university.

Vier Unis hat die Stadt zu bieten°. Die TU ist die zweitälteste°.

Nach vorn° präsentiert sie sich modern und sachlich°.

„Wir haben die Ideen° für die Zukunft°" heißt der Leitspruch°.

---

zu bieten *to offer* **zweitälteste** *second oldest* **Nach vorn** *From the front* **sachlich** *functional* **Ideen** *ideas* **Zukunft** *future* **Leitspruch** *motto*

 Verständnis Circle the correct answers.

1. What percentage of **TU** students come from abroad?
   a. 5   b. 10   c. 20   d. 30

2. Which of the following is *not* one of the key subjects (**Schwerpunkte**) offered by the **TU**?
   a. Mathematik   b. Architektur   c. Physik   d. Chemie

 Diskussion Discuss the following questions with a partner.

1. In what ways is the **TU Berlin** similar to your school? How is it different?

2. Would you like to study at the **TU Berlin**? Why or why not?

Sport und Freizeit  Vocabulary Tools

Wortschatz

Sportarten	sports
(der) (American) Football	football
(das) Golf	golf
(das) Hockey	hockey
(der) Volleyball	volleyball
das Schwimmbad, ⸚er	swimming pool
das Spiel, -e	game
der Sport	sports
das Stadion, Stadien	stadium
Fahrrad fahren (fährt)	to ride a bicycle
Ski fahren	to ski
schwimmen	to swim
trainieren	to practice
Freizeitaktivitäten	**leisure activities**
der Berg, -e	mountain
das Fahrrad, ⸚er	bicycle
die Freizeit	free time
das Hobby, -s	hobby
der Park, -s	park
der Strand, ⸚e	beach
der Wald, ⸚er	forest
angeln gehen	to go fishing
campen gehen	to go camping
essen gehen	to eat out
spazieren gehen	to go for a walk
klettern	to (rock) climb
kochen	to cook
(ein Pferd) reiten	to ride (a horse)
schreiben	to write
Spaß haben/machen	to have fun / to be fun
singen	to sing
tanzen	to dance
wandern	to hike

Labels in illustration:

die Spielerinnen (*sing.* die Spielerin)

Sie spielen Tennis (*n.*).

das Spielfeld, -er/ der Platz, ⸚e

der Ball, ⸚e

die Mannschaft, -en

der Spieler, -

Er spielt Fußball. (spielen)

Sie verliert nicht gern. (verlieren)

die Karten (*sing.* die Karte)

Er gewinnt. (gewinnen)

ACHTUNG

Infinitives can be used as nouns in German. **Freitags habe ich Schwimmen. Samstags habe ich Reiten.** Infinitives used as nouns are neuter.

Basketball (*m.*)

der Basketball

Sie spielen gern Schach (*n.*).

Baseball (*m.*)

Leichtathletik (*f.*)

ACHTUNG

Use **gern** or **nicht gern** after a verb to say that you *like* or *don't like* doing something.

Lisa singt gern.
Lisa likes to sing.

Ich spiele nicht gern Tennis.
I don't like playing tennis.

You will learn more about the uses of **gern** in **Lektion 4A**.

Anwendung

1 Was passt nicht? Indicate the word that doesn't belong.

1. a. Basketball
   b. Schach
   c. Golf
   d. Tennis

2. a. der Strand
   b. der Spieler
   c. das Stadion
   d. der Platz

3. a. reiten
   b. schwimmen
   c. singen
   d. klettern

4. a. der Rucksack
   b. das Camping
   c. der Berg
   d. das Spielfeld

5. a. spazieren gehen
   b. kochen
   c. wandern
   d. reiten

6. a. die Freizeit
   b. die Schule
   c. die Aktivität
   d. das Hobby

2 Was fehlt? Complete the sentences with words from the list.

| Fußball | Schwimmbad | Spaß | spazieren | Tennisspielerinnen |

1. Serena und Venus Williams sind _____.
2. Ski fahren macht im Winter viel _____.
3. Wir schwimmen im _____.
4. Auf dem Spielfeld spielen wir _____.
5. Im Park gehen wir _____.

3 Zuordnen Write the activity that describes each picture.

▶ **BEISPIEL**

Leichtathletik trainieren

1. _____

2. _____

3. _____

4. _____

4 Das Wochenende Listen to the conversation between Lukas, Max, and Michaela, and indicate who will be doing each activity.

	Lukas	Max	Michaela
1. Tennis spielen			
2. kochen			
3. lernen			
4. tanzen			
5. klettern			
6. Videospiele spielen			

Kommunikation

5 Berühmte Sportler
In pairs, match the athletes with the descriptions.

BEISPIEL

S1: Er spielt Fußball und kommt aus England.
S2: Es ist David Beckham.

____ 1. Er kommt aus der Schweiz und spielt Tennis.
____ 2. Er spielt Basketball.
____ 3. Sie ist eine Tennisspielerin aus Deutschland.
____ 4. Er schwimmt und hat viele olympische Medaillen (*medals*).
____ 5. Sie ist eine Skifahrerin aus Amerika.
____ 6. Er kommt aus Kalifornien und spielt Golf.

a. Lindsay Vonn
b. Steffi Graf
c. Roger Federer
d. Michael Phelps
e. Tiger Woods
f. LeBron James

6 Machst du das gern?
In pairs, take turns telling each other whether you like or dislike each activity.

▶ **BEISPIEL**

S1: Ich schwimme gern. Und du?
S2: Ich schwimme auch gern. /
Ich schwimme nicht gern.

1.

2.

3.

4.

7 Arbeitsblatt
Your instructor will give you a worksheet with information about activities. Ask your classmates what they like to do in their free time.

BEISPIEL Volleyball spielen

S1: Spielst du gern Volleyball?
S2: Ja. Ich spiele gern Volleyball./Nein. Ich spiele nicht gern Volleyball.

angeln gehen	reiten	Fußball spielen
campen gehen	schwimmen	Schach spielen
kochen	singen	tanzen
spazieren gehen	Baseball spielen	Tennis trainieren
klettern	Basketball spielen	wandern

8 Pantomime
Play charades in groups of four. Take turns acting out activities from the lesson vocabulary. The person who guesses the activity goes next.

BEISPIEL

S1: Ist es Baseball?
S2: Nein.
S3: Ist es Tennis?
S2: Ja, es ist Tennis!

Aussprache und Rechtschreibung  Audio

Diphthongs: *au, ei/ai, eu/äu*

When one vowel sound glides into another vowel sound in the same syllable, the complex sound produced is called a diphthong. In German, this complex sound is said quickly and is not drawn out as it is in English. There are three diphthongs in German: **au**, **ei/ai**, and **eu/äu**.

| f**au**l | **au**s | L**ei**ne | M**ai**s | n**eu**n | t**äu**schen |

The German diphthong written **au** begins with the vowel sound of the *o* in the English word *pod* and ends with a sound similar to the *oo* in the English word *loose*.

| **au**f | Fr**au** | B**au**ch | H**au**s | **au**ch |

The German diphthong written as **ei** or **ai** is pronounced very similarly to the *i* in the English word *time*. Remember that the German **ie** is not a diphthong, but simply a way of writing the long **i** sound, as in the word **sieben**.

| Fr**ei**tag | Z**ei**t | M**ai** | **Ei**s | schr**ei**ben |

The German diphthong written as **eu** or **äu** is pronounced very similarly to the *oi* in the English word *coin*.

| Z**eu**gnis | Fr**eu**nd | H**äu**ser | **Eu**ropa | D**eu**tsch |

---

1 **Aussprechen** Practice saying these words aloud.

1. laufen
2. Kaufhaus
3. Rauch
4. Maus
5. mein
6. Wein
7. Mainz
8. reiten
9. treu
10. freuen
11. Leute
12. läuft

2 **Nachsprechen** Practice saying these sentences aloud.

1. Die Mäuse laufen einfach im Zimmer herum.
2. Tausende Leute gehen an uns vorbei.
3. Am Freitag habe ich leider keine Zeit.
4. Paul macht eine Europareise mit Freunden.
5. Meine Frau kauft ein neues Haus außerhalb von Mainz.
6. Für den Sauerbraten brauchen wir Rotweinessig.

3 **Sprichwörter** Practice reading these sayings aloud.

Schuster, bleib bei deinen Leisten.[1]

Einem geschenkten Gaul schaut man nicht ins Maul.[2]

[1] Stick with what you know. (lit. Cobbler, stick with your shoe stretchers.)

[2] Don't look a gift horse in the mouth.

Ein Picknick im Park Video

George und Meline treffen Sabite und Torsten im Park. Sie sprechen über Sport und ihre Hobbys. Kommt Meline Torsten zu nahe (*too close*)?

1

> **TORSTEN** Das Fußballspiel beginnt um halb acht.
> **SABITE** Es ist Viertel nach sechs. Niemand ist hier. George kommt von der Uni.

2

> **TORSTEN** Spielt er Fußball?
> **SABITE** Er spielt Baseball in der Freizeit. Er ist in einer Uni-Mannschaft.
> **TORSTEN** Hat Meline Hobbys?
> **SABITE** Sie fährt Ski und spielt Tennis. Sie gewinnt alles.

3

> **GEORGE** Oh, vielen Dank! Wo sind Hans und Meline?
> **SABITE** Meline kommt aus der Bibliothek. Hans hat eine Vorlesung.
> **GEORGE** Studierst du auch, Torsten?
> **TORSTEN** Ja. Ich studiere Chemie und Biologie.

4

> **MELINE** Ich bringe Dessert!
> **GEORGE** Sabite, ich glaube, Hans...
> **MELINE** Hans. Hallo, Torsten, nett dich kennen zu lernen.
> **TORSTEN** Gleichfalls, Meline.

5

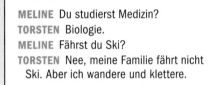

> **MELINE** Du studierst Medizin?
> **TORSTEN** Biologie.
> **MELINE** Fährst du Ski?
> **TORSTEN** Nee, meine Familie fährt nicht Ski. Aber ich wandere und klettere.

> **MELINE** Ich komme aus Wien. Alle fahren Ski in den österreichischen Alpen. Wir haben viele Sportarten: Skifahren, Klettern, Fahrradfahren, Golf und Tennis. Spielst du auch Tennis?
> **SABITE** Äh, Meline?
> **MELINE** Hmmm?
> **SABITE** Gehen wir spazieren.

6

---

1 **Was ist richtig?** Choose the words that best complete the sentences.

1. Torsten und Sabite sind (im Park / im Café).
2. George kommt (aus dem Stadion / von der Uni).
3. Meline fährt Ski und spielt (Golf / Tennis).
4. Torsten studiert Chemie und (Biologie / Physik).
5. Meline bringt (Kaffee / Dessert).
6. Alle fahren (Ski / Bob) in den österreichischen Alpen.
7. Sabite ist eifersüchtig auf (*jealous of*) (Meline / Torsten).
8. Meline trennt keine (Klassenkameraden / Paare).
9. (Frau Yilmaz / Herr Yilmaz) macht morgen Sauerbraten.
10. Hans weiß nicht, dass Sabite einen (Mitbewohner / Freund) hat.

PERSONEN

 Torsten   Sabite   George   Meline

7

SABITE Meline. Wir sind Mitbewohnerinnen. Freundinnen.
MELINE Und?
SABITE „Spielst du auch Tennis?"

8

MELINE Sabite. Keine Sorge. Ich trenne keine Paare.
SABITE Es ist okay, ich verstehe.

9

SABITE George, Meline, meine Mutter macht morgen Sauerbraten. Kommt ihr zum Abendessen?
MELINE Oh, danke, Sabite. Wir kommen.
TORSTEN Frau Yilmaz ist eine gute Köchin.
GEORGE Wow, vielen Dank. Und Hans?
SABITE Ich frage ihn.

10

MELINE Hans weiß nicht, dass Sabite einen Freund hat, oder?
GEORGE Er hat keine Ahnung.

Nützliche Ausdrücke

- **Niemand ist hier.**
  Nobody's here.
- **die Uni-Mannschaft**
  varsity team
- **Sie gewinnt alles.**
  She wins at everything.
- **glauben**
  to believe
- **aber**
  but
- **Alle fahren Ski in den österreichischen Alpen.**
  Everyone in the Austrian Alps skis.
- **Gehen wir spazieren.**
  Let's go for a walk.
- **Keine Sorge.**
  Don't worry.
- **das Abendessen**
  dinner
- **der Koch / die Köchin**
  cook
- **Hans weiß nicht, dass Sabite einen Freund hat, oder?**
  Hans doesn't know Sabite has a boyfriend, does he?
- **Er hat keine Ahnung.**
  He doesn't have a clue.

2B.1
- **Meine Familie fährt nicht Ski.**
  My family doesn't ski.

2B.2
- **Meine Mutter macht morgen Sauerbraten.**
  My mother is making sauerbraten tomorrow.

2B.3
- **Ich trenne keine Paare.**
  I wouldn't break up a couple.

2 **Zum Besprechen** In this episode, the characters talk about their favorite sports and pastimes. Interview your classmates to find out who shares your interests. Who likes the same sports? Who has the same hobbies?

3 **Vertiefung** Fußball is one of the most popular sports in Germany. What is the name of the German national soccer league? Find the names of four prominent German soccer teams. Which team won last year's championship?

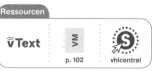

Ressourcen

v̂Text   VM   vhlcentral
         p. 102

IM FOKUS

Skifahren im Blut° Reading

In Alpine villages, learning to ski is like learning to walk. Almost everyone does it, starting at a very young age. The beginner slopes are full of preschool-aged children taking their first lessons. Skiing courses were required in Austrian schools until 1995, and many schools in Bavaria and Austria still offer **Skiwoche°**, a chaperoned week-long ski trip, as part of their curriculum.

Many of the world's best skiers come from German-speaking countries. Carina Vogt is a German **Skisprung-Weltmeisterin°** and **Olympiasiegerin°**.

Vogt won the first gold medal ever awarded for women's ski jumping at the 2014 Sochi Winter Olympic games, and in 2015 she won two World Cup gold medals for ski jumping, coming in third overall in women's events. In honor of her achievements, there is now a street named after her in her home town of Degenfeld in Baden-Württemberg.

Austrian Marcel Hirscher specializes in slalom and giant slalom. The son of two ski instructors, Hirscher has been skiing since age 2. In 2015, at the age of 26, he became the first **Weltmeister** ever to win the overall World Cup title for men's ski events four times in a row.

While the Alpine skiing tradition remains strong, environmental and economic sustainability have become major concerns. Ski tourism has had a serious impact on the ecology of the Alpine regions. With rising temperatures due to climate change, lack of snow is also becoming an issue. Snowmaking is expensive and uses vast amounts of water. And, while large ski resorts continue to draw visitors from all over the world, skiing is becoming less affordable for locals, with some smaller ski areas struggling to remain in business.

Blut blood **Skiwoche** ski week **Skisprung-Weltmeisterin** ski jump world champion **Olympiasiegerin** Olympic gold medalist **Jährliche Anzahl an** Annual number of **mehr als** more than **Einnahmen** revenue **Arbeitsplätze** jobs **Pistenfläche** skiable area

Österreich: Ski-Paradies	
Jährliche Anzahl an° Skitouristen	mehr als° 15,4 Millionen
Jährliche Einnahmen° durch Skifahren	mehr als 11 Milliarden Euro
Arbeitsplätze° im Skitourismus	312.625
Pistenfläche°	25.400 Hektar (254 km²)
Alpine Skiweltmeisterschaft 2015: Medaillen für Österreich	9 (5 Gold, 3 Silber, 1 Bronze)

QUELLE: Trend Wirtschaftsmagazin

ÜBUNGEN

1 **Was fehlt?** Complete the statements.

1. Austrian schools had mandatory ski classes until _____.

2. In Bavaria and Austria, many school classes travel to the mountains for _____.

3. _____ won the first ever Olympic gold medal for women's ski jumping.

4. Vogt won two _____ gold medals in 2015.

5. There is a street named after Vogt in the town of _____.

6. _____ started skiing at age 2.

7. Hirscher was the first ever four-time _____ in men's ski events.

8. _____ uses excessive quantities of water.

9. Ski tourism accounts for _____ jobs in Austria.

10. Austria won _____ medals in the 2015 Alpine Skiing World Championships.

Mehr Freizeit

der Fan, -s	fan
die Meisterschaft, -en	championship
der Spielstand, ⸚e	score
das Tor, -e	goal (in soccer, etc.)
faulenzen	to relax; to be lazy
joggen	to jog
fit	in good shape
sportlich	athletic
Los!	Start!; Go!

Die Deutschen und das Fahrrad

In Deutschland hat man im Schnitt° 6 Stunden und 34 Minuten Freizeit am Tag. Populäre Hobbys der Deutschen sind Videospiele, Lesen und natürlich° Sport. Die Deutschen sind leidenschaftliche° Fahrradfahrer. Kilometerlange Radwege° durchkreuzen° das Land, wie etwa° die Romantische Straße° in Bayern: sie führt an Schlössern° und vielseitigen Landschaften° vorbei°.

im Schnitt *on average* **natürlich** *of course*
leidenschaftliche *passionate* **Radwege** *bike trails*
durchkreuzen *cross* **wie etwa** *such as* **Straße** *road*
Schlössern *castles* **vielseitigen Landschaften** *varied landscapes* **führt an... vorbei** *leads past*

Toooooor!

Der talentierte und populäre Fußballer **Mesut Özil** spielt international für Deutschland. 2014 ist die deutsche Fußballnationalmannschaft in Brasilien bei der Weltmeisterschaft°. In allen sieben Spielen steht Mesut Özil in der Startelf°. Er erzielt° drei Tore und wird° mit der deutschen Nationalmannschaft Weltmeister. Özil ist Deutscher mit türkischer Abstammung° und kommt aus Gelsenkirchen. Er ist Moslem und betet vor jedem° Spiel. Man sagt, die Familie Özil ist ein gutes Beispiel für erfolgreiche° Integration von Ausländern° in Deutschland. Aber Özil spielt nicht nur° für deutsche Mannschaften. Seit° 2013 spielt er in England, für *Arsenal London*.

Weltmeisterschaft *World Cup* **Startelf** *starting line-up*
erzielt *scores* **wird** *becomes* **mit türkischer Abstammung** *of Turkish descent* **betet vor jedem** *prays before every* **erfolgreiche** *successful* **Ausländern** *foreigners* **nicht nur** *not only* **Seit** *Since*

🔗 IM INTERNET

Wandern: Was sind beliebte Wanderwege° in der Schweiz?

beliebte Wanderwege *popular hiking trails*

Find out more at **vhlcentral.com**.

---

2 **Richtig oder falsch?** In pairs, correct the false statements.

	richtig	falsch
1. On average, Germans have more than six hours of leisure time per day.	☐	☐
2. Biking is a popular sport in Germany.	☐	☐
3. Mesut Özil played in six games in the 2014 World Cup.	☐	☐
4. Mesut Özil grew up in Turkey.	☐	☐

3 **Bekannte Sportler** In pairs, take turns role-playing famous athletes who play each of the sports listed. Your partner must guess who you are.

BEISPIEL

S1: *Ich spiele Fußball und komme aus Deutschland.*
S2: *Bist du Mesut Özil?*

1. Golf
2. Baseball
3. Schwimmen
4. Tennis
5. Basketball
6. Fußball

Ressourcen
vText
vhlcentral

2B.1 Stem-changing verbs  Presentation

QUERVERWEIS

See **2A.1** to review the present-tense conjugations of regular verbs.

Startblock Certain irregular verbs follow predictable patterns of spelling changes in their present-tense conjugations. These verbs use the regular endings, but have changes to their stem vowels in the **du** and **er/sie/es** forms. Most stem-changing verbs follow one of four patterns in the present tense.

ACHTUNG

The formal **Sie** forms are the same as the plural **sie** forms for all verbs. Starting in this lesson, **Sie** and **sie** (*pl.*) forms will be listed together in verb tables.

- a ⟶ ä

schlafen (*to sleep*)			
ich schlafe	*I sleep*	wir schlafen	*we sleep*
du schläfst	*you sleep*	ihr schlaft	*you sleep*
er/sie/es schläft	*he/she/it sleeps*	Sie/sie schlafen	*you/they sleep*

Schläfst du jede Nacht acht Stunden?
Do you sleep eight hours every night?

Sie **schlafen** im Studentenwohnheim.
They sleep in the dormitory.

- au ⟶ äu

laufen (*to run*)			
ich laufe	*I run*	wir laufen	*we run*
du läufst	*you run*	ihr lauft	*you run*
er/sie/es läuft	*he/she/it runs*	Sie/sie laufen	*you/they run*

Mehmet **läuft** am Strand.
Mehmet runs on the beach.

Sie **laufen** über das Spielfeld.
They're running across the field.

- e ⟶ i

	essen (*to eat*)		sprechen (*to speak*)	
ich	esse	*I eat*	spreche	*I speak*
du	isst	*you eat*	sprichst	*you speak*
er/sie/es	isst	*he/she/it eats*	spricht	*he/she/it speaks*
wir	essen	*we eat*	sprechen	*we speak*
ihr	esst	*you eat*	sprecht	*you speak*
Sie/sie	essen	*you/they eat*	sprechen	*you/they speak*

Wir **essen** in der Mensa.
We're eating in the cafeteria.

Sprichst du Englisch?
Do you speak English?

- Besides an e ⟶ i vowel change, **nehmen** (*to take*) and **werden** (*to become*) have additional changes in the **du** and **er/sie/es** forms.

ACHTUNG

Remember: when the verb stem ends in **-s**, drop the **-s** from the second-person singular ending.

	nehmen (*to take*)		werden (*to become*)	
ich	nehme	*I take*	werde	*I become*
du	nimmst	*you take*	wirst	*you become*
er/sie/es	nimmt	*he/she/it takes*	wird	*he/she/it becomes*
wir	nehmen	*we take*	werden	*we become*
ihr	nehmt	*you take*	werdet	*you become*
Sie/sie	nehmen	*you/they take*	werden	*you/they become*

Du **nimmst** jeden Tag den Bus.
You take the bus every day.

Ein Anfänger **wird** mit der Zeit Experte.
A beginner becomes an expert over time.

- e ⟶ ie

lesen (*to read*)			sehen (*to see*)		
ich	lese	*I read*	sehe	*I see*	
du	liest	*you read*	siehst	*you see*	
er/sie/es	liest	*he/she/it reads*	sieht	*he/she/it sees*	
wir	lesen	*we read*	sehen	*we see*	
ihr	lest	*you read*	seht	*you see*	
Sie/sie	lesen	*you/they read*	sehen	*you/they see*	

Du **liest** viele Bücher.
*You **read** a lot of books.*

Seht ihr die Spieler?
*Do you **see** the players?*

- This table summarizes some common verbs with stem changes in the present tense. When a verb with a present-tense stem change is presented in this text, it will be listed with its third-person singular form: **lesen (liest)**.

common stem-changing verbs (present tense)			
a ⟶ ä		**e ⟶ i**	
braten	*to fry*	brechen	*to break*
fahren	*to go*	essen	*to eat*
fallen	*to fall*	geben	*to give*
fangen	*to catch*	helfen	*to help*
lassen	*to let, to allow*	nehmen	*to take*
schlafen	*to sleep*	sprechen	*to speak*
tragen	*to carry; to wear*	treffen	*to hit; to meet*
waschen	*to wash*	vergessen	*to forget*
		werden	*to become*
		werfen	*to throw*
au ⟶ äu		**e ⟶ ie**	
laufen	*to run*	empfehlen	*to recommend*
		lesen	*to read*
		sehen	*to see*
		stehlen	*to steal*

Fährst du nach Berlin?
*Are you **going** to Berlin?*

Es **gibt** dort ein sehr gutes Café.
*There **is** a very good café there.*

ACHTUNG

The verb **geben** is used in certain idiomatic expressions, such as **Es gibt** (*There is/There are*). Idiomatic expressions do not translate literally to English.

Ressourcen

v̂ Text

WB
pp. 27–28

LM
p. 78

vhlcentral

Jetzt sind Sie dran!   Write the appropriate form of the verb.

1. Ich ___esse___ (essen) viele Äpfel.
2. Du _____ (helfen) Sophie.
3. Ich _____ (geben) Tobias ein Buch.
4. Peter _____ (nehmen) ein Taxi.
5. Ihr _____ (fahren) gern Fahrrad.
6. Wir _____ (tragen) Rucksäcke.
7. Anna _____ (werden) Informatikprofessorin.
8. Du _____ (lesen) viele Bücher.
9. Er _____ (schlafen) bis 8 Uhr morgens.
10. Ihr _____ (sprechen) Deutsch.
11. Die Schüler _____ (sehen) einen Film.
12. Du _____ (vergessen) die Hausaufgaben.

Anwendung

1 **Was ist richtig?** Select the verb that best completes each sentence.

1. Hannah (schläft / isst) viele Äpfel.
2. Ich (lese / brate) ein Schnitzel.
3. Du (fährst / triffst) einen Porsche.
4. Wir (helfen / waschen) den Hund.
5. Alena und Daniel (treffen / sprechen) Deutsch, Englisch und Polnisch.
6. Ihr (lauft / fangt) 8 Kilometer.
7. Du (liest / wird) viele Bücher.
8. Du (gibst / triffst) Jasmin im Café.

2 **Schreiben** Write complete sentences using the cues.

1. Herr Schmidt / empfehlen / das Schnitzel
2. ich / wissen / die Antwort
3. du / fahren / das Auto
4. wir / treffen / Katrina und Paul
5. Angela / lesen / gern
6. du / sprechen / Deutsch
7. ich / werden / Architekt
8. Peter / stehlen / einen Apfel

3 **Was sehen Sie?** Complete the sentences.

▶ **BEISPIEL**

Peter ___*läuft*___ gern im Park.

1. Sie _____ in der Hängematte.

2. Tobi _____ das Auto.

3. Der Footballspieler _____ den Ball.

4. Hans _____ das Buch.

5. Er _____ eine Bratwurst.

6. Ingrid _____ Rolf im Museum.

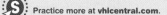

 Practice more at **vhlcentral.com**.

Kommunikation

4 **Bilden Sie Sätze** In pairs, create six logical sentences with items from each column. Some items may be used more than once.

> **BEISPIEL** *Du empfiehlst die Torte.*

A	B	C
ich	empfehlen	Fußball im Stadion
du	lesen	Goethes *Faust*
Nina	sehen	die Torte
Elsa und ich	spielen	23 Jahre alt
Bianca und du	sprechen	viele Fremdsprachen
Olivia und Markus	werden	einen Film

5 **Wie bitte?** Adele is talking to her mother on the phone. You hear only Adele's side of the conversation. In pairs, reconstruct her mother's questions.

> **BEISPIEL** Ich fahre am Wochenende nach Hause (*home*).
>
> *Wann fährst du nach Hause?*

1. Ja, ich schlafe gut.
2. Ich esse um 7 Uhr abends.
3. Ja, ich lese viel.
4. Ich sehe Matthias im Unterricht.
5. Ja, wir sprechen im Unterricht Deutsch.
6. Ja, Matthias und ich nehmen zusammen (*together*) den Bus.
7. Ich treffe Matthias nachmittags im Café.
8. Ja, ich fahre oft Fahrrad.

6 **Wer macht was?** Use the cues to ask your classmates whether they participate in these activities.

> **BEISPIEL**
>
> **S1:** *Spielst du Fußball im Stadion?*
> **S2:** *Nein, aber ich laufe im Park. Läufst du auch im Park?*

Fahrrad fahren	im Park laufen	im Stadion Fußball spielen
Ski fahren	im Schwimmbad schwimmen	Bälle werfen und fangen
viele Bücher lesen	den Bus nehmen	Freunde im Café treffen

7 **Im Park** In pairs, write a paragraph that describes the activities of the people shown. Use each of the verbs from the list at least once.

> **BEISPIEL**
>
> **S1:** *Die Frauen gehen im Park spazieren.*
> **S2:** *Die Kinder reiten im Park.*

fahren	sehen
laufen	gehen
reiten	spielen
schlafen	treffen

2B.2 Present tense used as future  Presentation

Startblock In German, as in English, you can use the present tense with certain time expressions to talk about the future.

Heute Abend spielen wir Fußball.

Morgen macht meine Mutter Sauerbraten.

- The adverbs **heute** (*today*), **morgen** (*tomorrow*), and **übermorgen** (*the day after tomorrow*) are commonly used with the present tense to express future ideas. Use them with these time expressions to specify the time of day at which a future action will occur.

common time expressions			
Morgen	*morning*	Nachmittag	*afternoon*
Vormittag	*midmorning*	Abend	*evening*
Mittag	*noon*	Nacht	*night*

Morgen gehen wir einkaufen.
Tomorrow *we're going shopping.*

Heute Nachmittag gehe ich schwimmen.
This afternoon *I'm going swimming.*

- In **2A.3**, you learned to use **am** before dates and days of the week. Also use **am** with **Morgen, Vormittag, Mittag, Nachmittag, Abend,** or **Wochenende** to specify when something will occur. When both the day of the week and the time of day are specified, they form a compound noun: **Dienstagmittag, Mittwochabend.**

Am Wochenende gehen wir angeln.
*We're going fishing **this weekend.***

Am Freitagnachmittag gehe ich zum Arzt.
*I'm going to the doctor's **Friday afternoon.***

- Use **im** with months and seasons (**Frühling, Sommer, Herbst, Winter**).

Im Februar fahre ich Ski.
*I'm going skiing **in February.***

Im Frühling gehe ich wandern.
*I'm going hiking **this spring.***

- The adjective **nächste** (*next*) can be used with time-related nouns such as days of the week, seasons, and months. In this usage, it takes accusative endings.

nächsten Sommer
next *summer*

nächste Woche
next *week*

nächstes Jahr
next *year*

Jetzt sind Sie dran!   Select the appropriate word or phrase.

1. Wir fahren (nächstes / nächste) Woche nach Polen.
2. (Am / Im) Montagvormittag gehe ich spazieren.
3. (Heute Abend / Abend) spielt ihr Karten.
4. Ursula fährt (am / im) Februar Ski.
5. Wir wandern (nächsten / nächstes) Freitag im Wald.
6. (Morgen Nachmittag / Nachmittag) fahre ich Fahrrad.
7. Wir gehen (Nacht / übermorgen) klettern.
8. (Nächsten / Nächstes) Wochenende spielst du Tennis.

Anwendung und Kommunikation

1 **Was passt?** Select the appropriate time expression.

1. Die nächste Prüfung ist (Nachmittag / übermorgen).
2. Ich fahre (im / am) März in Urlaub.
3. Spielst du (am / im) Abend Hockey?
4. Peter und Bettina fahren (nächstes / nächste) Wochenende in die Berge.
5. Gehst du (Nachmittag / heute Nachmittag) klettern?
6. (Nächstes / Nächsten) Sommer fahren wir an den Strand.

2 **Bilden Sie Sätze** Write sentences using the cues.

1. ich / gehen / heute Nachmittag / angeln
2. übermorgen / spielen / Roland / Baseball
3. nächstes Jahr / fahren / Anja / an den Strand
4. Patrick / treffen / Bianca / am Abend
5. am Sonntagabend / kochen / wir
6. du / fahren / im Winter / Ski

3 **Sätze** In pairs, use items from each column to make up sentences describing what each person is going to do.

BEISPIEL

Wir sehen heute Abend einen Film.

A	B	C	D
ich	Fahrrad fahren	am Freitag	für einen Marathonlauf
du	gehen	heute Nacht	im Park
Angelika	spazieren gehen	im Dezember	nach Österreich
wir	reisen	im Frühling	Freunde im Restaurant
ihr	trainieren	morgen Nachmittag	in die Disko
Otto und Gabi	treffen	nächstes Jahr	in den Bergen

4 **Fernsehen** In pairs, decide which TV programs you want to watch, and take turns asking each other when they will be on.

BEISPIEL

S1: *Wann kommt TV total?*
S2: *TV total kommt morgen Abend / Mittwochabend.*

	Dienstag (heute)	Mittwoch	Donnerstag
10.00 Uhr	Reisen für Genießer	Lindenstraße	Türkisch für Anfänger
15.00 Uhr	Sport Aktuell	Das Supertalent	Die Sendung mit der Maus
19.00 Uhr	Formel 1	Hallo Deutschland	Deutschland sucht den Superstar
23.00 Uhr	Bauer sucht Frau	TV total	Familien im Brennpunkt

2B.3  **Negation** **S** Presentation

Startblock In **1B.2**, you learned to make affirmative statements and ask yes-or-no questions. To negate a statement or ask a negative question, use **nicht** or **kein**.

Nein, meine Familie fährt **nicht** Ski.

Ich trenne **keine** Paare.

Nicht

QUERVERWEIS

You have already learned to use **nicht** in the expressions **nicht schlecht** and **nicht (so) gut** (in **1A Kontext**) and **nicht gern** (in **2B Kontext**)

ACHTUNG

Ich spiele kein Tennis means *I don't play tennis (at all)*. **Ich spiele nicht Tennis** means *I'm not playing tennis (at the moment)*.

- In negative statements or questions, place **nicht** after the subject, conjugated verb, direct object, and definite time expressions, but before other sentence elements.

Ich gehe heute in die Sporthalle.	▶ Ich gehe heute **nicht** in die Sporthalle.
I'm going to the gym today.	*I'm **not** going to the gym today.*
Brauchst du den Fußball?	▶ Brauchst du den Fußball **nicht**?
Do you need the soccer ball?	*Don't you need the soccer ball?*
Die Spieler sind hier.	▶ Die Spieler sind **nicht** hier.
The players are here.	*The players are **not** here.*
Mathematik ist einfach	▶ Mathematik ist **nicht** einfach.
Math is easy.	*Math is **not** easy.*

- In some cases, the placement of **nicht** depends on which element of a statement the speaker wants to emphasize.

Ich spiele **nicht** Golf mit Tobias. Ich spiele mit Tobias Tennis.	Ich spiele **nicht** mit Tobias Golf. Ich spiele mit Moritz Golf.
*I'm **not** playing golf with Tobias.* *I'm playing tennis with Tobias.*	*I'm **not** playing golf with Tobias.* *I'm playing golf with Moritz.*
Wir sehen den Film heute **nicht**.	Wir sehen den Film morgen, **nicht** heute.
*We're **not** seeing the film today.*	*We're seeing the film tomorrow, **not** today.*
Die Studenten essen **nicht** in der Mensa.	Die Studenten essen in der Mensa **nicht** gern.
The students aren't eating in the dining hall.	*The students don't like to eat in the dining hall.*

Hans weiß es **nicht**?

Er hat **keine** Ahnung.

Kein

- **Kein** is the negative form of the indefinite article **ein**. Use **kein** to negate a noun preceded by an indefinite article or by no article.

—Haben Sie Zeit?
—*Do you have time?*

▶ —Nein, wir haben **keine** Zeit.
—*No, we don't have time.*

—Hat er ein Hobby?
—*Does he have a hobby?*

▶ —Nein, er hat **keine** Hobbys.
—*No, he has **no** hobbies.*

- **Kein** follows the same patterns of gender and case endings as **ein**. Note that, unlike **ein**, **kein** has a plural form.

kein				
	masculine	**feminine**	**neuter**	**plural**
nominative	kein Ball	keine Freizeit	kein Spiel	keine Karten
accusative	keinen Ball	keine Freizeit	kein Spiel	keine Karten

—Hast du **einen** Fußball?
—*Do you have **a** soccer ball?*

▶ —Nein, ich habe **keinen** Fußball.
—*No, I don't have **a** soccer ball.*

—Ist das **ein** Stadion?
—*Is that **a** stadium?*

▶ —Nein, das ist **kein** Stadion.
—*No, that's **not a** stadium.*

—Sind das Basketballspieler?
—*Are those guys basketball players?*

▶ —Nein, das sind **keine** Basketballspieler.
—*No, those aren't basketball players.*

Doch

- The word **doch** has no exact equivalent in English. Use it to contradict a negative question or statement.

—Ich habe **keine** Freunde.
—*I don't have **any** friends.*

▶ —**Doch**, du hast viele Freunde!
—*No, you have lots of friends!*

—Gehst du **nicht** zum Strand?
—*Aren't you going to the beach?*

▶ —**Doch**, ich gehe zum Strand.
—*Yes, I'm going to the beach.*

QUERVERWEIS

Words that have the same endings as **ein** are often called **ein**-words. You will learn about other **ein**-words in **3A.1**.

Ressourcen

v̂ Text

WB
pp. 31–32

LM
p. 80

S
vhlcentral

Jetzt sind Sie dran!   **Complete the sentences with the appropriate form of nicht or kein.**

1. Der Volleyballspieler ist ___*nicht*___ so fit.
2. Stefan hat _____ Fußball.
3. Wir machen die Hausaufgaben _____.
4. Übermorgen habe ich _____ Vorlesung.
5. Uwe trainiert _____ und verliert das Spiel.
6. Ich habe _____ Foto.

7. Bernhard spielt viel Fußball, aber er gewinnt _____ Spiele.
8. Du schwimmst _____ im Schwimmbad.
9. Wir sehen den Film _____.
10. Ihr habt _____ Freizeit.
11. Am Donnerstag fahren wir _____ in die Berge.
12. Es gibt hier _____ Stadion.

Anwendung

1 **Verneinen Sie** Negate the sentences using **nicht**.

1. Wir haben die Karten.
2. Ich vergesse die Hausaufgaben.
3. Wir reiten am Wochenende.
4. Simon und Katrina sind hier.
5. Du gehst in die Bibliothek.

6. Ihr verliert das Volleyballspiel.
7. Thomas und Brigitte schwimmen am Nachmittag.
8. Am Sonntag gehen wir angeln.

2 **Antworten Sie** Answer the questions using **kein**.

BEISPIEL

S1: *Hast du Hobbys?*
S2: *Nein, ich habe keine Hobbys.*

1. Hat Peter ein Fahrrad?
2. Habt ihr Freizeit?
3. Sind das Spielerinnen?
4. Ist Berlin ein Land (*country*)?
5. Ist Alexandra eine Hockeyspielerin?

6. Hast du einen Basketball?
7. Gibt es dort ein Stadion?
8. Spielst du Volleyball?
9. Ist Salzburg ein Berg?
10. Haben Sie Karten?

3 **Was fehlt?** Complete the conversation with **nicht**, **kein**, or **doch**.

KARIN Hallo, Alina! Geht's dir gut? Kommst du (1) _____ heute Abend zum Training?

ALINA Heute Abend? (2) _____! Aber morgen komme ich (3) _____.

KARIN Warum (4) _____?

ALINA Ich habe (5) _____ Zeit! Wir haben sehr viele Biologiehausaufgaben und übermorgen habe ich auch eine Chemieprüfung!

KARIN Hast du nicht vier Klassen?

ALINA (6) _____, ich habe Biologie, Chemie, Physik und auch Mathematik.

Kommunikation

4 Partnerinterview In pairs, take turns asking each other questions. Contradict your partner's questions using **nicht**, **kein**, or **doch**.

> **BEISPIEL**
> **S1:** Hast du einen Basketball?
> **S2:** Nein, ich habe keinen Basketball.
> **S1:** Tanzt du nicht am Wochenende?
> **S2:** Doch, ich tanze am Wochenende.

1. Spielst du Hockey?
2. Wanderst du im Wald?
3. Fährst du im Dezember Fahrrad?
4. Hast du keine Hobbys?

5. Trainierst du für einen Marathonlauf?
6. Hast du nicht viele Hausaufgaben?
7. Schwimmst du im Schwimmbad?
8. Bist du Tennisspieler(in)?

5 Das stimmt nicht! In pairs, take turns making false statements about the photos. Correct your partner's false statements by negating them, then supply the correct answer.

> **BEISPIEL**
> **S1:** Die Frau fährt Auto.
> **S2:** Nein, sie fährt nicht Auto. Sie fährt Fahrrad.

1.

2.

3.

4.

5.

6.

6 Ich habe es schlecht In pairs, take turns coming up with exaggerations using **nicht** and **kein**. Contradict your partner's exaggerations using **doch**.

> **BEISPIEL**
> **S1:** Wir haben keine Freizeit!
> **S2:** Doch, wir haben viel Freizeit!

7 Trauriger Jörn In small groups, explain why Jörn is sad, using negative statements.

> **BEISPIEL**
> **S1:** Jörn hat keine Freunde.
> **S2:** Er lernt nicht und hat keine guten Noten.

Wiederholung

1 Gute Freunde

In pairs, look at the information provided about each person. Decide which of them are friends, based on their interests.

BEISPIEL

*Heidi fährt Ski und Florian fährt auch Ski.
Heidi und Florian sind Freunde.*

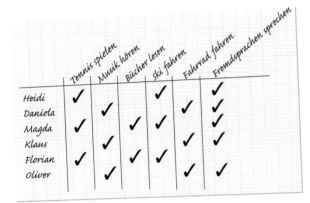

2 Begriffe raten

In small groups, take turns drawing pictures based on words or phrases you learned in **Lektionen 2A** and **2B**. The first person to guess the word or phrase draws next.

BEISPIEL

S1: *Spielt er Schach?*
S2: *Nein. Er spielt nicht Schach.*
S3: *Spielt er Karten?*
S2: *Ja, richtig!*

3 Viele Fragen

Start a conversation with a classmate using the questions as prompts. Ask follow-up questions using time expressions.

BEISPIEL

S1: *Machst du viele Hausaufgaben?*
S2: *Ja, ich mache viele Hausaufgaben.*
S1: *Hast du heute Hausaufgaben in Geschichte?*
S2: *Nein, ich habe heute keine Hausaufgaben in Geschichte.*

1. Liest du viele Bücher?
2. Reist du im Winter nach Kanada?
3. Sprichst du Deutsch?
4. Verstehst du Mathematik?
5. Machst du viel Sport?
6. Spielst du Schach?
7. Isst du viel Pizza?
8. Fährst du viel Fahrrad?

4 Diskutieren und kombinieren

Your instructor will give you and your partner different worksheets showing two schedules. Take turns asking and answering questions to find out the missing information from your partner's schedule.

BEISPIEL

S1: *Wann gehst du ins Stadion?*
S2: *Nächsten Montag um halb fünf nachmittags.*

5 Vermischtes

Use the cues to form questions. Then, in pairs, take turns asking and answering the questions.

BEISPIEL

S1: *Hast du heute Abend Freizeit?*
S2: *Nein, ich habe heute Abend keine Freizeit.*

1. angeln gehen / du / am Sonntag
2. Tennis spielen / du / samstags
3. gehen / du / oft / in die Sporthalle
4. Tennisschuhe / haben / keine / du
5. du / reiten / am Wochenende
6. du / schlafen / viel / sonntags
7. für die Prüfung / lernen / nicht / du
8. du / nicht / aus Berlin / kommen

6 Arbeitsblatt

Your instructor will give you and your partner each a worksheet. Take turns asking questions to find each other's battleships.

BEISPIEL

S1: *Liest Otto ein Buch?*
S2: *Treffer (Hit)! Er liest ein Buch./
Nein, kein Treffer. Er liest nicht.*

	lesen	arbeiten
Otto		
Lukas und Maria		🚢

7 **Marias Leben** In pairs, take turns asking and answering questions about Maria's activities.

▶ **BEISPIEL**

Dienstag, 9.15

S1: Was macht Maria am Dienstag um Viertel nach neun morgens?

S2: Am Dienstag um Viertel nach neun morgens macht Maria Hausaufgaben.

1. morgen, 10.30

2. heute, 12.00

3. Samstag, 14.00

4. heute Nachmittag, 14.25

5. nächsten Montag, 17.45

6. Freitag, 23.15

8 **Minigeschichte** In small groups, make up a story about the people in the picture. Be as detailed as possible. You may want to give the people names.

BEISPIEL

S1: Es ist Samstag und viele Studenten trainieren im Stadion.

S2: Niklas und David sind Basketballspieler, aber sie trainieren nicht...

fangen	trainieren
gewinnen	treffen
laufen	verlieren
spielen	werfen

Mein Wör|ter|buch

Add five words related to the themes **an der Universität** and **Sport und Freizeit** to your personalized dictionary.

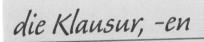

die Klausur, -en

Übersetzung
exam

Wortart
das Substantiv

Gebrauch
Ich lerne viel für die Klausur.

Synonyme
die Prüfung, das Examen, der Test

Antonyme
—

S Vocabulary Tools

Panorama ⓢ Interactive Map

Berlin

Die Stadt in Zahlen

▶ **Fläche:** *892 km² (Quadratkilometer)*

▶ **Einwohner° der Stadt Berlin:** *3.443.570*

▶ **Ausländer° in Berlin:** *503.945 (aus 186 Ländern)*

▶ **Touristen (2013):** *11.324.947*

▶ **Fastfood:** *Döner Kebap, erfunden° 1971 von Mehmet Aygün in Berlin; etwa 1.600 Verkaufsstellen° Currywurst (70 Millionen pro Jahr), erfunden 1949 von Herta Heuwer in Berlin; etwa 200 Verkaufsstellen*

▶ **Touristenattraktionen:** *das Brandenburger Tor, der Reichstag, die Gedächtniskirche, der Gendarmenmarkt, der Alexanderplatz, das Holocaust-Mahnmal, die Museumsinsel, der Potsdamer Platz, das Nikolaiviertel.*

QUELLE: Berlin - offizielles Hauptstadtportal

Berühmte Berliner

▶ **Friedrich II. (Friedrich der Große),** *König von Preußen° (1712–1786)*

▶ **Alexander von Humboldt,** *Naturforscher° (1769–1859)*

▶ **Gustav Langenscheidt,** *Deutschlehrer und Verlagsbuchhändler° (1832–1895)*

▶ **Berthold Brecht,** *Dramatiker° (1898–1956)*

▶ **Marlene Dietrich,** *Schauspielerin° und Sängerin° (1901–1992)*

▶ **Thomas „Icke" Häßler,** *Fußballspieler (1966–)*

▶ **Franziska van Almsick,** *Schwimmerin (1978–)*

Einwohner *inhabitants* **Ausländer** *foreigners* **erfunden** *invented*
Verkaufsstellen *points of sale* **König von Preußen** *King of Prussia*
Naturforscher *naturalist* **Verlagsbuchhändler** *publisher*
Dramatiker *playwright* **Schauspielerin** *actress* **Sängerin** *singer*
Weltkrieg *World War* **in Trümmern** *in ruins* **Gebäude zerstört** *buildings destroyed* **Wohnungen** *apartments* **Krankenhäuser** *hospitals*
beschädigt *damaged*

das Brandenburger Tor

der Alexanderplatz

die Museumsinsel

die Gedächtniskirche

Unglaublich aber wahr!

Am 2. Mai 1945 endet der 2. Weltkrieg° in Berlin. 28.5 km² der Stadt liegen in Trümmern°. Im Zentrum sind etwa 50% der Gebäude zerstört°. Etwa 600.000 Wohnungen° sind komplett zerstört. Die Infrastruktur der Stadt, Straßen, Schulen und Krankenhäuser° sind schwer beschädigt°. In Berlin leben noch 2,8 Millionen Menschen, vor dem Krieg sind es 4,3 Millionen.

Geschichte

Das DDR Museum

Seit 1989 sind Berlin und ganz Deutschland nicht mehr geteilt°. Das DDR Museum beleuchtet° das Leben in der ehemaligen° DDR: die Mauer, die Stasi° und den Alltag°. Die Ausstellung ist interaktiv. Man kann sich in einen echten° Trabant° oder ein authentisches DDR-Wohnzimmer° setzen. Geschichte zum Anfassen°!

Sport

Olympische Spiele 1936

Die Olympischen Sommerspiele 1936 finden vom 1. bis 16. August 1936 in Berlin statt°. 3.961 Athleten aus 49 Nationen nehmen an den Spielen teil° – ein neuer Rekord. Der bekannteste° Sportler dieser Spiele ist der amerikanische Leichtathlet Jesse Owens. Er gewinnt vier Goldmedaillen. Der erfolgreichste° deutsche Athlet ist der Kunstturner° Konrad Frey mit drei Goldmedaillen, einer Silbermedaille und zwei Bronzemedaillen. Die Nationalsozialisten missbrauchen° die Spiele als Propaganda.

Architektur

Der Reichstag°

Zwischen 1884 und 1894 errichtet der Architekt Paul Wallot den Reichstag. Er ist das wichtigste° Gebäude der deutschen Politik: Bis 1918 trifft sich hier der Reichstag des Deutschen Kaiserreichs°, danach das Parlament der Weimarer Republik, und seit 1999 der Deutsche Bundestag. 1933 ist der legendäre Reichstagsbrand°. Heute besuchen Touristen oft die Glaskuppel. Sie ist 23,5 Meter hoch°, 40 Meter breit° und 800 Tonnen schwer°. Im Sommer 1995 verhüllen° die Künstler Christo und Jeanne-Claude den Reichstag komplett. 5 Millionen Besucher° kommen nach Berlin, um den Reichstag zu sehen.

Kultur

Karneval der Kulturen

Berlin ist eine internationale Stadt mit mehr als 500.000 Menschen aus 186 Ländern. Seit 1996 gibt es jedes Jahr ein Fest, um die Internationalität und Kulturenvielfalt° Berlins zu feiern: den Karneval der Kulturen. Es gibt einen großen Umzug° mit etwa 5.000 Teilnehmern und ein viertägiges Straßenfest mit mehr als 800 Künstlern – Musik, Tanz, Performance – aus über 70 Ländern. 2011 besuchen fast 1,5 Millionen Menschen das Event in Berlin-Kreuzberg. 750.000 sehen den Umzug. An den vier Tagen kann man viele kulinarische und handwerkliche° Sachen genießen°.

⬯ IM INTERNET

1. Suchen Sie Informationen über Marlene Dietrich. Wann beginnt ihre (her) Karriere? Suchen Sie die drei bekanntesten Filme.

2. Was ist die Museumsinsel? Suchen Sie Informationen über mindestens (at least) drei Museen der Museumsinsel.

3. Suchen Sie Beispiele für „Ostalgie" (nostalgia for the East).

Find out more at **vhlcentral.com**.

geteilt *divided* beleuchtet *illuminates* ehemaligen *former* Stasi *secret police* Alltag *everyday* echten *real* Trabant *car produced in East Germany* Wohnzimmer *living room* zum Anfassen *to touch* finden... statt *take place* nehmen... teil *participate* bekannteste *most well-known* erfolgreichste *most successful* Kunstturner *gymnast* missbrauchen *misuse* Reichstag *parliament building* wichtigste *most important* des Deutschen Kaiserreichs *of the German empire* Reichstagsbrand *Reichstag fire* hoch *high* breit *wide* schwer *heavy* verhüllen *cover with fabric* Besucher *visitors* Kulturenvielfalt *cultural diversity* Umzug *parade* handwerkliche *crafts* genießen *enjoy*

⬯ Was haben Sie gelernt? Complete the sentences.

1. Die Fläche Berlins ist _____ Quadratkilometer.

2. Nach dem 2. Weltkrieg sind _____ Wohnungen in Berlin zerstört.

3. Seit _____ ist Berlin nicht mehr geteilt.

4. Im _____ kann man ein DDR-Wohnzimmer sehen.

5. Der erfolgreichste deutsche Athlet bei den Olympischen Spielen 1936 ist _____.

6. An den Olympischen Spielen 1936 nehmen 3.961 _____ teil.

7. Paul Wallot errichtet den Reichstag zwischen _____ und 1894.

8. Im Sommer 1995 kommen 5 Millionen _____ nach Berlin, um den Reichstag zu sehen.

9. Der Karneval der Kulturen dauert (*lasts*) _____ Tage.

10. Besucher sehen Künstler – Musiker, Tänzer etc. – aus über _____ Ländern beim Karneval der Kulturen.

 Practice more at **vhlcentral.com**.

Lesen  Audio: Reading

Vor dem Lesen

Texte verstehen

Briefly look at the document. What is its format? What kind of information is given? How is it organized? What are the visual components? What types of documents usually contain these elements?

Verwandte Wörter

You have already learned that you can use cognates, as well as format, to help you predict the content of a document. With a classmate, make a list of all the cognates you find in the reading selection. Based on these cognates and the format of the document, can you guess what this document is and what it is for?

Karlswald-Universität
Studienkolleg Mittelhessen

4 Stunden pro Tag (Montag–Freitag)
2 Tutorien pro Woche

Kurse

- Grundstufe: Anfänger°
- Stufe 1: Einführung° I
- Stufe 2: Einführung II
- Stufe 3: fortgeschritten° I
- Stufe 4: fortgeschritten II
- Stufe 5/6: Vorbereitung° auf die DSH-Prüfung

Kosten

- Einstufungstest: 50 Euro
- Stufe 1, 2, 3 und 4: 410 Euro pro Kurs
- Stufe 5/6: 620 Euro

Unterbringung°

- In Studentenwohnheimen
- In Privatwohnungen

Studienkolleg Mittelhessen
Friedrichstraße 3 | D-35032 Marburg

ausländische *foreign* **die... wollen** *who want* **Anfänger** *beginner* **Einführung** *introduction*
fortgeschritten *advanced* **Vorbereitung** *preparation* **Unterbringung** *accommodations*

Die Deutschkurse an der Karlswald-Universität:
Deutschtraining für ausländische° Studenten, die in Karlswald studieren wollen°.

Stufe 1–4 vom 3. Januar bis 14. Februar
Stufe 5/6 vom 3. Januar bis 22. März

Große Auswahl° zusätzlicher Aktivitäten:

- Tagesausflüge° zu Städten der Region (Frankfurt, Eisenach, Heidelberg)
- Besuche von Sehenswürdigkeiten° (Elisabethkirche, Marburger Schloss)
- Besuche von Kulturveranstaltungen° (Theaterproduktionen, Konzerte)
- Sport und andere Aktivitäten

Intensives Training in Hörverständnis°, Leseverständnis und Textproduktion.

Tel.: (06421) 28 23 651 - Fax.: (06421) 28 23 652
www.uni-karlswald.de/studienkolleg

Auswahl *selection* **Tagesausflüge** *day trips* **Sehenswürdigkeiten** *places of interest*
Kulturveranstaltungen *cultural events* **Hörverständnis** *listening comprehension*

Nach dem Lesen

Antworten Sie Select the option that best completes the statement.

1. Das ist eine Broschüre für...
   a. ein deutsches Gymnasium.
   b. ein Institut für Deutschkurse.
   c. Studenten, die Englisch lernen wollen.

2. Studenten, die kein Deutsch sprechen, nehmen den Kurs...
   a. Grundstufe.   b. Stufe 3.   c. Stufe 5/6.

3. Jeden (*Every*) Tag haben Studenten in einem Kurs...
   a. 4 Stunden Deutschunterricht.
   b. 4 Stunden Tutorien.
   c. 2 Stunden Deutschunterricht.

4. Der Test am Ende der Stufe 5/6...
   a. ist intensives Training.
   b. hat kein Hörverständnis.
   c. heißt DSH-Prüfung.

5. Studenten wohnen...
   a. bei deutschen Familien.
   b. im Studentenwohnheim.
   c. in Frankfurt.

6. An Wochenenden besuchen Studenten...
   a. Studentenheime und Privatwohnungen.
   b. Frankfurt und andere Städte.
   c. die Universität.

7. Kurse kosten...
   a. 50 Euro.
   b. 1.030 Euro.
   c. 410 oder 620 Euro.

8. Die Kurse der Stufe 1, 2, 3 und 4 dauern...
   a. 4 Wochen.   b. 6 Wochen.   c. 11 Wochen.

Richtig oder falsch? Mark the appropriate box.

	richtig	falsch
1. Das Studienkolleg Mittelhessen ist für deutsche Studenten.	☐	☐
2. Die Deutschkurse sind 5 Stunden jeden Tag.	☐	☐
3. Es gibt Tagesausflüge nach Frankfurt, Eisenach und Heidelberg.	☐	☐
4. Das Studienkolleg ist in der Friedrichstraße 3, D-35032 Marburg.	☐	☐

Hören

Vorbereitung

Based on the photograph, who do you think Julian and Anni are? Where are they? Do they know each other well? Where are they going this morning? What are they talking about?

Zuhören

 Listen to the conversation and list any cognates you hear. Listen again and complete the highlighted portions of Julian's schedule.

4. April   Montag

9.30	Kaffee mit Jasmin in der Cafeteria	14.30	
10.00	Seminar zur eng- lischen Literatur	15.00	
10.30		15.30	
11.00		16.00	
11.30		16.30	
12.00	Mittagessen mit Karl in der Mensa	17.00	
12.30		17.30	
13.00		18.00	
13.30		18.30	
14.00		19.00	Konzert im Kulturladen

Verständnis

 Richtig oder falsch? Indicate whether each sentence is **richtig** or **falsch**. Correct any false statements.

1. Anni lernt morgens in der Bibliothek.

_____

2. Julian und Anni studieren Architektur.

_____

3. Um 9.30 Uhr trinkt Julian mit Jasmin Kaffee.

_____

4. Anni hat um 2 Uhr eine Vorlesung.

_____

5. Anni findet Architektur interessant.

_____

6. Anni und Julian haben langweilige Professoren.

_____

7. Julian und Anni gehen am Nachmittag Fußball spielen.

_____

8. Julian geht am Abend in ein Konzert.

Pläne In pairs, discuss your plans for this weekend, including where and when you will do each activity.

Schreiben

Strategien

Brainstorming

Brainstorming can help you generate ideas on a specific topic. Before you begin writing, you should spend 10–15 minutes brainstorming, jotting down any ideas about the topic that occur to you. Whenever possible, try to write down your ideas in German. Express your ideas in single words or phrases, and jot them down in any order. While brainstorming, do not worry about whether your ideas are good or bad. Selecting and organizing ideas should be the second stage of your writing. The more ideas you write down while you are brainstorming, the more options you will have to choose from later on, when you start to organize your ideas.

Hobbys...
laufen
campen gehen
Tennis spielen
kochen
tanzen
schreiben
schwimmen
Fahrrad fahren

Thema

Eine persönliche Beschreibung

Write a description of yourself to post on a Web site in order to find a German-speaking e-pal. Your description should include:

- your name and where you are from.
- your birthday.
- the name of your school and where it is located.
- the courses you are currently taking and your opinion of each one.
- your hobbies and pastimes.
- any other information you would like to include.

Hallo!

Ich heiße Erik Schneider und ich komme aus Köln. Ich bin Schüler am Schiller-Gymnasium. Ich fahre Ski, spiele Tennis und fahre Fahrrad...

 **Vocabulary Tools**

Lektion 2A

das Studium

der Abschluss, ⸚e / das Diplom,
  -e *degree*
das Abschlusszeugnis, -se / das
  Diplom, -e *diploma*
der Dozent, -en / die Dozentin, -nen
  college/university instructor
das Fach, ⸚er *subject*
das Seminar, -e *seminar*
das Stipendium, -en *scholarship*
die Veranstaltung, -en *class; course*
die Vorlesung, -en *lecture*
(die) Architektur *architecture*
(die) Biologie *biology*
(die) Chemie *chemistry*
(die) Fremdsprache, -n *foreign
  language*
(die) Geschichte *history*
(die) Informatik *computer science*
(die) Kunst, ⸚e *art*
(die) Literatur *literature*
(die) Mathematik *math*
(die) Medizin *medicine*
(die) Naturwissenschaft, -en *science*
(die) Physik *physics*
(die) Psychologie *psychology*
(die) Wirtschaft *business*
belegen *to take (a class)*
gehen *to go*
lernen *to study; to learn*
studieren *to study; to major in*

Sportarten

spielen *to play*

der Stundenplan

der Montag, -e *Monday*
der Dienstag, -e *Tuesday*
der Mittwoch, -e *Wednesday*
der Donnerstag, -e *Thursday*
der Freitag, -e *Friday*
der Samstag, -e *Saturday*
der Sonntag, -e *Sunday*
die Stunde, -n *hour*
die Woche, -n *week*
das Wochenende, -n *weekend*
die Zeit, -en *time*
morgens *in the morning*
nachmittags *in the afternoon*
abends *in the evening*
montags *on Mondays*
dienstags *on Tuesdays*
mittwochs *on Wednesdays*
donnerstags *on Thursdays*
freitags *on Fridays*
samstags *on Saturdays*
sonntags *on Sundays*

Orte

das Café, -s *café*
der Hörsaal, Hörsäle *lecture hall*
der Seminarraum, -räume *(college/
  university) classroom*

zum Beschreiben

einfach *easy*
interessant *interesting*
langweilig *boring*
nützlich *useful*
nutzlos *useless*
schwierig *difficult*

Regular verbs *See pp. 56–57.*
Interrogative words *See p. 60.*
Telling time *See p. 62.*
Ordinal numbers and dates *See p. 63.*
gern/nicht gern *See p. 69.*

Lektion 2B

Sportarten

(der) Baseball *baseball*
(der) Basketball *basketball*
(der) (American) Football *football*
(der) Fußball *soccer*
(das) Golf *golf*
(das) Hockey *hockey*
(die) Leichtathletik *track and field*
(das) Tennis *tennis*
(der) Volleyball *volleyball*
der Ball, ⸚e *ball*
die Mannschaft, -en *team*
das Schwimmbad, ⸚er *swimming pool*
das Spiel, -e *game*
der Spieler, - / die Spielerin, -nen
  player
das Spielfeld, -er / der Platz, ⸚e
  field, court
der Sport *sports*
das Stadion, Stadien *stadium*
Fahrrad fahren *to ride a bicycle*
Ski fahren *to ski*
gewinnen *to win*
schwimmen *to swim*
trainieren *to practice*
verlieren *to lose*

Orte

die Sporthalle, -n *gym*

Freizeit

der Berg, -e *mountain*
das Fahrrad, ⸚er *bicycle*
die Freizeit *free time*
die Freizeitaktivität, -en *leisure activity*
das Hobby, -s *hobby*
die Karte, -n *card*
der Park, -s *park*
das Schach *chess*
der Strand, ⸚e *beach*
der Wald, ⸚er *forest*
angeln gehen *to go fishing*
campen gehen *to go camping*
essen gehen *to eat out*
spazieren gehen *to go for a walk*
klettern *to (rock) climb*
kochen *to cook*
(ein Pferd) reiten *to ride (a horse)*
schreiben *to write*
Spaß haben/machen *to have fun / to
  be fun*
singen *to sing*
tanzen *to dance*
wandern *to hike*

Ausdrücke

Sie spielen gern Schach. *They like to
  play chess.*
Sie verliert nicht gern. *She doesn't like
  to lose.*

Stem-changing verbs *See pp. 76–77.*
Common time expressions *See p. 80.*
Negative words *See pp. 82–83*

Ressourcen
vText **vhlcentral**

Johanna Schmidts Familie

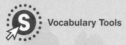 Vocabulary Tools

Walter Gärtner

mein Großvater/Opa (*m.*)

Peter Schmidt   **Marianne Schmidt**

mein Vater (*m.*),
Mariannes Mann (*m.*)

meine Mutter (*f.*),
Walter und Hannas
Tochter (*f.*)

Michaela Schmidt   **Daniel Schmidt**   **Johanna Schmidt**

meine Schwägerin   mein Bruder (*m.*)   ich, Peter und
Mariannes Tochter

Jonas Schmidt   **Greta Schmidt**

mein Neffe (*m.*)   meine Nichte (*f.*)
Peter und Mariannes Enkelkinder

Hanna Gärtner

meine Großmutter/Oma (f.)

Dieter Gärtner

mein Onkel (m.),
Walter und Hannas
Sohn (m.)

Renate Gärtner

meine Tante (f.),
Dieters Frau (f.)

Simon Gärtner

mein Cousin (m.),
Walter und Hannas
Enkelsohn (m.)

Sophia Gärtner

meine Cousine (f.),
Simon und Klaras
Schwester (f.)

Klara Gärtner

meine Cousine,
Simon und Sophias
Schwester,
Walter und Hannas
Enkeltochter (f.)

Zeus

Simon, Sophia und
Klaras Hund

Anwendung

1 Kombinieren Match the people with the descriptions.

____ 1. Mariannes Bruder
____ 2. Daniels Frau
____ 3. Marianne und Peter
____ 4. Dieter und Renates Sohn
____ 5. Mariannes Vater
____ 6. Peter und Mariannes Sohn
____ 7. Daniels Tochter
____ 8. Dieters Frau

a. Johannas Eltern
b. Johannas Tante
c. Johannas Cousin
d. Johannas Schwägerin
e. Johannas Nichte
f. Johannas Bruder
g. Johannas Onkel
h. Johannas Opa

2 Identifizieren Write each person's family relationship to Dieter Gärtner.

BEISPIEL Hanna: _____ *die Mutter* _____

1. Sophia: _____
2. Marianne: _____
3. Daniel: _____
4. Peter: _____
5. Simon: _____
6. Johanna: _____
7. Walter und Hanna: _____
8. Renate: _____

3 Kategorien List at least four roles each person could have in a family.

BEISPIEL eine Frau, 40 Jahre alt
eine Mutter   eine Tante   eine Cousine   eine Tochter

1. ein Mann, 62 Jahre alt:
_____   _____   _____   _____

2. ein Kind, 3 Jahre alt:
_____   _____   _____   _____

3. ein Mädchen, 15 Jahre alt:
_____   _____   _____   _____

4. eine Frau, 50 Jahre alt:
_____   _____   _____   _____

4 Hören Sie zu Listen to Johanna's descriptions and indicate whether each statement is **richtig** or **falsch**, based on her family tree.

	richtig	falsch		richtig	falsch
1.	☐	☐	7.	☐	☐
2.	☐	☐	8.	☐	☐
3.	☐	☐	9.	☐	☐
4.	☐	☐	10.	☐	☐
5.	☐	☐	11.	☐	☐
6.	☐	☐	12.	☐	☐

Kommunikation

5 Beschreibungen Use words from the list to describe the images.
Compare your answers with a classmate's, and correct each other's work.

| Enkelkinder | Großeltern | Neffe | Sohn | verheiratet | verlobt | Zwillinge |

▶ **BEISPIEL**
Das Paar ist verlobt.

1.

2.

3.

4.

5.

6.

6 Brieffreunde Read Eva's letter to her penpal. Then, in pairs, take turns answering the questions.

Liebe Andrea,

hast du eine große Familie? Meine Familie ist nicht sehr groß. Ich habe eine große Schwester Nicole und einen kleinen Halbbruder Peter. Und wir haben einen Hund, Cäsar, und Miezi, unsere kleine Katze.

Nicole studiert Sportmedizin in Heidelberg. Peter ist fünf und geht in den Kindergarten.

Meine Familie ist sehr sportlich. Mein Stiefvater spielt Golf, meine Mutter und Nicole spielen Tennis, Peter spielt Fußball und ich mache Ballett.

Und wie ist deine Familie?

Liebe Grüße
deine Eva

1. Wie viele Personen wohnen mit Eva zusammen?
2. Hat sie auch Haustiere?
3. Wie alt ist Peter?
4. Was macht Evas Familie in der Freizeit?
5. Wie groß ist Ihre (*your*) Familie?

7 Arbeitsblatt Your instructor will give you a worksheet with statements about family relationships. Use the cues to ask your classmates about their families.

BEISPIEL Ich habe zwei Schwestern.

S1: Hast du zwei Schwestern?
S2: Ja, ich habe zwei Schwestern.
(*You write his/her name.*)
OR
S2: Nein, ich habe keine Schwestern.
(*You ask another classmate.*)

8 Was machen sie gern? Use the vocabulary you learned in Kapitel 2 to talk with a classmate about what your family members enjoy doing.

BEISPIEL

S1: *Mein Bruder spielt gern Tennis. Was macht dein Bruder?*
S2: *Mein Bruder liest gern Bücher.*

Aussprache und Rechtschreibung  Audio

Final consonants

The German consonants **b**, **d**, and **g** generally sound quite similar to their English counterparts.

| **Ball** | **Bruder** | **Dezember** | **bringen** | **Golf** |

However, when **b** appears at the end of a word or syllable, or before a **t**, it is pronounced like a **p**.

| **ab** | **habt** | **gelb** | **Staub** | **liebt** |

When **d** appears at the end of a word or syllable, it is pronounced like a **t**. The **-dt** letter combination is also pronounced **t**.

| **Geld** | **Hund** | **Stadt** | **sind** | **Fahrrad** |

As you learned in **2A**, when **g** appears at the end of a word or before a **t**, it is pronounced like a **k**. In standard German, **-ig** at the end of a word is pronounced like the German **ch**.

| **klug** | **bringt** | **Tag** | **sagt** | **zwanzig** |

1 **Aussprechen** Practice saying these words aloud.

1. Bank	4. lobt	7. Abend	10. Berg
2. sieben	5. danken	8. gehen	11. fragt
3. Laub	6. Boden	9. Junge	12. schwierig

2 **Nachsprechen** Practice saying these sentences aloud.

1. Der Dieb klaut ein Fahrrad.
2. Der Besucher fragt Manfred ruhig um Rat.
3. Bernds Geschwister sind freundlich und großzügig.
4. Viele Diebe klauen viele Fahrräder.
5. Ingrids böser Bruder ist gierig und gemein.
6. Jörg sitzt im Zug und singt ein Lied.

3 **Sprichwörter** Practice reading these sayings aloud.

Kindermund tut Wahrheit kund.[1]

Geld regiert die Welt.[2]

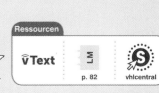

Ressourcen

v̂ Text   LM   S
p. 82   vhlcentral

Ein Abend mit der Familie Video

Die Freunde essen bei Familie Yilmaz. Alle wissen (*know*), Torsten ist Sabites Freund. Alle, nur einer nicht.

1

ANKE Hallo! Willkommen, ich bin Sabites Mutter.
GEORGE Freut mich sehr, Sie kennen zu lernen, Frau Yilmaz. Ich bin George Bachman.

2

SABITE George, das ist meine jüngere Schwester, Zeynep.
GEORGE Hallo, Zeynep, nett dich kennen zu lernen.
SABITE Und das ist unser Vater.
GEORGE Herr Yilmaz, freut mich.

ANKE Das sind die Patatesli Sigara Böregi von Faiks Großmutter.
MELINE Herr Yilmaz, Ihre Familie kommt aus der Türkei?
FAIK Ja. Ich komme aus Ankara. Ich habe dort Cousins und einen Onkel. Haben Sie Geschwister?
MELINE Ich habe drei ältere Schwestern. Eine ist verheiratet, eine ist getrennt, eine ist verlobt. Ich habe auch eine Nichte, sie heißt Ava und ist 12.

3

4

GEORGE Meine Eltern sind geschieden. Meine Urgroßeltern kommen aus Heidelberg.
TORSTEN Mein Onkel lebt in Heidelberg. Er ist Professor. Es ist eine schöne Stadt.

5

SABITE Hallo, Hans.
HANS Tut mir leid, dass ich zu spät komme.

HANS Hallo!
SABITE Hans, das sind meine Eltern, Anke und Faik.
HANS Guten Abend, Herr Yilmaz. Guten Abend, Frau Yilmaz. Für Sie.
ANKE Danke.
HANS Sehr erfreut.

6

ÜBUNGEN

1 **Richtig oder falsch?** Indicate whether each statement is **richtig** or **falsch**.

1. Sabite hat einen jüngeren Bruder.
2. Meline hat zwei ältere Schwestern.
3. Melines Nichte heißt Ava.
4. Faik kommt aus Ankara.
5. Es gibt Sauerbraten bei Familie Yilmaz.
6. Georges Eltern sind verheiratet.
7. Torstens Onkel lebt in München.
8. Georges Urgroßeltern kommen aus Berlin.
9. Hans' Familie kommt aus Bayern.
10. Max ist 18 und spielt Basketball.

PERSONEN

 Anke   Faik   George   Hans Meline Sabite Torsten   Zeynep

7

HANS Bist du ihr Bruder?
TORSTEN Nein, Sabite ist meine Freundin. Ich bin Torsten. Nett dich kennen zu lernen.
HANS Freut mich.
MELINE Börek?
HANS Nein danke.

8

MELINE Frau Yilmaz, Ihr Sauerbraten ist köstlich.
ANKE Danke, Meline. Hans? Alles in Ordnung? Du isst nichts.
HANS Hmm? Ja, danke.

9

FAIK Hans, Ihre Familie kommt aus Bayern?
HANS Ja.
TORSTEN Ich habe eine Tante in München. Hast du Geschwister, Hans?
HANS Mein Bruder, Max, ist 18. Er ist sportlich und spielt gern Fußball.
MELINE Hat er eine Freundin?

10

SABITE Hans, alles in Ordnung?
MELINE Sabite!
SABITE Was?
MELINE Hans.
SABITE Was ist mit Hans? Oh. Ooooh.
ANKE Wir haben Strudel!

Nützliche Ausdrücke

- **Freut mich sehr, Sie kennen zu lernen.**
  Pleased to meet you.
- **Das ist meine jüngere Schwester.**
  This is my younger sister.
- **die Türkei**
  Turkey
- **Haben Sie Geschwister?**
  Do you have any siblings?
- **die Urgroßeltern**
  great-grandparents
- **Tut mir leid, dass ich zu spät komme.**
  Sorry for being late.
- **der Sauerbraten**
  marinated beef
- **Ihr Sauerbraten ist köstlich.**
  Your sauerbraten is delicious.
- **Er ist sportlich und spielt gern Fußball.**
  He's athletic and likes to play soccer.
- **Alles in Ordnung?**
  Everything OK?
- **einladen**
  to invite
- **das Abendessen**
  dinner

  3A.1
- **Das ist unser Vater.**
  This is our father.

  3A.2
- **Es ist eine schöne Stadt.**
  It's a beautiful city.

---

2 **Zum Besprechen** Draw your family tree. Include your parents, siblings, aunts, uncles, and grandparents. Then "introduce" your family to a classmate.

BEISPIEL

S1: *Das ist meine Tante. Sie heißt Paula. Sie wohnt in New Jersey.*
S2: *Das ist mein Onkel. Er heißt...*

3 **Erweiterung** Boreks are a popular Turkish snack with many varieties. In pairs, research another popular Turkish dish, and share your findings with the class.

Ressourcen

v Text   VM   vhlcentral
         p. 103

Eine deutsche Familie Reading

TANJA UND JENS SIND EIN deutsches Ehepaar mit zwei Kindern. Sie haben zwei Söhne, Finn und Lukas. Finn ist 11 Jahre alt und in der 5. Klasse. Lukas ist zwei Jahre älter als Finn und geht schon° in die 7. Klasse. Die Familie hat eine große Wohnung° und einen schönen Garten vor dem Haus. Jens arbeitet den ganzen Tag in einem Büro°. Tanja arbeitet als Krankenschwester°, aber sie ist nachmittags immer zu Hause, wenn Finn und Lukas um eins von der Schule nach Hause kommen. Abends spielen sie zusammen Fußball im Park oder fahren Fahrrad am Rhein.

In der Familie macht auch Jens Hausarbeit°, aber Tanja kocht und putzt° trotzdem mehr. Die Familie fährt einmal im Jahr zusammen in den Urlaub°.

Sind Jens und Tanja also eine „typisch" deutsche Familie? Das Leben in Deutschland ist vielfältiger geworden°. In der Wohnung links neben Jens und Tanja lebt eine Einwandererfamilie°, rechts von ihnen lebt ein allein erziehender° Vater mit seiner Tochter. Was ist also „typisch" für die deutsche Familie von heute? Vielleicht einfach Zusammenhalt° und Liebe.

schon *already* **Wohnung** *apartment* **Büro** *office* **Krankenschwester** *nurse* **Hausarbeit** *housework* **putzt** *cleans* **Urlaub** *vacation* **ist vielfältiger geworden** *has become more diverse* **Einwandererfamilie** *family of immigrants* **allein erziehender** *single parent* **Zusammenhalt** *sticking together* **Mit wem** *With whom* **sonstige** *miscellaneous*

Mit wem° die Deutschen leben (%)

	Eltern	allein	Partner	allein mit Kind	sonstige°
18-24	63,5	15,9	15,8	1,4	3,4
25-29	19,8	25,2	48,6	3,1	3,3
30-34	6,8	20,1	66,9	4,5	1,7
35-44	3,3	14,9	74,1	6,3	1,4
45-54	1,3	13,6	78,8	5,0	1,4
55-64	0,3	16,9	79,4	2,2	1,3
65-74	0,1	25,0	70,8	2,1	2,1
75-79	0	41,8	52,0	2,2	3,9
80+	0	58,7	30,1	2,5	3,4

QUELLE: Bundesministerium

1 **Was fehlt?** Complete the statements.

1. Jens' Frau heißt _____.
2. Jens' _____ heißen Finn und Lukas.
3. Am Tag arbeitet _____ im Büro.
4. Tanja _____ als Krankenschwester.
5. Am Vormittag sind Finn und Lukas in der _____.
6. Am Abend spielen Jens, Finn, Lukas und Tanja Fußball oder _____ am Rhein.
7. Jens macht in der Familie auch _____.
8. Die Familie fährt gemeinsam in den _____.
9. In Deutschland leben die meisten (*most*) 18- bis 24-Jährigen mit ihren (*their*) _____.
10. Die meisten Deutschen, die älter als (*older than*) 80 Jahre sind, leben _____.

Die Familie

die Ehe	*marriage*
das Einzelkind	*only child*
die Hochzeit	*wedding*
die Mama	*mom*
der erste/zweite Mann	*first/second husband*
der Papa	*dad*
die Urgroßmutter	*great-grandmother*
der Urgroßvater	*great-grandfather*
der / die Verlobte	*fiancé(e)*
adoptieren	*to adopt*

Die Liebe

Ein Kuss° ist nicht nur° ein Kuss. In den
meisten Teilen° Deutschlands sagt man
„Kuss". Aber es gibt andere Möglichkeiten°,
„Kuss" in der deutschsprachigen Welt zu
sagen. **In der Schweiz** und **in Liechtenstein**
sagt man „Müntschi". **In Österreich** und
in Bayern ist ein Kuss ein „Bussi" oder ein
„Busserl". **Auf Kölsch** (der Dialekt von Köln)
ist das ein „Bütz".

Und wie sagt man „Ich liebe dich"?
Ein paar° Varianten:
In Bayern und **in Österreich** sagt man „I mog
di". **In der Schweiz** geht das so: „I liäbä di".
Und **die Berliner** sagen „Ick liebe Dir".

Kuss *kiss* **nur** *only* **meisten Teilen** *most parts*
Möglichkeiten *possibilities* **Ein paar** *A couple of*

Angela Merkel

Seit November 2005 hat Deutschland eine Bundeskanzlerin°: **Angela Merkel**. Viele
Deutsche finden Merkel pragmatisch und solide, und im Magazin Forbes steht, sie ist eine
der mächtigsten° Frauen der Welt. Die CDU°-Politikerin hat keine Kinder, aber sie hat einen
wichtigen Unterstützer°, ihren Mann, Joachim Sauer. Sauer ist Professor für Chemie an der
Humboldt-Universität in Berlin. Er hält sich am liebsten von den Medien fern°, aber wenn die
mächtigsten Politiker der Welt zusammen essen, ist Sauer oft dabei. Und wer wäscht im
Hause Sauer-Merkel die Wäsche°? Beide!

Bundeskanzlerin *female chancellor* **eine der mächtigsten** *one of the most powerful* **CDU** *Christian Democratic Union*
Unterstützer *supporter* **hält sich am liebsten von den Medien fern** *prefers to stay away from the media*
wäscht... die Wäsche *does the laundry*

**Scheidung (*Divorce*): Eine Epidemie in den
deutschsprachigen Ländern?**

Find out more at **vhlcentral.com**.

---

2 **Richtig oder falsch?** Indicate whether each statement is **richtig** or
falsch. Correct the false statements.

1. Der Dialekt, den man in Köln spricht, heißt „Bayerisch".

2. „I liäbä di" ist die schweizerische Art (*Swiss way*), „Ich liebe dich"
   zu sagen.

3. Angela Merkel hat zwei Kinder.

4. Joachim Sauer ist mit Angela Merkel verheiratet.

5. Joachim Sauer ist der deutsche Bundespräsident.

3 **Sie sind dran** Use vocabulary from **Deutsch im Alltag** to write six
sentences describing a famous American family. Then share
the description with your classmates.

Ressourcen

v Text

vhlcentral

3A.1 Possessive adjectives  Presentation

Startblock In both English and German, possessive adjectives indicate ownership or belonging.

Sabite ist **meine** Freundin.

Herr Yilmaz, **Ihre** Familie kommt aus der Türkei?

QUERVERWEIS

In **Kontext 3A**, you learned some possessive adjectives used with family vocabulary: <u>**mein**</u> Großvater, <u>**meine**</u> Mutter, <u>**meine**</u> Eltern.

- In **1A.1**, you learned about indefinite articles. Possessive adjectives are also referred to as **ein**-words since they take the same endings as the indefinite article **ein**. Each personal pronoun has a corresponding possessive adjective.

personal pronouns and possessive adjectives		
personal pronouns	possessive adjectives	
ich	mein	*my*
du	dein	*your* (sing., inf.)
er	sein	*his*
sie	ihr	*her*
es	sein	*its*
wir	unser	*our*
ihr	euer	*your* (pl., inf.)
Sie	Ihr	*your* (sing./pl., form.)
sie	ihr	*their*

Meine Schwester ist 16 Jahre alt.
My sister is 16 years old.

Wo ist **dein** Vater?
*Where is **your** father?*

- Possessive adjectives always precede the nouns they modify.

meine Mutter	**deine** Mutter	**unsere** Mutter	**seine** Mutter
my mother	*your mother*	*our mother*	*his mother*

Meine Schwester ist sehr sportlich.
My sister is very athletic.

- Like other **ein**-words, their endings change according to the gender, case, and number of the object possessed.

deine Mutter	**dein** Vater	**dein** Baby	**deine** Eltern
your mother	*your father*	*your baby*	*your parents*

Mein Großvater liebt **seine** Enkelkinder.
*My grandfather loves **his** grandchildren.*

- Like other **ein**-words, possessive adjectives have no added endings before singular masculine or neuter nouns in the nominative, or before singular neuter nouns in the accusative.

nominative and accusative of *ein*-words				
	masculine	**feminine**	**neuter**	**plural**
nominative	**ein** Vater **unser** Vater	**ein**e Mutter **unser**e Mutter	**ein** Kind **unser** Kind	**kein**e Brüder **unser**e Brüder
accusative	**ein**en Vater **unser**en Vater	**ein**e Mutter **unser**e Mutter	**ein** Kind **unser** Kind	**kein**e Brüder **unser**e Brüder

Ihr Kind ist 3 Jahre alt.   Tobias liebt **seinen** Bruder.
Her child is 3 years old.   *Tobias loves **his** brother.*

- The formal possessive adjective **Ihr** corresponds to the formal personal pronoun **Sie**. The possessive adjective **ihr** can mean either *her* or *their*, depending on context.

Wo sind **Ihre** Eltern?   Rolf und Heike kochen für **ihre** Kinder.
*Where are **your** parents?*   *Rolf and Heike cook for **their** children.*

Christa kocht für **ihre** Enkelkinder.
*Christa cooks for **her** grandchildren.*

- The possessive adjective **euer** drops the second **e** when an ending is added. The possessive adjective **unser** may drop the **e** in the stem when an ending is added, but this form is rare.

euer Enkelsohn   **eure** Familie   **unser** Sohn   **uns(e)re** Tochter
your grandson   *your family*   *our son*   *our daughter*

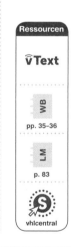

Ressourcen

v̂ Text

WB
pp. 35–36

LM
p. 83

vhlcentral

Jetzt sind Sie dran!   Write the correct forms of the possessive adjectives.

Nominativ

mein
1. ___*meine*___ Idee

dein
2. _____ Eltern

sein
3. _____ Wörterbuch

ihr
4. _____ Familienstand

Akkusativ

mein
5. _____ Bruder

dein
6. _____ Frage

sein
7. _____ Familie

ihr
8. _____ Kind

Nominativ

unser
9. _____ Fahrrad

euer
10. _____ Mannschaft

Ihr
11. _____ Nachname

ihr
12. _____ Hausaufgaben

Akkusativ

unser
13. _____ Verwandten

euer
14. _____ Sohn

Ihr
15. _____ Hunde

ihr
16. _____ Problem

Anwendung

1 **Was ist richtig?** Select the appropriate form of the possessive adjective.

1. (Mein / Meine) Eltern essen gern Spaghetti.
2. (Unser / Unsere) Sohn spielt gut Fußball.
3. Markus und Sabine lieben (ihren / ihre) Eltern.
4. Andrea liebt (euren / euer) Hund.
5. Hat (dein / deinen) Bruder einen Sohn?
6. Sind (Ihr / Ihre) Großeltern hier?
7. Ich lese (mein / meine) Bücher nicht.
8. Mein Vater und (sein / seinen) Freund spielen Schach.

2 **Was fehlt?** Complete each sentence with the appropriate possessive adjective.

BEISPIEL Treffen Sie ____*Ihren*____ Mann im Restaurant?

1. Das Baby braucht _____ Mutter.
2. Ali und Lara suchen _____ Hund.
3. Ich heiße Jan, und _____ Nachname ist Bauer.
4. Sarah und _____ Schwester kochen gern zusammen.
5. Herr Schulz und _____ Frau sind getrennt.
6. Siehst du _____ Großeltern oft?
7. Wir lieben _____ Verwandten.
8. Kinder, wo sind _____ Eltern?

3 **Schreiben** Write a sentence about each item saying whose it is.

▶ **BEISPIEL**
Das sind meine Hefte.

ich

1. du

2. er

3. wir

4. sie

5. Sie

6. ihr

4 **Antworten Sie** Answer the questions with complete sentences.

1. Wo wohnt Ihre Familie?
2. Wie heißt Ihre Mutter?
3. Wie ist ihr Nachname?
4. Wie alt ist Ihr Vater?
5. Welche Sportarten spielt Ihre Familie gern?
6. Spielen Ihre Großeltern Schach?
7. Wie heißt Ihr bester Freund / Ihre beste Freundin?
8. Welche Bücher lesen Ihre Freunde gern?

Kommunikation

5 **Familie und Freunde** With your partner, take turns asking and answering these questions.

> **BEISPIEL**
>
> **S1:** Hat deine Mutter Haustiere?
> **S2:** Ja, meine Mutter hat zwei Haustiere. Ihre Katze heißt Muffin und ihr Hund heißt Sam. Wie ist dein Vater?
> **S1:** Mein Vater ist Lehrer. Er ist vierzig Jahre alt und hat zwei Brüder.

1. Hat deine Mutter Haustiere?
2. Wie ist dein Vater?
3. Wieviele Kinder haben deine Eltern?

4. Wo wohnt deine Familie?
5. Was machen deine Freunde am Samstag?
6. Was studiert dein bester Freund oder deine beste Freundin?

6 **Meine Familie** Use the cues to form questions. Then interview your classmates about their family members.

> **BEISPIEL**
>
> **S1:** Spricht deine Mutter Deutsch?
> **S2:** Ja, meine Mutter spricht Deutsch.
> **S3:** Nein, meine Mutter spricht kein Deutsch.

1. Bruder / spielen / Fußball
2. Vater / haben / ein Hund
3. Eltern / lesen / Bücher
4. Großmutter / spielen / Tennis
5. Schwester / haben / grüne Augen
6. Onkel und Tante / fahren / Ski
7. Verwandte / schreiben / E-Mails
8. Familie / sein / groß

7 **Ich sehe etwas** Tell the class about something of yours that you can see in the classroom. Then, repeat what the people before you said they saw.

> **BEISPIEL**
>
> **S1:** Ich sehe meinen Fußball.
> **S2:** Ich sehe mein Buch und Stefan sieht seinen Fußball.
> **S3:** Ich sehe meine Fotos, Maria sieht ihr Buch und Stefan sieht seinen Fußball.

8 **Familienporträt** In small groups, take turns describing your family. Use possessive pronouns in the nominative and accusative case. After everyone has spoken, take turns describing your partners' families to the rest of the class.

> **BEISPIEL**
>
> **S1:** Das ist Inga. Ihre Mutter hat grüne Augen und braune Haare.
> **S2:** Das ist Michael. Seine Mutter ist Lehrerin.

3A.2 Descriptive adjectives and adjective agreement  Presentation

Startblock Adjectives can describe people, places, or things. Here are some adjectives commonly used to describe people and their physical attributes.

QUERVERWEIS

In **2A Kontext**, you learned a few adjectives to describe school subjects. In **3A Kontext**, you learned some additional adjectives to describe eye color, hair color, and marital status.

physical description			
alt	*old*	hübsch	*pretty*
blond	*blond*	jung	*young*
braunhaarig	*brown-haired*	klein	*small; short (stature)*
dick	*fat; thick*	kurz	*short (hair)*
dunkelhaarig	*dark-haired*	lang	*long (hair)*
dünn	*thin*	lockig	*curly*
glatt	*straight (hair)*	rothaarig	*red-headed*
groß	*big; tall*	schlank	*slim*
großartig	*terrific*	schön	*pretty; beautiful*
gut aussehend	*handsome*	schwarzhaarig	*black-haired*
hässlich	*ugly*	sportlich	*athletic*

- Use an adjective with no added endings after the verbs **sein**, **werden**, and **bleiben** (*to remain*).

Mein Bruder ist **klein**.	Seine Mutter bleibt **sportlich**.	Deine Schwester wird **groß**.
*My brother is **short**.*	*His mother stays **in shape**.*	*Your sister is getting **tall**.*

- When you use an adjective before a noun, you need to include an adjective ending.

Meine **großen** Schwestern spielen Fußball.	Das ist eine **schöne** Katze.
*My **big** sisters play soccer.*	*That's a **pretty** cat.*

- Adjective endings depend on the case, number, and gender of the noun they modify, and whether they are preceded by a **der**-word, an **ein**-word, or neither.

Sie lieben ihren **jungen** Sohn.	Das **kleine** Baby hat **blaue** Augen.
*They love their **young** son.*	*The **little** baby has **blue** eyes.*

- Adjectives after a **der**-word have these endings.

after *der*-words				
	masculine	**feminine**	**neuter**	**plural**
nominative	der **groß**e Bruder	die **blond**e Schwester	das **jung**e Kind	die **alt**en Großeltern
accusative	den **groß**en Bruder	die **blond**e Schwester	das **jung**e Kind	die **alt**en Großeltern

Der **alte** Mann dort ist mein Opa.	Die **große** Frau ist meine Tante.
*The **old** man over there is my grandpa.*	*The **tall** woman is my aunt.*
Ich liebe die **schönen** Häuser in dieser Straße.	Irene sucht ihren **kleinen** Cousin.
*I love the **pretty** houses on this street.*	*Irene is looking for her **little** cousin.*

- Adjectives preceded by an **ein**-word have these endings.

after *ein*-words	masculine	feminine	neuter	plural
nominative	ein **groß**er Bruder	eine **blond**e Schwester	ein **jung**es Kind	meine **alt**en Großeltern
accusative	einen **groß**en Bruder	eine **blond**e Schwester	ein **jung**es Kind	meine **alt**en Großeltern

Mein **großer** Bruder ist ein **guter** Golfspieler.
*My **big** brother is a **good** golf player.*

Ist deine **kleine** Schwester hier?
*Is your **little** sister here?*

Herr Wirth hat eine **sportliche** Tochter.
*Mr. Wirth has an **athletic** daughter.*

Seine Großmutter hat einen **schönen** Vogel.
*His grandmother has a **beautiful** bird.*

- Unpreceded adjectives have these endings.

unpreceded	masculine	feminine	neuter	plural
nominative	**rot**er Wein	**dick**e Milch	**alt**es Brot	**groß**e Fische
accusative	**rot**en Wein	**dick**e Milch	**alt**es Brot	**groß**e Fische

Kleine Kinder brauchen **gute** Eltern.
***Small** children need **good** parents.*

Altes Brot schmeckt nicht so gut.
***Old** bread doesn't taste so good.*

Mein Vater hat **braune** Augen.
*My father has **brown** eyes.*

Unsere Geschwister haben **lockige** Haare.
*Our siblings have **curly** hair.*

- If multiple adjectives precede the same noun, they all take the same ending.

Ist das **kleine**, **rothaarige** Mädchen deine Schwester?
*Is the **little**, **red-headed** girl your sister?*

Sie hat einen **großen**, **gut aussehenden** Bruder.
*She has a **tall**, **good-looking** brother.*

- Use **sehr** before an adjective to mean *very*. The adverb **sehr** does not take any additional endings.

Ihre Haare sind **sehr** lang.
*Her hair is **very** long.*

Ich lese ein **sehr** gutes Buch.
*I'm reading a **very** good book.*

ACHTUNG

Some adjectives ending in -**el**, such as **dunkel**, drop the **e** in the stem when an ending is added.

Das ist ein dunkles Foto.
That's a dark photo.

QUERVERWEIS

You learned the adverb **sehr** in **1A Kontext**, in the expression **sehr gut**. You will learn more about adverbs in **4A.1**.

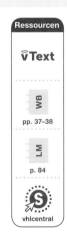

Ressourcen

vText

WB
pp. 37–38

LM
p. 84

vhlcentral

Jetzt sind Sie dran! Write the nominative or accusative form of the adjectives.

Nominativ

1. der ___schlanke___ (schlank) Vater
2. ein _____ (verheiratet) Mann
3. die _____ (groß) Familie
4. eine _____ (alt) Schwägerin
5. das _____ (verlobt) Paar
6. die _____ (sportlich) Enkelkinder

Akkusativ

7. einen _____ (jung) Vater
8. die _____ (ledig) Verwandten
9. einen _____ (dünn) Hund
10. ein _____ (hübsch) Mädchen
11. den _____ (klein) Sohn
12. das _____ (blond) Kind

Anwendung

1 **Kombinieren** Match each adjective with its opposite.

1. hässlich   a. jung
2. kurz   b. dick
3. blond   c. klein
4. alt   d. schön
5. groß   e. schwarzhaarig
6. dünn   f. lang
7. lockig   g. glatt

2 **Was fehlt?** Complete the sentences.

1. Ich habe einen _____ (groß) Bruder.
2. Mein _____ (groß) Bruder spielt Fußball.
3. Er hat einen _____ (klein) Hund.
4. Der _____ (klein) Hund hat sehr _____ Haare.
5. Seine _____ (kurz) Haare sind auch sehr _____ (dünn).
6. Hast du auch so einen _____ (klein), _____ (schön) Hund?

3 **Was ist richtig?** Select the adjective that best completes each sentence.

> **BEISPIEL**   Martin ist sehr nett und freundlich.
> Er ist ein _____*großartiger*_____ (hässlicher, sportlicher, großartiger) Junge.

1. Sein Vater fährt viel Fahrrad und Ski. Er ist ein sehr _____ (sportlicher, alter, blonder) Mann.
2. Deine Schwester hat schöne Haare. Sie ist ein _____ (großes, hässliches, hübsches) Mädchen.
3. Meine Mutter hat keine lockigen Haare. Sie hat _____ (kleine, lange, glatte) Haare.
4. Meine Eltern sind nicht mehr zusammen. Ich habe _____ (verheiratete, kurze, geschiedene) Eltern.
5. Ihre Enkeltochter ist 2 Jahre alt. Sie ist ein _____ (junges, hässliches, dickes) Kind.
6. Die Großeltern sind 80 Jahre alt. Die _____ (hübschen, alten, kleinen) Großeltern spielen Schach am Wochenende.

4 **Schreiben** Replace the underlined words with the words in parentheses and make any necessary changes.

> **BEISPIEL**   <u>Das</u> kleine Mädchen ist sehr sportlich. (die)
> *Die kleinen Mädchen sind sehr sportlich.*

1. <u>Der</u> rothaarige Sohn spielt Fußball. (mein)
2. Ihr Großvater liest <u>das</u> lange Buch. (ein)
3. Ich belege <u>einen</u> schwierigen Kurs. (den)
4. <u>Der</u> kurze, dünne Junge ist nicht sehr sportlich. (die)
5. Siehst du <u>die</u> kleinen Kinder? (das)

Kommunikation

5 **Die Familie Müller** In pairs, take turns describing the members of the Müller family.

BEISPIEL

Moritz ist alt und klein.

Michael · Petra · Inez · Rex · Alexander · Moritz

6 **Ein guter Freund** Interview a classmate to learn about one of his/her friends. Use the questions below and add three more of your own.

BEISPIEL

S1: *Hat deine beste Freundin lange Haare?*
S2: *Nein, sie hat kurze Haare.*

- Wie heißt er/sie?
- Wie alt ist er/sie?
- Ist er/sie groß oder klein?
- Hat er/sie blaue Augen?
- Ist er/sie dunkelhaarig?
- Ist er/sie sportlich?
- Ist er ein guter Schüler? / Ist sie eine gute Schülerin?

7 **Raten Sie** Choose a famous person. In small groups, take turns asking yes-or-no questions to determine the identity of each person.

▶ **BEISPIEL**

S1: *Ist sie eine Frau?*
S2: *Ja.*
S3: *Hat sie blaue Augen?*
S2: *Nein.*

8 **Beschreiben** Pick one of your family members and describe him or her to your partner. Take notes on your partner's description, and be prepared to describe his or her family member to the class.

BEISPIEL

Mein Onkel ist ein großer Mann. Er hat kurze schwarze Haare...

- Wie alt ist er/sie?
- Wie ist sein/ihr Familienstand?
- Hat er/sie Kinder?
- Macht er/sie Sport?
- Hat er/sie Haustiere?
- Woher kommt er/sie?

Wiederholung

1 **Wer ist wer?** In pairs, take turns choosing a person from the list and giving clues to help your partner guess which person you've chosen.

BEISPIEL

S1: *Mein Vater ist ihr Mann. Meine
Schwester ist ihre Tochter. Wer ist sie?*
S2: *Sie ist deine Mutter.*

Bruder	Schwester
Cousin	Schwiegermutter
Enkeltochter	Sohn
Großvater	Tante
Schwager	Vater

2 **Saras Familie** In pairs, say what each person in Sara's family is like and what he or she likes to do. Use vocabulary from **Kontext 2B**.

▶ **BEISPIEL**

S1: *Wie ist Saras Bruder?*
S2: *Ihr Bruder ist groß. Er spielt
gern Tennis.*

Bruder

1. Cousin

2. Neffe

3. Tante

4. Onkel

5. Großvater

6. Schwägerin

3 **Arbeitsblatt** Your instructor will give you a worksheet with instructions to play Family Bingo. Get a different name for each square of the grid, then share your findings with the class.

BEISPIEL

S1: *Paula, hast du einen großen Bruder?*
S2: *Ja, mein Bruder Stefan ist sehr groß.*
S1: *Paula hat einen großen Bruder.*

4 **Verschiedene Menschen** In small groups, take turns picking someone in the illustration and describing him/her. The next person repeats the description and adds to it. Keep going around the group, trying to add as many details as possible.

BEISPIEL

S1: *Die Frau heißt Fatima. Sie ist hübsch.*
S2: *Die Frau heißt Fatima. Sie ist hübsch und liest gern.*
S3: *Die Frau heißt Fatima. Sie ist hübsch und liest gern.
Morgen geht sie spazieren.*

Daniel   Fatima   Annika

Yusuf und
Tobias

Mert und Lara

Jana und
Alexander

Emil und Eva

5 **Diskutieren und kombinieren** Your instructor will give you and your partner each a picture of a family. Ask questions to find the six differences between the two pictures.

BEISPIEL

S1: *Ist Renate blond?*
S2: *Nein. Renate ist nicht blond. Sie ist dunkelhaarig.*

6 **Stammbaum** Create an illustrated family tree, and share it with a classmate. Tell your partner about each of your family members, including their names, how they are related to you, what they are like, and what they like or don't like to do.

BEISPIEL

S1: *Das ist meine Schwester. Sie heißt Steffi. Sie ist
sehr sportlich.*
S2: *Fährt Steffi gern Fahrrad?*

Zapping

S Video

Bauer Joghurt

The Bauer creamery was founded in 1887 in Wasserburg am Inn, Bavaria. Today, the company is managed by the fifth generation of the Bauer family. Known especially for their yogurt, Bauer also produces a variety of cheeses and other dairy products. The company has a reputation for excellent quality, using milk from cows fed on non-genetically modified food, with no added preservatives or artificial flavors.

Papa, wer ist dieser Bauer°?

Die Bauers, Schatz. Das ist eine Familie aus Bayern°.

Die machen alle Joghurt. Vom Opa bis zum Enkel.

Bauer *farmer* **Bayern** *Bavaria*

 Verständnis Answer the questions in German.

1. Who are the Bauers, according to the girl's father?
2. Which members of the Bauer family does the father mention?

 Diskussion In pairs, discuss the answers to these questions.

1. Do you know of other companies like Bauer that are family-owned? Are family-owned companies more likely to produce quality products? Explain.
2. What is the message of this commercial? Do you think it effectively conveys that message? Explain.

Wortschatz

persönliche Beschreibungen	*personal descriptions*
(un)angenehm	(un)pleasant
arm	poor; unfortunate
bescheiden	modest
egoistisch	selfish
ernst	serious
freundlich	friendly
gemein	mean
gierig	greedy
großzügig	generous
intellektuell	intellectual
intelligent	intelligent
langsam	slow
mutig	brave
naiv	naïve
nervös	nervous
nett	nice
neugierig	curious
reich	rich
schlecht	bad
schüchtern	shy
schwach	weak
stolz	proud
toll	great
lächeln	to smile
lachen	to laugh
weinen	to cry
Berufe	*professions*
der Architekt, -en / die Architektin, -nen	architect
der Geschäftsmann (*pl.* Geschäftsleute) / die Geschäftsfrau, -en	businessman / businesswoman
der Ingenieur, -e / die Ingenieurin, -nen	engineer
der Journalist, -en / die Journalistin, -nen	journalist
der Rechtsanwalt, ¨e / die Rechtsanwältin, -nen	lawyer

Ressourcen

v̂ Text | WB pp. 39–40 | LM p. 85 | vhlcentral

Wie sind sie?

Vocabulary Tools

Er ist stark.

der Kellner, - (die Kellnerin, -nen)

Er ist schnell.

Sie sind faul.

Er ist fleißig.

der Besitzer, - (die Besitzerin, -nen)

diskret

müde

eifersüchtig

Sie ist besorgt.

Er ist traurig.

ACHTUNG

Note that the plural of **der Geschäftsmann** is **die Geschäftsleute**; **die Leute** means *people*.

die Friseurin, -nen
(der Friseur, -e)

Er ist lustig.

Sie sind glücklich/froh.

Sie ist süß.

der Musiker, -
(die Musikerin, -nen)

Anwendung

1 Kombinieren
Match these famous people with their professions.

_____ 1. Sheryl Sandberg
_____ 2. Ferdinand Porsche
_____ 3. Walter Gropius
_____ 4. Diane Sawyer
_____ 5. Ludwig van Beethoven
_____ 6. Sonia Sotomayor

a. Architekt
b. Rechtsanwältin
c. Musiker
d. Geschäftsfrau
e. Journalistin
f. Ingenieur

2 Gegenteile
Complete each sentence with the opposite adjective.

1. Der Geschäftsmann ist nicht <u>arm</u>, er ist _____.
2. Die Musiker sind nicht <u>traurig</u>, sie sind _____.
3. Die Besitzerin ist nicht <u>gierig</u>, sie ist _____.
4. Die Kellnerin ist nicht <u>langsam</u>, sie ist _____.
5. Die Tennisspieler sind nicht <u>schwach</u>, sie sind _____.
6. Der Rechtsanwalt ist nicht <u>fleißig</u>, er ist _____.
7. Die Architektin ist nicht <u>stolz</u>, sie ist _____.
8. Unser Hund ist nicht <u>gemein</u>, er ist _____.

3 Was fehlt?
Select the word that best describes each person.

bescheiden	gierig	müde	stark
faul	glücklich	nervös	süß
fleißig	intelligent	neugierig	traurig

1. Klara arbeitet viel und schnell. Sie ist _____.
2. Ben hat sehr gute Noten. Er ist _____.
3. Philip hat viel Stress. Er ist _____.
4. Emma lacht und lächelt viel. Sie ist _____.
5. Maria macht keine Hausaufgaben. Sie ist _____.
6. Tom schläft nicht viel. Er ist _____.
7. Erik weint. Er ist _____.
8. Greta hat viele Fragen. Sie ist _____.

4 Hören Sie zu
You will hear descriptions of three people. Listen carefully and indicate whether the statements are **richtig** or **falsch**.

	richtig	falsch
1. Florian ist Journalist.	☐	☐
2. Stefanie hat zwei Kinder.	☐	☐
3. Franz' Hund heißt Argus.	☐	☐
4. Stefanies Mann findet seinen Beruf langweilig.	☐	☐
5. Florian ist ein angenehmer Boss.	☐	☐
6. Stefanie und Klaus sind reich.	☐	☐
7. Florians Auto ist sehr alt.	☐	☐
8. Franz ist ein stolzer Opa.	☐	☐

Kommunikation

5 **Berufe** In pairs, take turns replying to the questions based on the images.

▶ **BEISPIEL**

S1: Ist Karl Musiker?
S2: Nein, er ist Kellner.

1. Ist Helga Ingenieurin?

2. Ist Ulrich Architekt?

3. Sind Markus, Jan und Tobias Rechtsanwälte?

4. Ist Birgit Kellnerin?

5. Ist Stefan Friseur?

6. Ist Claudia Musikerin?

---

6 **Partnersuche** Read Georg's personal ad and discuss with a partner whether Maria or Jessica would be a better match for him. Be ready to defend your opinion to the class.

Georg, 32 Jahre ✉ ■ ☺ ⊞

Hallo! Ich heiße Georg, ich bin 32 Jahre alt, 182 cm groß, schlank, dunkelhaarig und habe braune Augen. Ich bin ein netter Mann, optimistisch und intelligent. Ich habe viele Hobbys, spiele Fußball, Tennis und Handball, sehe gern Filme und koche auch gern und gut. Ich bin geschieden und habe eine kleine Tochter. Meine ideale Partnerin ist zwischen 26 und 32 Jahre alt, nicht zu klein (ca. 168 cm), blond, schlank, aktiv und sportlich. Sie muss gern essen und sie muss Kinder gern haben! Wenn du das bist, dann schicke mir eine E-Mail an nettergeorg@gvz.de.

Maria
23 Jahre
groß (182 cm)
lustig
schüchtern
aktiv

Jessica
28 Jahre
klein (165 cm)
sportlich
intellektuell
schlank

---

7 **Wunschpartner** Now it's your turn to write a personal ad. Using Georg's ad as a model, describe yourself and your ideal girlfriend or boyfriend. Include details such as profession, age, physical characteristics, and personality. In groups, take turns reading the ads and guessing who wrote them.

8 **Klassentreffen** Imagine you are at the 10th reunion for your high-school class. With a partner, role-play a conversation between two old friends who haven't seen each other since graduation.

- Find out where your friend now lives and what his or her profession is.
- Ask about your friend's marital status, whether he or she has children, and, if so, what they are like.
- Ask your friend to describe his or her significant other.

9 **Klatsch und Tratsch** Heike is catching up with her cousin Lisa, who is a real **Klatschbase** (gossip). With a partner, write a conversation between Heike and Lisa in which Lisa gives her opinion of the guests at a recent family wedding.

BEISPIEL

S1: Wie ist Peters Frau?
S2: Sie ist hübsch und sehr schlank, aber eine unangenehme Person und ein bisschen gemein. Sie ist Journalistin, also der intellektuelle Typ.

Aussprache und Rechtschreibung

 Audio

Consonant clusters

Some German consonant combinations are not common in English. In the clusters **gn**, **kn**, **pf**, and **ps**, both consonants are pronounced. Do not add a vowel sound between these consonants when you pronounce them.

Gn**om**   **K**n**ödel**   **Pf**erd**   **Na**pf**   **ps**ychisch

The German **ng** is always pronounced like the English *ng* in *singer*, never like the consonant combination in *finger*, regardless of where it appears in a word.

Ring**   **fa**ng**en   **ju**ng**   **Prüfu**ng**en   **entla**ng

Some German letters represent the sound of a consonant cluster. The letter **x** is pronounced like the consonant combination **ks**. The letter **z** and the consonant combinations **tz** and **ts** are pronounced like the *ts* in the English word *hats*. The letter combination **qu** is pronounced *kv*.

e**x**tra   **Z**ahn   **Qu**alität   sit**z**t   **Äqu**ator

1 Aussprechen Practice saying these words aloud.

1. Gnade
2. knicken
3. Pfeil
4. Topf
5. Pseudonym
6. lang
7. bringen
8. Examen
9. Zoo
10. Mozart
11. Quatsch
12. Aquarell

2 Nachsprechen Practice saying these sentences aloud.

1. Die Katze streckt sich und legt den Kopf in den Nacken.
2. Felix fängt eine Qualle aus dem Ozean.
3. Der Zoowärter zähmt ein quergestreiftes Zebra.
4. Herr Quast brät Knödel in der Pfanne.
5. Der Gefangene bittet Xerxes um Gnade.
6. Das Taxi fährt kreuz und quer durch die Schweiz.

3 Sprichwörter Practice reading these sayings aloud.

Pferde lassen sich zum Wasser bringen, aber nicht zum Trinken zwingen.[1]

Nachts sind alle Katzen grau.[2]

[1] You can lead a horse to water, but you can't make it drink.

[2] At night, all cats are grey.

Unsere Mitbewohner Video

George trifft Meline im Museum und Hans trifft Sabite am Brandenburger Tor.
Sie reden über ihre Mitbewohner. Oder reden sie über mehr?

GEORGE Hallo, Meline. Wer ist das?
MELINE Fritz Sommer. Langweilig. George, du sollst nicht immer alles so ernst nehmen.
GEORGE Du bist lustig.
MELINE Und du bist süß, mein kleiner amerikanischer Freund.

HANS Hallo, Sabite!
SABITE Hallo, Hans! Wie geht's? Oh, sei nicht traurig. Du bist nett und großzügig. Können wir Freunde sein?

GEORGE Ist Sabite eine gute Mitbewohnerin?
MELINE Sabite ist eine liebenswürdige und bescheidene Person. Ihre Kunst ist hässlich und schlecht!

MELINE Oh, armer Hans!
GEORGE Sei nicht gemein, Meline.
MELINE Bin ich nicht. Sabite ist künstlerisch, lebhaft und verrückt.

SABITE Ich bin so stolz auf dich, Hans. Du bist ein echter Freund. Danke, dass du mir hilfst.
HANS Keine Ursache.
SABITE Meline ist gemein.
HANS Meline ist unangenehm.

MELINE Hans ist intellektuell, aber naiv.
GEORGE Ihn als Mitbewohner zu haben, ist langweilig. Er liest und sieht fern bis um zwei Uhr früh. Ich habe morgens Uni.
MELINE Kann er nicht ohne Fernsehen lernen?
GEORGE Nein, das kann er nicht.

1 Wer ist das? Which character does each statement describe: George, Meline, Sabite, or Hans?

1. _____ ist besorgt um seine Noten.

2. _____ hat schöne Augen.

3. _____ macht hässliche und schlechte Kunst.

4. Jungen finden _____ geheimnisvoll und faszinierend.

5. _____ ist nett und großzügig.

6. _____ ist ein echter Freund.

7. _____ ist ein netter Typ.

8. _____ ist künstlerisch, lebhaft und verrückt.

9. _____ ist süß.

10. _____ ist intellektuell, aber naiv.

Nützliche Ausdrücke

SABITE Ich möchte, dass sie einen neuen Freund hat.
HANS Bist du eifersüchtig?
SABITE Was?
HANS Sie ist lebhaft und hübsch. Sie hat sehr schöne Augen. Jungen finden sie geheimnisvoll und faszinierend.

- **etwas ernst nehmen**
  to take something seriously
- **Du bist lustig.**
  You should talk. (lit. You're funny.)
- **Ihn als Mitbewohner zu haben, ist langweilig.**
  Having him as a roommate is boring.
- **Sei nicht traurig.**
  Don't be sad.

SABITE Ist George ein guter Mitbewohner?
HANS Er ist ein netter Typ. Er ist besorgt um seine Noten. Ich sehe nachts fern und lese und er lernt bis zwei Uhr morgens.

- **Danke, dass du mir hilfst.**
  Thanks for helping me.
- **Keine Ursache.**
  You're welcome.
- **Ich möchte, dass sie einen neuen Freund hat.**
  I want her to get a new boyfriend.
- **Jungen finden sie geheimnisvoll und faszinierend.**
  Boys find her mysterious and fascinating.

SABITE Findest du sie hübsch?
HANS Wen?
SABITE Meline.
HANS Ich weiß nicht.

- **besorgt sein um**
  to be worried about
- **Du darfst nicht...**
  You mustn't...
- **Ich finde nicht, dass sie gut zusammenpassen.**
  I don't think they're a good match.
- **Schluss machen**
  to break up

3B.1
- **Ich kann sie nicht auseinanderbringen.**
  I can't break them up.

GEORGE Meline, Sabite meint es ernst mit Torsten. Du darfst nicht...
MELINE Ich finde nicht, dass sie gut zusammenpassen. Aber mach dir keine Sorgen. Ich kann sie nicht auseinanderbringen. Sie machen bald Schluss, auch ohne meine Hilfe.

3B.2
- **Er ist besorgt um seine Noten.**
  He's worried about his grades.

3B.3
- **Mach dir keine Sorgen.**
  Don't worry.

---

2 **Schreiben** Write a brief description of a well-known person in your school or community, using as many descriptive adjectives as you can. Do not mention his/her name. Be prepared to read your description to the class, who will guess this person's identity.

freundlich	intellektuell	schüchtern
glücklich	lustig	traurig
großzügig	mutig	...

3 **Vertiefung** Research a famous German person and present him/her to the class. Use adjectives to describe his/her physical appearance and personality. Be prepared to share your description with your classmates.

Auf unsere Freunde! Reading

IN DIESER° FACEBOOK-ZEIT HABEN wir alle viele „Freunde". Was ist also ein Kumpel°, mit dem Sie hin und wieder auf Partys gehen, und was ist ein echter° Freund? Deutsche sagen nicht so schnell „Freund" wie Amerikaner. In Deutschland ist es etwas Besonderes° ein „Freund" zu sein.

Wirklich gute Freunde hat man in Deutschland wahrscheinlich höchstens° vier oder fünf. Ein echter Freund zu sein bedeutet, dass° man sich sehr gut und vielleicht auch schon sehr lange kennt°. Die meisten Leute in Deutschland sagen, dass sie ihre Freunde schon aus der Schule oder aus der Kinderzeit kennen. Nur

weil° man einmal zusammen Kaffee getrunken hat°, ist man noch lange kein Freund.

In der Gruppe kennen sich alle mehr oder weniger gut. Trotzdem° nennen sich die Leute in einer Gruppe „Kumpel", nicht „Freunde". Die anderen Leute, die man kennt, nennt man meistens „Bekannte".

Es gibt also drei Gruppen von Menschen um eine Person: Die meisten Menschen sind Bekannte. Die größere Gruppe sind die Kumpel. Und nur eine sehr kleine Gruppe sind richtige Freunde. Aber mit diesen Freunden kann man alles teilen°. Also: Auf Freunde!

Auf unsere Freunde! *Here's to our friends!* **dieser** *this* **Kumpel** *buddy* **echter** *real* **etwas Besonderes** *something special* **wahrscheinlich höchstens** *probably at most* **bedeutet, dass** *means that* **sich... kennt** *know each other* **Nur weil** *Just because* **getrunken hat** *has drunk* **Trotzdem** *Nevertheless* **teilen** *share*

---

1 **Was fehlt?** Complete the statements.

1. In Deutschland sagt man nicht so schnell _____ zu einer neuen Person.

2. Viele Deutsche kennen ihre Freunde aus der _____ und aus der Kinderzeit.

3. Gute _____ nennt man in Deutschland nur vier oder fünf Personen.

4. Für _____ und für Deutsche hat das Wort „Freund" nicht die gleiche Bedeutung.

5. In _____ ist ein Freund jemand, den (*whom*) man sehr gut kennt.

6. Einen echten Freund kennt man sehr gut und oft auch sehr _____.

7. Es gibt _____ Gruppen von Menschen um eine Person.

8. In einer _____ sind alle gute Kumpel.

9. Die meisten Menschen, die man kennt, nennt man _____.

10. Die Gruppe der Freunde ist eine sehr _____ Gruppe.

Wie wir Menschen sind

aufrichtig	*sincere*
besserwisserisch	*know-it-all (adj.)*
eingebildet	*arrogant*
geduldig	*patient*
geizig	*stingy*
liebevoll	*loving*
locker	*easy-going*
oberflächlich	*superficial*
ruhig	*calm*
weise	*wise*
zuverlässig	*reliable*

Es wird geheiratet!°

Wie wünscht° man dem neuen Paar ein frohes Eheleben°? In **Bayern**, **Österreich** und **in der Schweiz** ist das **Brautstehlen°** eine lustige Tradition. Freunde stehlen die Braut und bringen sie von Gaststätte° zu Gaststätte. Der Bräutigam° muss sie finden... und alle Getränke bezahlen°! Die **Deutschen** und die **Österreicher** tragen den Ring meistens an der rechten° Hand. Aber **in der Schweiz** trägt man ihn an der linken° Hand. Die ist dem Herzen näher°.

Es wird geheiratet! *Someone's getting married!* **wünscht** *wishes* **Eheleben** *married life* **Brautstehlen** *stealing of the bride* **Gaststätte** *restaurant* **Bräutigam** *groom* **Getränke bezahlen** *pay for the drinks* **rechten** *right* **linken** *left* **dem Herzen näher** *closer to the heart*

Tokio Hotel

Die erfolgreiche° deutsche Band *Tokio Hotel* besteht° am Anfang aus den eineiigen° Zwillingen Bill und Tom Kaulitz. Schon als Kinder machen sie zusammen Musik. Als Duett treten sie unter dem Namen *Black Questionmark* auf°. Ihr Stiefvater ist auch Musiker und fördert° die Brüder. 2001 geben sie in ihrer Heimatstadt° Magdeburg ein Konzert. Dort treffen sie Gustav Schäfer und Georg Listing. Sie werden Freunde und treten zu viert unter dem Namen *Devilish* auf. 2005 nimmt die Universal Music Group die Band unter Vertrag°. Die vier nennen sich *Tokio Hotel* und sind schnell auf der ganzen Welt bekannt. Sie haben in Deutschland und Österreich vier Nummer-eins-Singles und verkaufen bis heute weltweit über 7 Millionen Alben°.

erfolgreich *successful* **besteht** *consists* **eineiigen** *identical* **treten...auf** *perform* **fördert** *supports* **Heimatstadt** *home town* **unter Vertrag** *under contract* **Alben** *albums*

🔊 IM INTERNET

Sind die Hochzeitsbräuche (*wedding traditions*) anders (*different*) in Deutschland als in den USA?

Find out more at **vhlcentral.com**.

---

2 **Richtig oder falsch?** Indicate whether each statement is **richtig** or **falsch**. Correct the false statements.

1. In Österreich ist es Tradition, den Bräutigam zu stehlen.
2. In Deutschland trägt man den Ehering an der rechten Hand.
3. *Tokio Hotel* ist eine erfolgreiche Band aus Österreich.
4. Bill und Tom Kaulitz sind Cousins.
5. *Tokio Hotel* verkauft bis heute über 7 Millionen Alben.

3 **Wie sind sie?** In pairs, describe each person in the photo on p. 120. How old do you think they are? What do you think their personalities are like? Are they friends or just classmates?

Modals Presentation

Startblock In both English and German, modal verbs modify the meaning of another verb.

Könnën wir Freunde sein?

Oh, George, du **darfst** nicht so ernst sein.

- Modals express an attitude towards an action, such as permission, obligation, ability, desire, or necessity. *May*, *can*, and *must* are examples of English modals.

modals	
dürfen	*to be allowed to, may*
können	*to be able to, can*
müssen	*to have to, must*
sollen	*to be supposed to*
wollen	*to want to*

- Except for **sollen**, all of the German modals are irregular in their present tense singular forms.

modals in the present tense					
	dürfen	**können**	**müssen**	**sollen**	**wollen**
ich	darf	kann	muss	soll	will
du	darfst	kannst	musst	sollst	willst
er/sie/es	darf	kann	muss	soll	will
wir	dürfen	können	müssen	sollen	wollen
ihr	dürft	könnt	müsst	sollt	wollt
Sie/sie	dürfen	können	müssen	sollen	wollen

- When you use a modal to modify the meaning of another verb, put the conjugated form of the modal in second position. Put the infinitive of the other verb at the end of the sentence.

Ich **muss** Französisch **lernen**.
*I **have to study** French.*

Ich **will** Französisch **lernen**.
*I **want to learn** French.*

- To form a yes-or-no question, move the modal verb to the beginning of the sentence, while the verb it modifies remains at the end.

  Willst du Wasser **trinken**?
  *Do you **want to drink** water?*

  Könnt ihr eurer Mutter **helfen**?
  *Can you **help** your mother?*

- **Dürfen** expresses permission.

  Mama, **darf** ich heute Nachmittag
   schwimmen gehen?
  *Mom, **may** I go swimming this afternoon?*

  Nein, Lina, du **darfst** heute nicht
   schwimmen gehen.
  *No, Lina, you **may** not go swimming today.*

- **Können** expresses ability.

  Peter **kann** Ski fahren.
  *Peter **can** ski.*

  Kannst du Fahrrad fahren?
  Can you ride a bicycle?

- **Müssen** expresses obligation.

  Jasmin und Moritz **müssen** viel lernen.
  *Jasmin and Moritz **have to** study a lot.*

  Muss Maria Spanisch lernen?
  *Does Maria **have to** learn Spanish?*

- **Sollen** conveys the expectation that a task be completed (*to be supposed to*). Note that, unlike the English *should* or *ought*, **sollen** implies an expectation that comes from someone other than the subject.

  Du **sollst** das Buch lesen.
  *You **are supposed to** read the book.*

  Soll ich nach Hause gehen?
  Should I go home?

- **Wollen** expresses desire.

  Sie **wollen** Musikerinnen werden.
  *They **want to** become musicians.*

  Willst du eine Katze haben?
  *Do you **want to** get a cat?*

Ressourcen

v̂Text

WB
pp. 41–42

LM
p. 87

vhlcentral

Jetzt sind Sie dran! **Complete the sentences.**

1. Die Lehrerin ___soll___ (sollen) langsam sprechen.
2. Ihr _____ (sollen) eure Hausaufgaben nicht vergessen.
3. Was _____ (sollen) wir heute machen?
4. Der Musiker _____ (können) Gitarre spielen.
5. Ich _____ (können) meinen Rucksack nicht finden.
6. _____ (Können) du nach Deutschland reisen?
7. Du _____ (müssen) ein Wörterbuch kaufen.
8. Ein Geschäftsmann _____ (müssen) sehr fleißig sein.

9. Wir _____ (müssen) das Matheproblem an die Tafel schreiben.
10. Das Paar _____ (dürfen) heiraten.
11. Die Kinder _____ (dürfen) hier Fußball spielen.
12. Du _____ (dürfen) nicht in das Klassenzimmer gehen.
13. Ich _____ (wollen) Architektin werden.
14. Die Kinder _____ (wollen) Fremdsprachen studieren.
15. _____ (Wollen) ihr die Fotos sehen?

Anwendung

1 **Entscheiden Sie** Select the correct form of the modal.

1. Ich (sollen / soll) Gitarre spielen.
2. Wir (dürfen / darf) keine Schokolade essen.
3. (Willst / Wollt) du in die Bibliothek gehen?
4. Ihr (musst / müsst) eure Großeltern begrüßen.
5. Annika (kann / können) ihre Cousine nicht finden.
6. Max und Nils (kann / können) samstags lange schlafen.

2 **Was fehlt?** Complete the sentences.

1. Die Kellner _____ (sollen) das Essen bringen.
2. Du _____ (können) Deutsch lernen.
3. Wir _____ (müssen) einen Beruf finden.
4. Ihr _____ (dürfen) einen Film sehen.
5. Ich _____ (wollen) Journalist werden.

3 **Schreiben** Rewrite the sentences using the cues.

> **BEISPIEL** Antonia ist Musikerin. (wollen)
> *Antonia will Musikerin sein.*

1. Die Ingenieure bauen eine neue Maschine. (müssen)
2. Der Journalist reist nach Deutschland. (dürfen)
3. Die Geschäftsfrau und der Geschäftsmann sind nicht gierig. (sollen)
4. Meine Tante und ich tanzen Tango. (können)
5. Ich werde Friseurin. (wollen)

4 **Fragen** Use the cues to form questions about the images.

> ▶ **BEISPIEL**
> ich / schwimmen
> gehen / dürfen
> *Darf ich schwimmen gehen?*

1. du / Ski fahren / können

2. ich / jetzt lernen / sollen

3. Erika / Fußball spielen / wollen

4. wir / Musik hören / dürfen

5. Thomas / Musiker werden / wollen

6. ihr / viele Bücher lesen / müssen

Kommunikation

5 **Viele Wünsche** In pairs, take turns saying what each person wants to do. Then, imagine what they must or should do to achieve that goal.

BEISPIEL mein Bruder / nach Deutschland fahren

S1: *Mein Bruder will nach Deutschland fahren.*
S2: *Er soll Deutsch lernen.*

1. meine Freundin / Architektin werden
2. ich / das Fußballspiel gewinnen
3. wir / einen Hund haben
4. mein Vater / ein neues Auto kaufen
5. meine Schwester / gute Noten haben
6. mein Onkel / kurze Haare haben

6 **Berufe** With a partner, offer advice to help these people get the jobs they want.

BEISPIEL Mira und Maria / Ingenieurinnen

S1: *Mira und Maria wollen Ingenieurinnen werden.*
S2: *Sie sollen viel lernen.*

1. Emil und Hasan / Rechtsanwälte
2. David und Hanna / Musiker
3. Julia / Journalistin
4. Greta und Dilara / Geschäftsfrauen

7 **Einladungen** In small groups, take turns inviting each other to take part in these activities. If you turn down an invitation, explain what you want to do, should do, or must do instead, and suggest a different activity.

BEISPIEL

S1: *Willst du Tennis spielen?*
S2: *Ich kann nicht. Ich muss Hausaufgaben machen.*
Aber wir können morgen spazieren gehen.

1.
2.
3.
4.
5.
6.

3B.2 **Prepositions with the accusative**  Presentation

Startblock In **1B.1**, you learned the accusative endings for definite and indefinite articles. You also learned that the direct object in German always takes the accusative case. In addition, the objects of certain prepositions are always in the accusative case.

Das Trinkgeld ist **für den Kellner**.
*The tip is **for the waiter.***

Der Hund läuft **durch die Wälder**.
*The dog is running **through the woods.***

- Prepositions and prepositional phrases describe time, manner, and place, and answer the questions *when*, *how*, and *where*.

um 8 Uhr
at 8 o'clock

ohne meinen Bruder
***without** my brother*

gegen die Wand
***against** the wall*

- Here are some common accusative prepositions.

prepositions with the accusative							
bis	*until, to*	entlang	*along*	gegen	*against*	pro	*per*
durch	*through*	für	*for*	ohne	*without*	um	*around; at (time)*

Der Besitzer kommt **durch die Tür**.
*The owner is coming **through the door.***

Was hast du **gegen meinen Freund**?
*What do you have **against my boyfriend?***

- The prepositions **durch**, **für**, and **um**, when followed by the neuter definite article **das**, may be contracted to **durchs**, **fürs**, and **ums**. These contractions are frequently used in speech and are acceptable in writing.

Das Spielzeug ist **fürs** Baby.
*The toy is **for the** baby.*

Die Kinder laufen **ums** Haus.
*The kids are running **around** the house.*

- The accusative preposition **bis** is frequently used with time expressions. When **bis** comes before a proper noun, such as **Samstag** or **März**, no article is necessary.

Ich bin **bis April** in Deutschland.
*I'm in Germany **until April.***

Wir bleiben **bis nächsten Monat** in Köln.
*We are staying in Cologne **until next month.***

- **Pro** is also an accusative preposition. The object it precedes takes no article.

Der Kellner verdient 300 Euro **pro Woche**.
*The waiter earns 300 euros **per week.***

Das Auto fährt 230 Kilometer **pro Stunde**.
*The car goes 230 kilometers **per hour.***

- The accusative is also used with objects that precede **entlang**.

Wir gehen **den Fluss entlang**.
*We are going **down the river.***

Ich fahre **die Straße entlang**.
*I'm driving **along the road.***

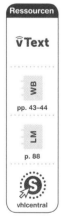

Ressourcen

v̂Text

WB
pp. 43–44

LM
p. 88

vhlcentral

Jetzt sind Sie dran! Select the preposition that best completes each sentence.

1. Die Frau geht (ohne / pro) ihren Mann einkaufen.
2. Der Hund läuft (durch / gegen) den Park.
3. Die Mutter braucht ein Spielzeug (um / für) ihre Tochter.
4. Was haben die Besitzer (gegen / bis) die Musik?
5. Die Kellnerin geht (durch / um) den Tisch.

6. Die Taxifahrt kostet 2 € (für / pro) Kilometer.
7. Ich gehe den Fluss (entlang / bis).
8. Die Journalisten arbeiten (gegen / bis) Mitternacht.

Anwendung und Kommunikation

1 Was ist richtig? Select the preposition that best completes each sentence.

> bis | entlang | für | gegen | ohne | um

1. _____ 8 Uhr muss ich arbeiten.
2. Der kleine Junge wirft den Ball _____ die Wand.
3. _____ meine Schwester gehe ich nicht campen.
4. Das Auto fährt die Straße _____.
5. Sara kauft einen Kaffee _____ ihre Mutter.
6. Mein Onkel spielt _____ 6 Uhr Fußball.

2 Bilden Sie Sätze Write eight sentences using items from each column. Pay attention to word order and accusative endings. Use each preposition once.

BEISPIEL Herr und Frau Becker / heute Abend eine Party geben / um / 8 Uhr
Heute Abend um 8 Uhr geben Herr und Frau Becker eine Party.

der Besitzer	angeln gehen	bis	Haustiere
du	beginnen	durch	Woche
ich	in Berlin bleiben	entlang	der Park
die Journalistin	50 Stunden arbeiten	für	19 Uhr
das Konzert	fahren	gegen	Samstag
Herr Bauer	laufen	ohne	die Straße
meine Schwester	lernen	pro	mein Bruder
wir	sein	um	die Prüfung

3 Umfrage In pairs, take turns asking and answering the questions.

BEISPIEL

S1: *Um wie viel Uhr fährst du zur Uni?*
S2: *Ich fahre um 8 Uhr zur Uni.*

1. Um wie viel Uhr beginnt dein Unterricht?
2. Wie viele Stunden schläfst du pro Nacht?
3. Für wen kaufst du gern Blumen?
4. Ohne was kannst du nicht leben?
5. Gegen welche Mannschaften spielst du gern?

4 Die Geburtstagsfeier In small groups, write four sentences describing the illustration. Use at least four prepositions with the accusative.

 Practice more at **vhlcentral.com**.

3B.3 The imperative  Presentation

Startblock Imperatives are used to express commands, requests, suggestions, directions, and instructions.

Sei nicht traurig.

Mach dir keine Sorgen!

- The imperative forms are based on the present-tense conjugation patterns of **du**, **wir**, **ihr**, and **Sie**.

the *Imperativ* conjugation	
Indikativ	**Imperativ**
du kaufst	kauf(e)
ihr kauft	kauft
Sie kaufen	kaufen Sie
wir kaufen	kaufen wir

Mach deine Hausaufgaben!
Do your homework!

Backen wir einen Kuchen!
Let's bake a cake!

- To form an informal singular command, drop the -st from the present-tense **du** form of the verb. As in English, omit the subject pronoun with the second-person imperative.

Antworte auf die Frage!
Answer the question!

Schreib deinen Eltern eine E-Mail.
Write your parents an email.

- Verbs with an **a** to **ä** vowel change do not retain this change in the imperative. However, **e** to **ie** and **e** to **i** changes are retained in the imperative for **du**.

Fahr langsam!
Drive slowly!

Lies das Buch.
Read the book.

Nimm den Bleistift.
Take the pencil.

- The informal plural **ihr** command is identical to the present-tense form, without the pronoun.

Esst die Äpfel, Kinder!
Eat the apples, kids!

Lernt für die Prüfung.
Study for the exam.

- For formal commands, keep the subject **Sie** and invert the subject/verb word order of the present tense. Remember that the singular and plural forms are identical.

Probieren Sie den Kuchen!
Try the cake!

Warten Sie bitte hier.
*Please **wait** here.*

- The first person plural command is equivalent to the English *Let's....* As with **Sie**, invert the subject/verb order of the present tense for **wir**.

Essen wir den Kuchen.
Let's eat the cake.

Gehen wir spazieren.
Let's go for a walk.

ACHTUNG

Verbs that contain a double **s** in the infinitive do not drop an **s** in the informal singular imperative.

Iss das Gemüse, Tanja!
Eat your vegetables, Tanja!

- In a negative command, **nicht** or **kein** follows the imperative form.

  Fahren Sie nicht so schnell!
  Don't drive so fast!

  Hör keine laute Musik!
  Don't listen to loud music!

  Arbeite nicht so langsam!
  Don't work so slowly!

  Macht kein Theater!
  Don't make a fuss!

- Use **bitte** to soften a command and make it polite. **Bitte** can be placed almost anywhere in a sentence, as long as it doesn't separate the verb from the subject pronoun **wir** or **Sie**.

  Öffnen Sie **bitte** Ihren Rucksack.
  *Open your backpack, **please**.*

  Schlaft **bitte** nicht im Unterricht!
  Please don't sleep in class!

  Geh nach Hause, **bitte**.
  *Go home, **please**.*

  Bitte nehmen Sie Platz.
  Please take a seat.

- The modals **können** and **wollen** are often used instead of the imperative for polite requests.

  Können Sie mir helfen?
  Can you help me?

  Wollen wir gehen?
  Shall we go?

- The verb **sein** has irregular imperative forms.

  Sei lieb!
  Be good! (sing., inf.)

  Seid diskret!
  Be discreet! (pl., inf.)

  Seien Sie mutig!
  Be brave! (form.)

  Seien wir realistisch!
  Let's be realistic!

- On signs or labels, and in recipes or printed instructions, infinitives are often used instead of imperatives. Here are some common commands and instructions found in everyday situations. Notice that in some cases, a command is conveyed by using an infinitive or the word **verboten** (*forbidden*), rather than the imperative.

common commands	
Drücken.	*Push.*
Ziehen.	*Pull.*
Bring mir...	*Bring me...*
Langsam fahren.	*Slow down.*
Warte.	*Wait.*
Sprechen Sie bitte langsamer.	*Please speak more slowly.*
Türen schließen.	*Keep doors closed.*
Rauchen verboten.	*No smoking.*
Betreten des Rasens verboten.	*Keep off the grass.*
Keine Zufahrt.	*Do not enter.*
Parkverbot.	*No parking.*

QUERVERWEIS

See **2B.3** to review the use of **nicht** and **kein**.

Ressourcen

v̂Text

WB
pp. 45–46

LM
p. 89

S
vhlcentral

 **Jetzt sind Sie dran!**   Select the correct imperative form to complete each sentence.

1. Herr Braun, (sprecht / sprechen Sie) bitte langsamer.
2. Schüler, (öffnen Sie / öffnet) eure Bücher auf Seite 34.
3. Philip, (vergiss / vergessen wir) deine Hausaufgaben nicht!
4. Kinder, (seid / sei) freundlich und nett!
5. Wir haben morgen eine Prüfung. (Lernen wir / Lernt) zusammen!
6. Nina, (fahrt / fahr) nicht so schnell!
7. Herr und Frau Schmidt, (warte / warten Sie) bitte einen Moment.
8. Wir haben Hunger. (Essen wir / Iss) den Strudel!

Anwendung

1 Was fehlt? Complete the sentences using the imperative.

BEISPIEL Sebastian, _____Komm_____ (kommen)!

1. Herr Schneider, _____ (wiederholen) bitte.
2. Marie und Lukas, _____ (essen) langsamer!
3. Felix, _____ (sein) nicht gemein!
4. Frau Fischer und Herr Wagner, _____ (nehmen) bitte eine Karte!
5. Paul und Else, _____ (machen) bitte kein Theater!
6. _____ (sprechen) wir Deutsch!

2 Bilden Sie Sätze Write imperative commands for each person using the cues.

BEISPIEL Herr Braun: nicht so schnell fahren
Herr Braun, fahren Sie nicht so schnell!

1. Klara: Tennis mit Jan spielen
2. Wir: durch den Park gehen
3. Max und Lara: den Text auf Seite 27 lesen
4. Herr Gärtner: heute bis 8 Uhr bleiben
5. Frau Weber: nicht nervös sein
6. Niklas: um 6 Uhr nach Hause kommen

3 Schreiben Tell these people not to do what they are doing.

BEISPIEL Lara ist eifersüchtig.
Sei nicht eifersüchtig, Lara!

1. Herr Becker ist gierig.
2. Tom und Jonas weinen.
3. Lukas spielt schlechte Musik.
4. Frau Weber kauft hässliche Sachen.

5. Max und Lukas schreiben an die Wand.
6. Wir bleiben hier.
7. Hanna telefoniert 4 Stunden pro Tag.
8. Otto und Emma essen den Kuchen.

4 Konjugieren Write a command for each image using the cues.

1. wir

2. Nils

3. Kinder / eure Bücher

4. Frau Schulze / ein Glas Wasser

5. wir

6. Greta / ein Bonbon

Kommunikation

5 **Befehle** In small groups, write eight sentences using **sollen**. Then, trade lists with another group and convert their sentences into commands.

S1: *Du sollst deine Hausaufgaben machen.*
S2: *Mach deine Hausaufgaben.*

6 **Guter Rat** In pairs, use the imperative to give advice to each person or group.

deine Lehrerin

      Sprechen Sie bitte langsamer.

1. deine Mitschueler
2. deine beste Freundin oder dein bester Freund
3. deine Eltern oder deine Großeltern
4. dein Bruder oder deine Schwester
5. dein Schuldirektorin oder deine Schuldirektor
6. deine Katze oder dein Hund

7 **Ein paar Ratschläge** In pairs, list ten pieces of advice that you would give to a new German exchange student at your school. Use the affirmative and negative forms of the imperative.

S1: *Sei fleißig, aber nicht zu ernst!*
S2: *Vergiss nicht deine Hausaufgaben!*

8 **Simon sagt** In groups of five, play Simon Says. One student gives commands using the **du**, **Sie**, **ihr**, and **wir** forms. The group members must perform or mime the activity, but only if the speaker says "**Simon sagt**". The first person to make a mistake becomes the new leader.

S1: *Simon sagt: „Tanzen wir!"*
OR
S1: *Laura und Michael, lauft um den Tisch!*

essen	laufen	schreiben
fahren	nehmen	sprechen
hören	öffnen	tanzen
fangen	sagen	weinen
lachen	schlafen	wiederholen

Wiederholung

1 Etwas unternehmen
In pairs, make plans for what you will do today in each location. Use prepositions with the accusative.

BEISPIEL

S1: Um 10 Uhr gehen wir in die Bibliothek.
S2: Ja, dort können wir gute Bücher für das Referat finden.

bis	gegen
durch	ohne
entlang	um
für	

1.

2.

3.

4.

2 Wollen und sollen
In small groups, take turns saying one thing that you want to do today, one thing you must do, one thing you can do, one thing you may do, and one thing you are supposed to do.

BEISPIEL

S1: Ich will heute Abend in die Sporthalle gehen, aber ich muss Hausaufgaben machen.
S2: Ich soll für meinen Deutschkurs lernen, aber ich kann auch Tennis spielen.
S3: Ich kann nicht Tennis spielen. Ich muss...

3 Diskutieren und kombinieren
Your instructor will give you and a partner different worksheets with a list of occupations and profiles of several students. Take turns describing the students and matching their qualities to appropriate occupations.

BEISPIEL

S1: Jana ist kreativ und gut in Mathe.
S2: Ah, dann ist Jana eine gute Architektin.

4 Meine ideale Familie
Survey your classmates about their ideal family situation, and write down their answers. Then, in pairs, compare your results.

BEISPIEL

S1: Wie ist deine ideale Familie?
S2: Meine ideale Familie ist sehr groß...

5 Arbeitsblatt
Your instructor will give you a worksheet with several activities listed. Survey your classmates to find someone who would like to do each of the activities with you. When someone says "yes", agree on a time and date. If someone says "no", they must give an excuse, explaining what they have to or are supposed to do instead.

BEISPIEL

S1: Gehen wir morgen Abend ins Theater!
S2: Ich kann nicht. Ich muss für die Prüfung lernen.
S3: Ich komme gern. Gehen wir morgen um 7 Uhr!

6 Geschwister
In pairs, role-play a conversation between two siblings. The younger sibling asks to do things, and the older sibling tells him/her what to do and what not to do.

BEISPIEL

S1: Darf ich Fußball spielen?
S2: Nein, das darfst du nicht! Iss dein Abendessen!

7 Die Familie

With a partner, write a brief description of these five family members. Use the vocabulary you learned in **Lektionen 2A**, **2B**, **3A**, and **3B** to describe their interests, activities, physical characteristics, and personalities.

Die Tochter heißt Mia. Sie ist zwölf Jahre alt. Sie hat blonde Haare und blaue Augen. Sie ist sehr aktiv und spielt gern Fußball.

Die Familie

der Sohn   der Vater   der Cousin
die Tochter   die Mutter

8 Am Wochenende

In small groups, prepare a skit in which a group of friends makes plans for the weekend. Use vocabulary from **Kapitel 2**.

S1: *Ich spiele gern Basketball! Können wir morgen Basketball spielen?*
S2: *Nein, bleiben wir hier! Wir müssen unsere Hausaufgaben machen!*
S3: *Ihr könnt hier bleiben, aber ich will...*

Mein Wör | ter | buch

Add five words related to **die Familie** and **persönliche Beschreibungen** to your personalized dictionary.

klug

Übersetzung
clever, smart

Wortart
Adjektiv (Beschreibungswort)

Gebrauch
Der Mann ist klug. Ein kluger Mann spricht nicht zu viel.

Synonyme
intelligent, schlau

Antonyme
unintelligent, dumm

Vocabulary Tools

Panorama

S Interactive Map

Die Vereinigten Staaten und Kanada

Anteil der Amerikaner mit deutschen Wurzeln: 15% (50 Millionen)

- ▶ **Kalifornien:** *5.517.470*
- ▶ **Pennsylvania:** *3.491.269*
- ▶ **Ohio:** *3.231.788*
- ▶ **Illinois:** *2.668.955*
- ▶ **Texas:** *2.542.996*
- ▶ **Wisconsin:** *2.455.980*
- ▶ **Michigan:** *2.271.091*
- ▶ **Florida:** *2.270.456*
- ▶ **New York:** *2.250.309*
- ▶ **Minnesota:** *1.949.346*
- ▶ **Indiana:** *1.629.766*
- ▶ **Missouri:** *1.576.813*

QUELLE: U.S. Census 2010

Anteil der Kanadier mit deutschen Wurzeln: 10% (3 Millionen)

- ▶ **Toronto:** *220.135*
- ▶ **Vancouver:** *187.410*
- ▶ **Winnipeg::** *109.355*
- ▶ **Kitchener:** *93.325*
- ▶ **Montreal:** *83.850*

QUELLE: Canadian Census 2011

Die ersten deutschen Siedler in Kanada kommen zwischen 1750 und 1753 nach Nova Scotia. Die meisten von ihnen° sind Bauern und Kaufleute°. Zwischen 1919 und 1939 kommen fast 100.000 Deutsche nach Kanada. Auch von ihnen sind die meisten Bauern. Sie alle bringen ihre Familien mit und starten ein neues Leben in Nordamerika.

Berühmte Deutschamerikaner und Deutschkanadier

- ▶ **Levi Strauss,** *Unternehmer° (1829–1902)*
- ▶ **Frederick Louis Maytag I,** *Unternehmer (1857–1937)*
- ▶ **Dwight D. Eisenhower,** *Fünf-Sterne General und US-Präsident (1890–1969)*
- ▶ **Lou Gehrig,** *Baseballspieler (1903–1941)*
- ▶ **Henry Kissinger,** *Politiker (1923–)*
- ▶ **Almuth Lütkenhaus,** *Künstlerin° (1930–1996)*
- ▶ **Dany Heatley,** *Eishockeyspieler (1981–)*
- ▶ **Justin Bieber,** *Sänger° (1994–)*

Die meisten von ihnen *most of them* **Kaufleute** *tradespeople*
Unternehmer *entrepreneur* **Künstlerin** *artist* **Sänger** *singer*
verlässt *leaves* **Flöten** *flutes* **Immobilien** *real estate*
Fellhandel *fur trade* **reichste** *richest* **Vermögen** *fortune*

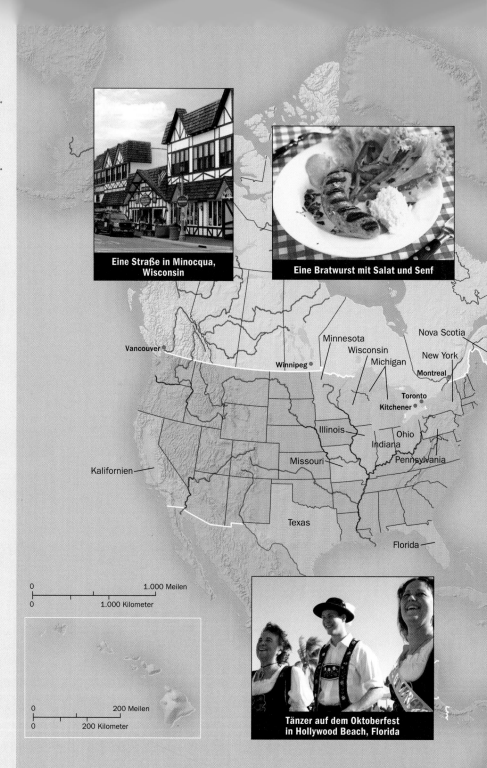

Eine Straße in Minocqua, Wisconsin

Eine Bratwurst mit Salat und Senf

Vancouver · Winnipeg · Minnesota · Wisconsin · Michigan · Nova Scotia · New York · Montreal · Toronto · Kitchener · Illinois · Ohio · Indiana · Pennsylvania · Kalifornien · Missouri · Texas · Florida

0 — 1.000 Meilen
0 — 1.000 Kilometer

0 — 200 Meilen
0 — 200 Kilometer

Tänzer auf dem Oktoberfest in Hollywood Beach, Florida

Unglaublich, aber wahr!

1784 verlässt° **John Jacob Astor** (1763–1848) das Dorf Walldorf in Deutschland mit $25 und 7 Flöten° in Richtung USA. Durch Immobilien°– und Fellhandel° wird er reich und ist zur Zeit seines Todes der reichste° Mann Amerikas. Sein Vermögen° beträgt ungefähr $90 Millionen.

Menschen

Sandra Bullock

Sandra Bullock wurde 1964 in Arlington, Virginia geboren°. Ihre Mutter ist Helga D. Meyer, eine deutsche Opernsängerin. Deshalb verbringt° Bullock, die neben Englisch fließend° Deutsch spricht, auch die ersten 12 Jahre ihres Lebens in der deutschen Stadt Fürth, bevor sie mit ihrer Familie in die USA zieht. Ihre erfolgreiche Karriere beinhaltet Filme wie *Gravity, Speed* und *Blind Side – Die große Chance*, für den sie einen Oscar als beste Hauptdarstellerin° erhält.

Essen

Hamburger

Der Hamburger – ein Sandwich aus einer Frikadelle° in einer Semmel° mit einem Salatblatt und einer Scheibe Tomate – hat etwas mit der Stadt Hamburg zu tun. Als deutsche Immigranten und Matrosen° Ende des 18. Jahrhunderts nach New York kommen, bekommen Sie hier „Steak im Hamburger Stil". Diese Steaks damals hatten mit heutigen Hamburgern außer dem Namen noch nicht viel zu tun. Erst mit der Erfindung des Fleischwolfs° im 19. Jahrhunderts werden aus Steaks im Hamburger Stil die heutigen Hamburger.

Feiern

German Fest

Das German Fest in Milwaukee ist das größte „deutsche" Event Nordamerikas. Seit 1981 feiern die Menschen hier am letzten Juliwochenende Kultur deutschsprachiger° Länder und Regionen wie Österreich, Deutschland, Liechtenstein, Südtirol und der Schweiz. Besucher° tragen teilweise Dirndl und Lederhosen, hören traditionelle Blaskapellen° oder moderne Popmusik und bekommen Informationen über ihre deutsche Abstammung°. Im Jahr 2010 essen die Besucher unter anderem 20.000 Bratwürste, 9.000 Knödel°, 200 Spanferkel° und 15.000 Stück Strudel.

Geschichte

Deutsche in Texas

1848 gibt es in Deutschland und vielen anderen europäischen Ländern (Frankreich, Dänemark, Österreich) Revolutionen und Aufstände° auf Grund von sozialen und wirtschaftlichen° Problemen. Nach der Mairevolution verlassen° viele Revolutionäre Deutschland und gehen in die USA. Sie leben in Städten wie zum Beispiel New Braunfels und Fredericksburg in Texas. Diesen deutschen Einfluss° kann man heute hier immer noch sehen. Unter anderem gibt es in Texas eine Form des Deutschen, die man Texas-Deutsch nennt.

🔗 IM INTERNET

1. Welche anderen Gerichte (*dishes*) haben ihren Ursprung (*origin*) in deutschsprachigen Ländern?
2. Suchen Sie ein Rezept für ein deutsch-amerikanisches (oder österreichisch-amerikanisches) Gericht.
3. Suchen Sie Informationen über eine berühmte deutsch-amerikanische Person.

Find out more at **vhlcentral.com**.

---

wurde... geboren *was born* **verbringt** *spends (time)* **fließend** *fluent* **Hauptdarstellerin** *lead actress* **Aufstände** *uprisings* **wirtschaftlichen** *economic* **verlassen** *leave* **Einfluss** *influence* **Frikadelle** *meatball* **Semmel** *bun* **Matrosen** *sailors* **Erfindung des Fleischwolfs** *invention of the meat grinder* **deutschsprachiger** *German-speaking* **Besucher** *Visitors* **Blaskapellen** *brass bands* **Abstammung** *descent* **Knödel** *dumplings* **Spanferkel** *suckling pigs*

🔗 Was haben Sie gelernt? Complete the sentences.

1. Die meisten Amerikaner mit deutschen Wurzeln leben in _____.
2. Ungefähr _____ der amerikanischen Bevölkerung haben deutsche Wurzeln.
3. John Astor verlässt 1784 Deutschland mit _____ und 7 Flöten.
4. Eine Schauspielerin, die fließend Deutsch spricht, ist _____.
5. Sandra Bullock wohnt in Fürth, bis sie _____ alt ist.
6. Zwei deutsche Städte in Texas sind _____.
7. Hamburger haben ihren Namen von der deutschen Stadt _____.
8. Die Besucher essen jedes Jahr 200 Spanferkel und 20.000 Bratwürste auf dem _____.
9. Beim *German Fest* sehen _____ viele Facetten deutschsprachiger Kultur.

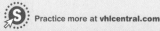

Lesen  Audio: Reading

Vor dem Lesen

Die beliebtesten° Haustiere

In Deutschland gibt es Haustiere in mehr als° 12 Millionen Haushalten.

Katzen	**16,5%**	der Haushalte
Hunde	**13,8%**	der Haushalte
Kleintiere	**5,9%**	der Haushalte
Vögel	**5,7%**	der Haushalte
Aquarien°	**5,7%**	der Haushalte

Auch in Österreich und der Schweiz sind Katzen und Hunde die beliebtesten Haustiere.

beliebtesten *most popular* **mehr als** *more than*
Aquarien *fish tanks*

Texte verstehen Take a quick look at the visual elements of the article in order to generate a list of ideas about its content. Then compare your list with a classmate's. What elements did you both notice? What aspects did your partner notice that didn't catch your eye? Discuss and consolidate your ideas to produce a final list to share with the class.

Hunde und Katzen

Für viele Deutsche, Österreicher und Schweizer sind Haustiere sehr wichtig. Allerdings gibt es in diesen Ländern weit weniger vierbeinige° Freunde als in anderen europäischen Ländern. Zum Beispiel hat in Deutschland nur etwa jeder Vierte ein Haustier.

Welche Tiere findet man bei Deutschen, Österreichern und Schweizern am häufigsten°? Oft hört man, der Hund ist des Deutschen bester Freund. Statistiken zeigen° allerdings, dass nicht Hunde, sondern Katzen das Haustier Nummer 1 im deutschsprachigen Raum sind. Hunde stehen nur an Nummer 2.

vierbeinige *four-legged* **am häufigsten** *most frequently* **zeigen** *show*

Außerdem geht der allgemeine° Trend hin zu mehr° Katzen und weniger° Hunden. Andere beliebte Tiere sind Kleintiere wie Kaninchen° und Hamster. Vögel singen immer weniger in deutschsprachigen Haushalten°.

Haustiere sind oft ein wichtiger Teil° der Familie. Kinder lernen durch sie, soziale Kontakte zu pflegen°. Großstadtkinder, die mit einem Hund leben, haben später° oft weniger Probleme mit Kriminalität. Vor allem bei Singles sind Katzen beliebt, da sie alleine sein können, aber auch eine Art Partnerersatz sind.

Wer hat welches Haustier?

Status	Katzen	Hunde	Fische	Vögel
Ledig	23%	18%	7%	5%
Verheiratet	18%	18%	6%	5%
Frauen	17%	18%	7%	5%
Männer	17%	18%	6%	5%

allgemeine *general* mehr *more* weniger *fewer* Kaninchen *bunnies* Haushalten *households*
ein wichtiger Teil *an important part* pflegen *to cultivate* später *later*

Nach dem Lesen

 Richtig oder falsch? Indicate whether each statement is **richtig** or **falsch**.

	richtig	falsch
1. Fast jede Familie in Deutschland hat ein Haustier.	☐	☐
2. Katzen sind das Haustier Nummer 1.	☐	☐
3. Der Trend in den nächsten Jahren geht zu mehr Hunden.	☐	☐
4. Immer weniger Menschen haben Vögel.	☐	☐
5. Großstadtkinder mit Hunden haben mehr Probleme.	☐	☐
6. Viele Ledige haben Katzen als Haustiere.	☐	☐

 Was ist richtig? Select the correct response according to the article.

1. Wie viel Prozent der Deutschen besitzen ein Haustier?
   a. 10%-20%   b. 20%-30%   c. 30%-40%
2. Welche Haustiere werden immer beliebter?
   a. Katzen   b. Vögel   c. Hunde
3. Welches Tier passt in die Kategorie Kleintiere?
   a. Katzen   b. Hunde   c. Hamster
4. Welches Haustier besitzen die meisten Deutschen?
   a. Hunde   b. Fische   c. Katzen
5. Welche Bevölkerungsgruppe hat die meisten Haustiere?
   a. Frauen   b. Ledige   c. Verheiratete

Meine Haustiere With a partner, talk about the pets you or your family and friends have. Use the verb **haben** and possessive adjectives.

BEISPIEL

S1: *Hast du eine Katze?*
S2: *Nein, ich habe einen Fisch, aber mein Onkel hat zwei Katzen…*

Hören

Vorbereitung

Based on the photograph, where do you think Lena and Jasmin are? What do you think they are talking about?

◁)) Zuhören

 Now you are going to hear Lena and Jasmin's conversation. Write **M** next to adjectives that describe Jasmin's friend Maria. Write **T** next to adjectives that describe Lena's ex-boyfriend, Tobias. Some adjectives will not be used.

_____ fleißig   _____ langweilig

_____ hübsch   _____ intelligent

_____ eifersüchtig   _____ egoistisch

_____ sportlich   _____ langsam

_____ großartig   _____ verlobt

_____ ernst   _____ faul

Verständnis

Wer ist das? Write the name of the person described by each statement.

1. _____ ist Jasmins neue Freundin.
2. _____ ist egoistisch und eifersüchtig.
3. _____ lernt mit Maria für die Literaturprüfungen.
4. _____ ist allein glücklich.
5. _____ ist mit Antonia verlobt.
6. _____ will mit Lena schwimmen gehen.

Richtig oder falsch Indicate whether each statement is **richtig** or **falsch**. Correct the false statements.

1. Lena studiert Literatur.
2. Tobias hilft Jasmin.
3. Maria ist großartig.
4. Lena ist ledig.
5. Geschichte ist Jasmins Hobby.
6. Tobias ist intelligent und fleißig.

Schreiben

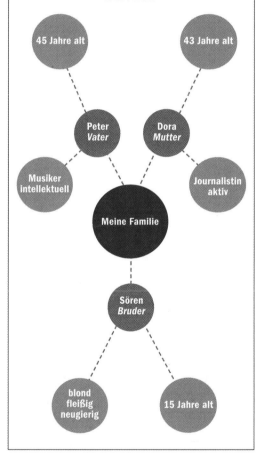

Thema

Briefe schreiben

A German friend you met online wants to know about your family. Using the verbs and grammar structures you learned in this unit, write a brief description of your family or an imaginary family, including:

- Names and relationships
- Physical characteristics
- Hobbies and interests

Here are some useful expressions for writing a letter or e-mail in German:

Salutations	
Lieber Erik,	*Dear Erik,*
Liebe Anna,	*Dear Anna,*

Asking for a response	
Ich hoffe, bald von dir zu hören.	*I hope to hear from you soon.*
Erzähl, was es Neues bei dir gibt!	*Let me know what's new with you!*

Closings	
Bis bald!/Tschüss!	*So long!*
Mach's gut!	*All the best!*
Mit freundlichen Grüßen	*Yours sincerely*
Hochachtungsvoll	*Respectfully*

Lektion 3A

die Familie

das Baby, -s *baby*
der Bruder, ⸚ *brother*
der Cousin, -s *cousin (m.)*
die Cousine, -n *cousin (f.)*
die Eltern *parents*
das Enkelkind, -er *grandchild*
der Enkelsohn, ⸚e *grandson*
die Enkeltochter, ⸚ *granddaughter*
die Frau, -en *wife*
das Geschwister, - *sibling*
die Großeltern *grandparents*
die Großmutter, ⸚ *grandmother*
der Großvater, ⸚ *grandfather*
der Halbbruder, ⸚ *half brother*
die Halbschwester, -n *half sister*
das Kind, -er *child*
der Mann, ⸚er *husband*
die Mutter, ⸚ *mother*
der Nachname, -n *last name*
der Neffe, -n *nephew*
die Nichte, -n *niece*
die Oma, -s *grandma*
der Onkel, - *uncle*
der Opa, -s *grandpa*
das Paar, -e *couple*
der Schwager, ⸚ *brother-in-law*
die Schwägerin, -nen *sister-in-law*
die Schwester, -n *sister*
die Schwiegermutter, ⸚ *mother-in-law*
der Schwiegervater, ⸚ *father-in-law*
der Sohn, ⸚e *son*
der Stiefbruder, ⸚ *stepbrother*
die Stiefmutter, ⸚ *stepmother*
die Stiefschwester, -n *stepsister*
der Stiefsohn, ⸚e *stepson*
die Stieftochter, ⸚ *stepdaughter*
der Stiefvater, ⸚ *stepfather*
die Tante, -n *aunt*
die Tochter, ⸚ *daughter*
der Vater, ⸚ *father*
der / die Verwandte, -n *relative*
der Zwilling, -e *twin*

der Familienstand

die Witwe, -n *widow*
der Witwer, - *widower*
geschieden *divorced*
getrennt *separated*
ledig *single*
verheiratet *married*
verlobt *engaged*
zusammen *together*
heiraten *to marry*

die Haustiere

der Fisch, -e *fish*
der Hund, -e *dog*
die Katze, -n *cat*
der Vogel, ⸚ *bird*

zum Beschreiben

blaue / grüne / braune Augen
 blue / green / brown eyes
blonde / braune / schwarze Haare
 blond / brown / black hair
dunkel *dark*
hell *light*

Possessive adjectives *See p. 104.*
Descriptive adjectives *See p. 108.*

Lektion 3B

zum Beschreiben

(un)angenehm *(un)pleasant*
arm *poor; unfortunate*
bescheiden *modest*
besorgt *worried*
diskret *discreet*
egoistisch *selfish*
eifersüchtig *jealous*
ernst *serious*
faul *lazy*
fleißig *hard-working*
freundlich *friendly*
froh *happy*
gemein *mean*
gierig *greedy*
glücklich *happy*
großzügig *generous*
intellektuell *intellectual*
intelligent *intelligent*
langsam *slow*
lustig *funny*
müde *tired*
mutig *brave*
naiv *naïve*
nervös *nervous*
nett *nice*
neugierig *curious*
reich *rich*
schlecht *bad*
schnell *fast*
schüchtern *shy*
schwach *weak*
stark *strong*
stolz *proud*
süß *sweet; cute*
toll *great*
traurig *sad*
lächeln *to smile*
lachen *to laugh*
weinen *to cry*

Berufe

der Architekt, -en / die Architektin, -nen
 architect
der Besitzer, - / die Besitzerin, -nen
 owner
der Friseur, -e / die Friseurin, -nen
 hairdresser
der Geschäftsmann (*pl.* Geschäftsleute)
 / die Geschäftsfrau, -en
 businessman / businesswoman
der Ingenieur, -e / die Ingenieurin, -nen
 engineer
der Journalist, -en / die Journalistin, -nen
 journalist
der Kellner, - / die Kellnerin, -nen
 waiter / waitress
der Musiker, - / die Musikerin, -nen
 musician
der Rechtsanwalt, ⸚e / die
 Rechtsanwältin, -nen *lawyer*

Modalverben

dürfen *to be allowed to, may*
können *to be able to, can*
müssen *to have to, must*
sollen *to be supposed to*
wollen *to want to*

Prepositions with the accusative
 See p. 126.
Common commands *See p. 129.*

Lebensmittel

 **Vocabulary Tools**

Wortschatz	
Geschäfte	*stores*
die Bäckerei, -en	bakery
die Eisdiele, -n	ice cream shop
das Feinkostgeschäft, -e	delicatessen
das Fischgeschäft, -e	fish store
die Konditorei, -en	pastry shop
das Lebensmittelgeschäft, -e	grocery store
der Markt, ⸚e	market
die Metzgerei, -en	butcher shop
der Supermarkt, ⸚e	supermarket
einkaufen gehen	to go shopping
verkaufen	to sell
Essen	*food*
das Brot, -e	bread
das Brötchen, -	roll
die Butter	butter
der Joghurt, -s	yogurt
der Käse, -	cheese
das Öl, -e	oil
das Olivenöl, -e	olive oil
die Pasta	pasta
der Reis	rice
das Rezept, -e	recipe
die Zutat, -en	ingredient
Fleisch und Fisch	*meat and fish*
die Garnele, -n	shrimp
das Hähnchen, -	chicken
die Meeresfrüchte (*pl.*)	seafood
das Rindfleisch	beef
der Schinken, -	ham
das Schweinefleisch	pork
der Thunfisch	tuna
das Würstchen, -	sausage
Obst und Gemüse	*fruits and vegetables*
die Ananas, -	pineapple
die Artischocke, -n	artichoke
die Himbeere, -n	raspberry
die Melone, -n	melon
die Traube, -n	grape

Ressourcen

v̂Text | WB pp. 47–48 | LM p. 90 | S vhlcentral

die Orange, -n

die Birne, -n

die Erdbeere, -n

Obst

der Pfirsich, -e

die Banane, -n

der Apfel, ⸚

die Kartoffel, -n

Gemüse

die Zwiebel, -n

die rote Paprika (*pl.* die roten Paprika)

die Karotte, -n

die Aubergine, -n

die grüne Bohne (*pl.* die grünen Bohnen)

der Knoblauch

der Pilz, -e

die Tomate, -n

die Marmelade, -n

der Kuchen, -

die grüne Paprika
(*pl.* die grünen Paprika)

der Salat, -e

das Ei, -er

Anwendung

1 Was passt zusammen? Welche Wörter in Liste 1 passen zu (*match*) den Wörtern in Liste 2?

Liste 1	Liste 2
____ 1. die Paprika	a. der Fisch
____ 2. das Rindfleisch	b. das Fleisch
____ 3. die Banane	c. das Obst
____ 4. der Thunfisch	d. das Gemüse
____ 5. die Orange	
____ 6. das Würstchen	
____ 7. der Salat	
____ 8. die Garnele	

2 Lebensmittel Schreiben Sie die Namen der Lebensmittel unter die Fotos.

▶ BEISPIEL *die Tomaten*

1. _____

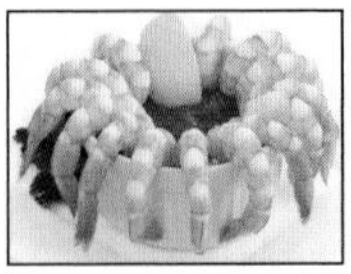

2.  _____ 3.  _____ 4. 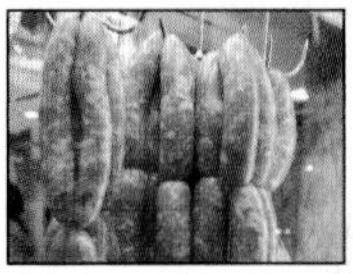 _____ 5. _____

3 Was essen Sie gern? Schreiben Sie die Namen der Lebensmittel, die (*that*) Sie gern, nicht so gern und nicht gern essen.

gern	nicht so gern	nicht gern
1. _____	_____	_____
2. _____	_____	_____
3. _____	_____	_____

4 Samstag ist Markttag Hören Sie die Dialoge an und entscheiden Sie (*decide*), ob die Sätze (*sentences*) **richtig** oder **falsch** sind.

	richtig	falsch
1. Annika geht im Supermarkt einkaufen.	☐	☐
2. Sie kauft Garnelen und Thunfisch.	☐	☐
3. Thunfisch ist heute im Angebot (*on sale*).	☐	☐
4. Ein Kilo Garnelen kostet 8,30 €.	☐	☐
5. Am Obststand kauft Annika nur Äpfel und Bananen.	☐	☐
6. Annika macht einen Salat.	☐	☐

Practice more at **vhlcentral.com**.

Kommunikation

5 Was kann man hier kaufen?
Welche drei Lebensmittel können Sie in den Geschäften kaufen? Vergleichen Sie (*Compare*) die Antworten mit einem Partner / einer Partnerin.

▶ **BEISPIEL**

in der Eisdiele
das Eis
der Kaffee
die Cola

1. beim Bäcker
_____
_____
_____

2. in der Metzgerei
_____
_____
_____

3. auf dem Markt
_____
_____
_____

4. im Supermarkt
_____
_____
_____

5. im Fischgeschäft
_____
_____
_____

6 Kochen mit Freunden
Sie und Ihre Freunde wollen am Abend zusammen kochen. Diskutieren Sie, was Sie alles brauchen und wer was kaufen soll (*who should buy what*).

BEISPIEL

S1: *Wer bringt Obst und Gemüse?*
S2: *Ich bringe Salat. Thomas, bringst du das Obst?*
S3: *Ja, ich kann Trauben und Birnen bringen.*

7 Arbeitsblatt
Sie sind Geschäftsbesitzer und Ihre Mitstudenten müssen erraten (*guess*), was man bei Ihnen kaufen kann und welches Geschäft Sie haben.

BEISPIEL

S1: *Verkaufen Sie Bananen?*
S2: *Nein.*
S3: *Verkaufen Sie Wurst?*
S2: *Ja.*
S1: *Haben Sie eine Metzgerei?*

8 Essen und trinken
Fragen Sie Ihre Mitstudenten, was sie gern oder nicht gern essen und trinken. Finden Sie mindestens (*at least*) eine Person, die denselben Geschmack (*the same taste*) hat wie Sie.

BEISPIEL

S1: *Ich esse gern Brot und Nutella am Morgen. Isst du auch Nutella?*
S2: *Nein, ich esse nicht gern Nutella.*
S3: *Ich esse gern Brot und Nutella. Und ich trinke morgens Kaffee. Du auch?*

Aussprache und Rechtschreibung  Audio

The German *s, z,* and *c*

The *s* sound in German is represented by **s**, **ss**, or **ß**. At the end of a word, **s**, **ss**, and **ß** are pronounced like the *s* in the English word *yes*. Before a vowel, **s** is pronounced like the *s* in the English word *please*.

Reis	**Profe**ss**or**	**wei**ß	**Supermarkt**	**Kä**s**e**

The German **z** is pronounced like the *ts* in the English word *bats*, whether it appears at the beginning, middle, or end of a word. The combination **tz** is also pronounced *ts*. The ending -**tion** is always pronounced -*tsion*.

Pilz**e**	**Z**wiebel	**Plat**z	**Besit**z**er**	**Kau**tion

Only in loan words does the letter **c** appear directly before a vowel. Before **e** or **i**, the letter **c** is usually pronounced *ts*. Before other vowels, it is usually pronounced like the *c* in *cat*. The letter combination **ck** is pronounced like the *ck* in the English word *packer*.

Cent	**C**elsius	**C**omputer	**ba**ck**en**	**Bä**ck**erei**

1   **Aussprechen** Wiederholen Sie die Wörter, die Sie hören.

1. lassen	4. weiser	7. selbst	10. letztes
2. lasen	5. sinnlos	8. Zeile	11. Campingplatz
3. weißer	6. seitens	9. Katzen	12. Fleck

2   **Nachsprechen** Wiederholen Sie die Sätze, die Sie hören.

1. Der Musiker geht am Samstag zum Friseur.
2. Es geht uns sehr gut.
3. Die Zwillinge essen eine Pizza mit Pilzen, Zwiebeln und Tomaten.
4. Jetzt ist es Zeit in den Zoo zu gehen.
5. Der Clown sitzt im Café und spielt Computerspiele.
6. Ich esse nur eine Portion Eis.

3   **Sprichwörter** Wiederholen Sie die Sprichwörter, die Sie hören.

Aus den Augen, aus dem Sinn.[1]

Gegensätze ziehen sich an.[2]

[1] Out of sight, out of mind.
[2] Opposites attract.

Ressourcen

vText   LM p. 91   vhlcentral

Börek für alle Video

George und Hans treffen Meline und Sabite im Supermarkt. George hat eine
Idee: Er macht Börek für seine Freunde. Aber kann George kochen?

1

GEORGE Was möchtest du heute essen?
HANS Hmmm. Ich esse gerne Fleisch.
Rindfleisch, Schweinefleisch und Wurst...
GEORGE Los! Auf zur Fleischtheke!
HANS Ja!

5

2

SABITE Ich esse gern Tofu mit Pilzen
und Erdbeeren.
HANS Erdbeeren und was?
SABITE Pilze. Mit Tofu.

MELINE Müssen wir mit Hans und
George essen?
SABITE Ach, Meline, sei nett.

3

GEORGE Sabite, welche Zutaten kommen
in die Börek von deiner Mutter? Wir können
sie kochen.
SABITE Hmm. Lass mich überlegen. Kartoffeln,
Blätterteig, Zwiebeln. Kartoffeln kochen,
Zwiebeln braten, Teig aufrollen. Backen.

HANS Muss Meline mit uns essen? Sie ist
extrem unangenehm. Ich finde, das ist
eine ausgesprochen schlechte Idee.
GEORGE Meline ist lustig. Du magst
sie bestimmt.
HANS Das glaube ich kaum.
GEORGE Sie mag dich bestimmt.

6

4

GEORGE Ich mache heute Abend Börek!
SABITE Wir bringen Käse und Brot mit. Wann
sollen wir kommen?
GEORGE Kommt um halb sieben vorbei.
SABITE Perfekt.
MELINE Was ist perfekt?

1 **Was fehlt?** Ergänzen Sie die Sätze mit den richtigen Informationen.

1. Hans isst gern Schweinefleisch und (Rindfleisch / Tofu).
2. Sabite isst gern Tofu mit Pilzen und (Wurst / Erdbeeren).
3. In die Börek von Frau Yilmaz kommen (Pilze / Zwiebeln).
4. Man muss die Zwiebeln (waschen / braten).
5. Meline und Sabite sollen um (zehn nach sieben / halb sieben)
bei Hans und George sein.

6. Sie bringen (Käse und Brot / Käse und Wurst) mit.
7. Hans findet die Idee ausgesprochen (schlecht / gut).
8. In Georges Börek ist kein (Blätterteig / Schafskäse).
9. Sabite ruft morgen (ihre Mutter / ihre Oma) an.
10. Hans und George haben noch (Milch und Äpfel / Joghurt
und Bananen).

7

GEORGE Tada! Prost!
HANS Prost!

8

SABITE George! Was...
GEORGE Ich weiß es nicht!

9

SABITE Wo ist der Schafskäse? Er gibt ihnen erst noch den Geschmack.
GEORGE Schafskäse? Wieso...
SABITE Oh, nein. Oh, George, es tut mir leid! Ich rufe morgen meine Mutter an und schreibe es dann auf.

10

GEORGE Es ist schon okay. Der Butterkäse und das Brot liegen dort.
MELINE Ich brate Eier und Kartoffeln.
HANS Gute Idee. Wir haben hier oben noch Joghurt und Bananen.
SABITE Hier stehen noch Butter und Marmelade für das Brot!

Nützliche Ausdrücke

- **die Wurst**
  cold cuts
- **Los! Auf zur Fleischtheke!**
  Let's go! To the butcher's counter!
- **der Blätterteig**
  phyllo dough
- **aufrollen**
  roll up
- **Kommt um halb sieben vorbei!**
  Come over at half past six!
- **Brauchen wir noch etwas?**
  Do we need anything else?
- **Ich finde, das ist eine ausgesprochen schlechte Idee.**
  I think it's an extremely bad idea.
- **Das glaube ich kaum.**
  I hardly think so.
- **Ich weiß es nicht!**
  I don't know!
- **der Schafskäse**
  Feta cheese

4A.1
- **Ich mache heute Abend Börek!**
  I'm making boreks tonight!

4A.2
- **Du magst sie bestimmt.**
  You really will like her.

4A.3
- **Ich rufe morgen meine Mutter an und schreibe es dann auf.**
  I'll call my mother tomorrow, and I'll write it down.

---

2 **Zum Besprechen** Sie und ein Freund möchten heute Abend eine Party geben. Spielen Sie mit einem Partner einen Dialog. Welches Essen wollen Sie servieren? Welche Zutaten brauchen Sie? Müssen Sie einkaufen gehen? Wie kochen Sie das Essen?

3 **Vertiefung** Suchen Sie bekannte Lebensmittelhersteller (*food brands*) in Deutschland, wie Knorr, Maggi oder Haribo. Finden Sie drei bekannte Produkte. Präsentieren Sie der Klasse Ihre Resultate.

Ressourcen

v̂Text

VM
p. 105

vhlcentral

Der Wiener Naschmarkt Reading

IN DEUTSCHLAND, ÖSTERREICH und der Schweiz hat fast jede Stadt° einen Marktplatz°. Er ist normalerweise im Zentrum der Stadt.

Stände am Naschmarkt	
Lebensmittel	31
Gastronomie°	27
Obst und Gemüse	20
Fleischwaren	9
Backwaren°	8
Fisch	5
Blumen	2
Milchprodukte	2
Wein	1
Bier	1
Sonstiges°	1
QUELLE: Edition moKKa	

Große Städte haben oft mehr als einen Marktplatz. Berühmte° Marktplätze sind der Viktualienmarkt in München, der Alexanderplatz in Berlin, der Helvetiaplatz in Zürich und der Naschmarkt in Wien.

Der Naschmarkt ist einer der 26 Märkte in Wien. Er existiert seit über° 80 Jahren und liegt° sehr zentral. Viele Stände° auf dem Naschmarkt sind von Montag bis Samstag zwischen° 9 und 21 Uhr offen. Vor allem° samstagmorgens bei gutem Wetter° findet man alte und junge Menschen an den Ständen. Die Atmosphäre ist lebendig°: Menschen unterhalten sich° und Kunden handeln mit den Verkäufern°.

Märkte wie der Wiener Naschmarkt haben auch viele verschiedene° Waren: Es gibt Käse, Fleisch, Wurst, Obst und Gemüse. Natürlich gibt es auch Milchprodukte wie Käse und Joghurt. Außerdem° kann man Blumen oder Seife° kaufen. Der Markt ist auch sehr international mit italienischen, griechischen, türkischen und asiatischen Ständen.

fast jede Stadt almost every city **Marktplatz** market square **Berühmte** Famous **existiert seit über** has existed for more than **liegt** is located **Stände** stands **zwischen** between **Vor allem** Especially **bei gutem Wetter** when the weather is nice **lebendig** lively **unterhalten sich** chat **Kunden handeln mit den Verkäufern** buyers negotiate with the vendors **verschiedene** different **Außerdem** In addition **Seife** soap **Gastronomie** prepared foods **Backwaren** baked goods **Sonstiges** Other

ÜBUNGEN

1 **Der Wiener Naschmarkt** Ergänzen Sie die Sätze.

1. Jede Stadt in Deutschland, _____ und der Schweiz hat einen Marktplatz.
2. Der Marktplatz ist normalerweise im _____ der Stadt.
3. Ein berühmter Marktplatz in Berlin heißt _____.
4. In Wien gibt es _____ Märkte.
5. Der Naschmarkt existiert seit über _____ Jahren.
6. Viele Stände sind zwischen 9 und _____ Uhr offen.
7. Die Atmosphäre auf dem Naschmarkt ist _____.
8. Der Naschmarkt ist sehr international mit italienischen, griechischen, _____ und asiatischen Waren.
9. An fünf Ständen kann man _____ kaufen.
10. Auf dem Naschmarkt gibt es _____ Obst- und Gemüsestände.

DIE DEUTSCHSPRACHIGE WELT

Das ist eine Tomate, oder?

Deutsche und Österreicher sprechen Deutsch, aber es gibt verschiedene Vokabeln. Deutsche sagen „Tomate". Was sagen Österreicher? Hier ist eine kurze Liste mit Essensvokabeln:

In Deutschland	In Österreich
die Aprikose°	die Marille
grüne Bohnen	Fisolen
das Brötchen	die Semmel
das Hackfleisch°	das Faschierte
die Kartoffel	der Erdapfel
der Meerrettich°	der Kren
der Quark°	der Topfen
die Sahne°	der Obers
die Tomate	der Paradeiser

Aprikose *apricot* **Hackfleisch** *ground meat* **Meerrettich** *horseradish* **Quark** *curd cheese* **Sahne** *cream*

PORTRÄT

Wolfgang Puck

Wolfgang Puck ist ein österreichischer Koch°. Er lebt und arbeitet in den USA, hat aber auch Restaurants in Toronto, Dubai, London, Singapur und Tokio. Er ist sehr erfolgreich°: Der Umsatz° seiner Firmen ist mehr als 300 Millionen Dollar pro Jahr. In den USA hat er mehr als 70 Restaurants: Bistros, Cafés und Gourmetrestaurants. Ein sehr berühmtes und sehr teures° Restaurant ist das Spago in Beverly Hills. Das Essen in seinen Restaurants ist nicht nur amerikanisch. In fast jedem Restaurant kann man neben amerikanischen Burgern auch Wiener Schnitzel° und Kärntner Kasnudeln° bestellen.

Koch *chef* **erfolgreich** *successful* **Umsatz** *total revenue* **teures** *expensive* **Wiener Schnitzel** *Viennese schnitzel* **Kärntner Kasnudeln** *South Austrian cheese noodles*

∞ IM INTERNET

Wie viele Christkindlmärkte gibt es in Österreich? Wo sind sie? Welche Christkindlmärkte sind sehr berühmt?

Find out more at **vhlcentral.com**.

---

2 **Richtig oder falsch?** Korrigieren Sie die falschen Aussagen.

1. Das Brötchen heißt Semmel in Österreich.
 2. Eine Tomate heißt Marille in Österreich.
3. Wolfgang Puck ist ein deutscher Koch.
4. Wolfgang Puck hat Restaurants nur in den USA.
5. In fast jedem Restaurant von Wolfgang Puck kann man Wiener Schnitzel bestellen.

3 **Auf dem Naschmarkt** Spielen Sie ein Gespräch zwischen einem Kunden (*customer*) und einem Verkäufer auf dem Naschmarkt. Integrieren Sie die folgenden Informationen: Grüße, zwei Produkte, Preise, Bezahlung (*payment*), Abschiede.

BEISPIEL

S1: *Guten Tag.*
S2: *Grüß Gott. Kann ich Ihnen helfen?*
S1: *Ja. Ich hätte gerne...*

Ressourcen

vText

vhlcentral

Adverbs  Presentation

Startblock In German, as in English, adverbs are words or phrases that modify a verb, an adjective, or another adverb. Adverbs describe *when*, *how*, or *where* an action takes place.

QUERVERWEIS

In **2B**, you learned to use the adverb **gern(e)** (*lit. gladly*) with a verb to say that you enjoy an activity.

See **1B.2** to review basic word order in German.

See **2A.3** to review other adverbs related to time and date.

- An adverb usually comes immediately before the adjective or adverb it modifies. Adverbs that frequently modify adjectives or other adverbs include **fast** (*almost*), **noch** (*yet; still; in addition*), **nur** (*only*), **schon** (*already*), **sehr, so** (*so*), **wirklich** (*really*), **ziemlich** (*quite*), and **zu** (*too*).

  Der Kuchen ist **fast** fertig.
  *The cake is **almost** ready.*

  Du isst **viel zu** schnell.
  *You eat **much too** quickly.*

- When an adverb modifies a verb, it generally comes immediately after the verb it modifies. Adverbs of time or place can also come directly before the verb.

  Ich esse **täglich** Gemüse.
  *I eat vegetables **every day**.*

  Morgens trinken wir **immer** Kaffee.
  *We **always** drink coffee **in the morning**.*

- Here are some common adverbs of time, manner, and place.

adverbs					
Wann?		**Wie?**		**Wo?**	
immer	*always*	allein	*alone*	da/dort	*there*
jetzt	*now*	bestimmt	*definitely*	drüben	*over there*
nie	*never*	leider	*unfortunately*	hier	*here*
oft	*often*	vielleicht	*maybe*	überall	*everywhere*
selten	*rarely*	zusammen	*together*	woanders	*somewhere else*
täglich	*daily*				

ACHTUNG

In English, you can turn an adjective into an adverb by adding the ending *-ly*.

In German, you can turn an adjective into an adverb by placing it after the verb you want to modify:

Peter ist ein gesunder Junge.
Peter is a healthy boy.

Peter isst sehr gesund.
Peter eats very healthily.

- Adverbs of time indicate *when* or *how frequently* an event occurs and answer the questions **wann?** and **wie oft?** (*how often?*).

  Wir gehen **morgen** einkaufen.
  *We're going shopping **tomorrow**.*

  Ich esse **selten** Kuchen.
  *I **rarely** eat cake.*

- If there is more than one time expression in a sentence, general time references are placed before adverbs of specific time.

  Die Bäckerei öffnet **am Sonntag um 9 Uhr**.
  *The bakery opens at **9 o'clock on Sunday**.*

  Samstag morgens um 11 Uhr frühstücke ich mit meinem Vater.
  *I have breakfast with my father **every Saturday morning at 11 o'clock**.*

- Adverbs of manner indicate *how* an action is done. They answer the question **wie?**

  Ich mache das **allein**.
  *I'm doing this **by myself**.*

  Du spielst **wirklich gut** Tennis.
  *You play tennis **really well**.*

- Adverbs of place describe locations or directions and answer the questions **wo?**, **wohin?**, and **woher?**

  Woher kommst du?
  *Where are you **from**?*

  Ich komme **aus Deutschland**.
  *I'm **from Germany**.*

  Wohin geht ihr?
  Where are you going?

  Wir gehen **in die Eisdiele**.
  *We're going **to the ice cream shop**.*

- When there is more than one adverbial expression in a sentence, adverbs of time come first, followed by adverbs of manner, then adverbs of place.

  Papa kauft **heute in der Konditorei** eine Geburtstagstorte.
  *Dad is getting a birthday cake **today at the pastry shop**.*

  Wir fahren **zusammen zum Supermarkt**.
  *We're going **to the supermarket together**.*

  Heute Abend esse ich **vielleicht im Restaurant**.
  *Maybe I'll eat **at a restaurant tonight**.*

  Sie essen **morgen Abend bestimmt woanders**.
  *They are **definitely** eating **somewhere else tomorrow night**.*

- In **2B.3** you learned how to negate sentences with **nicht**. In sentences with adverbial expressions, **nicht** usually *precedes* general expressions of time, manner, and place, but *follows* adverbs of specific time.

  Wir kaufen **nicht oft** Fleisch im Supermarkt.
  *We don't **often** buy meat at the supermarket.*

  Ich will **am Montag nicht** in die Schule gehen.
  *I don't want to go to school **on Monday**.*

  Die Gäste sind **noch nicht hier**.
  *The guests aren't **here yet**.*

  Wir können **nicht mehr hier** warten.
  *We can't wait **here anymore**.*

Jetzt sind Sie dran!   Geben Sie an (*Indicate*), ob die Adverbien die Zeit, die Art und Weise (*manner*) oder den Ort beschreiben.

1. Wir kochen heute Abend <u>zusammen</u>.   *Art und Weise*
2. Marina ist <u>immer</u> besorgt. _____
3. Die Eltern trinken <u>gern</u> Rotwein. _____
4. Das Lebensmittelgeschäft ist <u>dort drüben</u>. _____
5. Meine Schwester isst <u>nie</u> Obst und Gemüse. _____
6. Ihr trinkt <u>selten</u> Kaffee. _____
7. Du machst deine Hausaufgaben <u>allein</u>. _____
8. Ich fahre <u>schnell</u> zur Universität. _____
9. Petra hat <u>jetzt</u> keine Zeit. _____
10. Ich esse <u>oft</u> Käse und Brot. _____
11. Kann man Auberginen <u>überall</u> kaufen? _____
12. Wir bleiben <u>hier</u> in Berlin. _____

Anwendung

1 **Was ist richtig?** Wählen Sie (*Choose*) das adverbiale Element, das am besten passt.

BEISPIEL Ich gehe (die ganze Nacht / im Restaurant / morgens) in den Unterricht.

1. Yusuf macht (in der Bibliothek / im Fitnessstudio / in der Bäckerei) Hausaufgaben.
2. Wir möchten später (selten / beim Bäcker / im Park) ein Picknick machen.
3. Efe geht (im Hörsaal / im Supermarkt / im Café) einkaufen.
4. Das Restaurant ist (oft / überall / zusammen) voll (*crowded*).
5. Das Rezept ist (jetzt / fast / wirklich) einfach.
6. Thomas isst (dort / selten / allein) Fleisch.
7. Der Kuchen ist (abends / am Wochenende / sehr) gut.
8. Zum Mittagessen gehen wir (leider / in die Mensa / überall).

2 **Auf dem Campus** Setzen Sie das Adverb an die richtige Stelle.

BEISPIEL Wir essen um 6 Uhr. (immer)
Wir essen immer um 6 Uhr.

1. David vergisst immer seine Hausaufgaben. (fast)
   _____
2. Ich gehe im Supermarkt einkaufen. (oft)
   _____
3. Paula geht nachmittags spazieren. (auf dem Campus)
   _____
4. Die Studenten essen in der Mensa. (nicht gern)
   _____
5. Ihr lernt in der Bibliothek. (abends)
   _____
6. Du gehst freitags tanzen. (im Club)
   _____
7. Die Professorin korrigiert die Prüfungen. (am Sonntag)
   _____
8. Julius fährt nach Berlin. (am Wochenende)
   _____

3 **Was machen diese Leute?** Bilden Sie Sätze mit zwei Adverbien. Setzen Sie die Wörter in die richtige Reihenfolge (*order*).

Subjekt	Objekt	Verb	Adverbien	
ich	das Auto	backen	gern	selten
du	die Hausaufgaben	fahren	jetzt	im Sommer
mein Vater	den Hund	kaufen	nächstes Jahr	überall
wir	einen Kuchen	machen	nie	um 9 Uhr
du und Dieter	einen Obstsalat	wandern	oft	am Wochenende
meine Freunde	einen Snack	waschen	schnell	zusammen

 Practice more at **vhlcentral.com**.

Kommunikation

4 **Wie und warum?** Was machen die Personen, wie machen Sie das und warum? Erfinden Sie (*Make up*) ein kurzes Szenario. Benutzen Sie (*Use*) jedes der folgenden Adverbien nur einmal (*once*): allein, langsam, oft, selten, vielleicht, zusammen.

▶ **BEISPIEL**

S1: Wie geht er?
S2: Er geht schnell. Wohin geht er?
S3: Er geht vielleicht in den Park.

1._____

 2._____

 3._____

 4._____

 5._____

5 **Partnergespräch** Stellen Sie Ihrem Partner / Ihrer Partnerin Fragen.

BEISPIEL

S1: Wie oft kochst du?
S2: Ich koche sehr oft. / Ich koche selten.

1. Wann lernst du?
2. Wann sind deine Kurse?
3. Wie oft gehst du in die Mensa?

4. Wann machst du deine Mittagspause?
5. Wie oft gehst du tanzen?
6. Wie oft fährst du zu den Großeltern?

6 **Meine Mitstudenten** Finden Sie für jede Aktivität eine Person aus Ihrer Klasse.

BEISPIEL

S1: Isst du oft Fisch?
S2: Nein, ich esse nicht oft Fisch.
S3: Und du?

oft / Fisch essen
gut / Gitarre spielen
täglich / in der Sporthalle trainieren
selten / Gemüse essen
gern / am Wochenende tanzen gehen
oft / Schokomilch trinken
nie / samstags im Haus bleiben
immer / Eier zum Frühstück essen
gut / kochen können

4A.2

The modal *mögen*

 Presentation

Startblock In 2B **Kontext**, you learned to express likes and dislikes using **gern** and **nicht gern**. Another way of expressing liking is with the modal **mögen**.

ACHTUNG

While **gern** is always used with a verb, **mögen** is typically used with a noun:
Wir <u>mögen</u> Erdbeeren.
But: **Wir <u>essen gern</u> Erdbeeren.**

Ich <u>mag keinen</u> Tee.
But: **Ich <u>trinke nicht gern</u> Tee.**

Since **gern** is an adverb, it can also be used in combination with **mögen**, for emphasis:

Was <u>magst</u> du <u>gern</u>?
Das <u>mag</u> ich <u>nicht so gern</u>.

QUERVERWEIS

See **3B.1** to review the other modal verbs: **dürfen**, **können**, **müssen**, **sollen**, and **wollen**.

See **2B.3** to review negation.

Hey! Ich **mag** das! Danke.

Meline ist lustig. Du **magst** sie bestimmt.

- Like all the modal verbs, **mögen** is irregular in the singular.

mögen (*to like*)			
ich mag	*I like*	wir mögen	*we like*
du magst	*you like*	ihr mögt	*you like*
er/sie/es mag	*he/she/it likes*	Sie/sie mögen	*you/they like*

- While most modals modify another verb, **mögen** almost always modifies a noun.

Mögt ihr diesen Joghurt?
*Do you **like** this yogurt?*

Nein, diesen Joghurt **mögen** wir **nicht**.
*No, we **don't like** that yogurt.*

- Depending on context, you can use either **nicht** or **kein** to negate a statement with **mögen**.

Ich **mag keine** grünen Paprika.
*I **don't like** green peppers.*

Magst du rote Paprika?
*Do you **like** red peppers?*

Nein, rote Paprika **mag** ich auch **nicht**.
*No, I **don't like** red peppers either.*

- **Möchten** is the subjunctive form of **mögen**. Use **möchten** for polite requests and to say what you *would like* to have or do. **Möchten** may be followed by either a verb or a noun.

möchten			
ich möchte	*I would like*	wir möchten	*we would like*
du möchtest	*you would like*	ihr möchtet	*you would like*
er/sie/es möchte	*he/she/it would like*	Sie/sie möchten	*you/they would like*

Wir **möchten** Fußball spielen.
*We **would like** to play soccer.*

Möchten Sie Kaffee oder Tee?
***Would** you **like** coffee or tea?*

Ressourcen

v̄Text

WB
pp. 51–52

LM
p. 93

vhlcentral

Jetzt sind Sie dran!   Ergänzen Sie die Lücken mit den richtigen Formen der Modalverben **mögen** oder **möchten**.

1. Die Kinder ___*mögen*___ (mögen) Schokolade.
2. Ich _____ (mögen) keinen Fußball.
3. Julia _____ (möchten) in die Konditorei gehen.
4. _____ (Möchten) du Pasta oder Reis?
5. Anne _____ (mögen) russische Literatur.
6. _____ (Möchten) Sie einen Tisch am Fenster?
7. Ihr _____ (möchten) zur Bäckerei gehen.
8. _____ (Mögen) du Meeresfrüchte nicht?
9. Ich _____ (möchten) kein Fleisch essen.
10. Unsere Katzen _____ (mögen) unseren Hund nicht.
11. _____ (Mögen) ihr Garnelen?
12. Wir _____ (möchten) Pasta.

Anwendung und Kommunikation

1 **Wer mag was?** Schreiben Sie die Sätze um. Benutzen Sie **mögen** anstatt **essen** oder **trinken gern**.

> **BEISPIEL** Ich esse nicht gern Garnelen.
>
> *Ich mag keine Garnelen. / Ich mag Garnelen nicht.*

1. Meine Schwester isst gern Schokolade.
2. Meine Eltern essen gern Bananen zum Frühstück.
3. Ich esse nicht gern Auberginen.
4. Mein Mann und ich essen gern Pizza.
5. Esst ihr gern Würstchen?
6. Trinkst du nicht gern Kaffee?

2 **Pläne** Ergänzen Sie die Sätze mit der richtigen Form von **möchten** und mit Wörtern aus der Liste.

am Wochenende Fußball spielen	schlafen
im Biergarten essen	tanzen
heiraten	Tennis spielen

▶ **BEISPIEL**
Ben und Simon
möchten am Wochenende Fußball spielen.

1. Elias und Emma
_____

2. Paula, du
_____

3. Professor Klein
_____

4. Alex und du, ihr
_____

5. Marie und ich, wir
_____

3 **Was magst du?** Fragen Sie Ihren Partner / Ihre Partnerin, was er/sie (nicht) mag. Fragen Sie auch nach den anderen Personen in seiner/ihrer Familie.

> **BEISPIEL**
>
> **S1:** *Magst du Thunfisch?*
> **S2:** *Nein, aber ich mag Käse.*
> **S1:** *Und dein Bruder? Mag er Thunfisch?*
> **S2:** *Nein, aber er mag Würstchen.*

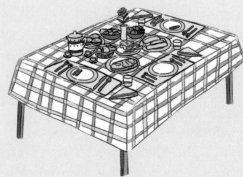

4A.3 Separable and inseparable prefix verbs  Presentation

Startblock In German, many verbs have a prefix in their infinitive form.

Ich gehe wirklich gern **einkaufen**.

Lass mich **überlegen**.

- A verb with a prefix has the same conjugations as its base form, but the added prefix changes the meaning.

  Sucht ihr eure Eltern?
  *Are you **looking for** your parents?*

  Besucht ihr eure Verwandten?
  *Do you **visit** your relatives?*

- Some prefixes are always attached to the verb and others can be separated from it.

  Jakob **verkauft** sein Fahrrad.
  *Jakob **is selling** his bike.*

  Ich **kaufe** im Supermarkt **ein**.
  *I **shop** at the supermarket.*

- Here are some of the most common separable and inseparable prefix verbs.

QUERVERWEIS

See **2B.1** to review the present tense of irregular verbs like **fangen** and **schlafen**.

verbs with separable prefixes	
anfangen	*to begin*
ankommen	*to arrive*
anrufen	*to call*
aufstehen	*to get up*
ausgehen	*to go out*
einkaufen	*to shop*
einschlafen	*to fall asleep*
mitbringen	*to bring along*
mitkommen	*to come along*
vorbereiten	*to prepare*
vorstellen	*to introduce*
zuschauen	*to watch*
zurückkommen	*to come back*

verbs with inseparable prefixes	
beantworten	*to answer*
besprechen	*to discuss*
bestellen	*to order*
besuchen	*to visit*
bezahlen	*to pay (for)*
erklären	*to explain*
verkaufen	*to sell*
verbringen	*to spend (time)*
überlegen	*to think over*
wiederholen	*to repeat*

- Separable prefixes are generally prepositions (**an, aus, mit**) or other parts of speech that carry meaning and can stand alone. In contrast, most inseparable prefixes (**be-, er-, ver-**) have no independent meaning and never stand alone.

  Heute Abend **gehen** wir zusammen **aus**.
  *Tonight we**'re going out** together.*

  Ich **bestelle** die Pasta mit Garnelen.
  *I**'m ordering** the pasta with shrimp.*

  Stefan **steht** jeden Morgen um 6 Uhr **auf**.
  *Stefan **gets up** at 6 o'clock every morning.*

  Ihr **verkauft** euer Auto?
  *You**'re selling** your car?*

ACHTUNG

When speaking, place the stress on the prefix of a separable prefix verb: **<u>an</u>rufen**, **<u>ein</u>schlafen**. The prefix of an inseparable prefix verb is never stressed: **ver<u>kau</u>fen**, **wieder<u>ho</u>len**.

- When using a separable prefix verb in the present tense or the imperative, move the prefix to the end of the sentence or clause.

  Wir **kaufen** auf dem Markt **ein**.
  We're shopping at the market.

  Bitte **stellen** Sie die Frau **vor**.
  Please introduce the woman.

  Kommst du **zurück**?
  Are you coming back?

  Ruf deine Eltern **an**!
  Call your parents!

Wir **bringen** Käse und Brot **mit**.

Wir **laden** Meline und Sabite zu uns zu Börek **ein**?

ACHTUNG

In this book, separable prefix verbs will be presented with their third person present-tense form in parentheses: **einkaufen (kauft... ein)**

- To make the sentence negative, add **nicht** immediately before the separable prefix.

  Ich komme **nicht** zurück.
  *I'm **not** coming back.*

  Ruf deine Eltern **nicht** an!
  Don't call your parents!

- When using a modal with a separable prefix verb, move the infinitive of the separable prefix verb to the end of the sentence.

  Die Mädchen **möchten** morgen Abend **ausgehen**.
  *The girls **want to go out** tomorrow night.*

  Ich **muss** mit meinen Hausaufgaben **anfangen**.
  *I **need to start** my homework.*

- The prefix of an inseparable prefix verb always remains attached to the beginning of the verb.

  Ich **bezahle** die Lebensmittel.
  *I'll **pay for** the groceries.*

  Wiederholen Sie den Satz.
  Repeat the sentence.

Ressourcen

v̂Text

WB
pp. 53–54

LM
p. 94

S
vhlcentral

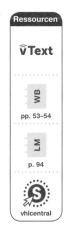

Jetzt sind Sie dran!   Schreiben Sie die richtige Form des Verbs in Klammern.

1. Ich ___wiederhole___ den Satz. (wiederholen)
2. Wir _____ unsere Freunde _____. (anrufen)
3. Erwin und Marta _____ ihr Haus. (verkaufen)
4. Du musst heute Abend noch _____. (einkaufen)
5. Der Student _____ seine Eltern _____. (vorstellen)
6. _____ wir am Wochenende _____? (ausgehen)
7. Papa _____ gern Meeresfrüchte. (bestellen)
8. Ich _____ eine Woche in Zürich. (verbringen)
9. Kannst du Brot _____? (mitbringen)
10. Wir _____ unsere Verwandten in Salzburg. (besuchen)

Anwendung

1 **Befehle** Geben Sie Befehle (*commands*) in der **Sie**-Form.

BEISPIEL

aufstehen
Stehen Sie auf.

1. anrufen
2. einkaufen
3. bezahlen
4. zuschauen
5. nicht mitkommen

6. überlegen
7. anfangen
8. nicht einschlafen
9. zurückkommen
10. nicht ausgehen

2 **Fragen** Formulieren Sie die Fragen um und benutzen Sie (*use*) dabei die angegebenen (*indicated*) Modalverben.

BEISPIEL

Kommst du mit? (können)
Kannst du mitkommen?

1. Gehst du aus? (wollen)
2. Kaufen wir ein? (sollen)
3. Kommt Lisa mit? (müssen)

4. Fangt ihr an? (möchten)
5. Schläfst du ein? (dürfen)
6. Schaut Nils zu? (können)

3 **Was machen sie?** Schreiben Sie zu jedem (*each*) Foto einen Satz und benutzen Sie Präfixverben.

Freunde anrufen	einschlafen
heute Abend ausgehen	die Grammatik erklären
die Bücher bezahlen	euren Hund mitbringen
einkaufen	

▶ **BEISPIEL**

Herr Schröder
Herr Schröder erklärt die Grammatik.

ich
1._____

Jana und Lina
2._____

Emma und
ihre Freunde
3._____

Stefanie
4._____

Frau Neumann und
ihre Tochter
5._____

ihr
6._____

Kommunikation

4 **Mein Tag** Füllen Sie einen Terminkalender mit Ihren Informationen aus und diskutieren Sie dann mit Ihrem Partner / Ihrer Partnerin, was Sie täglich so machen.

S1: Ich stehe um 8 Uhr auf. Und du?
S2: Ich stehe um 8.30 Uhr auf. Meine erste Vorlesung fängt um 10 Uhr an. Und deine?

8.00	Ich stehe auf.
9.00	
10.00	
11.00	
12.00	
13.00	
14.00	
15.00	

5 **Wer ist das?** Wählen Sie eine Person und schreiben Sie zwei Dinge auf, die diese (*this*) Person macht. Ihre Mitstudenten müssen raten (*guess*), wer es ist.

S1: Sie kommt um 8 Uhr zur Uni.
    Sie erklärt die Hausaufgaben und beantwortet unsere Fragen.
S2: Ist es die Professorin?

anfangen	ausgehen	besuchen	erklären	verbringen
ankommen	beantworten	bezahlen	mitbringen	vorbereiten
anrufen	besprechen	einkaufen	mitkommen	zurückkommen

6 **Ein Picknick machen** Sie und Ihre Freunde planen ein Picknick. Diskutieren Sie, wer was kauft, wer was mitbringt und was Sie alles machen müssen.

S1: Sollen wir viele Freunde anrufen?
S2: Ja, und wir müssen auch viel Essen mitbringen.
S3: Ich bringe Wurst und Käse mit!

Wiederholung

1
Was magst du? Fragen Sie einen Partner / eine Partnerin, was er/sie mag oder nicht mag.

BEISPIEL

S1: *Magst du Hähnchen mit Reis?*
S2: *Ja, ich mag Hähnchen mit Reis. Und du?*
S1: *Nein, ich mag Hähnchen mit Reis nicht. Magst du…?*

Würstchen mit Brot	Schweinefleisch mit Kartoffeln
Thunfisch mit Zwiebeln	Auberginen mit Tomaten
Pasta mit Pilzen	Schinken mit Brot
Hähnchen mit Reis	Pasta mit Käse
Garnelen mit Tomaten	Rindfleisch mit Salat

2
Das Wochenende Sagen Sie, was die Personen am Wochenende machen möchten. Wechseln Sie sich (*Take turns*) mit einem Partner / einer Partnerin ab.

Klara

▶ **BEISPIEL**

S1: *Was möchte Klara am Wochenende machen?*
S2: *Klara möchte am Wochenende gern lesen.*

1. Petra und Klaus

2. Paul, Manfred, Andrea und Monika

3. Inge

4. Robert

3
Arbeitsblatt Fragen Sie Ihre Mitstudenten, wie oft, wie und wo sie diese Lebensmittel essen.

BEISPIEL

S1: *Wie oft isst du Eier in der Mensa?*
S2: *Ich esse selten Eier in der Mensa.*

4
Was machen sie? Ein Student / Eine Studentin spielt eine Situation. Die anderen Studenten raten (*guess*) die Situation. Benutzen Sie vollständige (*complete*) Sätze.

BEISPIEL

S1: *Fährst du Fahrrad?*
S2: *Nein.*
S1: *Reitest du ein Pferd?*
S2: *Ja.*

aufstehen	im Restaurant	einschlafen
ausgehen	bestellen	Fahrrad fahren
einen Kuchen	einen Freund	ein Pferd reiten
backen	besuchen	Volleyball spielen

5
Diskutieren und kombinieren Sie bekommen eine Tabelle von Ihrem Professor / Ihrer Professorin. Fragen Sie einen Partner / eine Partnerin, wann die Personen die Aktivitäten machen.

BEISPIEL

S1: *Wann geht Alex Lebensmittel einkaufen?*
S2: *Alex geht am Samstag Lebensmittel einkaufen.*

6
Der Wochenplan Entscheiden Sie (*Decide*), was Sie diese Woche machen wollen. Suchen Sie andere Studenten in der Gruppe, die das Gleiche planen und finden Sie eine gemeinsame Zeit, wann sie das machen können.

BEISPIEL

S1: *Willst du diese Woche einkaufen gehen?*
S2: *Ja, ich will diese Woche einkaufen gehen.*
S1: *Können wir zusammen einkaufen gehen?*
S2: *Ja, gern.*
S1: *Hast du am Mittwoch Zeit?*
S2: *Nein, am Mittwoch habe ich keine Zeit. Hast du am Donnerstag Zeit?*
S1: *Ja, am Donnerstag habe ich Zeit. Um wie viel Uhr…*

Zapping

S Video

Yello Strom

Die Firma Yello Strom ist eine deutsche Stromfirma°. In Deutschland können Kunden° zwischen verschiedenen° Stromfirmen wählen. Kundenservice° ist deshalb aber auch ein wichtiger Aspekt, um neue Kunden zu gewinnen. Yello Strom ist eine kreative Firma mit neuen Ideen. Kundenservice ist sehr wichtig für diese Firma. In diesem Werbeclip zeigt° die Firma, dass Kunden bei Yello Strom nur mit echten Menschen reden!

Auf dem Wochenmarkt°

„Sie haben drei gelbe° Bananen gewählt°.“

„Guter Service geht anders°.“

Stromfirma *electric company* **Kunden** *customers* **verschiedenen** *different* **Kundenservice** *customer service* **zeigt** *shows* **Wochenmarkt** *farmer's market* **gelbe** *yellow* **gewählt** *selected* **anders** *differently*

Verständnis Beantworten Sie die Fragen mit den Informationen aus dem Video.

1. Was möchte die Frau auf dem Markt?
   Sie möchte drei _____.

2. Was versteht der Verkäufer?
   Er versteht drei _____.

Diskussion Diskutieren Sie die folgenden Fragen mit einem Partner / einer Partnerin.

1. Wie finden Sie Telefonmenüs? Funktionieren sie gut? Sind sie praktisch oder frustrierend?

2. Wie findest du die Werbung (*commercial*)? Ist die Situation lustig oder nicht so lustig?

Communicative Goals

You will learn how to:
- talk about food and meals
- describe flavors

Im Restaurant

Vocabulary Tools

Wortschatz	
im Restaurant	***at the restaurant***
die Beilage, -n	side dish
das Besteck	silverware
die Flasche, -n	bottle
der erste/zweite Gang	first/second course
das Gericht, -e	dish
die Hauptspeise, -n	main course
der Nachtisch, -e	dessert
die Rechnung, -en	check
die Tasse, -n	cup
das Trinkgeld	tip
die Vorspeise, -n	appetizer
Mahlzeiten	***meals***
das Abendessen	dinner
das Frühstück	breakfast
das Mittagessen	lunch
der Snack, -s	snack
Getränke	***drinks***
das Bier	beer
der Kaffee	coffee
die Milch	milk
das Mineralwasser	sparkling water
der Saft, ⁻e	juice
der Tee	tea
das stille Wasser	still water
der Wein	wine
Essen beschreiben	***talking about food***
der Geschmack, ⁻e	flavor; taste
fade	bland
lecker	delicious
leicht	light
salzig	salty
scharf	spicy
schwer	rich, heavy
süß	sweet
Ausdrücke	***expressions***
Ich hätte gern(e)...	I would like...
auf Diät sein	to be on a diet
hausgemacht	homemade

Labels in illustration:

der Koch, ⁻e (die Köchin, -nen *f.*)

Die Suppe schmeckt gut. (schmecken)

der Kellner, - (die Kellnerin, -nen *f.*)

die Gabel, -n

die Speisekarte, -n

Speisekarte

die Serviette, -n

der Teller, -

das Messer, -

die Tischdecke, -n

Sie bestellen.
(bestellen)

Speisekarte

eisekarte

das Salz

das Glas, ¨er

der Pfeffer

der Esslöffel, -

der Teelöffel, -

Anwendung

1 Was passt nicht? Welches Wort passt nicht zu den anderen?

1. a. die Gabel
   b. das Messer
   c. die Serviette
   d. der Löffel

2. a. die Milch
   b. der Saft
   c. der Kaffee
   d. das Salz

3. a. die Speisekarte
   b. die Flasche
   c. die Tasse
   d. das Glas

4. a. salzig
   b. stolz
   c. scharf
   d. süß

5. a. die Kellnerin
   b. die Köchin
   c. der Saft
   d. der Koch

6. a. das Mittagessen
   b. die Beilage
   c. das Abendessen
   d. das Frühstück

2 Wie schmeckt's? Beschreiben Sie (*Describe*) den Geschmack der Lebensmittel.

▶ **BEISPIEL** Die Bratwurst ist
_____scharf_____

1. Der Saft ist
   _____.

2. Die Suppe ist
   _____.

3. Der Salat ist
   _____.

4. Der Käse ist
   _____.

5. Das Brot ist
   _____.

6. Der Kuchen ist
   _____.

3 Was bestellen wir? Hören Sie den Dialog an und markieren Sie, was Tom, Klara und Murat bestellen.

Essen	Tom	Klara	Murat
1. Steak	☐	☐	☐
2. Cola	☐	☐	☐
3. Meeresfrüchtesalat	☐	☐	☐
4. stilles Wasser	☐	☐	☐
5. gemischter Salat	☐	☐	☐
6. Brot	☐	☐	☐
7. Mineralwasser	☐	☐	☐
8. Rindfleisch	☐	☐	☐

Kommunikation

4 Verschiedene Mahlzeiten
Fragen Sie Ihren Partner / Ihre Partnerin, welche Mahlzeiten auf den Fotos zu sehen sind. Wechseln Sie sich ab (*Take turns*).

▶ **BEISPIEL**

das Frühstück
S1: *Ist das das Frühstück?*
S2: *Nein, das ist das Abendessen.*

1. die Vorspeise

2. die Hauptspeise

3. der Nachtisch

4. das Abendessen

5. ein Snack

6. das Mittagessen

5 Wo möchten wir heute Abend essen?
Sie möchten heute Abend ins Restaurant essen gehen. Lesen Sie die Speisekarte und überlegen Sie, was Sie zu jedem (*for each*) Gang bestellen wollen.

BEISPIEL

S1: *Ich möchte gern den Tomatensalat mit Mozzarella als ersten Gang.*
S2: *Ich auch! Und als zweiten Gang bestelle ich das Hähnchen mit Reis.*
S3: *Wollt ihr auch Getränke bestellen?*

Speisekarte

Vorspeisen
Tagessuppe
Chef-Salat mit Schinken, Käse und Ei
Bauern-Salat mit Schafskäse, Zwiebeln
   und Oliven
Tomatensalat mit Mozzarella

Beilagen
Kartoffelsalat
Karottensalat
Grüner Salat
Kartoffelpuffer
Sauerkraut

Nachspeisen
Apfelkuchen
Bananen mit Schokolade
hausgemachter Joghurt mit
   Himbeermarmalade
Obstsalat

Hauptspeisen
Würstchen mit Brötchen
Thunfisch mit Salat
Hähnchen mit Reis
Rindfleisch mit Pommes frites
Schweinefleisch mit Kartoffeln
Pasta mit Garnelen
Pasta mit Käse

Getränke
stilles Wasser   Milch
Mineralwasser   Kaffee
Orangensaft   Tee

6 Stress im Restaurant!
Sie sind im Restaurant und der Kellner bringt Ihr Essen. Aber auf dem Tisch gibt es kein Besteck, kein Brot, keine Getränke, kein Salz und so weiter. Sagen Sie dem Kellner, was er noch alles bringen soll.

BEISPIEL

S1: *Kann ich bitte auch Gabel und Messer haben?*
S2: *Und bitte zwei Glas Wasser!*
S3: *Natürlich. Möchten sie noch etwas (anything else)?*

7 Diskutieren und kombinieren
Wie sind die Restaurants „Zum Grünen Baum" und „Zur Stadtmauer"? Fragen Sie Ihren Partner / Ihre Partnerin, und ergänzen Sie die fehlenden (*missing*) Informationen.

BEISPIEL

S1: *Was für ein Restaurant ist „Zur Stadtmauer"?*
S2: *Es ist ein vegetarisches Bistro. Und was für ein Restaurant ist „Zum Grünen Baum"?*
S1: *Dort gibt es traditionelle deutsche Gerichte. Welche Vorspeisen gibt es im Bistro?*

Aussprache und Rechtschreibung  Audio

The German *s* in combination with other letters

The letter combination **sch** is pronounced like the *sh* in the English word *fish*.

Fisch	Schinken	Geschäft	Fleisch	Schule

When an **s** appears at the beginning of a word in front of the letter **p** or **t**, it is also pronounced like the *sh* in *fish*. A prefix added to the word will not change the pronunciation of the **s**. However, if the **sp** or **st** letter combination occurs in the middle or at the end of a word, the **s** is pronounced like the *s* in the English word *restore*.

Speise	stoppen	versprechen	Aspirin	Fenster

In a few words borrowed from other languages, **sh** and **ch** are also pronounced like the *sh* in *fish*.

Chauffeur	Cashewnuss	Shampoo	Champignon	charmant

At the beginning of a word, the letter combination **tsch** is pronounced like the *ch* in *chat*. In the middle or at the end of a word, **tsch** is pronounced like the *tch* in *catch*.

tschüss	Tschad	Tschechien	Rutsch	Klatschbase

1 **Aussprechen** Wiederholen Sie die Wörter, die Sie hören.

1. Schaft   3. Sport   5. aufstehen   7. Aspekt   9. platschen
2. waschen   4. Strudel   6. Kasten   8. Putsch   10. Kutscher

2 **Nachsprechen** Wiederholen Sie die Sätze, die Sie hören.

1. Im Lebensmittelgeschäft kaufst du Schinken und Fisch.
2. In der Schule schwimmen alle Schüler im Schwimmbad.
3. Studenten spielen gern Videospiele.
4. Auf der Speisekarte steht Käsespätzle.
5. Der Tscheche sagt nicht mal tschüss.
6. Ich wünsche dir einen guten Rutsch ins neue Jahr!

3 **Sprichwörter** Wiederholen Sie die Sprichwörter, die Sie hören.

Besser spät als nie.[1]

Reden ist Silber; Schweigen ist Gold.[2]

[1] Better late than never.
[2] Talk is silver; silence is golden.

Ressourcen

vText   LM   vhlcentral
             p. 96

Die Rechnung, bitte! 🔊 Video

Torsten und Sabite sind bei einem romantischen Abendessen in einem
schönen Restaurant. Aber es bleibt nicht so romantisch...

KELLNER Wir bieten eine leckere hausgemachte
Pilzsuppe an. Nicht zu schwer.
SABITE Davon nehme ich einen Teller,
bitte. Und als zweiten Gang nehme ich
die Rindsrouladen.
KELLNER Sehr gerne. Und für Sie, mein Herr?
TORSTEN Als Vorspeise nehme ich den Salat
und als Hauptspeise das Wiener Schnitzel,
mit Salzkartoffeln, bitte.
KELLNER Ausgezeichnet.

SABITE Sie haben sehr gutes Essen in
diesem Restaurant.
TORSTEN Ja. Meine ältere Schwester empfiehlt
es guten Freunden wärmstens.

KELLNER Möchten Sie gerne noch
einen Nachtisch?
MELINE Ach, ich muss auf meine Figur achten!
KELLNER Oh, nein, Sie sind doch extrem...
LORENZO Wir nehmen ein Stück Schwarzwälder
Kirschtorte. Zwei Gabeln.
MELINE Und zwei Kaffee bitte.

SABITE Hallo!
MELINE Sabite! Hallo! Sabite, das ist Lorenzo.
Lorenzo, das ist meine Mitbewohnerin, Sabite.
LORENZO Ciao.

LORENZO Ich komme aus Milano.
MELINE Lorenzo ist geschäftlich in
Berlin. Er arbeitet im Bereich
internationale Finanzen.
LORENZO Bist du auch Studentin?
SABITE Ja, ich studiere Kunst.

SABITE Ich liebe die Kunst von Kandinsky
und Klee. Aber Italien hat die Meister...
Michelangelo... Da Vinci...
LORENZO Ja. Du musst sie mal aus der
Nähe sehen.
SABITE Ich hoffe, sie eines Tages sehen
zu können. Mein Vater kommt aus
der Türkei. Ich möchte dort gern ein
Semester lang studieren.

ÜBUNGEN

1 **Richtig oder falsch?** Entscheiden Sie, ob die folgenden Sätze
richtig oder **falsch** sind.

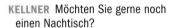

1. Sabite nimmt die Pilzsuppe und die Roulade.
2. Torsten bestellt ein Schnitzel mit Salzkartoffeln.
3. Torstens Schwester empfiehlt ihren Freunden das Restaurant.
4. Meline und Lorenzo bestellen zwei Stück Schwarzwälder Kirschtorte.
5. Lorenzo kommt aus Italien.

6. Er studiert Kunst.
7. Sabite mag die Kunst von Klee und Picasso.
8. Sie möchte ein Jahr in der Türkei studieren.
9. Sie möchte Istanbul kennen lernen.
10. Sabite findet Torsten egoistisch.

7

SABITE Torsten, ist alles in Ordnung?
TORSTEN Türkei? Du möchtest in der Türkei studieren?
SABITE Ich möchte Istanbul kennen lernen.

8

SABITE Hör auf. Noch studiert niemand in der Türkei. Entschuldige bitte.
TORSTEN Sabite!

9

SABITE Torsten ist... ist... ist so egoistisch!

10

TORSTEN Frauen. Und du bist also nicht Lukas?
LORENZO Die Rechnung, bitte!

Nützliche Ausdrücke

- **anbieten**
  to offer
- **Davon nehme ich einen Teller, bitte.**
  I would like a bowl of that, please.
- **die Rindsroulade**
  beef roulade
- **die Salzkartoffeln**
  boiled potatoes
- **Ich muss auf meine Figur achten.**
  I have to watch my weight.
- **die Schwarzwälder Kirschtorte**
  Black Forest cake
- **Er ist geschäftlich in Berlin.**
  He's in Berlin on business.
- **Er arbeitet im Bereich internationale Finanzen.**
  He works in international finance.
- **Ich hoffe, sie eines Tages sehen zu können.**
  I hope to see them someday.
- **ein Semester lang**
  for one semester
- **Hör auf!**
  Cut it out!
- **Noch studiert niemand in der Türkei.**
  No one's studying in Turkey just yet.

4B.1
- **Meine ältere Schwester empfiehlt es guten Freunden wärmstens.**
  My older sister highly recommends it to her close friends.

4B.2
- **Du musst sie mal aus der Nähe sehen.**
  You should see them up close.

---

2 **Zum Besprechen** Wählen Sie zu dritt ein Gericht aus Deutschland, Österreich oder der Schweiz und machen Sie eine Liste mit Zutaten. Präsentieren Sie der Klasse dann die Liste. Ihre Kommilitonen müssen das Gericht erraten (*guess*).

3 **Vertiefung** In den USA ist Wiener Schnitzel vielleicht das berühmteste (*most famous*) Gericht aus den deutschsprachigen Ländern. Wissen Sie, woher es kommt? Kennen Sie andere Gerichte, die den Namen von Städten haben?

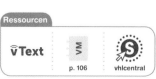

Ressourcen — v̂Text · VM p. 106 · vhlcentral

Wiener Kaffeehäuser Reading

KAFFEEHÄUSER IN ÖSTERREICH HABEN eine lange Tradition. Kaffeehäuser gibt es seit dem 18. Jahrhundert. In Wien findet man heute mindestens° 1.100 Kaffeehäuser. Typischerweise serviert ein Kellner einen Kaffee auf einem silbernen Tablett° mit einem Löffel, einem Glas Wasser und einem Keks. In den Kaffeehäusern trinkt man aber auch andere Getränke wie Kakao, Wasser und Wein. Zum Kaffee isst man oft Apfelstrudel, Gugelhupf° oder Sachertorte°. Oft besuchen Gäste° ein Kaffeehaus, bestellen einen Kaffee und bleiben viele Stunden. Hier diskutieren Gäste auch über Politik, Sport und andere Themen.

Wiener Kaffeehäuser haben spezielle Vokabeln: Sahne° heißt Obers. Ein kleiner oder großer Brauner ist ein Kaffee serviert mit Obers in einer kleinen Schale°. Eine Melange ist halb° Kaffee und halb geschäumte° Milch. Ein Kapuziner ist ein kleiner Mokka (ein Schwarzer oder Espresso pur) mit wenig Milch.

Es gibt auch andere Cafés in Wien. In einer Espresso-Bar trinkt man vor allem° Espresso und Cappuccino wie in Italien. In Stehcafés trinken Gäste Kaffee sehr schnell oder nehmen den Kaffee mit. Café-Konditoreien sind nicht nur Cafés. In der Konditorei kaufen Kunden hausgemachte Kuchen und Süßigkeiten°. Die neueste Version eines Cafés ist der amerikanische Import Starbucks. Hier findet man vor allem jüngere Österreicher.

Typische Cafépreise	
Kleiner Schwarzer	2,80 €
Kleiner Brauner	2,90 €
Melange	3,90 €
Großer Schwarzer	4,20 €
Großer Brauner	4,30 €
Einspänner	4,90 €
Kapuziner	4,90 €
Pharisäer	6,60 €

QUELLE: Café Korb in Wien

mindestens at least **Tablett** tray **Gugelhupf** Bundt cake **Sachertorte** chocolate torte **Gäste** guests **Sahne** cream **Schale** dish **halb** half **geschäumte** foamed **vor allem** above all **Süßigkeiten** sweets

ÜBUNGEN

1 **Wiener Kaffeehäuser** Ergänzen Sie die Sätze.

1. Wiener Kaffeehäuser haben eine _____ Tradition.

2. In Wien findet man mehr als _____ Kaffeehäuser.

3. Auf einem Tablett serviert der Kellner den Kaffee, einen Löffel, ein _____ und einen Keks.

4. Gäste bleiben oft _____ Stunden.

5. Neben Kaffee kann man auch _____, Wasser oder Wein trinken.

6. Typisches Essen in Kaffeehäusern sind _____, Gugelhupf und Sachertorte.

7. Ein Melange ist halb Kaffee und halb _____.

8. In Wien gibt es auch Espresso-Bars, _____ und Café-Konditoreien.

9. In einer Espresso-Bar trinken Gäste Kaffee wie in _____.

10. Ein Kapuziner im Café Korb kostet _____.

Am Tisch

Die Rechnung, bitte!	*Check, please!*
Die Speisekarte, bitte!	*The menu, please!*
Guten Appetit!	*Enjoy your meal!*
Noch einen Wunsch?	*Anything else?*
Herr Ober!	*Waiter!*
Prost!	*Cheers!*
Zum Wohl!	*Cheers!*

Ausländische Spezialitäten

In Deutschland besteht die Bevölkerung° ungefähr zu 8% aus° Ausländern°, in der Schweiz sind es fast 23%. Die Ausländer kommen aus vielen Ländern wie Italien, Griechenland°, der Türkei, Nordafrika und dem ehemaligen° Jugoslawien. Deshalb° ist die Restaurantszene in Deutschland, Österreich und der Schweiz auch sehr international. In jeder° Stadt gibt es Restaurants mit italienischen, griechischen und verschiedenen° asiatischen Speisen. Vor allem in Großstädten ist die Auswahl° sehr groß. Die populärsten Restaurants sind definitiv italienisch, aber man findet auch sehr viele asiatische Restaurants.

Bevölkerung *population* **besteht... aus** *consists of* **Ausländern** *foreigners* **Griechenland** *Greece* **ehemaligen** *former* **Deshalb** *Therefore* **jeder** *every* **verschiedenen** *various* **Auswahl** *selection*

Figlmüller

Das Figlmüller ist ein sehr altes Restaurant in Wien. Es ist „die Heimat° des Schnitzels", ein Paradies für Schnitzelfans. Man findet das Restaurant in der Wollzeile im Zentrum Wiens. Das Restaurant existiert seit über 100 Jahren und ist berühmt° für seine Schnitzel, ein Stück Schweinefleisch mit Semmelbröselhülle°. Die Schnitzel sind ziemlich groß, dünn und sehr knusprig°. Dazu gibt es österreichische Weine. Bier und Kaffee gibt es hier nicht. Auch Süßspeisen finden Gäste nicht auf der Speisekarte. Aber Schnitzel sind hier sehr wichtig. Alle Ober servieren die Schnitzel in einem schwarzen Smoking°!

Heimat *home* **berühmt** *famous* **Semmelbröselhülle** *bread crumb crust* **knusprig** *crisp* **Smoking** *tuxedo*

🔗 IM INTERNET

Suchen Sie Informationen über die Mensa an der Universität Wien. Was können Studenten essen? Was können Studenten trinken? Wie viel kostet das Essen?

Find out more at **vhlcentral.com**.

---

2 **Richtig oder falsch?** Korrigieren Sie die falschen Aussagen.

1. In deutschsprachigen Ländern gibt es viele internationale Restaurants.
2. Die beliebtesten internationalen Restaurants sind italienisch.
3. Das Restaurant Figlmüller ist ein sehr altes Restaurant in Wien.
4. Das Restaurant Figlmüller hat eine Spezialität: Apfelstrudel.
5. Fast 23% der Bevölkerung in Deutschland sind Ausländer.

3 **Eine Speisekarte** Schreiben Sie eine Speisekarte für ein Restaurant in Deutschland, Österreich oder der Schweiz. Geben Sie die Preise für die Speisen und die Getränke an.

BEISPIEL *Restaurant „Zur Post"*

Hauptspeisen		Nachtische	
Schweinebraten	6,90 €	*Obstsalat*	3,10 €
Pizza Marinara	5,50 €	*Tiramisu*	3,50 €

4B.1 The dative  Presentation

Startblock In **1B.1**, you learned that the direct object of a verb is always in the accusative case. When a verb has an indirect object, it is always in the dative case.

QUERVERWEIS

See **1A.3** and **1B.1** to review the use of the nominative and accusative case.

- An object in the dative case indicates *to whom* or *for whom* an action is performed.

Ich bringe **dem Lehrer** einen Apfel.
*I'm bringing **the teacher** an apple.*

Zeig **der Lehrerin** deine Arbeit.
*Show your work **to the teacher**.*

- Verbs that are frequently used with a dative object include **zeigen** (*to show*), **geben**, **bringen**, **empfehlen**, and **gehören** (*to belong to*). Note that the verbs **helfen** and **danken** also take a dative object, even though their English equivalents normally take a direct object.

Wir helfen **den Kindern**.
*We're helping (giving help to) **the kids**.*

Sie dankt **dem Kellner**.
*She's thanking (giving thanks to) **the waiter**.*

- The forms of the definite and indefinite articles that accompany dative nouns differ from the forms in the nominative or accusative case.

definite articles				
	masculine	**feminine**	**neuter**	**plural**
nominative	der Kellner	die Kellnerin	das Kind	die Kinder
accusative	den Kellner	die Kellnerin	das Kind	die Kinder
dative	dem Kellner	der Kellnerin	dem Kind	den Kindern

indefinite articles				
	masculine	**feminine**	**neuter**	**plural**
nominative	ein Kellner	eine Kellnerin	ein Kind	keine Kinder
accusative	einen Kellner	eine Kellnerin	ein Kind	keine Kinder
dative	einem Kellner	einer Kellnerin	einem Kind	keinen Kindern

Der Kellner bringt **der Frau** einen Salat.
*The waiter is bringing **the woman** a salad.*

Ich empfehle **einem Freund** das Restaurant.
*I'm recommending the restaurant **to a friend**.*

QUERVERWEIS

See **3A.1** to review the use of possessive adjectives.

- The endings for possessive adjectives are the same as the endings for the indefinite articles.

possessive adjectives				
	masculine	**feminine**	**neuter**	**plural**
nominative	mein Koch	meine Köchin	mein Kind	meine Kinder
accusative	meinen Koch	meine Köchin	mein Kind	meine Kinder
dative	meinem Koch	meiner Köchin	meinem Kind	meinen Kindern

Der Kellner bringt **meiner Frau** einen Salat.
*The waiter is bringing **my wife** a salad.*

Wir empfehlen unseren **Freunden** das Restaurant.
*We recommend the restaurant **to our friends**.*

- When using plural nouns in the dative case, add **-n** to any noun whose plural form does not already end in **-n** or **-s**.

nominative plural	dative plural
die Teller	den Teller**n**
die Esslöffel	den Esslöffel**n**
die Kaffees	den Kaffees
die Rechnungen	den Rechnungen

- A small number of singular masculine nouns also add the ending **-n** or **-en** in the accusative and dative cases. The **n**-nouns you have learned so far are: **der Architekt**, **der Journalist**, **der Junge**, **der Neffe**, and **der Student**.

  Nils backt **seinem Neffen** einen Apfelkuchen.
  *Nils is baking an apple pie **for his nephew**.*

  Ich schreibe **dem Journalisten** eine E-Mail.
  *I'm writing an e-mail **to the journalist**.*

- In the dative case, an adjective preceded by an **ein**-word or a **der**-word always ends in **-en**.

  Anna kauft **dem kleinen** Jungen ein Eis.
  *Anna is buying an ice cream for **the little** boy.*

  Ich gebe **meiner kleinen** Schwester eine Banane.
  *I'm giving **my little** sister a banana.*

- Adjectives in the dative that are not preceded by an article have endings similar to the definite article endings.

unpreceded adjective endings	masculine	feminine	neuter	plural
nominative	süß**er** Kuchen	süß**e** Melone	süß**es** Getränk	süß**e** Äpfel
accusative	süß**en** Kuchen	süß**e** Melone	süß**es** Getränk	süß**e** Äpfel
dative	süß**em** Kuchen	süß**er** Melone	süß**em** Getränk	süß**en** Äpfeln

  Ich biete **guten** Freunden immer gutes Essen an.
  *I always serve good food to **good** friends.*

  Die Lehrerin hilft **neuen** Studenten gern.
  *The teacher likes to help **new** students.*

- Use the dative question word **wem** to ask *to whom?*

nominative	accusative	dative
wer?	**wen?**	wem?

  Wem gibst du das Geschenk?
  ***To whom** are you giving the present?*

  Ich gebe **meiner Mutter** das Geschenk.
  *I'm giving the present **to my mother**.*

  Wem gehört diese Tasse?
  ***Who** does this cup belong **to**?*

  Sie gehört **meinem Opa**.
  *It belongs to **my grandpa**.*

QUERVERWEIS

See **3A.2** to review adjective agreement in the nominative and accusative case.

See **2A.2** to review question words.

ACHTUNG

In sentences with both direct and indirect objects, the dative object comes before the accusative object.

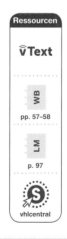

Ressourcen

v̂Text

WB
pp. 57–58

LM
p. 97

S
vhlcentral

Jetzt sind Sie dran! **Wählen Sie den richtigen Artikel.**

1. Mama dankt (der / dem) Kellner.
2. Ich gebe (dem / der) Lehrerin die Hausaufgaben.
3. Moritz gibt (seiner / seinem) Mutter ein Parfüm.
4. Die Lehrerin hilft (ihren / ihrem) Schüler mit der Grammatik.
5. Die Großmutter backt (ihrem / ihrer) Enkelkind einen Kuchen.
6. Ich schreibe (dem / der) Besitzer eine E-Mail.

Anwendung

1 **Was fehlt?** Ergänzen Sie die Sätze mit den richtigen Substantivformen im Dativ.

BEISPIEL deine Freundin: Kaufst du _deiner Freundin_ einen MP3-Player?

1. meine Partnerin: Ich zeige _____ die Hausaufgaben.
2. ihr Mann: Sie gibt _____ einen Kuss.
3. die Freunde: Er macht _____ ein leckeres Essen.
4. unser Opa: Ich schreibe _____ eine lange E-Mail.
5. die alte Frau: Er bringt _____ ein Mineralwasser.
6. die Kellnerin: Der Koch gibt _____ eine Tasse Tee.

2 **Pluralformen** Geben Sie die richtigen Pluralformen im Dativ an.

1. dem alten Hund: _____
2. seiner lieben Tante: _____
3. der netten Katze: _____
4. einem neugierigen Journalisten: _____
5. dem kleinen Mädchen: _____
6. keiner stolzen Frau: _____
7. dem mutigen Kind: _____
8. ihrem großen Neffen: _____
9. meinem faulen Bruder: _____

3 **Dativobjekte** Ergänzen Sie die Sätze mit der richtigen Form im Dativ.

1. Die Kellnerin empfiehlt _____ (meine Brüder) die Vorspeise.
2. _____ (Wer) bringst du die Flasche Apfelsaft?
3. Ich gebe _____ (die Kellnerin) ein Trinkgeld.
4. Der gute Student hilft _____ (schlechte Studenten) oft.
5. Du gibst _____ (ein schönes Mädchen) rote Rosen.
6. _____ (Wer) soll ich das Besteck geben?
7. Kannst du _____ (meine Mutter) einen Nachtisch empfehlen?
8. Ich zeige _____ (mein Freund) die Rechnung.
9. Die Kinder helfen _____ (ihre Eltern) gern.
10. Der Junge gibt _____ (die alten Hunde) Würstchen.

4 **Nettigkeiten** Bilden Sie Sätze.

BEISPIEL sie / der Kellner / ein Trinkgeld / geben
Sie geben dem Kellner ein Trinkgeld.

1. die Frau / ihre Mutter / ein Kuchen / geben
2. ich / der Hund / sein Essen / vorbereiten
3. der Schüler / die Lehrerin / eine Postkarte / schreiben
4. er / seine Tochter / eine Vorspeise / bestellen
5. die Köchin / das Kind / ein Brötchen / geben
6. meine Frau / die Oma / eine Beilage / mitbringen

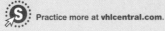
Practice more at **vhlcentral.com**.

Kommunikation

5 **Was für ein Chaos!** Ihr Haus ist ein totales Chaos. Fragen Sie Ihren Partner / Ihre Partnerin, wem die Sachen gehören, die im Haus herumliegen.

▶ **BEISPIEL**

S1: *Wem gehört der Pullover?*
S2: *Er gehört meiner Schwester.*

meine Eltern	die Köchin
eine Freundin	meine Schwester
der Kellner	ein Student

1. 2. 3.

4. 5. 6.

6 **Geschenke** Sehen Sie die Speisekarte auf Seite 164 an und erzählen Sie Ihrem Partner / Ihrer Partnerin, welche Gerichte Sie Ihrer Familie und Ihren Freunden empfehlen.

BEISPIEL meine Tante

S1: *Ich empfehle meiner Tante den Chef-Salat.*
Was empfiehlst du deiner Oma?
S2: *Ich empfehle meiner Oma einen kleinen*
Tomatensalat mit Mozzarella!

1. Mutter/Vater
2. Großeltern
3. Lehrer/Lehrerin
4. Cousin/Cousine

5. Onkel/Tante
6. bester Freund/beste Freundin
7. Bruder/Schwester
8. Kommilitonen

7 **Wem tust du einen Gefallen?** Beantworten Sie die Fragen von Ihrem Partner / Ihrer Partnerin.

BEISPIEL

S1: *Wem zeigst du dein Zeugnis?*
S2: *Ich zeige meinen Eltern mein Zeugnis. Und du?*

1. Wem schreibst du Postkarten im Sommer?
2. Wem kochst du ein Essen?
3. Wem kaufst du ein Buch?

4. Wem hilfst du bei den Hausaufgaben?
5. Wem stellst du deine Eltern vor?
6. Wem backst du einen Kuchen?

4B.2

Prepositions with the dative  Presentation

Startblock Certain prepositions are always followed by an object in the dative case.

Mein Vater kommt **aus der Türkei**.

Ich glaube, es ist alles okay **mit den beiden**.

QUERVERWEIS

See **3B.2** to review prepositions that take an object in the accusative case.

ACHTUNG

The prepositions **nach** and **zu** are also used in the set expressions **nach Hause** (*home*) and **zu Hause** (*at home*). **Ich gehe jetzt nach Hause. Er bleibt immer zu Hause.**

- Most dative prepositional phrases provide information about time and location.

prepositions with the dative			
aus	*from*	nach	*after; to*
außer	*except for*	seit	*since; for*
bei	*at; near; with*	von	*from*
mit	*with*	zu	*to; for; at*

Willst du **bei meinen Eltern** essen?
*Do you want to eat **at my parents' house**?*

Zum Geburtstag bekomme ich Geschenke.
*I get presents **on my birthday**.*

- Use **nach** before the names of countries or cities. Use **zu** with people, businesses, or other locations.

Wir fliegen morgen **nach Berlin**.
*We're flying **to Berlin** tomorrow.*

Gehst du **zur Bäckerei**?
*Are you going **to the bakery**?*

- The preposition **seit** is used with time expressions to indicate *since when* or *for how long* something has been taking place.

Seit wann wohnst du in Berlin?
***Since when** have you been living in Berlin?*

Ich wohne **seit einem Jahr** in Berlin.
*I've been living in Berlin **for one year**.*

- The prepositions **bei**, **von**, and **zu** can combine with the definite article **dem** to form contractions. The preposition **zu** also forms a contraction with the definite article **der**.

bei + dem = **beim**   zu + dem = **zum**
von + dem = **vom**   zu + der = **zur**

Wir kaufen oft **beim** Supermarkt ein.
*We often shop **at the** supermarket.*

Ich esse immer Eier **zum** Frühstück.
*I always have eggs **for** breakfast.*

Ressourcen

v̂Text

WB
pp. 59–60

LM
p. 98

vhlcentral

Jetzt sind Sie dran!   Wählen Sie die passenden Präpositionen.

1. Der beste Tisch ist (aus dem / beim) Fenster.
2. Wann fährst du (zum / mit dem) Supermarkt?
3. (Vom / Außer dem) Supermarkt gibt es hier keine Geschäfte.
4. Deine Familie kommt (mit / aus) den USA.
5. (Seit / Außer) zwei Jahren lerne ich Spanisch.
6. Ninas Freund fährt (nach der / zur) Universität.
7. Ich wohne (zu / bei) meinen Eltern.
8. Wir essen Pizza (mit / bei) Besteck.

Anwendung und Kommunikation

1 Was ist richtig? Wählen Sie die passenden Präpositionen.

BEISPIEL Wir wohnen (seit / um) fünf Jahren hier.

1. Daniel kommt (mit / aus) Hamburg.
2. Er studiert (bei / seit) sechs Semestern an der Uni Heidelberg.
3. Er wohnt (mit / von) drei Freunden zusammen.
4. Alle drei Monate fährt er (nach / zu) Hause zu seinen Eltern.
5. Seine Mutter ist immer extrem glücklich, wenn ihr Sohn (nach / zu) Hause ist.
6. Am Wochenende spielt er (aus / mit) seinem Vater Tennis.
7. (Außer / Aus) seinen Eltern besucht er auch seine Großeltern.
8. Daniel hat nächste Woche Geburtstag und er bekommt (nach / von) seinem Opa ein neues Auto.

2 Wer ist das? Setzen Sie die fehlenden Dativpräpositionen ein.

Christoph Waltz kommt (1) _____ Österreich. Seine Großmutter arbeitet als junge Frau als Schauspielerin (*actress*) (2) _____ einem Theater und (3) _____ dieser Großmutter hat er sein Talent. Waltz ist (4) _____ vielen Jahren als ein großartiger Schauspieler berühmt. Für seine Rollen in den Filmen *Inglourious Basterds* und *Django Unchained* gewinnt er zwei Oscars. Beide Filme sind (5) _____ Quentin Tarantino. Waltz wohnt (6) _____ seiner Frau in Hollywood, London und Berlin.

3 Seit wann? Seit wann macht Ihr Partner / Ihre Partnerin die folgenden Aktivitäten?

BEISPIEL heute Vorlesungen haben

S1: *Seit wann hast du heute Vorlesungen?*
S2: *Ich habe seit 10 Uhr Vorlesung. Und du?*

1. hier studieren
2. Deutsch lernen
3. Kaffee trinken
4. einen Computer haben
5. ein Handy haben
6. Auto fahren

4 Fotoalbum Sehen Sie die Fotos an und beantworten Sie die Fragen von Ihrem Partner / Ihrer Partnerin.

▶ **BEISPIEL**

S1: *Woher kommt Eriks Opa?*
S2: *Er kommt aus der Schweiz.*

1. Mit wem spricht Anna?

2. Wohin reisen Lena und Jasmin?

3. Wohin geht Annika?

4. Seit wann arbeitet Felix im Restaurant?

Wiederholung

1 Ankes Familie

Ankes Familie ist in einem Restaurant. Was bringt der Kellner den Familienmitgliedern (*family members*) zu trinken?

BEISPIEL die Schwester

S1: Was bringt der Kellner Ankes Schwester?
S2: Er bringt ihrer Schwester ein Glas Milch.

der Kaffee die Milch	das Mineralwasser der Orangensaft	das stille Wasser der Tee

1. der Onkel
2. die Eltern
3. der Bruder
4. die Oma
5. die Tante
6. der Opa

2 Der Koch

Fragen Sie den Koch, was er den Personen zum Essen macht. Wechseln Sie sich ab.

der Musiker / das Frühstück

BEISPIEL

S1: Herr Müller, was machen Sie dem Musiker zum Frühstück?
S2: Ich mache dem Musiker ein Schinkenbrot.

1. die Journalistin / das Abendessen

2. die Architektin / das Mittagessen

3. die Friseurin / das Mittagessen

4. der Geschäftsmann / das Abendessen

5. die Dozentin / das Abendessen

6. der Ingenieur / das Mittagessen

3 Wie schmeckt's?

Sagen Sie einem Partner / einer Partnerin, was die Personen essen und wie sie es finden.

BEISPIEL

S1: Wie findet die Frau die Erdbeeren?
S2: Sie sind der Frau zu süß.

fade	lecker	leicht	salzig	scharf	süß

1. der Mann

2. die Frau

3. das Mädchen

4. die Studenten

5. der Junge

6. die Kinder

4 Diskutieren und kombinieren

Sie sind Kellner / Kellnerin im Restaurant. Was sollen Sie den Gästen bringen? Fragen Sie Ihren Partner / Ihre Partnerin.

BEISPIEL

S1: Was braucht der junge Mann?
S2: Bring dem jungen Mann eine Serviette.
S1: Was braucht die alte Frau?
S2: Bring der alten Frau eine Gabel.

5 Arbeitsblatt

Sie bekommen von Ihrem Professor / Ihrer Professorin eine Liste mit diversen Aktivitäten. Suchen Sie Kommilitonen, die diese Aktivitäten machen.

BEISPIEL

S1: Isst du täglich Eier zum Frühstück?
S2: Ja, ich esse täglich Eier zum Frühstück.
OR
S1: Wohnst du bei deinen Eltern?
S2: Nein, ich wohne nicht bei meinen Eltern.

6 Wie lange?

Wie lange? Finden Sie vier Dinge heraus, die Ihr Partner / Ihre Partnerin gern macht. Fragen Sie ihn/sie, seit wann er/sie das schon macht.

S1: Was spielst du gern?
S2: Ich spiele gern Tennis.
S1: Seit wann spielst du Tennis?
S2: Seit drei Jahren.

7 Interview

Interview Führen Sie ein Interview mit einem Partner / einer Partnerin. Wenn eine Person fertig ist, tauschen Sie (exchange) Rollen.

S1: Bei wem wohnst du im Sommer?
S2: Ich wohne bei meinem Bruder.

1. Woher kommst du?
2. Seit wann studierst du an der Uni?
3. Gehst du gern zum Supermarkt einkaufen?
4. Mit wem telefonierst du gern?
5. Bei wem wohnst du im Sommer?
6. Wohin möchtest du reisen?

8 Poetische Präpositionen

Poetische Präpositionen Schreiben Sie mit einem Partner / einer Partnerin ein Gedicht aus fünf Sätzen. Außer der letzten Zeile (line) soll jede Zeile mit einer Dativ- oder Akkusativpräposition beginnen.

Mit dem Ball spiele ich.
Bei dem Metzger kaufen wir ein.
Durch die Stadt läuft die Mutter.
Außer Anton isst die Familie.
Der Hund schläft ein.

Mein Wör|ter|buch

Schreiben Sie noch fünf weitere Wörter in Ihr persönliches Wörterbuch zu den Themen **Lebensmittel** und **im Restaurant**.

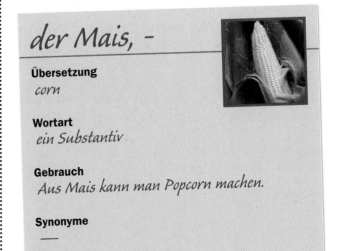

der Mais, -

Übersetzung
corn

Wortart
ein Substantiv

Gebrauch
Aus Mais kann man Popcorn machen.

Synonyme
—

Antonyme
—

Vocabulary Tools

Panorama Interactive Map

Österreich

Österreich in Zahlen

▶ **Fläche°:** *83.855 km² (Quadratkilometer) (60% der Fläche sind gebirgig°)*

▶ **Bevölkerung:** *8,2 Millionen Menschen*

▶ **9 Bundesländer°:** *Burgenland, Kärnten, Niederösterreich, Oberösterreich, Salzburg, Steiermark, Tirol, Vorarlberg, Wien*

▶ **Städte:** *Wien (1,7 Mio. Einwohner), Graz (264.000), Linz (190.000), Salzburg (148.000) und Innsbruck (121.000)*

▶ **Berge:** *der Großglockner (3.797 m), die Wildspitze (3.774 m)*

▶ **Flüsse°:** *die Donau, der Inn*

▶ **Währung°:** *der Euro (€) (seit 2002)*

▶ **Wichtige Industriezweige°:** *Banken, Tourismus*

▶ **Touristenattraktionen:** *Bergsport, Salzburger Festspiele°, Spanische Hofreitschule°, Wintertourismus*

Touristen können in Städten wie Wien und Salzburg viel Kultur genießen° oder in den Alpen Berg- und Wintersport betreiben. Für Firmen ist Österreich interessant, weil die Unternehmenssteuer° sehr niedrig° ist.

QUELLE: Österreichische Botschaft, Washington

Berühmte Österreicher

▶ **Maria Theresia,** *Kaiserin° (1717–1780)*

▶ **Wolfgang Amadeus Mozart,** *Komponist (1756–1791)*

▶ **Sigmund Freud,** *Neurologe (1856–1939)*

▶ **Gustav Klimt,** *Künstler° (1862–1918)*

▶ **Lise Meitner,** *Physikerin (1878–1968)*

▶ **Friedensreich Hundertwasser,** *Architekt (1928–2000)*

▶ **Elfriede Jelinek,** *Autorin (1946–)*

▶ **Falco,** *Musiker (1957–1998)*

Fläche surface area **gebirgig** mountainous **Bundesländer** states
Flüsse rivers **Währung** currency **Wichtige Industriezweige** Important
industries **Festspiele** festivals **Hofreitschule** Riding School
genießen enjoy **Unternehmenssteuer** business tax **niedrig** low
Kaiserin empress **Künstler** artist **Pfefferminzbonbons** peppermint candies
Geschmacksrichtung flavor **jedem** every **Lakritz** licorice **Köpfe** heads
Spendern dispensers

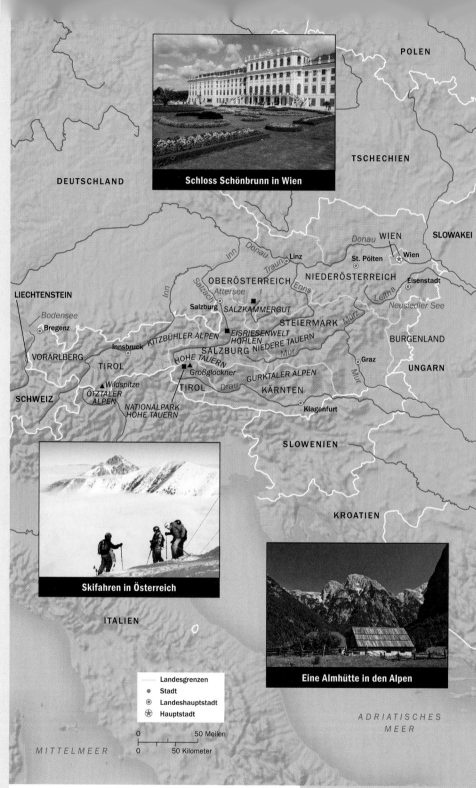

Schloss Schönbrunn in Wien

Skifahren in Österreich

Eine Almhütte in den Alpen

— Landesgrenzen
● Stadt
◉ Landeshauptstadt
✪ Hauptstadt

0   50 Meilen
0   50 Kilometer

Unglaublich, aber wahr!

Der Österreicher Eduard Haas III. fängt 1927 an, Pfefferminzbonbons° mit dem Namen PEZ zu verkaufen. Der Name PEZ kommt von der ersten Geschmacksrichtung°, PfeffErminZ. PEZ gibt es heute mit jedem° Geschmack, sogar Chlorophyll und Lakritz°! Seit 1952 gibt es lustige Köpfe° auf den Spendern° wie Mickey Mouse und Donald Duck.

Politik

Internationale Institutionen in Wien

Politisch ist Österreich ein neutrales Land. Es ist Mitglied° in der Europäischen Union, aber nicht in der NATO. Seit 1980 ist Wien einer von vier Hauptsitzen° der Vereinten Nationen°. Die anderen Hauptsitze sind New York, Genf und Nairobi. Andere internationale Organisationen in Wien sind die IAEA (Internationale Organisation für Atomenergie) und die OPEC.

Sport

Olympische Spiele

Olympische Spiele und Österreich bedeuten vor allem° Olympische Winterspiele und alpiner Skisport. 1964 und 1976 treffen sich° Sportler aus aller Welt zu den Olympischen Winterspielen in Innsbruck. Erfolgreiche° österreichische Olympioniken° sind Felix Gottwald (nordischer Kombinierer°) mit drei Gold-, einer Silber- und drei Bronzemedaillen. Der Skispringer° Thomas Morgenstern und der Skifahrer Toni Sailer gewinnen jeweils° drei Goldmedaillen. In alpinen Skidisziplinen gewinnen Österreicher mehr Medaillen als jedes andere Land der Welt (34 Gold-, 39 Silber- und 41 Bronzemedaillen).

Musik

Familie von Trapp in Amerika

Viele kennen° die Familie von Trapp aus dem Film *The Sound of Music*. Aber was passiert° mit der Familie nach der Emigration? 1939 emigriert die Familie mit nur vier Dollar in der Tasche° nach Amerika. Die von Trapps machen als „Trapp Family Singers" Karriere und kaufen 1942 eine Farm in Stowe, Vermont. Auch heute kann man die Farm als Gasthaus° besuchen — und man kann mit den von Trapps Weihnachten° feiern.

Architektur

Friedensreich Hundertwasser

Hundertwasser ist ein kontroverser österreichischer Architekt und Künstler. Er beginnt in den 50er Jahren in Österreich als Künstler mit revolutionären Ideen. Die Beziehung° zwischen Mensch und Natur ist ein zentrales Thema in seiner Kunst. Heute kann man seine Häuser in der ganzen Welt finden: in Magdeburg und Essen (Deutschland), in Napa Valley (USA), in Tel Aviv (Israel) und in Kawakawa (Neuseeland). Das Hundertwasserhaus in Wien ist ein Touristenmagnet und auch die Fassade der Müllverbrennungsanlage° Spittelau ist sehr berühmt.

🔊 IM INTERNET

1. Wer sind die besten österreichischen Frauen bei Olympischen Spielen?
2. Was bedeuten dem Architekten Hundertwasser die Ideen Fensterrecht, Baummieter und Spiralhaus?

Find out more at **vhlcentral.com**.

Mitglied *member* **Hauptsitzen** *head offices* **Vereinten Nationen** *United Nations* **vor allem** *especially* **treffen sich** *meet* **Erfolgreiche** *Successful* **Olympioniken** *Olympic champions* **nordischer Kombinierer** *Nordic combined skier* **Skispringer** *ski jumper* **jeweils** *each* **kennen** *know* **passiert** *happens* **Tasche** *pocket* **Gasthaus** *inn* **Weihnachten** *Christmas* **Beziehung** *relationship* **Müllverbrennungsanlage** *waste incineration plant*

🔊 **Was haben Sie gelernt?** Ergänzen Sie die Sätze.

1. Der Name _____ kommt von Pfefferminz.
2. Seit _____ gibt es lustige Köpfe auf den PEZ-Spendern.
3. Offiziell ist Österreich ein _____ Land.
4. Wien ist seit _____ einer von vier Hauptsitzen der Vereinten Nationen.
5. 1939 emigriert die Familie _____ nach Amerika.
6. Die Familie von Trapp kauft 1942 eine Farm in _____ in Vermont.
7. 1964 und _____ sind die Olympischen Winterspiele in Innsbruck.
8. In alpinen Skidisziplinen gewinnen die Österreicher _____ Medaillen als jedes andere Land.
9. Hundertwasser ist ein kontroverser österreichischer _____ und Künstler.
10. Hundertwassers Häuser kann man in Österreich, Deutschland, den USA, Israel und _____ finden.

 Practice more at **vhlcentral.com**.

Lesen  Audio: Reading

Vor dem Lesen

Textart Was für ein Text ist das? Erklären Sie Ihre Antwort einem Partner / einer Partnerin.

eine E-Mail	ein Blog
eine Broschüre	ein Memo
eine Einkaufsliste	ein Artikel

Auf einen Blick Sehen Sie sich mit einem Partner / einer Partnerin den Text an.

A. Schreiben Sie drei Aktivitäten auf, die Sie im Text finden.

_____

_____

_____

B. Welche Lehnwörter (loan words) und Kognate können Sie im Text finden? Diskutieren Sie Ihre Antworten.

_____   _____

_____   _____

_____   _____

http://www.die-ersten-monate-in-graz.com

Die ersten Monate in Graz

über mich   Hauptseite   Fotos   Kontakt

Besuch!   12. Oktober

Das Kunsthaus

Am Freitag besuchen mich meine Freunde Lukas, Jan und Paul für ein Wochenende in Graz. Super! Vier Jahre lang haben wir zusammen in Wien studiert. Jetzt sehen wir uns nur selten. Jan wohnt in Linz, Lukas arbeitet in Wien und Paul studiert immer noch. Alle können bei mir übernachten. Ich habe ein Gästezimmer° und zwei Sofas im Wohnzimmer°. Das funktioniert prima! Schlafen werden wir an diesem Wochenende ohnehin° nicht! Am Freitag geht's erstmal in die Hopfenlaube, eine tolle Konzerthalle, für eine Jamsession. Da ist die Musik immer toll und wir können über die guten alten Zeiten reden. Am Samstag geht's dann ins Café Schwalbennest frühstücken. Nach der langen Nacht ist ein guter Brunch extrem wichtig°. Das Café ist ganz in der Nähe° meiner Wohnung°. Anschließend° gehen wir bei schönem Wetter° eine Runde im Volksgarten Inlineskates fahren. Der Volksgarten ist total

Gästezimmer guest bedroom **Wohnzimmer** living room **ohnehin** anyhow
wichtig important **in der Nähe** near to **Wohnung** apartment
Anschließend Afterwards **bei schönem Wetter** in nice weather

Suche

schön und sehr zentral gelegen°. Später können wir auch noch die Treppen° zum Grazer Schlossberg hochklettern°. Vom Uhrturm kann man die ganze Stadt super sehen inklusive der wunderschönen Innenstadt. Und was machen wir bei Regen°? Dann können wir das Kunsthaus Graz besuchen. Dort gibt es immer moderne Ausstellungen°. Ich freue mich schon auf° das Wochenende und auf meine alten Freunde.

Archiv

▶ Prüfungsstress ☹
▶ Glücklich!
▶ Die Uni
▶ Es ist schon wieder° Montag…
▶ September
▶ August
▶ Juli
▶ Juni
▶ Mai
▶ April
▶ März

Der Uhrturm

Nach dem Lesen

Das richtige Wort Ergänzen Sie die Aussagen mit den richtigen Informationen.

1. Am Freitag besuchen drei Freunde die Stadt _____ für ein Wochenende.
2. Am _____ gehen die Freunde in die Hopfenlaube.
3. Am Samstag essen die Freunde _____ im Café Schwalbennest.
4. Anschließend gehen sie Inlineskates fahren im _____.
5. Später können sie die _____ zum Grazer Schlossberg hochklettern.
6. Bei Regen besuchen sie _____.

Informationen Schreiben Sie die richtigen Antworten. Schreiben Sie ganze Sätze.

> **BEISPIEL** Wo wohnt Lukas?
> *Lukas wohnt in Wien.*

1. Wer besucht Graz am Wochenende?

   _____

2. Warum wollen die Freunde in die Hopfenlaube gehen?

   _____

3. Wann frühstücken die Freunde im Café Schwalbennest?

   _____

4. Was machen die Freunde im Volksgarten?

   _____

5. Was kann man vom Uhrturm sehen?

   _____

6. Was kann man im Kunsthaus Graz sehen?

   _____

Ihre Heimatstadt Stellen Sie einem Partner / einer Partnerin Fragen: Was kann oder soll man in Ihrer Heimatstadt (*hometown*) machen?

> **BEISPIEL**
> **S1:** *Was muss man in deiner Heimatstadt sehen?*
> **S2:** *In meiner Heimatstadt muss man das Kunstmuseum sehen.*
> **S1:** *Wo kann man gut essen?*

zentral gelegen *centrally located* **Treppen** *stairs* **hochklettern** *to climb up* **Regen** *rain* **Ausstellungen** *exhibits* **freue mich…auf** *look forward to* **schon wieder** *once again*

Hören

Vorbereitung

Schauen Sie sich das Foto an. Wer ist auf dem Foto? Wo sind sie? Was machen sie?

Zuhören

 Hören Sie sich den Podcast mit Andrea und der Reporterin an. Lesen Sie dann die Liste. Hören Sie sich den Podcast ein zweites Mal an und markieren Sie die Zutaten, die Sie hören.

Pilze	Nudeln
Kartoffel	Zwiebeln
Butter	Salz
Milch	Pfirsiche
Tomaten	Paprika
Schinken	Pfeffer
Knoblauch	Eier

Verständnis

Eine Zusammenfassung Ergänzen Sie die Zusammenfassung (*summary*) von dem Podcast mit Wörtern von der Liste.

den Schinken	die Nudeln	eine Reporterin
findet	frische Pilze	salzig
lecker	einen Podcast	schmeckt
Pfeffer	probieren	Zwiebeln

1. Wir hören _____ mit der Köchin Andrea.
2. In der Küche sind Andrea und _____.
3. Im Moment kann man auf dem Markt _____ kaufen.
4. Heute kocht Andrea Nudeln mit Pfifferlingen (*chanterelles*). Sie sind sehr _____.
5. Die Pfifferlinge passen gut zum Schinken — er ist ziemlich _____.
6. Man braucht auch Vollmilch, Butter und _____.
7. Erst kocht Andrea _____.
8. Dann brät sie _____ mit Butter.
9. Am Ende kommen noch Salz und _____ dazu.
10. Die Reporterin _____ das Gericht lecker!

Und Sie? Bereiten Sie mit einem Partner / einer Partnerin ein Rezept für eine Pizza vor. Welche Zutaten sollen auf die Pizza?

BEISPIEL

S1: *Was soll alles auf die Pizza?*
S2: *Pilze, Zwiebeln, Tomaten...*

Schreiben

Adding details

How can you make your writing more informative or more interesting? You can add details by answering the "W" questions: Who? What? When? Where? Why? The answers to these questions will provide useful information that can be incorporated into your writing. Here are some useful question words that you have already learned.

Wer?	Wo?
Was?	Warum?
Wann?	Wie?

Compare these two statements.

„Ich muss einkaufen gehen."

„Nach der Schule muss ich Eier kaufen. Mit den Eiern kann ich eine leckere Omelette kochen."

While both statements give the same basic information (the writer needs to go shopping), the details provided in the second statement are much more informative.

Thema

✏ Grüße nach Salzburg

Sie entschließen sich (*decide*), ein Jahr in Österreich zu verbringen und bei einer Familie zu leben. Schreiben Sie eine Karte an Ihre Gastfamilie (*host family*). Sagen Sie der Familie, was Sie gern sehen wollen und was Sie machen wollen. Schreiben Sie fünf Sätze. Nennen Sie (*Give*) Details. Beantworten Sie dabei Fragen mit **wer?**, **was?**, **wo?**, **wie?** und **wann?**

Liebe Gastfamilie, bald komme ich nach Salzburg. Dann können wir zusammen den Uhrturm besuchen…

Lektion 4A

Obst und Gemüse

die Ananas, - *pineapple*
der Apfel, ⁝ *apple*
die Artischocke, -n *artichoke*
die Aubergine, -n *eggplant*
die Banane, -n *banana*
die Birne, -n *pear*
die grüne Bohne (*pl.* die grünen
  Bohnen) *green bean*
die Erdbeere, -n *strawberry*
die Himbeere, -n *raspberry*
die Karotte, -n *carrot*
die Kartoffel, -n *potato*
der Knoblauch *garlic*
die Melone, -n *melon*
die Orange, -n *orange*
die grüne Paprika (*pl.* die grünen
  Paprika) *green pepper*
die rote Paprika (*pl.* die roten
  Paprika) *red pepper*
der Pfirsich, -e *peach*
der Pilz, -e *mushroom*
der Salat, -e *lettuce; salad*
die Tomate, -n *tomato*
die Traube, -n *grape*
die Zwiebel, -n *onion*

Geschäfte

die Bäckerei, -en *bakery*
die Eisdiele, -n *ice cream shop*
das Feinkostgeschäft, -e *delicatessen*
das Fischgeschäft, -e *fish store*
die Konditorei, -en *pastry shop*
das Lebensmittelgeschäft, -e
  grocery store
der Markt, ⁝e *market*
die Metzgerei, -en *butcher shop*
der Supermarkt, ⁝e *supermarket*
einkaufen gehen *to go shopping*
verkaufen *to sell*

Essen

das Brot, -e *bread*
das Brötchen, - *roll*
die Butter *butter*
das Ei, -er *egg*
der Joghurt, -s *yogurt*
der Käse, - *cheese*
der Kuchen, - *cake; pie*
die Marmelade, -n *jam*
das Öl, -e *oil*
das Olivenöl, -e *olive oil*
die Pasta *pasta*
der Reis *rice*
das Rezept, -e *recipe*
die Zutat, -en *ingredient*

Fleisch und Fisch

die Garnele, -n *shrimp*
das Hähnchen, - *chicken*
die Meeresfrüchte (*pl.*) *seafood*
das Rindfleisch *beef*
der Schinken, - *ham*
das Schweinefleisch *pork*
der Thunfisch *tuna*
das Würstchen, - *sausage*

Ausdrücke

mögen *to like*

im Restaurant

der Pfeffer *pepper*
bestellen *to order*

....

Adverbs *See p. 150.*
Separable and inseparable prefix
  verbs *See p. 156.*

Lektion 4B

im Restaurant

die Beilage, -n *side dish*
das Besteck *silverware*
der Esslöffel, - *soup spoon*
die Flasche, -n *bottle*
die Gabel, -n *fork*
der erste/zweite Gang, ⁝ *first/second
  course*
das Glas, ⁝er *glass*
das Gericht, -e *dish*
die Hauptspeise, -n *main course*
der Kellner, - / die Kellnerin,
  -nen *waiter / waitress*
der Koch, ⁝e / die Köchin, -nen *cook*
das Messer, - *knife*
der Nachtisch, -e *dessert*
die Rechnung, -en *check*
das Salz *salt*
die Serviette, -n *napkin*
die Speisekarte, -n *menu*
die Suppe, -n *soup*
die Tasse, -n *cup*
der Teelöffel, - *teaspoon*
der Teller, - *plate*
die Tischdecke, -n *tablecloth*
das Trinkgeld *tip*
die Vorspeise, -n *appetizer*
schmecken *to taste*

Mahlzeiten

das Abendessen *dinner*
das Frühstück *breakfast*
das Mittagessen *lunch*
der Snack, -s *snack*

Getränke

das Bier *beer*
der Kaffee *coffee*
die Milch *milk*
das Mineralwasser *sparkling water*
der Saft, ⁝e *juice*
der Tee *tea*
das stille Wasser *still water*
der Wein *wine*

Essen beschreiben

der Geschmack, ⁝e *flavor; taste*
fade *bland*
lecker *delicious*
leicht *light*
salzig *salty*
scharf *spicy*
schwer *rich, heavy*
süß *sweet*

Ausdrücke

Ich hätte gern(e)... / Ich möchte
  I would like...
auf Diät sein *to be on a diet*
hausgemacht *homemade*

....

Dative articles and possessive
  adjectives *See pp. 170–171.*
Dative prepositions *See p. 174.*

Appendix A

Appendix B

Appendix C

die Welt

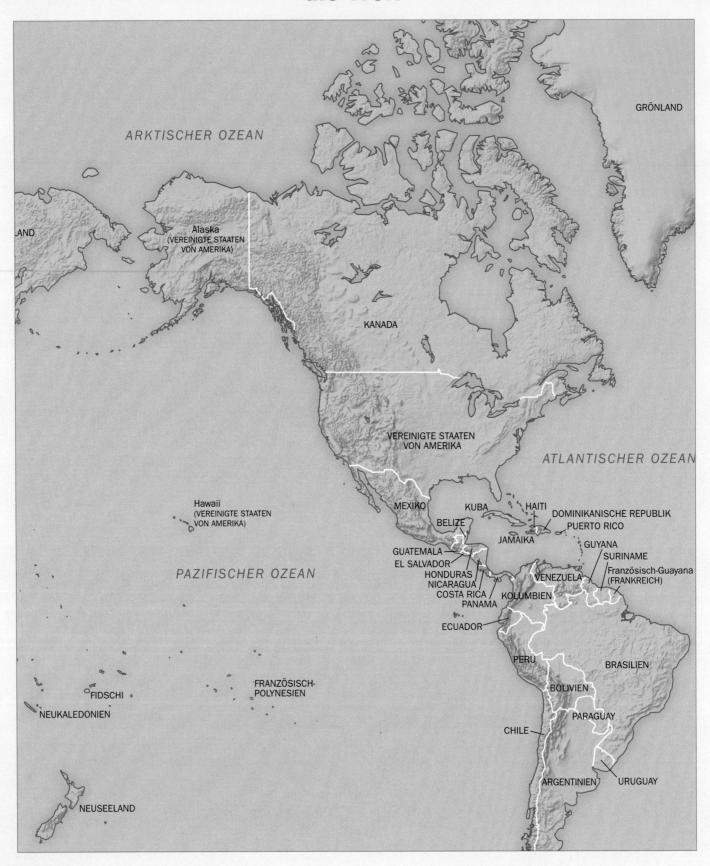

GRÖNLAND

ARKTISCHER OZEAN

...LAND

Alaska
(VEREINIGTE STAATEN
VON AMERIKA)

KANADA

VEREINIGTE STAATEN
VON AMERIKA

ATLANTISCHER OZEAN

Hawaii
(VEREINIGTE STAATEN
VON AMERIKA)

MEXIKO

KUBA
HAITI
DOMINIKANISCHE REPUBLIK
PUERTO RICO

BELIZE
JAMAIKA

PAZIFISCHER OZEAN

GUATEMALA
EL SALVADOR
HONDURAS
NICARAGUA
COSTA RICA
PANAMA

GUYANA
SURINAME
Französisch-Guayana
(FRANKREICH)

VENEZUELA

KOLUMBIEN

ECUADOR

PERU

BRASILIEN

BOLIVIEN

FRANZÖSISCH-
POLYNESIEN

FIDSCHI

PARAGUAY

NEUKALEDONIEN

CHILE

ARGENTINIEN
URUGUAY

NEUSEELAND

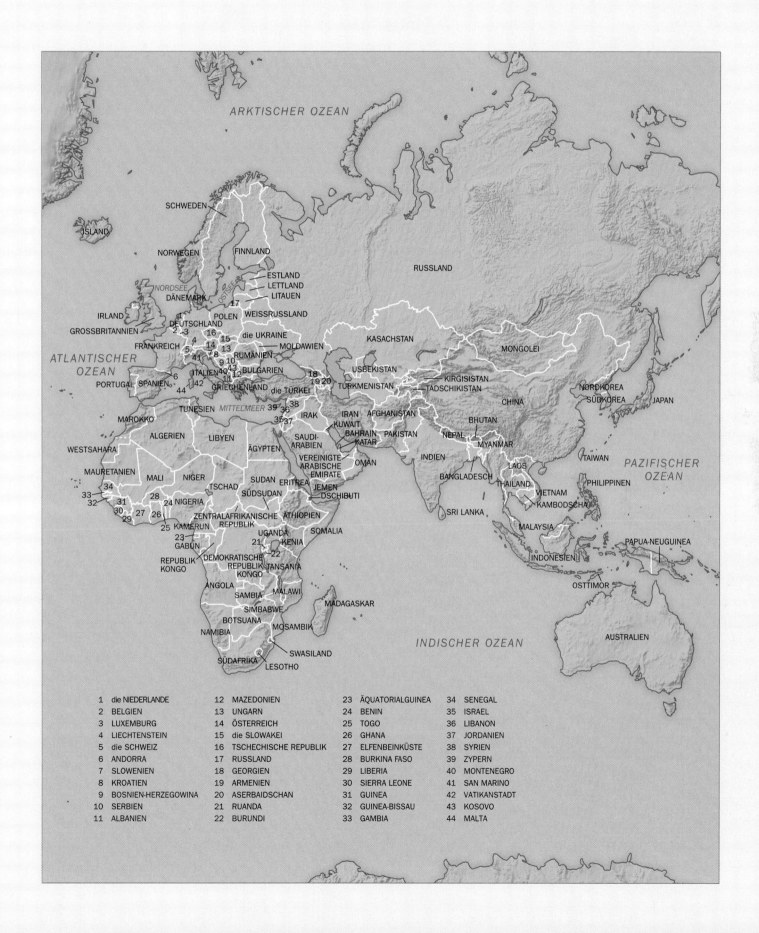

ARKTISCHER OZEAN

ISLAND

SCHWEDEN

NORWEGEN   FINNLAND

RUSSLAND

NORDSEE

DÄNEMARK   ESTLAND
                  LETTLAND
                  LITAUEN

IRLAND

GROSSBRITANNIEN   POLEN   WEISSRUSSLAND
                  DEUTSCHLAND

FRANKREICH   die UKRAINE   KASACHSTAN

ATLANTISCHER   MOLDAWIEN   MONGOLEI
OZEAN   RUMÄNIEN

                                       USBEKISTAN   NORDKOREA
ITALIEN   BULGARIEN   SÜDKOREA
PORTUGAL SPANIEN   die TÜRKEI   KIRGISISTAN   JAPAN
                  GRIECHENLAND   TADSCHIKISTAN
                                       TURKMENISTAN   CHINA

                  TUNESIEN MITTELMEER   PAZIFISCHER
                                       IRAK   IRAN   AFGHANISTAN   OZEAN
MAROKKO   BHUTAN
                                       KUWAIT   NEPAL   TAIWAN
          ALGERIEN   LIBYEN   ÄGYPTEN   BAHRAIN PAKISTAN   MYANMAR
                                  SAUDI-   KATAR
WESTSAHARA   ARABIEN   INDIEN
                                       VEREINIGTE   LAOS
MAURETANIEN MALI   NIGER   ARABISCHE   OMAN   BANGLADESCH   THAILAND PHILIPPINEN
                        TSCHAD   EMIRATE   VIETNAM
                  SUDAN ERITREA   JEMEN   SRI LANKA   KAMBODSCHA
NIGERIA SÜDSUDAN   DSCHIBUTI
                                                                                         MALAYSIA
ZENTRALAFRIKANISCHE ÄTHIOPIEN   PAPUA-NEUGUINEA
KAMERUN REPUBLIK   INDONESIEN
          UGANDA   OSTTIMOR
GABUN   KENIA
          DEMOKRATISCHE SOMALIA
REPUBLIK REPUBLIK
KONGO   KONGO   TANSANIA

ANGOLA
          SAMBIA   MALAWI
          SIMBABWE   MADAGASKAR

          BOTSUANA
NAMIBIA   MOSAMBIK   INDISCHER OZEAN   AUSTRALIEN

SÜDAFRIKA SWASILAND
           LESOTHO

1	die NIEDERLANDE	12	MAZEDONIEN	23	ÄQUATORIALGUINEA	34	SENEGAL
2	BELGIEN	13	UNGARN	24	BENIN	35	ISRAEL
3	LUXEMBURG	14	ÖSTERREICH	25	TOGO	36	LIBANON
4	LIECHTENSTEIN	15	die SLOWAKEI	26	GHANA	37	JORDANIEN
5	die SCHWEIZ	16	TSCHECHISCHE REPUBLIK	27	ELFENBEINKÜSTE	38	SYRIEN
6	ANDORRA	17	RUSSLAND	28	BURKINA FASO	39	ZYPERN
7	SLOWENIEN	18	GEORGIEN	29	LIBERIA	40	MONTENEGRO
8	KROATIEN	19	ARMENIEN	30	SIERRA LEONE	41	SAN MARINO
9	BOSNIEN-HERZEGOWINA	20	ASERBAIDSCHAN	31	GUINEA	42	VATIKANSTADT
10	SERBIEN	21	RUANDA	32	GUINEA-BISSAU	43	KOSOVO
11	ALBANIEN	22	BURUNDI	33	GAMBIA	44	MALTA

Europa

Länder, in denen Deutsch eine Amtssprache ist

BARENTSSEE

ISLAND
Reykjavik

EUROPÄISCHES NORDMEER

SCHWEDEN
FINNLAND
Helsinki
NORWEGEN
Stockholm
Tallinn
ESTLAND
Oslo
Riga
LETTLAND
Moskau
RUSSLAND

NORDSEE
DÄNEMARK
OSTSEE
LITAUEN
Vilnius
Minsk
Kopenhagen
RUSSLAND
WEISSRUSSLAND

ÖSTERREICH
LIECHTENSTEIN
Vaduz
die SCHWEIZ

Dublin
IRLAND
die NIEDERLANDE
Berlin
Warschau
GROSS-BRITANNIEN
Amsterdam
London
DEUTSCHLAND
POLEN
Kiew
Brüssel
die SLOWAKEI
die UKRAINE
LUXEMBURG
BELGIEN
Luxemburg
Prag
Paris
TSCHECHISCHE REPUBLIK
Bratislava
MOLDAWIEN
Kischinau
LIECHTENSTEIN
Wien
FRANKREICH
Bern Vaduz
ÖSTERREICH
Budapest
ATLANTISCHER OZEAN
die SCHWEIZ
SLOWENIEN
UNGARN
RUMÄNIEN
SCHWARZES MEER
Ljubljana
Zagreb
Belgrad
Bukarest
ITALIEN
KROATIEN
Monaco
BOSNIEN HERZEGOWINA
SERBIEN
KOSOVO
PORTUGAL
Andorra la Vella
SAN MARINO
Sarajevo
Pristina
BULGARIEN
MONACO
MONTENEGRO
Sofia
Ankara
ANDORRA
Rom
Podgorica
Skopje
Madrid
Korsika
Tirana
MAZEDONIEN
die TÜRKEI
Lissabon
VATIKANSTADT
ALBANIEN
SPANIEN
GRIECHENLAND
Sardinien
Athen
Nicosia
Balearische Inseln
Sizilien
Kreta
ZYPERN
Algier
Tunis
Rabat
Valletta MALTA
MITTELMEER
MAROKKO
TUNESIEN
Tripolis
Kairo
ALGERIEN
LIBYEN
ÄGYPTEN

0   500 Meilen
0   500 Kilometer

Deutschland

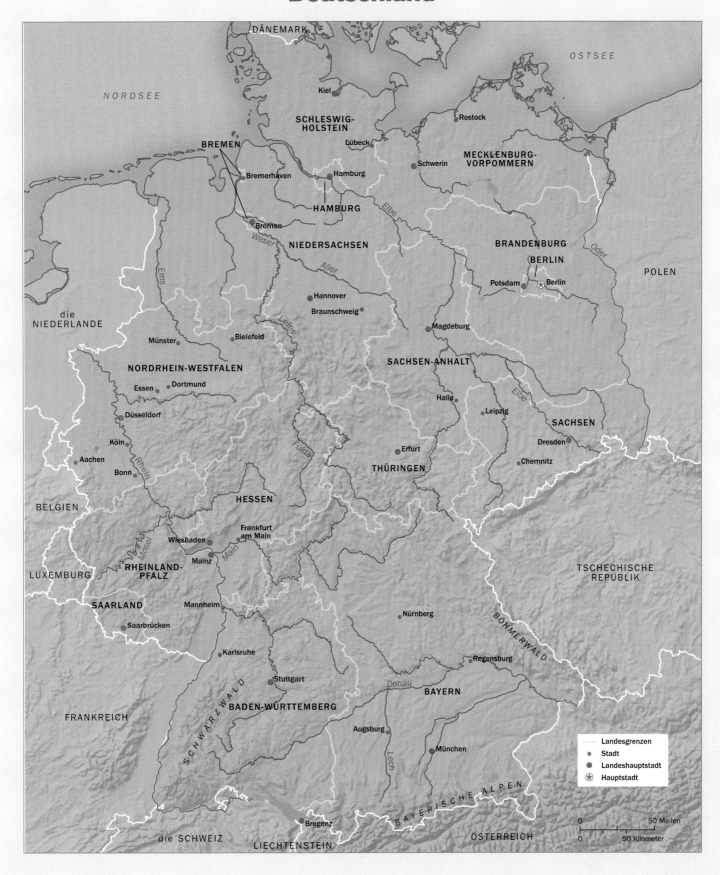

Österreich

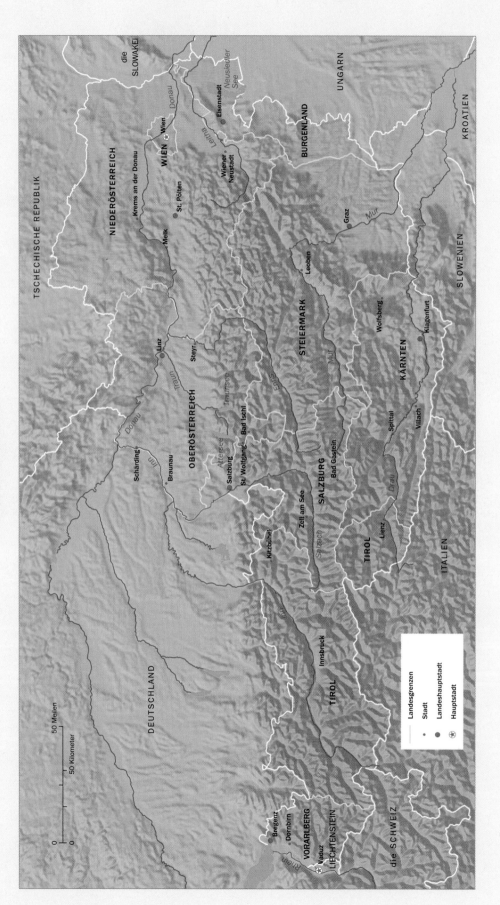

Liechtenstein

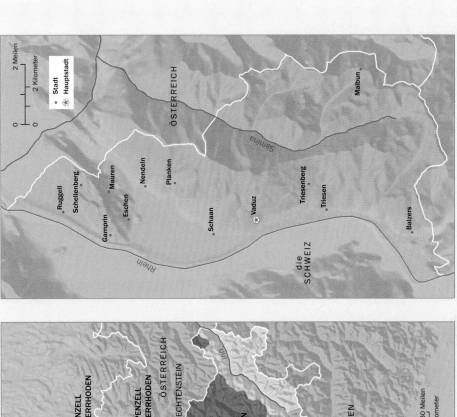

die Schweiz

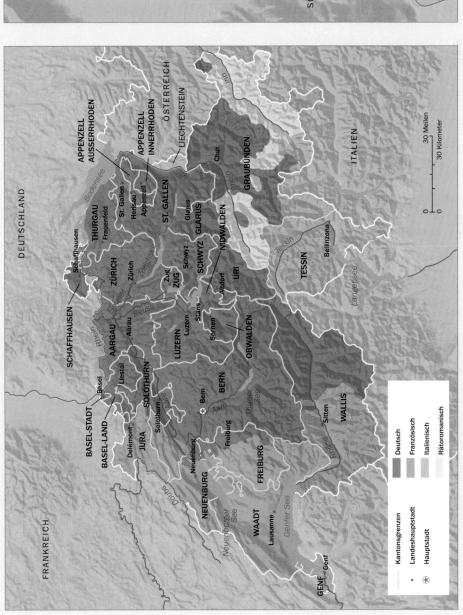

Declension of articles

definite articles			
	masculine	**feminine**	**neuter**	**plural**
nominative	der	die	das	die
accusative	den	die	das	die
dative	dem	der	dem	den
genitive	des	der	des	der

der-words			
	masculine	**feminine**	**neuter**	**plural**
nominative	dieser	diese	dieses	diese
accusative	diesen	diese	dieses	diese
dative	diesem	dieser	diesem	diesen
genitive	dieses	dieser	dieses	dieser

indefinite articles			
	masculine	**feminine**	**neuter**	**plural**
nominative	ein	eine	ein	-
accusative	einen	eine	ein	-
dative	einem	einer	einem	-
genitive	eines	einer	eines	-

ein-words			
	masculine	**feminine**	**neuter**	**plural**
nominative	mein	meine	mein	meine
accusative	meinen	meine	mein	meine
dative	meinem	meiner	meinem	meinen
genitive	meines	meiner	meines	meiner

Declension of nouns and adjectives

nouns and adjectives with *der*-words			
	masculine	**feminine**	**neuter**	**plural**
nominative	der gute Rat	die gute Landschaft	das gute Brot	die guten Freunde
accusative	den guten Rat	die gute Landschaft	das gute Brot	die guten Freunde
dative	dem guten Rat	der guten Landschaft	dem guten Brot	den guten Freunden
genitive	des guten Rates	der guten Landschaft	des guten Brotes	der guten Freunde

nouns and adjectives with *ein*-words			
	masculine	**feminine**	**neuter**	**plural**
nominative	ein guter Rat	eine gute Landschaft	ein gutes Brot	meine guten Freunde
accusative	einen guten Rat	eine gute Landschaft	ein gutes Brot	meine guten Freunde
dative	einem guten Rat	einer guten Landschaft	einem guten Brot	meinen guten Freunden
genitive	eines guten Rates	einer guten Landschaft	eines guten Brotes	meiner guten Freunde

unpreceded adjectives			
	masculine	**feminine**	**neuter**	**plural**
nominative	guter Rat	gute Landschaft	gutes Brot	gute Freunde
accusative	guten Rat	gute Landschaft	gutes Brot	gute Freunde
dative	gutem Rat	guter Landschaft	gutem Brot	guten Freunden
genitive	guten Rates	guter Landschaft	guten Brotes	guter Freunde

Declension of pronouns

personal pronouns									
nominative	ich	du	Sie	er	sie	es	wir	ihr	Sie	sie
accusative	mich	dich	Sie	ihn	sie	es	uns	euch	Sie	sie
accusative reflexive	mich	dich	sich	sich	sich	sich	uns	euch	sich	sich
dative	mir	dir	Ihnen	ihm	ihr	ihm	uns	euch	Ihnen	ihnen
dative reflexive	mir	dir	sich	sich	sich	sich	uns	euch	sich	sich

Glossary of Grammatical Terms

ADJECTIVE Words that describe people, places, or things. An attributive adjective comes before the noun it modifies and takes an ending that matches the gender and case of the noun. A predicate adjective comes after the verb **sein**, **werden**, or **bleiben** and describes the noun that is the subject of the sentence. Predicate adjectives take no additional endings.

Thomas hat eine sehr **gute** Stelle gefunden.
*Thomas found a really **good** job.*

Hast du mein **kleines** Adressbuch gesehen?
*Have you seen my **little** address book?*

Mein Bruder ist **klein**.
*My brother is **short**.*

Deine Schwester wird **groß**.
*Your sister is getting **tall**.*

Possessive adjectives Words that are placed before a noun to indicate ownership or belonging. Each personal pronoun has a corresponding possessive adjective. Possessive adjectives take the same endings as the indefinite article **ein**.

Meine Schwester ist hier.
My sister is here.

Wo ist **dein** Vater?
*Where is **your** father?*

ADVERB Words or phrases that modify a verb, an adjective, or another adverb. Adverbs and adverbial phrases describe *when*, *how*, or *where* an action takes place.

Der Kuchen ist **fast** fertig.
*The cake is **almost** ready.*

Du isst **viel zu** schnell.
*You eat **much too** quickly.*

ARTICLE A word that precedes a noun and indicates its gender, number, and case.

Definite article Equivalent to *the* in English. Its form indicates the gender and case of the noun, and whether it is singular or plural.

der Tisch (*m. s.*)
the table
die Tische (*m. pl.*)
the tables
die Tür (*f. s.*)
the door

die Türen (*f. pl.*)
the doors
das Fenster (*n. s.*)
the window
die Fenster (*n. pl.*)
the windows

Indefinite article Corresponds to *a* or *an* in English. It precedes the noun and matches its gender and case. There is no plural indefinite article in German.

ein Tisch (*m.*)
a table
eine Tür (*f.*)
a door

ein Fenster (*n.*)
a window

CASE There are four cases in German. The case indicates the function of each noun in a sentence. The case of a noun determines the form of the definite or indefinite article that precedes the noun, the form of any adjectives that modify the noun, and the form of the pronoun that can replace the noun.

Nominativ (*nominative*): **Der Professor** ist alt.
The professor is old.

Akkusativ (*accusative*): Ich verstehe **den Professor**.
I understand the professor.

Dativ (*dative*): Der Assistent zeigt **dem Professor** den neuen Computer.
The assistant is showing the professor the new computer.

Genitiv (*genitive*): Das ist der Assistent **des Professors**.
This is the professor's assistant.

The nominative case The grammatical subject of a sentence is always in the nominative case. The nominative case is also used for nouns that follow a form of **sein**, **werden**, or **bleiben**. In German dictionaries, nouns, pronouns, and numbers are always listed in their nominative form.

Das ist **eine gute Idee.**
*That's **a good idea.***

Die Kinder schlafen.
***The kids** are sleeping.*

The accusative case A noun that functions as a direct object is in the accusative case.

Der Lehrer hat **den Stift**.
*The teacher has **the pen**.*

Ich kaufe **einen Tisch**.
*I'm going to buy **a table**.*

Sie öffnet **die Tür**.
*She's opening **the door**.*

Ich habe **ein Problem**.
*I have **a problem**.*

The dative case An object in the dative case indicates to whom or for whom an action is performed.

Ich bringe **dem Lehrer** einen Apfel.
*I'm bringing **the teacher** an apple.*

Zeig **der Professorin** deine Arbeit.
*Show your work **to the professor**.*

The genitive case A noun in the genitive case modifies another noun. The genitive case indicates ownership or a close relationship between the genitive noun and the noun it modifies, which may be a subject or an object.

Thorsten hat die Rede **des Bundespräsidenten** heruntergeladen.
*Thorsten downloaded **the president's** speech.*

Das Mikrofon **der Professorin** funktioniert nicht.
***The professor's** microphone doesn't work.*

CLAUSE A group of words that contains both a conjugated verb and a subject, either expressed or implied.

Main (or independent) clause A clause that can stand alone as a complete sentence.

Ich bezahle immer bar, weil ich keine Kreditkarte habe.
I always pay cash, because I don't have a credit card.

Subordinate clause A subordinate clause explains how, when, why, or under what circumstances the action in the main clause occurs. The conjugated verb of a subordinate clause is placed at the end of that clause.

Ich lese die Zeitung, **wenn** ich Zeit **habe**.
*I read the newspaper **when** I **have** the time.*

COMPARATIVE The form of an adjective or adverb that compares two or more people or things.

Meine Geschwister sind alle **älter** als ich.
*My siblings are all **older** than I am.*

Die Fahrt dauert mit dem Auto **länger** als mit dem Zug.
*The trip takes **longer** by car than by train.*

CONJUNCTION A word used to connect words, clauses, or phrases.

Coordinating conjunctions Words that combine two related sentences, words, or phrases into a single sentence. There are five coordinating conjunctions in German: **aber** (*but*), **denn** (*because; since*), **oder** (*or*), **sondern** (*but, rather*), und (*and*). All other conjunctions are subordinating.

Ich möchte eine große Küche, **denn** ich koche gern.
*I want a big kitchen, **because** I like to cook.*

Lola braucht einen Schrank **oder** eine Kommode.
*Lola needs a closet **or** a dresser.*

Subordinating conjunctions Words used to combine a subordinate clause with a main clause.

Ich lese die Zeitung, **wenn** ich Zeit **habe**.
*I read the newspaper **when** I **have** the time.*

DEMONSTRATIVE Pronouns or adjectives that refer to something or someone that has already been mentioned, or that point out a specific person or thing.

Ist Greta online? –Ja, **die** schreibt eine E-Mail.
*Is Greta online? –Yes, **she's** writing an e-mail.*

Gefällt dir dieser Sessel? –Ja, **der** ist sehr bequem!
*Do you like that chair? –Yes, **it's** very comfortable!*

DER-WORDS Words that take the same endings as the forms of the definite article **der**. These include the demonstrative pronouns **dieser** (*this; that*), **jeder** (*each, every*), **jener** (*that*), **mancher** (*some*), and **solcher** (*such*), and the question word **welcher** (*which*).

Welcher Laptop gefällt dir am besten?
Which laptop do you like best?

Ich finde **diesen** Laptop am schönsten.
*I think **this** laptop is the nicest.*

DIRECT OBJECT A noun or pronoun that directly receives the action of the verb. Direct objects are in the accusative.

Kennst du **diesen Mann**?   Ich mache **eine Torte**.
*Do you know **that man**?   I'm making **a cake**.*

EIN-WORDS Words that take the same endings as the forms of the indefinite article **ein**. These include the negation **kein** and all of the possessive adjectives.

Hast du **einen** Hund?   Ich habe **keinen** Fußball.
*Do you have **a** dog?   I don't have **a** soccer ball.*

GENDER The grammatical categorization of nouns, pronouns, and adjectives as masculine, feminine, or neuter.

Masculine
articles: **der, ein**
pronouns: **er, der**
adjectives: **guter, schöner**

Feminine
articles: **die, eine**
pronouns: **sie, die**
adjectives: **gute, schöne**

Neuter
articles: **das, ein**
pronouns: **es, das**
adjectives: **gutes, schönes**

HELPING VERB *See* VERB, *Auxiliary verb.*

IMPERATIVE Imperatives are verb forms used to express commands, requests, suggestions, directions, or instructions.

Mach deine Hausaufgaben!   **Backen wir** einen Kuchen!
Do your homework!   Let's bake a cake!

INDIRECT OBJECT A noun or pronoun that receives the action of the verb indirectly. The indirect object is often a person to whom or for whom the action of the sentence is performed. Indirect objects are in the dative case.

Manfred hat **seinem Bruder** ein Buch geschenkt.
*Manfred gave **his brother** a book.*

INFINITIVE The basic, unconjugated form of a verb. Most German infinitives end in **-en**. A few end in **-ern** or **-eln**.

sehen, essen, lesen, wandern, sammeln
to see, to eat, to read, to hike, to collect

NOUN A word that refers to one or more people, animals, places, things, or ideas. Nouns in German may be masculine, feminine, or neuter, and are either singular or plural.

der **Junge**, die **Katze**, das **Café**
*the **boy**, the **cat**, the **café***

Compound noun Two or more simple nouns can be combined to form a compound noun. The gender of a compound noun matches the gender of the last noun in the compound.

die Nacht + das Hemd = **das Nachthemd**
*night + shirt = **nightshirt***

NUMBER A grammatical term that refers to the quantity of a noun. Nouns in German are either singular or plural. The plural form of a noun may have an added umlaut and/or an added ending. Adjectives, articles, and verbs also have different endings, depending on whether they are singular or plural.

Singular:
der **Mann**, die **Frau**, das **Kind**
*the **man**, the **woman**, the **child***

Plural:
die **Männer**, die **Frauen**, die **Kinder**
*the **men**, the **women**, the **children***

NUMBERS Words that represent quantities.

Cardinal numbers Numbers that indicate specific quantities. Cardinal numbers typically modify nouns, but do not add gender or case endings.

zwei Männer, **fünfzehn** Frauen, **sechzig** Kinder
two men, fifteen women, sixty children

Ordinal numbers Words that indicate the order of a noun in a series. Ordinal numbers add the same gender and case endings as adjectives.

der **erste** Mann, die **zweite** Frau, das **dritte** Kind
*the **first** man, the **second** woman, the **third** child*

PARTICIPLE A participle is formed from a verb but may be used as an adjective or adverb. Present participles are used primarily in written German. Past participles are used in compound tenses, including the **Perfekt** and the **Plusquamperfekt**.

Der **aufgehende** Mond war sehr schön.
*The **rising** moon was beautiful.*

Habt ihr schon **gegessen**?
*Have you already **eaten**?*

PREPOSITION A preposition links a noun or pronoun to other words in a sentence. Combined with a noun or pronoun, it forms a prepositional phrase, which can be used like an adverb to answer the question *when, how,* or *where.* In German, certain prepositions are always followed by a noun in the accusative case, while others are always followed by a noun in the dative case. A small number of prepositions are used with the genitive case.

ohne das Buch   **mit** dem Auto
***without** the book*   ***by** car*

trotz des Regens
***in spite of** the rain*

Two-way prepositions can be followed by either the dative or the accusative, depending on the situation. They are followed by the accusative when used with a verb that indicates movement toward a destination. With all other verbs, they are followed by the dative.

Stell deine Schuhe nicht **auf den Tisch**!
*Don't put your shoes **on the table**!*

Dein Schal liegt **auf dem Tisch**.
*Your scarf is lying **on the table**.*

PRONOUN A word that takes the place of a noun.

Subject pronouns Words used to replace a noun in the nominative case.

Maria ist nett.   **Der Junge** ist groß.
***Maria** is nice.*   ***The boy** is tall.*

Sie ist nett.   **Er** ist groß.
***She** is nice.*   ***He** is tall.*

Accusative pronouns Words used to replace a noun that functions as the direct object.

Wer hat **die Torte** gebacken?   Ich habe **sie** gebacken.
*Who baked **the cake**?*   *I baked **it**.*

Dative pronouns Words used to replace a noun that functions as the indirect object.

Musst du **deiner Oma** eine E-Mail schicken?
*Do you need to send an e-mail **to your grandma**?*

Nein, ich habe **ihr** schon geschrieben.
*No, I already wrote **to her**.*

Indefinite pronouns Words that refer to an unknown or nonspecific person or thing.

Jemand hat seinen Personalausweis vergessen.
Someone forgot his I.D. card.

Herr Klein will mit **niemandem** sprechen.
Mr. Klein doesn't want to speak with anyone.

Reflexive pronouns The pronouns used with reflexive verbs. When the subject of a reflexive verb is also its direct object, it takes an accusative reflexive pronoun. When the subject of a reflexive verb is not its direct object, it takes a dative reflexive pronoun.

Ich wasche **mich**.
I'm washing (myself).

Ich wasche **mir** das Gesicht.
I'm washing my face.

SUBJUNCTIVE A verb form (**der Konjunktiv II**) used to talk about hypothetical, unlikely or impossible conditions, to express wishes, and to make polite requests. German also has an additional subjunctive tense, der **Konjunktiv I**, used to report what someone else has said without indicating whether the information is true or false.

Ich **hätte** gern viel Geld.
I'd like to have a lot of money.

Wenn er sportlicher **wäre**, **würde** er häufiger trainieren.
If he were more athletic, he would exercise more.

SUPERLATIVE The form of an adjective or adverb used to indicate that a person or thing has more of a particular quality than anyone or anything else.

Welches ist **das größte** Tier der Welt?
What's the biggest animal in the world?

Wie komme ich **am besten** zur Tankstelle?
What's the best way to get to the gas station?

TENSE A set of verb forms that indicates if an action or state occurs in the past, present, or future.

Compound tense A tense made up of an auxiliary verb and a participle or infinitive.

Wir **haben** ihren Geburtstag **gefeiert**.
We celebrated her birthday.

VERB A word that expresses actions or states of being. German verbs are classified as *weak, mixed,* or *strong,* based on the way their past participles are formed.

weak: Ich **habe** eine Torte **gemacht**.
I made a cake.

strong: Wir **haben** Kekse **gegessen**.
We ate cookies.

mixed: Er **hat** eine CD **gebrannt**.
He burned a CD.

Auxiliary verb A conjugated verb used with the participle or infinitive of another verb. The auxiliary verbs **haben** and **sein** are used with past participles to form compound tenses including the **Perfekt** and **Plusquamperfekt**. **Werden** is used with an infinitive to form the future tense, and with a past participle to form a passive construction. Modals are also frequently used as auxiliary verbs.

Habt ihr den Tisch **gedeckt**?
Did you set the table?

Jasmin **war** noch nie nach Zürich **gefahren**.
Jasmin had never been to Zurich.

Wir **werden** uns in einer Woche wieder **treffen**.
We'll meet again in one week.

Es **wird** hier nur Deutsch **gesprochen**.
Only German is spoken here.

Modal verbs Verbs that modify the meaning of another verb. Modals express an attitude toward an action, such as permission, obligation, ability, desire, or necessity.

Ich **muss** Französisch **lernen**.
I have to study French.

Ich **will** Französisch **lernen**.
I want to learn French.

Principal parts German verbs are usually listed in dictionaries by their *principal parts* (**Stammformen**): the infinitive, the third-person singular present tense form (if the verb is irregular in the present), the third-person singular **Präteritum** form, and the past participle. Knowing the principal parts of a verb allows you to produce all of its conjugations in any tense.

geben (gibt)	gab	gegeben
to give (gives)	gave	given

Reflexive verbs Verbs that indicate an action you do to yourself or for yourself. The subject of a reflexive verb is also its object.

Ich **fühle mich** nicht **wohl**.
I don't feel well.

Wir **haben uns entspannt**.
We've been relaxing.

Reciprocal reflexive verbs Verbs that express an action done by two or more people or things to or for one another.

Wir rufen **uns** jeden Tag an.
We call each other every day.

Meine Großeltern lieben **sich** sehr.
My grandparents love each other very much.

Verb conjugation tables

Here are the infinitives of all verbs introduced as active vocabulary in **Mosaik**. Each verb is followed by a model verb that follows the same conjugation pattern. The number in parentheses indicates where in the verb tables, pages **A16–A25**, you can find the conjugated forms of the model verb. The word (**sein**) after a verb means that it is conjugated with **sein** in the **Perfekt** and **Plusquamperfekt**. For irregular reflexive verbs, the list may point to a non-reflexive model verb. A full conjugation of the simple forms of a reflexive verb is presented in Verb table 6 on page **A17**. Verbs followed by an asterisk (*) have a separable prefix.

abbiegen* (*sein*) like schieben (42)	**beschreiben** like bleiben (20)	**(sich) erkälten** like arbeiten (1)	**joggen** (*sein*) like machen (3)
abbrechen* like sprechen (47)	**besprechen** like sprechen (47)	**erkennen** like rennen (17)	**(sich) kämmen** like machen (3)
abfahren* (*sein*) like tragen (51)	**bestehen** like stehen (48)	**erklären** like machen (3)	**kaufen** like machen (3)
abfliegen* (*sein*) like schieben (42)	**bestellen** like machen (3)	**erzählen** like machen (3)	**kennen** like rennen (17)
abheben* like heben (29)	**besuchen** like machen (3)	**essen** (21)	**klettern** (*sein*) like fordern (26)
abschicken* like machen (3)	**(sich) bewegen** like heben (29)	**fahren** (*sein*) like tragen (51)	**klingeln** like sammeln (5)
abstauben* like machen (3)	**(sich) bewerben** like helfen (31)	**fallen** (*sein*) (22)	**kochen** like machen (3)
(sich) abtrocknen* like arbeiten (1)	**bezahlen** like machen (3)	**fangen** (23)	**kommen** (*sein*) (32)
adoptieren like probieren (4)	**bieten** like schieben (42)	**(sich) färben** like machen (3)	**können** (11)
anbieten* like schieben (42)	**bleiben** (*sein*) (20)	**faulenzen** like machen (3)	**korrigieren** like probieren (4)
anfangen* like fangen (23)	**braten** like schlafen (43)	**fegen** like machen (3)	**kosten** like arbeiten (1)
angeln like sammeln (5)	**brauchen** like machen (3)	**feiern** (2)	**küssen** like machen (3)
ankommen* (*sein*) like kommen (32)	**brechen** like sprechen (47)	**fernsehen*** like geben (27)	**lächeln** like sammeln (5)
anmachen* like machen (3)	**brennen** like rennen (17)	**finden** like trinken (52)	**lachen** like machen (3)
anrufen* like rufen (40)	**bringen** like denken (16)	**fliegen** (*sein*) like schieben (42)	**laden** like tragen (51)
anschauen* like machen (3)	**buchen** like machen (3)	**folgen** (*sein*) like machen (3)	**landen** (*sein*) like arbeiten (1)
anstoßen* like stoßen (50)	**büffeln** like sammeln (5)	**(sich) fragen** like machen (3)	**lassen** like fallen (22)
antworten like arbeiten (1)	**bügeln** like sammeln (5)	**(sich) freuen** (6)	**laufen** (*sein*) (33)
(sich) anziehen* like schieben (42)	**bürsten** like arbeiten (1)	**(sich) fühlen** like sich freuen (6)	**leben** like machen (3)
arbeiten (1)	**danken** like machen (3)	**füllen** like machen (3)	**legen** like machen (3)
(sich) ärgern like fordern (26)	**decken** like machen (3)	**funktionieren** like probieren (4)	**leiten** like arbeiten (1)
aufgehen* (*sein*) like gehen (28)	**denken** like denken (16)	**geben** (27)	**lernen** like machen (3)
auflegen* like machen (3)	**drücken** like machen (3)	**gefallen** like fallen (22)	**lesen** (34)
aufmachen* like machen (3)	**drucken** like machen (3)	**gehen** (*sein*) (28)	**lieben** like machen (3)
aufnehmen* like nehmen (38)	**durchfallen*** (*sein*) like fallen (22)	**gehören** like machen (3)	**liegen** (35)
aufräumen* like machen (3)	**durchmachen*** like machen (3)	**genießen** like fließen (25)	**löschen** like tragen (51)
aufstehen* (*sein*) like stehen (48)	**dürfen** (10)	**gewinnen** like schwimmen (44)	**lügen** (36)
aufwachen* (*sein*) like machen (3)	**(sich) duschen** like sich freuen (6)	**(sich) gewöhnen** like sich freuen (6)	**machen** (3)
ausfüllen like machen (3)	**einkaufen*** like machen (3)	**glauben** like machen (3)	**meinen** like machen (3)
ausgehen like gehen (28)	**einladen*** like tragen (51)	**gratulieren** like probieren (4)	**mieten** like arbeiten (1)
ausmachen like machen (3)	**einschlafen*** (*sein*) like schlafen (43)	**grüßen** like machen (3)	**mitbringen*** like denken (16)
(sich) ausruhen like sich freuen (6)	**einzahlen*** like machen (3)	**haben** like haben (7)	**mitkommen*** (*sein*) like kommen (32)
ausschalten* like arbeiten (1)	**empfehlen** like stehlen (49)	**handeln** like sammeln (5)	**mitmachen*** like machen (3)
(sich) ausziehen* like schieben (42)	**entdecken** like machen (3)	**hängen** like machen (3)	**mitnehmen*** like nehmen (38)
backen like mahlen (37)	**entfernen** like machen (3)	**heiraten** like arbeiten (1)	**mögen** (12)
(sich) baden like arbeiten (1)	**entgegennehmen*** like nehmen (38)	**heißen** (30)	**müssen** (13)
bauen like machen (3)	**entlassen** like fallen (22)	**helfen** (31)	**nachmachen*** like machen (3)
beantworten like arbeiten (1)	**(sich) entschließen** like fließen (25)	**heruntergehen*** (*sein*) like gehen (28)	**nehmen** (38)
bedeuten like arbeiten (1)	**(sich) entschuldigen** like machen (3)	**herunterladen*** like tragen (51)	**(sich) nennen** like rennen (17)
bedienen like machen (3)	**(sich) entspannen** like sich freuen (6)	**(sich) hinlegen*** like machen (3)	**niesen** like machen (3)
(sich) beeilen like sich freuen (6)	**entwerten** like arbeiten (1)	**(sich) hinsetzen*** like machen (3)	**öffnen** like arbeiten (1)
beginnen like schwimmen (44)	**entwickeln** like sammeln (5)	**hinterlassen** like fallen (22)	**packen** like machen (3)
behaupten like arbeiten (1)	**erfinden** like trinken (52)	**hochgehen*** (*sein*) like gehen (28)	**parken** like machen (3)
bekommen like kommen (32)	**erforschen** like machen (3)	**hören** like machen (3)	**passen** like machen (3)
belegen like machen (3)	**ergänzen** like machen (3)	**husten** like arbeiten (1)	**passieren** (*sein*) like probieren (4)
benutzen like machen (3)	**erhalten** like fallen (22)	**(sich) informieren** like probieren (4)	**probieren** (4)
berichten like arbeiten (1)	**(sich) erinnern** like fordern (26)	**(sich) interessieren** like probieren (4)	**putzen** like machen (3)

(sich) rasieren like probieren (4)
rauchen like machen (3)
recyceln like sammeln (5)
reden like arbeiten (1)
regnen like arbeiten (1)
reisen (*sein*) like machen (3)
reiten (*sein*) like pfeifen (39)
rennen (*sein*) (17)
reparieren like probieren (4)
retten like arbeiten (1)
sagen like machen (3)
schauen like machen (3)
scheitern (*sein*) like fordern (26)
schenken like machen (3)
schicken like machen (3)
schlafen (43)
schmecken like machen (3)
(sich) schminken like machen (3)
schneien like machen (3)
schreiben like bleiben (20)
schützen like machen (3)
schwänzen like machen (3)
schwimmen (*sein*) (44)
sehen like lesen (34)
sein (*sein*) (8)
(sich) setzen like machen (3)
singen like trinken (52)
sitzen (46)

sollen (14)
sortieren like probieren (4)
spazieren (*sein*) like probieren (4)
speichern like fordern (26)
spielen like machen (3)
sprechen (47)
springen (*sein*) like trinken (52)
spülen like machen (3)
starten (*sein*) like arbeiten (1)
staubsaugen like saugen (41)
stehen (48)
stehlen (49)
steigen (*sein*) like bleiben (20)
stellen like machen (3)
sterben (*sein*) like helfen (31)
(sich) streiten like pfeifen (39)
studieren like probieren (4)
suchen like machen (3)
surfen (*sein*) like machen (3)
tanken like machen (3)
tanzen like machen (3)
tragen (51)
träumen like machen (3)
(sich) treffen (*sein*) like sprechen (47)
treiben (*sein*) like bleiben (20)
(sich) trennen like sich freuen (6)
trinken (52)
tun (53)

üben like machen (3)
(sich) überlegen like machen (3)
übernachten like arbeiten (1)
überqueren like machen (3)
überraschen like machen (3)
umtauschen* like machen (3)
(sich) umziehen* (*sein*) like schieben (42)
untergehen* (*sein*) like gehen (28)
(sich) unterhalten* like fallen (22)
unterschreiben like bleiben (20)
(sich) verbessern like fordern (26)
verbringen like denken (16)
verdienen like machen (3)
vereinbaren like machen (3)
vergessen like essen (21)
verkaufen like machen (3)
verkünden like arbeiten (1)
(sich) verlaufen like laufen (33)
(sich) verletzen like machen (3)
(sich) verlieben like machen (3)
verlieren like schieben (42)
verschmutzen (*sein*) like machen (3)
(sich) verspäten like sich freuen (6)
(sich) verstauchen like machen (3)
verstehen like stehen (48)
versuchen like machen (3)
(sich) vorbereiten* like arbeiten (1)

vormachen* like machen (3)
vorschlagen* like tragen (51)
(sich) vorstellen* like machen (3)
wachsen (*sein*) like waschen (54)
wandern (*sein*) like fordern (26)
warten like arbeiten (1)
(sich) waschen (54)
wegräumen* like machen (3)
wegwerfen* like helfen (31)
weinen like machen (3)
werden (*sein*) (9)
wettmachen* like machen (3)
wiederholen like machen (3)
wiegen like schieben (42)
wischen like machen (3)
wissen (55)
wohnen like machen (3)
wollen (15)
(sich) wünschen like machen (3)
zeigen like machen (3)
ziehen (*sein*) like schieben (42)
zubereiten* like arbeiten (1)
zumachen* like machen (3)
(sich) zurechtfinden* like trinken (52)
zurückkommen* (*sein*) like kommen (32)
zuschauen* like machen (3)

Regular verbs: simple tenses

Infinitiv Partizip I Partizip II Perfekt	INDIKATIV			KONJUNKTIV I	KONJUNKTIV II		IMPERATIV
	Präsens	Präteritum	Plusquamperfekt	Präsens	Präsens	Perfekt	
1 arbeiten	arbeite	arbeitete	hatte gearbeitet	arbeite	arbeitete	hätte gearbeitet	
(to work)	arbeitest	arbeitetest	hattest gearbeitet	arbeitest	arbeitetest	hättest gearbeitet	arbeite
	arbeitet	arbeitete	hatte gearbeitet	arbeite	arbeitete	hätte gearbeitet	
arbeitend	arbeiten	arbeiteten	hatten gearbeitet	arbeiten	arbeiteten	hätten gearbeitet	arbeiten wir
gearbeitet	arbeitet	arbeitetet	hattet gearbeitet	arbeitet	arbeitetet	hättet gearbeitet	arbeitet
gearbeitet haben	arbeiten	arbeiteten	hatten gearbeitet	arbeiten	arbeiteten	hätten gearbeitet	arbeiten Sie
2 feiern	feiere	feierte	hatte gefeiert	feiere	feierte	hätte gefeiert	
(to celebrate)	feierst	feiertest	hattest gefeiert	feierest	feiertest	hättest gefeiert	feiere
	feiert	feierte	hatte gefeiert	feiere	feierte	hätte gefeiert	
feiernd	feiern	feierten	hatten gefeiert	feiern	feierten	hätten gefeiert	feiern wir
gefeiert	feiert	feiertet	hattet gefeiert	feiert	feiertet	hättet gefeiert	feiert
gefeiert haben	feiern	feierten	hatten gefeiert	feiern	feierten	hätten gefeiert	feiern Sie
3 machen	mache	machte	hatte gemacht	mache	machte	hätte gemacht	
(to make; to do)	machst	machtest	hattest gemacht	machest	machtest	hättest gemacht	mache/mach
	macht	machte	hatte gemacht	mache	machte	hätte gemacht	
machend	machen	machten	hatten gemacht	machen	machten	hätten gemacht	machen wir
gemacht	macht	machtet	hattet gemacht	machet	machtet	hättet gemacht	macht
gemacht haben	machen	machten	hatten gemacht	machen	machten	hätten gemacht	machen Sie
4 probieren	probiere	probierte	hatte probiert	probiere	probierte	hätte probiert	
(to try)	probierst	probiertest	hattest probiert	probierest	probiertest	hättest probiert	probiere/probier
	probiert	probierte	hatte probiert	probiere	probierte	hätte probiert	
probierend	probieren	probierten	hatten probiert	probieren	probierten	hätten probiert	probieren wir
probiert	probiert	probiertet	hattet probiert	probieret	probiertet	hättet probiert	probiert
probiert haben	probieren	probierten	hatten probiert	probieren	probierten	hätten probiert	probieren Sie
5 sammeln	sammle	sammelte	hatte gesammelt	sammle	sammelte	hätte gesammelt	
(to collect)	sammelst	sammeltest	hattest gesammelt	sammlest	sammeltest	hättest gesammelt	sammle
	sammelt	sammelte	hatte gesammelt	sammle	sammelte	hätte gesammelt	
sammelnd	sammeln	sammelten	hatten gesammelt	sammlen	sammelten	hätten gesammelt	sammeln wir
gesammelt	sammelt	sammeltet	hattet gesammelt	sammlet	sammeltet	hättet gesammelt	sammelt
gesammelt haben	sammeln	sammelten	hatten gesammelt	sammlen	sammelten	hätten gesammelt	sammeln Sie

Reflexive verbs

Infinitiv / Partizip I / Partizip II / Perfekt	INDIKATIV			KONJUNKTIV I	KONJUNKTIV II		IMPERATIV
	Präsens	Präteritum	Plusquamperfekt	Präsens	Präsens	Perfekt	
6 **sich freuen**	freue mich	freute mich	hatte mich gefreut	freue mich	freute mich	hätte mich gefreut	
(to be happy)	freust dich	freutest dich	hattest dich gefreut	freuest dich	freutest dich	hättest dich gefreut	freue/freu dich
	freut sich	freute sich	hatte sich gefreut	freue sich	freute sich	hätte sich gefreut	
sich freuend	freuen uns	freuten uns	hatten uns gefreut	freuen uns	freuten uns	hätten uns gefreut	freuen wir uns
sich gefreut	freut euch	freutet euch	hattet euch gefreut	freuet euch	freutet euch	hättet euch gefreut	freut euch
sich gefreut haben	freuen sich	freuten sich	hatten sich gefreut	freuen sich	freuten sich	hätten sich gefreut	freuen Sie sich

Auxiliary verbs

Infinitiv / Partizip I / Partizip II / Perfekt	INDIKATIV			KONJUNKTIV I	KONJUNKTIV II		IMPERATIV
	Präsens	Präteritum	Plusquamperfekt	Präsens	Präsens	Perfekt	
7 **haben**	habe	hatte	hatte gehabt	habe	hätte	hätte gehabt	
(to have)	hast	hattest	hattest gehabt	habest	hättest	hättest gehabt	habe/hab
	hat	hatte	hatte gehabt	habe	hätte	hätte gehabt	
habend	haben	hatten	hatten gehabt	haben	hätten	hätten gehabt	haben wir
gehabt	habt	hattet	hattet gehabt	habet	hättet	hättet gehabt	habt
gehabt haben	haben	hatten	hatten gehabt	haben	hätten	hätten gehabt	haben Sie
8 **sein**	bin	war	war gewesen	sei	wäre	wäre gewesen	
(to be)	bist	warst	warst gewesen	seiest/seist	wärst/wärest	wärst/wärest gewesen	sei
	ist	war	war gewesen	sei	wäre	wäre gewesen	
seiend	sind	waren	waren gewesen	seien	wären	wären gewesen	seien wir
gewesen	seid	wart	wart gewesen	seiet	wärt/wäret	wärt/wäret gewesen	seid
gewesen sein	sind	waren	waren gewesen	seien	wären	wären gewesen	seien Sie
9 **werden**	werde	wurde	war geworden	werde	würde	wäre geworden	
(to become)	wirst	wurdest	warst geworden	werdest	würdest	wärst geworden	werde
	wird	wurde	war geworden	werde	würde	wäre geworden	
werdend	werden	wurden	waren geworden	werden	würden	wären geworden	werden wir
geworden	werdet	wurdet	wart geworden	werdet	würdet	wärt geworden	werdet
geworden sein	werden	wurden	waren geworden	werden	würden	wären geworden	werden Sie

Compound tenses

Hilfsverb	INDIKATIV		KONJUNKTIV I		KONJUNKTIV II	
	Perfekt	**Plusquamperfekt**	**Präsens** **Perfekt**		**Präsens** **Perfekt**	
haben	habe	hatte	habe		hätte	
	hast gemacht	hattest gemacht	habest gemach		hättest gemach	
	hat gearbeitet	hatte gearbeitet	habe gearbeitet		hätte gearbeitet	
	haben studiert	hatten studiert	haben studiert		hätten studiert	
	habt gefeiert	hattet gefeiert	habet gefeiert		hättet gefeiert	
	haben gesammelt	hatten gesammelt	haben gesammelt		hätten gesammelt	
sein	bin gegangen	war gegangen	sei gegangen		wäre gegangen	
	bist gegangen	warst gegangen	seiest/seist gegangen		wärst/wärest gegangen	
	ist gegangen	war gegangen	sei gegangen		wäre gegangen	
	sind gegangen	waren gegangen	seien gegangen		wären gegangen	
	seid gegangen	wart gegangen	seiet gegangen		wärt/wäret gegangen	
	sind gegangen	waren gegangen	seien gegangen		wären gegangen	

	Futur I/II	**Futur I/II**	**Futur I/II**
werden	werde machen / gemacht haben	werde machen / gemacht haben	würde machen / gemacht haben
	wirst machen / gemacht haben	werdest machen / gemacht haben	würdest machen / gemacht haben
	wird machen / gemacht haben	werde machen / gemacht haben	würde machen / gemacht haben
	werden machen / gemacht haben	werden machen / gemacht haben	würden machen / gemacht haben
	werdet machen / gemacht haben	werdet machen / gemacht haben	würdet machen / gemacht haben
	werden machen / gemacht haben	werden machen / gemacht haben	würden machen / gemacht haben

Modal verbs

Infinitiv Partizip I Partizip II Perfekt	INDIKATIV			KONJUNKTIV I	KONJUNKTIV II		IMPERATIV
	Präsens	Präteritum	Plusquamperfekt	Präsens	Präsens	Perfekt	
10 **dürfen**	darf	durfte	hatte gedurft	dürfe	dürfte	hätte gedurft	*Modal verbs are*
(to be permitted to)	darfst	durftest	hattest gedurft	dürfest	dürftest	hättest gedurft	*not used in the*
	darf	durfte	hatte gedurft	dürfe	dürfte	hätte gedurft	*imperative.*
dürfend	dürfen	durften	hatten gedurft	dürfen	dürften	hätten gedurft	
gedurft/dürfen	dürft	durftet	hattet gedurft	dürfet	dürftet	hättet gedurft	
gedurft haben	dürfen	durften	hatten gedurft	dürfen	dürften	hätten gedurft	
11 **können**	kann	konnte	hatte gekonnt	könne	könnte	hätte gekonnt	*Modal verbs are*
(to be able to)	kannst	konntest	hattest gekonnt	könnest	könntest	hättest gekonnt	*not used in the*
	kann	konnte	hatte gekonnt	könne	könnte	hätte gekonnt	*imperative.*
könnend	können	konnten	hatten gekonnt	können	könnten	hätten gekonnt	
gekonnt /können	könnt	konntet	hattet gekonnt	könnet	könntet	hättet gekonnt	
gekonnt haben	können	konnten	hatten gekonnt	können	könnten	hätten gekonnt	
12 **mögen**	mag	mochte	hatte gemocht	möge	möchte	hätte gemocht	*Modal verbs are*
(to like)	magst	mochtest	hattest gemocht	mögest	möchtest	hättest gemocht	*not used in the*
	mag	mochte	hatte gemocht	möge	möchte	hätte gemocht	*imperative.*
mögend	mögen	mochten	hatten gemocht	mögen	möchten	hätten gemocht	
gemocht /mögen	mögt	mochtet	hattet gemocht	möget	möchtet	hättet gemocht	
gemocht haben	mögen	mochten	hatten gemocht	mögen	möchten	hätten gemocht	
13 **müssen**	muss	musste	hatte gemusst	müsse	müsste	hätte gemusst	*Modal verbs are*
(to have to)	musst	musstest	hattest gemusst	müssest	müsstest	hättest gemusst	*not used in the*
	muss	musste	hatte gemusst	müsse	müsste	hätte gemusst	*imperative.*
müssend	müssen	mussten	hatten gemusst	müssen	müssten	hätten gemusst	
gemusst /müssen	müsst	musstet	hattet gemusst	müsset	müsstet	hättet gemusst	
gemusst haben	müssen	mussten	hatten gemusst	müssen	müssten	hätten gemusst	
14 **sollen**	soll	sollte	hatte gesollt	solle	sollte	hätte gesollt	*Modal verbs are*
(to be supposed to)	sollst	solltest	hattest gesollt	sollest	solltest	hättest gesollt	*not used in the*
	soll	sollte	hatte gesollt	solle	sollte	hätte gesollt	*imperative.*
sollend	sollen	sollten	hatten gesollt	sollen	sollten	hätten gesollt	
gesollt /sollen	sollt	solltet	hattet gesollt	sollet	solltet	hättet gesollt	
gesollt haben	sollen	sollten	hatten gesollt	sollen	sollten	hätten gesollt	
15 **wollen**	will	wollte	hatte gewollt	wolle	wollte	hätte gewollt	*Modal verbs are*
(to want to)	willst	wolltest	hattest gewollt	wollest	wolltest	hättest gewollt	*not used in the*
	will	wollte	hatte gewollt	wollev	wollte	hätte gewollt	*imperative.*
wollend	wollen	wollten	hatten gewollt	wollen	wollten	hätten gewollt	
gewollt/wollen	wollt	wolltet	hattet gewollt	wollet	wolltet	hättet gewollt	
gewollt haben	wollen	wollten	hatten gewollt	wollen	wollten	hätten gewollt	

Mixed verbs

Infinitiv Partizip I Partizip II Perfekt	INDIKATIV			KONJUNKTIV I	KONJUNKTIV II		IMPERATIV
	Präsens	Präteritum	Plusquamperfekt	Präsens	Präsens	Perfekt	
16 denken	denke	dachte	hatte gedacht	denke	dächte	hätte gedacht	
(to think)	denkst	dachtest	hattest gedacht	denkest	dächtest	hättest gedacht	denke/denk
	denkt	dachte	hatte gedacht	denke	dächte	hätte gedacht	
denkend	denken	dachten	hatten gedacht	denken	dächten	hätten gedacht	denken wir
gedacht	denkt	dachtet	hattet gedacht	denket	dächtet	hättet gedacht	denkt
gedacht haben	denken	dachten	hatten gedacht	denken	dächten	hätten gedacht	denken Sie
17 rennen	renne	rannte	war gerannt	renne	rennte	wäre gerannt	
(to run)	rennst	ranntest	warst gerannt	rennest	renntest	wärest gerannt	renne/renn
	rennt	rannte	war gerannt	renne	rennte	wäre gerannt	
denkend	rennen	rannten	waren gerannt	rennen	rennten	wären gerannt	rennen wir
gerannt	rennt	ranntet	wart gerannt	rennet	renntet	wärt gerannt	rennt
gerannt sein	rennen	rannten	waren gerannt	rennen	rennten	wären gerannt	rennen Sie
18 senden	sende	sandte	hatte gesandt	sende	sendete	hätte gesandt	
(to send)	sendest	sandtest	hattest gesandt	sendest	sendetest	hättest gesandt	sende
	sendet	sandte	hatte gesandt	sende	sendete	hätte gesandt	
sendend	senden	sandten	hatten gesandt	senden	sendeten	hätten gesandt	senden wir
gesendet	sendet	sandtet	hattet gesandt	sendet	sendetet	hättet gesandt	sendet
gesendet haben	senden	sandten		senden	sendeten	hätten gesandt	senden Sie

Irregular verbs

Infinitiv Partizip I Partizip II Perfekt	INDIKATIV			KONJUNKTIV I	KONJUNKTIV II		IMPERATIV
	Präsens	Präteritum	Plusquamperfekt	Präsens	Präsens	Perfekt	
19 bitten	bitte	bat	hatte gebeten	bitte	bäte	hätte gebeten	
(to ask)	bittest	batest	hattest gebeten	bittest	bätest	hättest gebeten	bitte
	bittet	bat	hatte gebeten	bitte	bäte	hätte gebeten	
bittend	bitten	baten	hatten gebeten	bitten	bäten	hätten gebeten	bitten wir
gebeten	bittet	batet	hattet gebeten	bittet	bätet	hättet gebeten	bittet
gebeten haben	bitten	baten	hatten gebeten	bitten	bäten	hätten gebeten	bitten Sie
20 bleiben	bleibe	bliebe	war geblieben	bleibe	bliebe	wäre geblieben	
(to stay)	bleibst	bliebst	warst geblieben	bleibest	bliebest	wärest geblieben	bleibe/bleib
	bleibt	blieb	war geblieben	bleibe	bliebe	wäre geblieben	
bleibend	bleiben	blieben	waren geblieben	bleiben	blieben	wären geblieben	bleiben wir
geblieben	bleibt	bliebt	wart geblieben	bleibet	bliebet	wärt geblieben	bleibt
geblieben sein	bleiben	blieben	waren geblieben	bleiben	blieben	wären geblieben	bleiben Sie

Infinitiv Partizip I Partizip II Perfekt	INDIKATIV			KONJUNKTIV I	KONJUNKTIV II		IMPERATIV
	Präsens	Präteritum	Plusquamperfekt	Präsens	Präsens	Perfekt	
21 essen	esse	aß	hatte gegessen	esse	äße	hätte gegessen	
(to eat)	isst	aßest	hattest gegessen	essest	äßest	hättest gegessen	iss
	isst	aß	hatte gegessen	esse	äße	hätte gegessen	
essend	essen	aßen	hatten gegessen	essen	äßen	hätten gegessen	essen wir
gegessen	esst	aß	hattet gegessen	esset	äßet	hättet gegessen	esst
gegessen haben	essen	aßen	hatten gegessen	essen	äßen	hätten gegessen	essen Sie
22 fallen	falle	fiel	war gefallen	falle	fiele	wäre gefallen	
(to fall)	fällst	fielst	warst gefallen	fallest	fielest	wärest gefallen	falle/fall
	fällt	fiel	war gefallen	falle	fiele	wäre gefallen	
fallend	fallen	fielen	waren gefallen	fallen	fielen	wären gefallen	fallen wir
gefallen	fallt	fielt	wart gefallen	fallet	fielet	wäret gefallen	fallt
gefallen sein	fallen	fielen	waren gefallen	fallen	fielen	wären gefallen	fallen Sie
23 fangen	fange	fing	hatte gemacht	fange	finge	hätte gefangen	
(to catch)	fängst	fingst	hattest gemacht	fangest	fingest	hättest gefangen	fange/fang
	fängt	fing	hatte gemacht	fange	finge	hätte gefangen	
fangend	fangen	fingen	hatten gemacht	fangen	fingen	hätten gefangen	fangen wir
gefangen	fangt	fingt	hattet gemacht	fanget	finget	hättet gefangen	fangt
gefangen haben	fangen	fingen	hatten gemacht	fangen	fingen	hätten gefangen	fangen Sie
24 flechten	flechte	flocht	hatte geflochten	flechte	flöchte	hätte geflochten	
(to braid)	flichtst	flochtest	hattest geflochten	flechtest	flöchtest	hättest geflochten	flicht
	flicht	flocht	hatte geflochten	flechte	flöchte	hätte geflochten	
flechtend	flechten	flochten	hatten geflochten	flechten	flöchten	hätten geflochten	flechten wir
geflochten	flechtet	flochtet	hattet geflochten	flechtet	flöchtet	hättet geflochten	flechtet
geflochten haben	flechten	flochten	hatten geflochten	flechten	flöchten	hätten geflochten	flechten Sie
25 fließen	fließe	floss	war geflossen	fließe	flösse	wäre geflossen	
(to flow)	fließt	flossest/flosst	warst geflossen	fließest	flössest	wärest geflossen	fließe/fließ
	fließt	floss	war geflossen	fließe	flösse	wäre geflossen	
fließend	fließen	flossen	waren geflossen	fließen	flössen	wären geflossen	fließen wir
geflossen	fließt	flosst	wart geflossen	fließet	flösset	wärt geflossen	fließt
geflossen sein	fließen	flossen	waren geflossen	fließen	flössen	wären geflossen	fließen Sie
26 fordern	ford(e)re	forderte	hatte gefordert	fordere	forderte	hätte gefordert	
(to demand)	forderst	fordertest	hattest gefordert	forderest	fordertest	hättest gefordert	fordere/fordre
	fordert	forderte	hatte gefordert	fordere	forderte	hätte gefordert	
fordernd	fordern	forderten	hatten gefordert	forderen	forderten	hätten gefordert	fordern wir
gefordert	fordert	fordertet	hattet gefordert	forderet	fordertet	hättet gefordert	fordert
gefordert haben	fordern	forderten	hatten gefordert	forderen	forderten	hätten gefordert	fordern Sie
27 geben	gebe	gab	hatte gegeben	gebe	gäbe	hätte gegeben	
(to give)	gibst	gabst	hattest gegeben	gebest	gäbest	hättest gegeben	gib
	gibt	gab	hatte gegeben	gebe	gäbe	hätte gegeben	
gebend	geben	gaben	hatten gegeben	geben	gäben	hätten gegeben	geben wir
gegeben	gebt	gabt	hattet gegeben	gebet	gäbet	hättet gegeben	gebt
gegeben haben	geben	gaben	hatten gegeben	geben	gäben	hätten gegeben	geben Sie

Infinitiv / Partizip I / Partizip II / Perfekt	INDIKATIV			KONJUNKTIV I	KONJUNKTIV II		IMPERATIV
	Präsens	Präteritum	Plusquamperfekt	Präsens	Präsens	Perfekt	
28 gehen	gehe	ging	war gegangen	gehe	ginge	wäre gegangen	
(to go)	gehst	gingst	warst gegangen	gehest	gingest	wärest gegangen	gehe/geh
	geht	ging	war gegangen	gehe	ginge	wäre gegangen	
gehend	gehen	gingen	waren gegangen	gehen	gingen	wären gegangen	gehen wir
gegangen	geht	gingt	wart gegangen	gehet	ginget	wäret gegangen	geht
gegangen sein	gehen	gingen	waren gegangen	gehen	gingen	wären gegangen	gehen Sie
29 heben	hebe	hob	hatte gehoben	hebe	höbe	hätte gehoben	
(to lift)	hebst	hobst	hattest gehoben	hebest	höbest/höbst	hättest gehoben	hebe/heb
	hebt	hob	hatte gehoben	hebe	höbe	hätte gehoben	
hebend	heben	hoben	hatten gehoben	heben	höben	hätten gehoben	heben wir
gehoben	hebt	hobt	hattet gehoben	hebet	höbet/höbt	hättet gehoben	hebt
gehoben haben	heben	hoben	hatten gehoben	heben	höben	hätten gehoben	heben Sie
30 heißen	heiße	hieß	hatte geheißen	heiße	hieße	hätte geheißen	
(to be called)	heißt	hießest	hattest geheißen	heißest	hießest	hättest geheißen	heiß/heiße
	heißt	hieß	hatte geheißen	heiße	hieße	hätte geheißen	
heißend	heißen	hießen	hatten geheißen	heißen	hießen	hätten geheißen	heißen wir
geheißen	heißt	hießt	hattet geheißen	heißet	hießet	hättet geheißen	heißt
geheißen haben	heißen	hießen	hatten geheißen	heißen	hießen	hätten geheißen	heißen Sie
31 helfen	helfe	half	hatte geholfen	helfe	hälfe	hätte geholfen	
(to help)	hilfst	halfst	hattest geholfen	helfest	hälfest/hälfst	hättest geholfen	hilf
	hilft	half	hatte geholfen	helfe	hälfe	hätte geholfen	
helfend	helfen	halfen	hatten geholfen	helfen	hälfen	hätten geholfen	helfen wir
geholfen	helft	halft	hattet geholfen	helfet	hälfet/hälft	hättet geholfen	helft
geholfen haben	helfen	halfen	hatten geholfen	helfen	hälfen	hätten geholfen	helfen Sie
32 kommen	komme	kam	war gekommen	komme	käme	wäre gekommen	
(to come)	kommst	kamst	warst gekommen	kommest	kämest	wärest gekommen	komme/komm
	kommt	kam	war gekommen	komme	käme	wäre gekommen	
kommend	kommen	kamen	waren gekommen	kommen	kämen	wären gekommen	kommen wir
gekommen	kommt	kamt	wart gekommen	kommet	kämet	wäret gekommen	kommt
gekommen sein	kommen	kamen	waren gekommen	kommen	kämen	wären gekommen	kommen Sie
33 laufen	laufe	lief	war gelaufen	laufe	liefe	wäre gelaufen	
(to run)	läufst	liefst	warst gelaufen	laufest	liefest	wärest gelaufen	laufe/lauf
	läuft	lief	war gelaufen	laufe	liefe	wäre gelaufen	
laufend	laufen	liefen	waren gelaufen	laufen	liefen	wären gelaufen	laufen wir
gelaufen	lauft	lieft	wart gelaufen	laufet	liefet	wäret gelaufen	lauft
gelaufen sein	laufen	liefen	waren gelaufen	laufen	liefen	wären gelaufen	laufen Sie
34 lesen	lese	las	hatte gelesen	lese	läse	hätte gelesen	
(to read)	liest	la(se)st	hattest gelesen	lesest	läsest	hättest gelesen	lies
	liest	las	hatte gelesen	lese	läse	hätte gelesen	
lesend	lesen	lasen	hatten gelesen	lesen	läsen	hätten gelesen	les en wir
gelesen	lest	last	hattet gelesen	leset	läset	hättet gelesen	lest
gelesen haben	lesen	lasen	hatten gelesen	lesen	läsen	hätten gelesen	lesen Sie

Infinitiv Partizip I Partizip II Perfekt	INDIKATIV			KONJUNKTIV I	KONJUNKTIV II		IMPERATIV
	Präsens	Präteritum	Plusquamperfekt	Präsens	Präsens	Perfekt	
35 liegen	liege	lag	hatte gelegen	liege	läge	hätte gelegen	
(to lie; to be lying)	liegst	lagst	hattest gelegen	liegest	lägest	hättest gelegen	liege/lieg
	liegt	lag	hatte gelegen	liege	läge	hätte gelegen	
liegend	liegen	lagen	hatten gelegen	liegen	lägen	hätten gelegen	liegen wir
gelegen	liegt	lagt	hattet gelegen	lieget	läget	hättet gelegen	liegt
gelegen haben	liegen	lagen	hatten gelegen	liegen	lägen	hätten gelegen	liegen Sie
36 lügen	lüge	log	hatte gelogen	lüge	löge	hätte gelogen	
(to lie)	lügst	logst	hattest gelogen	lügest	lögest	hättest gelogen	lüge/lüg
	lügt	log	hatte gelogen	lüge	löge	hätte gelogen	
lügend	lügen	logen	hatten gelogen	lügen	lögen	hätten gelogen	lügen wir
gelogen	lügt	logt	hattet gelogen	lüget	löget	hättet gelogen	lügt
gelogen haben	lügen	logen	hatten gelogen	lügen	lögen	hätten gelogen	lügen Sie
37 mahlen	mahle	mahlte	hatte gemahlt/gemahlen	mahle	mahlte	hätte gemahlt/gemahlen	
(to grind)	mahlst	mahltest	hattest gemahlt/gemahlen	mahlest	mahltest	hättest gemahlt/gemahlen	mahle/mahl
mahlend	mahlt	mahlte	hatte gemahlt/gemahlen	mahle	mahlte	hätte gemahlt/gemahlen	
gemahlt/gemahlen	mahlen	mahlten	hatten gemahlt/gemahlen	mahlen	mahlten	hätten gemahlt/gemahlen	mahlen wir
gemahlt/gemahlen	mahlt	mahltet	hattet gemahlt/gemahlen	mahlet	mahltet	hättet gemahlt/gemahlen	mahlt
haben	mahlen	mahlten	hatten gemahlt/gemahlen	mahlen	mahlten	hätten gemahlt/gemahlen	mahlen Sie
38 nehmen	nehme	nahm	hatte genommen	nehme	nähme	hätte genommen	
(to take)	nimmst	nahmst	hattest genommen	nehmest	nähmest	hättest genommen	nimm
	nimmt	nahm	hatte genommen	nehme	nähme	hätte genommen	
nehmend	nehmen	nahmen	hatten genommen	nehmen	nähmen	hätten genommen	nehmen wir
genommen	nehmt	nahmt	hattet genommen	nehmet	nähmet	hättet genommen	nehmt
genommen haben	nehmen	nahmen	hatten genommen	nehmen	nähmen	hätten genommen	nehmen Sie
39 pfeifen	pfeife	pfiff	hatte gepfiffen	pfeife	pfiffe	hätte gepfiffen	
(to whistle)	pfeifst	pfiffst	hattest gepfiffen	pfeifest	pfiffest	hättest gepfiffen	pfeife/pfeif
	pfeift	pfiff	hatte gepfiffen	pfeife	pfiffe	hätte gepfiffen	
pfeifend	pfeifen	pfiffen	hatten gepfiffen	pfeifen	pfiffen	hätten gepfiffen	pfeifen wir
gepfiffen	pfeift	pfifft	hattet gepfiffen	pfeifet	pfiffet	hättet gepfiffen	pfeift
gepfiffen haben	pfeifen	pfiffen	hatten gepfiffen	pfeifen	pfiffen	hätten gepfiffen	pfeifen Sie
40 rufen	rufe	rief	hatte gerufen	rufe	riefe	hätte gerufen	
(to call)	rufst	riefst	hattest gerufen	rufest	riefest	hättest gerufen	rufe/ruf
	ruft	rief	hatte gerufen	rufe	riefe	hätte gerufen	
rufend	rufen	riefen	hatten gerufen	rufen	riefen	hätten gerufen	rufen wir
gerufen	ruft	rieft	hattet gerufen	rufet	riefet	hättet gerufen	ruft
gerufen haben	rufen	riefen	hatten gerufen	rufen	riefen	hätten gerufen	rufen Sie
41 saugen	sauge	saugte/sog	hatte gesaugt/gesogen	sauge	saugte/söge	hätte gesaugt/gesogen	
(to suck)	saugst	saugtest/sogst	hattest gesaugt/gesogen	saugest	saugtest/sögest	hättest gesaugt/gesogen	sauge/saug
saugend	saugt	saugte/sog	hatte gesaugt/gesogen	sauge	saugte/söge	hätte gesaugt/gesogen	
gesaugt/gesogen	saugen	saugten/sogen	hatten gesaugt/gesogen	saugen	saugten/sögen	hätten gesaugt/gesogen	saugen wir
gesaugt/gesogen	saugt	saugtet/sogt	hattet gesaugt/gesogen	sauget	saugtet/söget	hättet gesaugt/gesogen	saugt
haben	saugen	saugten/sogen	hatten gesaugt/gesogen	saugen	saugten/sögen	hätten gesaugt/gesogen	saugen Sie

Infinitiv Partizip I Partizip II Perfekt	INDIKATIV			KONJUNKTIV I	KONJUNKTIV II		IMPERATIV
	Präsens	Präteritum	Plusquamperfekt	Präsens	Präsens	Perfekt	
42 **schieben**	schiebe	schob	hatte geschoben	schiebe	schöbe	hätte geschoben	
(to push)	schiebst	schobst	hattest geschoben	schiebest	schöbest	hättest geschoben	schiebe/schieb
	schiebt	schob	hatte geschoben	schiebe	schöbe	hätte geschoben	
schiebend	schieben	schoben	hatten geschoben	schieben	schöben	hätten geschoben	schieben wir
geschoben	schiebt	schobt	hattet geschoben	schiebet	schöbet	hättet geschoben	schiebt
geschoben haben	schieben	schoben	hatten geschoben	schieben	schöben	hätten geschoben	schieben Sie
43 **schlafen**	schlafe	schlief	hatte geschlafen	schlafe	schliefe	hätte geschlafen	
(to sleep)	schläfst	schliefst	hattest geschlafen	schlafest	schliefest	hättest geschlafen	schlafe/schlaf
	schläft	schlief	hatte geschlafen	schlafe	schliefe	hätte geschlafen	
schlafend	schlafen	schliefen	hatten geschlafen	schlafen	schliefen	hätten geschlafen	schlafen wir
geschlafen	schlaft	schlieft	hattet geschlafen	schlafet	schliefet	hättet geschlafen	schlaft
geschlafen haben	schlafen	schliefen	hatten geschlafen	schlafen	schliefen	hätten geschlafen	schlafen Sie
44 **schwimmen**	schwimme	schwamm	war geschwommen	schwimme	schwömme	wäre geschwommen	
(to swim)	schwimmst	schwammst	warst geschwommen	schwimmest	schwömmest	wärest geschwommen	schwimme/schwimm
	schwimmt	schwamm	war geschwommen	schwimme	schwömme	wäre geschwommen	
schwimmend	schwimmen	schwammen	waren geschwommen	schwimmen	schwömmen	wären geschwommen	schwimmen wir
geschwommen	schwimmt	schwammt	wart geschwommen	schwimmet	schwömmet	wäret geschwommen	schwimmt
geschwommen sein	schwimmen	schwammen	waren geschwommen	schwimmen	schwömmen	wären geschwommen	schwimmen Sie
45 **schwören**	schwöre	schwor	hatte geschworen	schwöre	schwüre	hätte geschworen	
(to swear)	schwörst	schworst	hattest geschworen	schwörest	schwürest/schwürst	hättest geschworen	schwöre/schwör
	schwört	schwor	hatte geschworen	schwöre	schwüre	hätte geschworen	
schwörend	schwören	schworen	hatten geschworen	schwören	schwüren	hätten geschworen	schwören wir
geschworen	schwört	schwort	hattet geschworen	schwöret	schwüret	hättet geschworen	schwört
geschworen haben	schwören	schworen	hatten geschworen	schwören	schwüren	hätten geschworen	schwören Sie
46 **sitzen**	sitze	saß	hatte gesessen	sitze	säße	hätte gesessen	
(to sit)	sitzt	saßest	hattest gesessen	sitzest	säßest	hättest gesessen	sitze/sitz
	sitzt	saß	hatte gesessen	sitze	säße	hätte gesessen	
sitzend	sitzen	saßen	hatten gesessen	sitzen	säßen	hätten gesessen	sitzen wir
gesessen	sitzt	saßet	hattet gesessen	sitzet	säßet	hättet gesessen	sitzt
gesessen haben	sitzen	saßen	hatten gesessen	sitzen	säßen	hätten gesessen	sitzen Sie
47 **sprechen**	spreche	sprach	hatte gesprochen	spreche	spräche	hätte gesprochen	
(to speak)	sprichst	sprachst	hattest gesprochen	sprechest	sprächest	hättest gesprochen	sprich
	spricht	sprach	hatte gesprochen	spreche	spräche	hätte gesprochen	
sprechend	sprechen	sprachen	hatten gesprochen	sprechen	sprächen	hätten gesprochen	sprechen wir
gesprochen	sprecht	spracht	hattet gesprochen	sprechet	sprächet	hättet gesprochen	sprecht
gesprochen haben	sprechen	sprachen	hatten gesprochen	sprechen	sprächen	hätten gesprochen	sprechen Sie
48 **stehen**	stehe	stand	hatte gestanden	stehe	stünde/stände	hätte gestanden	
(to stand)	stehst	standest/standst	hattest gestanden	stehest	stündest/ständest	hättest gestanden	stehe/steh
	steht	stand	hatte gestanden	stehe	stünde/stände	hätte gestanden	
stehend	stehen	standen	hatten gestanden	stehen	stünden/ständen	hätten gestanden	stehen wir
gestanden	steht	standet	hattet gestanden	stehet	stündet/ständet	hättet gestanden	steht
gestanden haben	stehen	standen	hatten gestanden	stehen	stünden/ständen	hätten gestanden	stehen Sie

Infinitiv Partizip I Partizip II Perfekt	INDIKATIV			KONJUNKTIV I	KONJUNKTIV II		IMPERATIV
	Präsens	Präteritum	Plusquamperfekt	Präsens	Präsens	Perfekt	
49 stehlen	stehle	stahl	hatte gestohlen	stehle	stähle/stöhle	hätte gestohlen	
(to steal)	stiehlst	stahlst	hattest gestohlen	stehlest	stählest/stöhlest	hättest gestohlen	stiehl
	stiehlt	stahl	hatte gestohlen	stehle	stähle/stöhle	hätte gestohlen	
stehlend	stehlen	stahlen	hatten gestohlen	stehlen	stählen/stöhlen	hätten gestohlen	stehlen wir
gestohlen	stehlt	stahlt	hattet gestohlen	stehlet	stählet/stöhlet	hättet gestohlen	stehlt
gestohlen haben	stehlen	stahlen	hatten gestohlen	stehlen	stählen/stöhlen	hätten gestohlen	stehlen Sie
50 stoßen	stoße	stieß	hatte gestoßen	stoße	stieße	hätte gestoßen	
(to bump)	stößt	stießest/stießt	hattest gestoßen	stoßest	stießest	hättest gestoßen	stoße/stoß
	stößt	stieß	hatte gestoßen	stoße	stieße	hätte gestoßen	
stoßend	stoßen	stießen	hatten gestoßen	stoßen	stießen	hätten gestoßen	stoßen wir
gestoßen	stoßt	stießt	hattet gestoßen	stoßet	stießet	hättet gestoßen	stoßt
gestoßen haben	stoßen	stießen	hatten gestoßen	stoßen	stießen	hätten gestoßen	stoßen Sie
51 tragen	trage	trug	hatte getragen	trage	trüge	hätte getragen	
(to carry)	trägst	trugst	hattest getragen	tragest	trügest	hättest getragen	trage/trag
	trägt	trug	hatte getragen	trage	trüge	hätte getragen	
tragend	tragen	trugen	hatten getragen	tragen	trügen	hätten getragen	tragen wir
getragen	tragt	trugt	hattet getragen	traget	trüget	hättet getragen	tragt
getragen haben	tragen	trugen	hatten getragen	tragen	trügen	hätten getragen	tragen Sie
52 trinken	trinke	trank	hatte getrunken	trinke	tränke	hätte getrunken	
(to drink)	trinkst	trankst	hattest getrunken	trinkest	tränkest	hättest getrunken	trinke/trink
	trinkt	trank	hatte getrunken	trinke	tränke	hätte getrunken	
trinkend	trinken	tranken	hatten getrunken	trinken	tränken	hätten getrunken	trinken wir
getrunken	trinkt	trankt	hattet getrunken	trinket	tränket	hättet getrunken	trinkt
getrunken haben	trinken	tranken	hatten getrunken	trinken	tränken	hätten getrunken	trinken Sie
53 tun	tue	tat	hatte getan	tue	täte	hätte getan	
(to do)	tust	tatest	hattest getan	tuest	tätest	hättest getan	tue/tu
	tut	tat	hatte getan	tue	täte	hätte getan	
tuend	tun	taten	hatten getan	tuen	täten	hätten getan	tun wir
getan	tut	tatet	hattet getan	tuet	tätet	hättet getan	tut
getan haben	tun	taten	hatten getan	tuen	täten	hätten getan	tun Sie
54 waschen	wasche	wusch	hatte gewaschen	wasche	wüsche	hätte gewaschen	
(to wash)	wäschst	wuschest/wuschst	hattest gewaschen	waschest	wüschest/wüschst	hättest gewaschen	wasche/wasch
	wäscht	wusch	hatte gewaschen	wasche	wüsche	hätte gewaschen	
waschend	waschen	wuschen	hatten gewaschen	waschen	wüschen	hätten gewaschen	waschen wir
gewaschen	wascht	wuscht	hattet gewaschen	waschet	wüschet/wüscht	hättet gewaschen	wascht
gewaschen haben	waschen	wuschen	hatten gewaschen	waschen	wüschen	hätten gewaschen	waschen Sie
55 wissen	weiß	wusste	hatte gewusst	wisse	wüsste	hätte gewusst	
(to know)	weißt	wusstest	hattest gewusst	wissest	wüsstest	hättest gewusst	wisse
	weiß	wusste	hatte gewusst	wisse	wüsste	hätte gewusst	
wissend	wissen	wussten	hatten gewusst	wissen	wüssten	hätten gewusst	wissen wir
gewusst	wisst	wusstet	hattet gewusst	wisset	wüsstet	hättet gewusst	wisst
gewusst haben	wissen	wussten	hatten gewusst	wissen	wüssten	hätten gewusst	wissen Sie

Irregular verbs

The following is a list of the principal parts of all strong and mixed verbs that are introduced as active vocabulary in **Mosaik**, as well as other sample verbs. For the complete conjugations of these verbs, consult the verb list on pages **A14–A15** and the verb charts on pages **A16–A25**. The verbs listed here are base forms. See **Strukturen Volume 2, 2B.2** and **3A.1** to review **Perfekt** and **Präteritum** forms of separable and inseparable prefix verbs.

Infinitiv		Präteritum	Partizip II
backen	to bake	backte	gebacken
beginnen	to begin	begann	begonnen
bieten	to bid, to offer	bot	geboten
binden	to tie, to bind	band	gebunden
bitten	to request	bat	gebeten
bleiben	to stay	blieb	(ist) geblieben
braten (brät)	to fry, to roast	briet	gebraten
brechen (bricht)	to break	brach	gebrochen
brennen	to burn	brannte	gebrannt
bringen	to bring	brachte	gebracht
denken	to think	dachte	gedacht
dürfen (darf)	to be allowed to	durfte	gedurft
empfehlen (empfiehlt)	to recommend	empfahl	empfohlen
essen (isst)	to eat	aß	gegessen
fahren (fährt)	to go, to drive	fuhr	(ist) gefahren
fallen (fällt)	to fall	fiel	(ist) gefallen
fangen (fängt)	to catch	fing	gefangen
finden	to find	fand	gefunden
fliegen	to fly	flog	(ist) geflogen
fließen	to flow, to pour	floss	(ist) geflossen
frieren	to freeze	fror	(hat/ist) gefroren
geben (gibt)	to give	gab	gegeben
gehen	to go, to walk	ging	(ist) gegangen
gelten (gilt)	to be valid	galt	gegolten
genießen	to enjoy	genoss	genossen
geschehen (geschieht)	to happen	geschah	(ist) geschehen
gewinnen	to win	gewann	gewonnen
gleichen	to resemble	glich	geglichen
graben (gräbt)	to dig	grub	gegraben
haben (hat)	to have	hatte	gehabt
halten (hält)	to hold, to keep	hielt	gehalten
hängen	to hang	hing	gehangen
heben	to raise, to lift	hob	gehoben
heißen	to be called, to mean	hieß	geheißen
helfen (hilft)	to help	half	geholfen
kennen	to know	kannte	gekannt
klingen	to sound, to ring	klang	geklungen
kommen	to come	kam	(ist) gekommen
können (kann)	to be able to, can	konnte	gekonnt
laden (lädt)	to load, to charge	lud	geladen
lassen (lässt)	to let, to allow	ließ	gelassen
laufen (läuft)	to run, to walk	lief	(ist) gelaufen

Infinitiv		Präteritum	Partizip II
leiden	*to suffer*	litt	gelitten
leihen	*to lend*	lieh	geliehen
lesen (liest)	*to read*	las	gelesen
liegen	*to lie, to rest*	lag	gelegen
lügen	*to lie, to tell lies*	log	gelogen
meiden	*to avoid*	mied	gemieden
messen (misst)	*to measure*	maß	gemessen
mögen (mag)	*to like*	mochte	gemocht
müssen (muss)	*to have, to must*	musste	gemusst
nehmen (nimmt)	*to take*	nahm	genommen
nennen	*to name, to call*	nannte	genannt
preisen	*to praise*	pries	gepriesen
raten (rät)	*to guess*	riet	geraten
reiben	*to rub, to grate*	rieb	gerieben
riechen	*to smell*	roch	gerochen
rufen	*to call, to shout*	rief	gerufen
schaffen	*to create*	schuf	geschaffen
scheiden	*to divorce*	schied	geschieden
scheinen	*to shine, to appear*	schien	geschienen
schieben	*to push, to shove*	schob	geschoben
schießen	*to shoot*	schoss	geschossen
schlafen (schläft)	*to sleep*	schlief	geschlafen
schlagen (schlägt)	*to beat, to hit*	schlug	geschlagen
schließen	*to close*	schloss	geschlossen
schlingen	*to loop, to gulp*	schlang	geschlungen
schneiden	*to cut*	schnitt	geschnitten
schreiben	*to write*	schrieb	geschrieben
schwimmen	*to swim*	schwamm	(ist) geschwommen
sehen (sieht)	*to see*	sah	gesehen
sein (ist)	*to be*	war	(ist) gewesen
senden	*to send*	sandte/sendete	gesandt/gesendet
singen	*to sing*	sang	gesungen
sinken	*to sink*	sank	(ist) gesunken
sitzen	*to sit*	saß	gesessen
sollen (soll)	*to be supposed to*	sollte	gesollt
sprechen (spricht)	*to speak*	sprach	gesprochen
stehen	*to stand*	stand	gestanden
stehlen (stiehlt)	*to steal*	stahl	gestohlen
steigen	*to climb, to rise*	stieg	(ist) gestiegen
sterben (stirbt)	*to die*	starb	(ist) gestorben
stoßen	*to push, to thrust*	stieß	(hat/ist) gestoßen
streichen	*to paint, to cancel*	strich	gestrichen
streiten	*to argue*	stritt	gestritten
tragen (trägt)	*to carry*	trug	getragen
treffen (trifft)	*to hit, to meet*	traf	getroffen
treten (tritt)	*to kick, to step*	trat	(hat/ist) getreten
trinken	*to drink*	trank	getrunken
tun	*to do*	tat	getan
vergessen (vergisst)	*to forget*	vergaß	vergessen

Infinitiv		Präteritum	Partizip II
verlieren	*to lose*	verlor	verloren
wachsen (wächst)	*to grow*	wuchs	(ist) gewachsen
waschen (wäscht)	*to wash*	wusch	gewaschen
weisen	*to indicate, to show*	wies	gewiesen
wenden	*to turn, to flip*	wandte/wendete	gewandt/gewendet
werben (wirbt)	*to advertise*	warb	geworben
werden (wird)	*to become*	wurde	(ist) geworden
werfen (wirft)	*to throw*	warf	geworfen
winden	*to wind*	wand	gewunden
wissen (weiß)	*to know*	wusste	gewusst
wollen (will)	*to want*	wollte	gewollt
ziehen	*to pull, to draw, to move*	zog	(hat/ist) gezogen

Glossary

This glossary includes all active vocabulary introduced in **Mosaik**, as well as some additional words and expressions. The singular and plural endings listed for adjectival nouns are those that occur after a definite article. The numbers following each entry are as follows:

(2) **1A** = (**Mosaik** Volume) **Chapter, Lesson**

The entry would be in **Mosaik 2**, Chapter 1, Lesson A.

Abbreviations used in this glossary

acc.	accusative	*gen.*	genitive	*poss.*	possessive
adj.	adjective	*inf.*	informal	*prep.*	preposition
adv.	adverb	*interr.*	interrogative	*pron.*	pronoun
conj.	conjunction	*m.*	masculine noun	*sing.*	singular
dat.	dative	*n.*	neuter noun	*v.*	verb
f.	feminine noun	*nom.*	nominative		
form.	formal	*pl.*	plural		

Deutsch-Englisch

A

abbiegen *v.* to turn (2) **4A**
  rechts/links abbiegen *v.* to turn right/left (2) **4A**
abbrechen *v.* to cancel (2) **3B**
Abend, -e *m.* evening (1) **2B**
  abends *adv.* in the evening (1) **2A**
Abendessen, - *n.* dinner (1) **4B**
aber *conj.* but (1) **1B**
abfahren *v.* to leave (2) **4A**
Abfall, -̈e *m.* waste (3) **4B**
abfliegen *v.* to take off (2) **3B**
Abflug, -̈e *m.* departure (2) **3B**
abheben *v.* to withdraw (money) (3) **3A**
Absatz, -̈e *m.* paragraph (2) **1B**
abschicken *v.* to send (3) **3B**
Abschied, -e *m.* leave-taking; farewell (1) **1A**
Abschluss, -̈e *m.* degree (1) **2A**
  einen Abschluss machen *v.* to graduate (2) **1A**
Abschlusszeugnis, -se *n.* diploma (transcript) (1) **2A**
abstauben *v.* to dust (2) **2B**
sich abtrocknen *v.* to dry oneself off (3) **1A**
acht eight (1) **2A**
Achtung! Attention!
adoptieren *v.* to adopt (1) **3A**
Adresse, -n *f.* address (3) **2A**
Allee, -n *f.* avenue (3) **2B**
allein *adv.* alone; by oneself (1) **4A**
Allergie, -n *f.* allergy (3) **1B**
allergisch (gegen) *adj.* allergic (to) (3) **1B**
alles *pron.* everything (2) **3B**
  Alles klar? Everything OK? (1) **1A**
  alles Gute all the best (3) **2A**
  Alles Gute zum Geburtstag! Happy birthday! (2) **1A**
Alltagsroutine, -n *f.* daily routine (3) **1A**
  im Alltag in everyday life
als *conj.* as; when (2) **4A**
  als ob as if (3) **2A**
also *conj.* therefore; so (3) **1B**
alt *adj.* old (1) **3A**
Altkleider *pl.* second-hand clothing (3) **4B**
Altpapier *n.* used paper (3) **4B**
Amerika *n.* America (3) **2B**
amerikanisch *adj.* American (3) **2B**
Amerikaner, - / Amerikanerin, -nen *m./f.* American (3) **2B**
Ampel, -n *f.* traffic light (3) **2B**
an *prep.* at; on; by; in; to (2) **1B**, (3) **2B**
Ananas, - *f.* pineapple (1) **4A**
anbieten *v.* to offer (3) **4B**

anfangen *v.* to begin (1) **4A**
Angebot, -e *n.* offer
  im Angebot on sale (2) **1B**
angeln gehen *v.* to go fishing (1) **2B**
angenehm *adj.* pleasant (1) **3B**
  Angenehm. Nice to meet you. (1) **1A**
angesagt *adj.* trendy (2) **1B**
Angestellte, -n *m./f.* employee (3) **3A**
Angst, -̈e *f.* fear (2) **3A**
  Angst haben (vor) *v.* to be afraid (of) (2) **3A**
ankommen *v.* to arrive (1) **4A**
Ankunft, -̈e *f.* arrival (2) **3B**
Anlass, -̈e *m.* occasion (2) **1A**
  besondere Anlässe *m. pl.* special occasions (2) **1A**
anmachen *v.* to turn on (2) **4B**
Anruf, -e *m.* phone call (3) **3A**
  einen Anruf entgegennehmen *v.* to answer the phone (3) **3A**
anrufen *v.* to call (1) **4A**
  sich anrufen *v.* to call each other (3) **1A**
anschauen *v.* to watch, look at (2) **3A**
anspruchsvoll *adj.* demanding (3) **3B**
anstatt *prep.* instead of (2) **4B**
anstoßen *v.* to toast (2) **1A**
Antwort, -en *f.* answer
antworten (auf) *v.* to answer (1) **2A**
Anwendung *f.* application; usage
anziehen *v.* to put on (2) **1B**
  sich anziehen *v.* to get dressed (3) **1A**
Anzug, -̈e *m.* suit (2) **1B**
Apfel, -̈ *m.* apple (1) **1A**
Apotheke, -n *f.* pharmacy (3) **1B**
April *m.* April (1) **2A**, (2) **3A**
Arbeit, -en *f.* work (3) **3B**
  Arbeit finden *v.* to find a job (3) **3A**
arbeiten (an) *v.* to work (on) (1) **2A**, (2) **3A**
arbeitslos *adj.* unemployed (3) **2A**
Arbeitszimmer, - *n.* home office (2) **2A**
Architekt, -en / Architektin, -nen *m./f.* architect (1) **3B**
Architektur, -en *f.* architecture (1) **2A**
sich ärgern (über) *v.* to get angry (about) (3) **1A**
arm *adj.* poor; unfortunate (1) **3B**
Arm, -e *m.* arm (3) **1A**
Art, -en *f.* species; type (3) **4B**
Artischocke, -n *f.* artichoke (1) **4A**
Arzt, -̈e / Ärztin, -nen *m./f.* doctor (3) **1B**
  zum Arzt gehen *v.* to go to the doctor (3) **1B**
Assistent, -en / Assistentin, -nen *m./f.* assistant (3) **3A**
Aubergine, -n *f.* eggplant (1) **4A**
auch *adv.* also (1) **1A**

auf *prep.* on, onto, to (2) **1B**
  Auf Wiedersehen. Good-bye. (1) **1A**
aufgehen *v.* to rise (sun) (3) **4A**
auflegen *v.* to hang up (3) **3A**
aufmachen *v.* to open (2) **4B**
aufnehmen *v.* to record (2) **4B**
aufräumen *v.* to clean up (2) **2B**
aufregend *adj.* exciting (3) **4A**
aufrichtig *adj.* sincere (1) **3B**
aufstehen *v.* to get up (1) **4A**
aufwachen *v.* to wake up (3) **1A**
Auge, -n *n.* eye (1) **3A**; (3) **1A**
Augenbraue, -n *f.* eyebrow (3) **1A**
August *m.* August (1) **2A**, (2) **3A**
aus *prep.* from (1) **4A**
Ausbildung, -en *f.* education (3) **3A**
Ausdruck, -̈e *m.* expression
Ausfahrt, -en *f.* exit (2) **4A**
ausfüllen *v.* to fill out (3) **2A**
  ein Formular ausfüllen *v.* to fill out a form (3) **2A**
Ausgang, -̈e *m.* exit (2) **3B**
ausgefallen *adj.* offbeat (2) **1B**
ausgehen *v.* to go out (1) **4A**
Ausland *n.* abroad (2) **3B**
ausmachen *v.* to turn off (2) **4B**
sich ausruhen *v.* to rest (3) **1A**
ausschalten *v.* turn out, to turn off (3) **4B**
Aussehen *n.* look (style) (2) **1B**
außer *prep.* except (for) (1) **4B**
außerhalb *prep.* outside of (2) **4B**
Aussprache *f.* pronunciation
Aussterben *n.* extinction (3) **4B**
sich ausziehen *v.* to get undressed (3) **1A**
Auto, -s *n.* car (1) **1A**, (2) **4A**
Autobahn, -en *f.* highway (2) **4A**

B

Baby, -s *n.* baby (1) **3A**
Bäckerei, -en *f.* bakery (1) **4A**
Badeanzug, -̈e *m.* bathing suit (2) **1B**
Bademantel, -̈ *m.* bathrobe (3) **1A**
sich baden *v.* to bathe, take a bath (3) **1A**
Badewanne, -n *f.* bathtub (2) **2A**
Badezimmer, - *n.* bathroom (2) **2A**, (3) **1A**
Bahnsteig, -e *m.* track; platform (2) **4A**
bald *adv.* soon
  Bis bald. See you soon. (1) **1A**
Balkon, -e/-s *m.* balcony (2) **2A**
Ball, -̈e *m.* ball (1) **2B**
Ballon, -e/-s *m.* balloon (2) **1A**
Banane, -n *f.* banana (1) **4A**

Bank, ⁼e *f.* bench (3) **2B**
Bank, -en *f.* bank (3) **2A**
  auf der Bank *f.* at the bank (3) **2B**
Bankangestellte, -n *m./f.* bank employee (3) **3B**
bar *adj.* cash (3) **2A**
  bar bezahlen *v.* to pay in cash (3) **2A**
Bargeld *n.* cash (3) **2A**
Bart, ⁼e *m.* beard (3) **1A**
Baseball *m.* baseball (1) **2B**
Basketball *m.* basketball (1) **2B**
Bauch, ⁼e *m.* belly (3) **1A**
Bauchschmerzen *m. pl.* stomachache (3) **1B**
bauen *v.* to build (1) **2A**
Bauer, -n / Bäuerin, -nen *m./f.* farmer (3) **3B**
Bauernhof, ⁼e *m.* farm (3) **4A**
Baum, ⁼e *m.* tree (3) **4A**
Baumwolle *f.* cotton (2) **1B**
Baustelle, -n *f.* construction zone (2) **4A**
beantworten *v.* to answer (1) **4B**
bedeuten *v.* to mean (1) **2A**
bedeutend *adj.* important (3) **4A**
bedienen *v.* to operate, use (2) **4B**
sich beeilen *v.* to hurry (3) **1A**
Beförderung, -en *f.* promotion (3) **3B**
beginnen *v.* to begin (2) **2A**
Begrüßung, -en *f.* greeting (1) **1A**
behaupten *v.* to claim (3) **4B**
bei *prep.* at; near; with (1) **4A**
Beilage, -n *f.* side dish (1) **4B**
Bein, -e *n.* leg (3) **1A**
Beitrag ⁼e *m.* contribution (3) **4B**
bekannt *adj.* well-known (3) **2A**
bekommen *v.* to get, to receive (2) **1A**
belegen *v.* to take (a class) (1) **2A**
benutzen *v.* to use (2) **4A**
Benutzername, -n *m.* screen name (2) **4B**
Benzin, -e *n.* gasoline (2) **4A**
Berg -e *m.* mountain (1) **2B**, (3) **4A**
berichten *v.* to report (3) **4B**
Beruf, -e *m.* profession; job (1) **3B**, (3) **3A**
Berufsausbildung, -en *f.* professional training (3) **3A**
bescheiden *adj.* modest (1) **3B**
beschreiben *v.* to describe (1) **2A**
Beschreibung, -en *f.* description (1) **3B**
Besen, - *m.* broom (2) **2B**
Besitzer, - / Besitzerin, -nen *m./f.* owner (1) **3B**
besonderes *adj.* special (3) **2A**
  nichts Besonderes *adj.* nothing special (3) **2A**
besorgt *adj.* worried (1) **3B**
Besorgung, -en *f.* errand (3) **2A**
  Besorgungen machen *v.* to run errands (3) **2A**
besprechen *v.* to discuss (2) **3A**
Besprechung, -en *f.* meeting (3) **3A**
besser *adj.* better (2) **4A**
Besserwisser, - / Besserwisserin, -nen *m./f.* know-it-all (1) **2A**
beste *adj.* best (2) **4A**
Besteck *n.* silverware (1) **4B**
bestehen *v.* to pass (a test) (1) **1B**
bestellen *v.* to order (1) **4A**
bestimmt *adv.* definitely (1) **4B**

besuchen *v.* to visit (1) **4A**
Bett, -en *n.* bed (2) **2A**
  das Bett machen *v.* to make the bed (2) **2B**
  ins Bett gehen *v.* to go bed (3) **1A**
Bettdecke, - n *f.* duvet (2) **2B**
bevor *conj.* before (2) **4A**
sich bewegen *v.* to move (around)
sich bewerben *v.* to apply (3) **3A**
Bewerber, - / die Bewerberin, -nen *m./f.* applicant (3) **3A**
Bewertung, -en *f.* rating (2) **3B**
bezahlen *v.* to pay (for) (1) **4A**
Bibliothek, -en *f.* library (1) **1B**
Bier, -e *n.* beer (1) **4B**
bieten *v.* to offer (3) **1B**
Bild, -er *n.* picture (2) **2A**
Bildschirm, -e *m.* screen (2) **4B**
Bioladen, ⁼ *m.* health-food store (3) **1B**
Biologie *f.* biology (1) **2A**
biologisch *adj.* organic (3) **4B**
Birne, -n *f.* pear (1) **4A**
bis *prep.* until (1) **3B**
  Bis bald. See you soon. (1) **1A**
  Bis dann. See you later. (1) **1A**
  Bis gleich. See you soon. (1) **1A**
  Bis morgen. See you tomorrow. (1) **1A**
  Bis später. See you later. (1) **1A**
  bis zu *prep.* up to; until (3) **2B**
Bitte. Please.; You're welcome. (1) **1A**
Blatt, ⁼er *n.* leaf (3) **4A**
blau *adj.* blue (1) **3A**
  blaue Fleck, -e *m.* bruise (3) **B1**
bleiben *v.* to stay (2) **1B**
  Bleiben Sie bitte am Apparat. *v.* Please hold. (3) **3A**
Bleistift, -e *m.* pencil (1) **1B**
Blitz, -e *m.* lightning (2) **3A**
blond *adj.* blond (1) **3A**
  blonde Haare *n. pl.* blond hair (1) **3A**
Blume, -n *f.* flower (1) **1A**
Blumengeschäft, -e *n.* flower shop (3) **2A**
Bluse, -n *f.* blouse (2) **1B**
Blutdruck *m.* blood pressure (3) **1B**
Boden, ⁼ *m.* floor; ground (2) **2A**
Bohne, -n *f.* bean (1) **4A**
  grüne Bohne *f.* green bean (1) **4A**
Boot, -e *n.* boat (2) **4A**
Bordkarte, -n *f.* boarding pass (3) **3B**
braten *v.* to fry (1) **2B**
brauchen *v.* to need (1) **2A**
braun *adj.* brown (2) **1B**
braunhaarig *adj.* brown-haired, brunette (1) **3A**
brechen *v.* to break (1) **2B**
  sich (den Arm / das Bein) brechen *v.* to break (an arm / a leg) (3) **1B**
Bremse, -n *f.* brake (2) **4A**
brennen *v.* to burn (2) **1A**
Brief, -e *m.* letter (3) **2A**
  einen Brief abschicken *v.* to mail a letter (3) **2A**
Briefkasten, ⁼ *m.* mailbox (3) **2A**
Briefmarke, -n *f.* stamp (3) **2A**
Briefträger, - / Briefträgerin, -nen *m./f.* mail carrier (3) **2A**

Briefumschlag, ⁼e *m.* envelope (3) **2A**
Brille, -n *f.* glasses (2) **1B**
bringen *v.* to bring (1) **2A**
Brot, -e *n.* bread (1) **4A**
Brötchen, - *n.* roll (1) **4A**
Brücke, -n *f.* bridge (3) **2B**
Bruder, ⁼ *m.* brother (1) **1A**
Brunnen, - *m.* fountain (3) **2B**
Buch, ⁼er *n.* book (1) **1A**
buchen *v.* to make a (hotel) reservation (2) **3B**
Bücherregal, -e *n.* bookshelf (2) **2A**
Buchhalter, - / Buchhalterin, -nen *m./f.* accountant (3) **3B**
büffeln *v.* to cram (for a test) (1) **2A**
Bügelbrett, -er *n.* ironing board (2) **2B**
Bügeleisen, -. *n.* iron (2) **2B**
bügeln *v.* to iron (2) **2B**
Bundespräsident, -en / Bundespräsidentin, -nen *m./f.* (federal) president (2) **4B**
bunt *adj.* colorful (3) **2A**
Bürgermeister, - / Bürgermeisterin, -nen *m./f.* mayor (3) **2B**
Bürgersteig, -e *m.* sidewalk (3) **2B**
Büro, -s *n.* office (3) **3B**
Büroklammer, -n *f.* paperclip (3) **3A**
Büromaterial *n.* office supplies (3) **3A**
Bürste, -n *f.* brush (3) **1A**
bürsten *v.* to brush
  sich die Haare bürsten *v.* to brush one's hair (3) **1A**
Bus, -se *m.* bus (2) **4A**
Busch, ⁼e *m.* bush (3) **4A**
Bushaltestelle, -n *f.* bus stop (2) **4A**
Businessklasse *f.* business class (2) **3B**
Bußgeld, -er *n.* fine (monetary) (2) **4A**
Butter *f.* butter (1) **4A**

C

Café, -s *n.* café (1) **2A**
Camping *n.* camping (1) **2B**
CD, -s *f.* compact disc, CD (2) **4B**
Chef, -s / Chefin, -nen *m./f.* boss (3) **3B**
Chemie *f.* chemistry (1) **2A**
China *n.* China (3) **2B**
Chinese, -n / Chinesin, -nen *m./f.* Chinese (person) (3) **2B**
Chinesisch *n.* Chinese (language) (3) **2B**
Computer, - *m.* computer (1) **1B**
Cousin, -s / Cousine, -n *m./f.* cousin (1) **3A**

D

da there (1) **1A**
  Da ist/sind... There is/are... (1) **1A**
Dachboden, ⁼ *m.* attic (2) **2A**
dafür *adv.* for it (2) **2A**
daher *adv.* from there (2) **2A**
dahin *adv.* there (2) **2A**
damit *conj.* so that (3) **2A**
danach *conj.* then, after that (3) **1B**
danken *v.* to thank (1) **2A**
  Danke. Thank you. (1) **1A**
dann *adv.* then (2) **3B**
daran *adv.* on it (2) **2A**

darauf *adv.* on it (2) **2A**
darin *adv.* in it (2) **2A**
das *n.* the; this/that (1) **1A**
dass *conj.* that (3) **2A**
Datei, - en *f.* file (2) **4B**
Datum (*pl.* Daten) *n.* date (2) **3A**
davon *adv.* of it (2) **2A**
davor *adv.* before it (2) **2A**
Decke, -n *f.* blanket (2) **2B**
decken *v.* to cover (2) **2B**
  den Tisch decken *v.* to set the table (2) **2B**
denken *v.* to think (2) **1A**
  denken an *v.* to think about (2) **3A**
denn *conj.* for; because (2) **2A**
der *m.* the (1) **1A**
deshalb *conj.* therefore; so (3) **1B**
deswegen *conj.* that's why; therefore (3) **1B**
deutsch *adj.* German (3) **2B**
Deutsch *n.* German (language) (3) **2B**
Deutsche *m./f.* German (man/woman) (3) **2B**
Deutschland *n.* Germany (1) **4A**
deutschsprachig *adj.* German-speaking
Dezember *m.* December (1) **2A**, (2) **3A**
Diät, -en *f.* diet (1) **4B**
  auf Diät sein *v.* to be on a diet (1) **4B**
dick *adj.* fat (1) **3A**
die *f./pl.* the (1) **1A**
Dienstag, -e *m.* Tuesday (1) **2A**
  dienstags *adv.* on Tuesdays (1) **2A**
dieser/diese/dieses *m./f./n.* this; these (2) **4B**
diesmal *adv.* this time (2) **3B**
Digitalkamera, -s *f.* digital camera (2) **4B**
Ding, -e *n.* thing
Diplom, -e *n.* diploma (degree) (2) **2A**
diskret *adj.* discreet (1) **3B**
doch *adv.* yes (contradicting a negative statement or question) (1) **2B**
Dokument, -e *n.* document (2) **4B**
Donner, - *m.* thunder (2) **3A**
Donnerstag, -e *n.* Thursday (1) **2A**
  donnerstags *adv.* on Thursdays (1) **2A**
dort *adv.* there (1) **1A**
Dozent, -en / Dozentin, -nen *m./f.* college instructor (1) **2A**
draußen *prep.* outside; *adv.* out (2) **3A**
  Es ist schön draußen. It's nice out. (2) **3A**
dreckig *adj.* filthy (2) **2B**
drei three (1) **2A**
dritte *adj.* third (1) **2A**
Drogerie, -n *f.* drugstore (3) **2A**
drüben *adv.* over there (1) **4A**
drücken *v.* to push (1) **3B**; to print (2) **4B**
Drucker, - *m.* printer (2) **4B**
du *pron. (sing. inf.)* you (1) **1A**
dumm *adj.* dumb (2) **4A**
dunkel *adj.* dark (1) **3A**
dunkelhaarig *adj.* dark-haired (1) **3A**
dünn *adj.* thin (1) **3A**
durch *prep.* through (1) **3B**
durchfallen *v.* to flunk; to fail (1) **1B**
durchmachen *v.* to experience (2) **4B**
dürfen *v.* to be allowed to; may (1) **3B**
(sich) duschen *v.* to take a shower (3) **1A**

Dutzend, -e *n.* dozen (1) **4A**
DVD, -s *f.* DVD (2) **4B**
DVD-Player, - *m.* DVD-player (2) **4B**

E

Ecke, -n *f.* corner (3) **2B**
egoistisch *adj.* selfish (1) **3B**
Ehe, -n *f.* marriage (2) **1A**
Ehefrau, -en *f.* wife (1) **3A**
Ehemann, ¨er *m.* husband (1) **3A**
Ei, -er *n.* egg (1) **4A**
Eichhörnchen, - *n.* squirrel (3) **4A**
eifersüchtig *adj.* jealous (1) **3B**
ein/eine *m./f./n.* a (1) **1A**
Einbahnstraße, -n *f.* one-way street (2) **4A**
einfach *adj.* easy (1) **2A**
einfarbig *adj.* solid colored (2) **1B**
eingebildet *adj.* arrogant (1) **3B**
einkaufen *v.* to shop (1) **4A**
  einkaufen gehen *v.* to go shopping (1) **4A**
Einkaufen *n.* shopping (2) **1B**
Einkaufszentrum, (*pl.* Einkaufszentren) *n.* mall; shopping center (3) **2B**
Einkommensgruppe, -n *f.* income bracket (2) **2B**
einladen *v.* to invite (2) **1A**
einmal *adv.* once (2) **3B**
eins one (1) **2A**
einschlafen *v.* to go to sleep (1) **4A**
einzahlen *v.* to deposit (money) (3) **2A**
Einzelkind, -er *n.* only child (1) **3A**
Eis *n.* ice cream (2) **1A**
Eisdiele, -n *f.* ice cream shop (1) **4A**
Eishockey *n.* ice hockey (1) **2B**
Eiswürfel, - *m.* ice cube (2) **1A**
elegant *adj.* elegant (2) **1B**
Elektriker, - / Elektrikerin, -nen *m./f.* electrician (3) **3B**
elf eleven (1) **2A**
Ell(en)bogen, - *m.* elbow (3) **1A**
Eltern *pl.* parents (1) **3A**
E-Mail, -s *f.* e-mail (2) **4B**
empfehlen *v.* to recommend (1) **2B**
Empfehlungsschreiben, - *n.* letter of recommendation (3) **3A**
endlich *adv.* finally (3) **1B**
Energie, -n *f.* energy (3) **4B**
energiesparend *adj.* energy-efficient (2) **2B**
eng *adj.* tight (2) **1B**
England *n.* England (3) **2B**
Engländer, - / Engländerin, -nen *m./f.* English (person) (3) **2B**
Englisch *n.* English (language) (3) **2B**
Enkelkind, -er *n.* grandchild (1) **3A**
Enkelsohn, ¨e *m.* grandson (1) **3A**
Enkeltochter, ¨ *f.* granddaughter (1) **3A**
entdecken *v.* to discover (2) **2B**
entfernen *v.* to remove (2) **2B**
entlang *prep.* along, down (1) **3B**
entlassen *v.* to fire; to lay off (3) **3B**
sich entschließen *v.* to decide (1) **4B**
(sich) entschuldigen *v.* to apologize; to excuse
  Entschuldigen Sie. Excuse me. (*form.*) (1) **1A**

Entschuldigung. Excuse me. (1) **1A**
sich entspannen *v.* to relax (3) **1A**
entwerten *v.* to validate (2) **4A**
  eine Fahrkarte entwerten *v.* to validate a ticket (2) **4A**
entwickeln *v.* to develop (3) **4B**
er *pron.* he (1) **1A**
Erdbeben, - *n.* earthquake (3) **4A**
Erdbeere, -n *f.* strawberry (1) **4A**
Erde, -n *f.* earth (3) **4B**
Erderwärmung *f.* global warming (3) **4B**
Erdgeschoss, -e *n.* ground floor (2) **2A**
Erfahrung, -en *f.* experience (3) **3A**
erfinden *v.* to invent (2) **3A**
Erfolg, -e *m.* success (3) **3B**
erforschen *v.* to explore (3) **4A**
ergänzen *v.* complete
Ergebnis, -se *n.* result; score (1) **1B**
erhalten *v.* to preserve (3) **4B**
sich erinnern (an) *v.* to remember (3) **1A**
sich erkälten *v.* to catch a cold (3) **1A**
Erkältung, -en *f.* cold (3) **1B**
erkennen *v.* to recognize (2) **3A**
erklären *v.* to explain (1) **4A**
erneuerbare Energie, -n *f.* renewable energy (3) **4B**
ernst *adj.* serious (1) **3B**
erster/erste/erstes *adj.* first (1) **2A**
erwachsen *adj.* grown-up (3) **2A**
erzählen *v.* to tell (2) **3A**
  erzählen von *v.* to talk about (2) **3A**
es *pron.* it (1) **1A**
  Es geht. (I'm) so-so. (1) **1A**
  Es gibt... There is/are... (1) **2B**
Essen, - *n.* food (1) **4A**
essen *v.* to eat (1) **2B**
  essen gehen *v.* to eat out (1) **2B**
Esslöffel, - *m.* soup spoon (1) **4B**
Esszimmer, - *n.* dining room (2) **2A**
etwas *pron.* something (2) **3B**
  etwas anderes something else (3) **2A**
euer (*pl. inf.*) *poss. adj.* your (1) **3A**

F

Fabrik, -en *f.* factory (3) **4B**
Fabrikarbeiter, - / Fabrikarbeiterin, -nen *m./f.* factory worker (3) **3B**
Fach, ¨er *n.* subject (1) **2A**
fade *adj.* bland (1) **4B**
fahren *v.* to drive; to go (1) **2B**
  Auto fahren *v.* to drive a car (2) **4A**
  Fahrrad fahren *v.* to ride a bicycle (1) **2B**
  geradeaus fahren *v.* to go straight ahead (2) **4A**
Fahrer, - / Fahrerin, -nen *m./f.* driver (2) **4A**
Fahrgemeinschaft, -en *f.* carpool (3) **4B**
Fahrkarte, -n *f.* ticket (2) **4A**
  eine Fahrkarte entwerten *v.* to validate a ticket (2) **4A**
Fahrkartenschalter, - *m.* ticket office (2) **4A**
Fahrplan, ¨e *m.* schedule (2) **4A**
Fahrrad, ¨er *n.* bicycle (1) **2B**, (2) **4A**
Fahrstuhl, ¨e *m.* elevator (2) **3B**
fallen *v.* to fall (1) **2B**

Familie, -n *f.* family (1) **3A**
Familienstand, ⸚e *m.* marital status (1) **3A**
Fan, -s *m.* fan (1) **2B**
fangen *v.* to catch (1) **2B**
fantastisch *adj.* fantastic (3) **2A**
Farbe, -n *f.* color (2) **1B**
färben *v.* to dye
  sich die Haare färben *v.* to dye one's hair (3) **1A**
fast *adv.* almost (1) **4A**
faul *adj.* lazy (1) **3B**
Februar *m.* February (1) **2A**, (2) **3A**
fegen *v.* to sweep (2) **2B**
feiern *v.* to celebrate (2) **1A**
Feiertag, -e *m.* holiday (2) **1A**
Feinkostgeschäft, -e *n.* delicatessen (1) **4A**
Feld, -er *n.* field (3) **4A**
Fenster, - *n.* window (1) **1A**
Ferien *pl.* vacation (2) **3A**
Fernbedienung, -en *f.* remote control (2) **4B**
fernsehen *v.* to watch television (2) **4B**
Fernsehen *n.* television (programming)
Fernseher, - *m.* television set (2) **4B**
fertig *adj.* ready; finished (3) **3B**
Fest, -e *n.* festival; celebration (2) **1A**
Festplatte, -n *f.* hard drive (2) **4B**
Feuerwehrmann, ⸚er **/ Feuerwehrfrau, -en**
  (pl. Feuerwehrleute) *m./f.* firefighter (3) **3B**
Fieber, - *n.* fever (3) **1B**
  Fieber haben *v.* to have a fever (3) **1B**
finden *v.* to find (1) **2A**
Finger, - *m.* finger (3) **1A**
Firma (pl. die Firmen) *f.* firm; company (3) **3A**
Fisch, -e *m.* fish (1) **4A**, (3) **4A**
Fischgeschäft, -e *n.* fish store (1) **4A**
fit *adj.* in good shape (1) **2B**
Flasche, -n *f.* bottle (1) **4B**
Fleisch *n.* meat (1) **4A**
fleißig *adj.* hard-working (1) **3B**
fliegen *v.* to fly (2) **3B**
Flug, ⸚e *m.* flight (2) **3B**
Flughafen, ⸚ *m.* airport (2) **3B**
Flugticket, -s *n.* (plane) ticket (2) **3B**
Flugzeug, -e *n.* airplane (2) **3B**
Flur, -e *m.* hall (2) (1) **2A**
Fluss, ⸚e *m.* river (1) **3B**, (3) **4A**
folgen *v.* to follow (2) **1A**, (3) **2B**
Form, -en *f.* shape, form
  in guter/schlechter Form sein *v.* to be in/out of shape (3) **1B**
Formular, -e *n.* form (3) **2A**
  ein Formular ausfüllen *v.* to fill out a form (3) **2A**
Foto, -s *n.* photo, picture (1) **1B**
Frage, -n *f.* question (1) **1B**
fragen *v.* to ask (1) **2A**
  fragen nach *v.* to ask about (2) **3A**
  sich fragen *v.* to wonder, ask oneself (3) **1A**
Frankreich *n.* France (3) **2B**
Franzose, -n / Französin, -nen *m./f.* French (person) (3) **2B**
Französisch *n.* French (language) (3) **2B**
Frau, -en *f.* woman (1) **1A**; wife (1) **3A**
  Frau... Mrs./Ms.... (1) **1A**
Freitag, -e *m.* Friday (1) **2A**

freitags *adv.* on Fridays (1) **2A**
Freizeit, -en *f.* free time, leisure (1) **2B**
Freizeitaktivität, - en *f.* leisure activity (1) **2B**
Fremdsprache, -n *f.* foreign language (1) **2A**
sich freuen (über) *v.* to be happy (about) (3) **1A**
  Freut mich. Pleased to meet you. (1) **1A**
  sich freuen auf *v.* to look forward to (3) **1A**
Freund, -e / Freundin, -nen *m./f.* friend (1) **1A**
freundlich *adj.* friendly (1) **3B**
  Mit freundlichen Grüßen Yours sincerely (1) **3B**
Freundschaft, -en *f.* friendship (2) **1A**
Frischvermählte, -n *m./f.* newlywed (2) **1A**
Friseur, -e / Friseurin, -nen *m./f.* hairdresser (1) **3B**
froh *adj.* happy (1) **3B**
  Frohe Ostern! Happy Easter! (2) **1A**
  Frohe Weihnachten! Merry Christmas! (2) **1A**
früh *adj.* early; in the morning (1) **2B**
  morgen früh tomorrow morning (1) **2B**
Frühling, -e *m.* spring (1) **2B**, (2) **3A**
Frühstück, -e *n.* breakfast (1) **4B**
fühlen *v.* to feel (1) **2A**
  sich (wohl) fühlen *v.* to feel (well) (3) **1A**
füllen *v.* to fill
fünf five (1) **2A**
funktionieren *v.* to work, function (2) **4B**
für *prep.* for (1) **3B**
furchtbar *adj.* awful (2) **3A**
Fuß, ⸚e *m.* foot (3) **1A**
Fußball *m.* soccer (1) **2B**
Fußgänger, - / Fußgängerin, -nen *m./f.* pedestrian (3) **2B**

G

Gabel, -n *f.* fork (1) **4B**
Gang, ⸚e *m.* course (1) **4B**
  erster/zweiter Gang *m.* first/second course (1) **4B**
ganz *adj.* all, total (2) **3B**
ganztags *adj.* full-time (3) **3B**
Garage, -n *f.* garage (2) **1B**
Garnele, -n *f.* shrimp (1) **4A**
Gartenabfall, ⸚e *m.* yard waste (3) **4B**
Gärtner, - /Gärtnerin, -nen *m./f.* gardener (3) **3B**
Gast, ⸚e *m.* guest (2) **1A**
Gastfamilie, -n *f.* host family (1) **4B**
Gastgeber, - / Gastgeberin, -nen *m./f.* host/hostess (2) **1A**
Gebäck, -e *n.* pastries; baked goods (2) **1A**
Gebäude, - *n.* building (3) **2A**
geben *v.* to give (1) **2B**
  Es gibt... There is/are... (1) **2B**
Geburt, -en *f.* birth (2) **1A**
Geburtstag, -e *m.* birthday (2) **1A**
  Wann hast du Geburtstag? When is your birthday? (2) **3A**
geduldig *adj.* patient (1) **3B**
Gefahr, -en *f.* danger (3) **4B**
gefährdet *adj.* endangered; threatened (3) **4B**
gefallen *v.* to please (2) **1A**
Gefrierschrank, ⸚e *m.* freezer (2) **2B**
gegen *prep.* against (1) **3B**
gegenüber (von) *prep.* across (from) (3) **2B**
Gehalt, ⸚er *n.* salary (3) **3A**

hohes/niedriges Gehalt, ⸚er *n.* high/low salary (3) **3A**
Gehaltserhöhung, -en *f.* raise (3) **3B**
gehen *v.* to go (1) **2A**
  Es geht. (I'm) so-so. (1) **1A**
  Geht es dir/Ihnen gut? *v.* Are you all right? (inf./form.) (1) **1A**
  Wie geht es Ihnen? (form.) How are you? (1) **1A**
  Wie geht's (dir)? (inf.) How are you? (1) **1A**
gehören *v.* to belong to (1) **4B**
Geländewagen, - *m.* SUV (2) **4B**
gelb *adj.* yellow (2) **1B**
Geld, -er *n.* money (3) **2A**
  Geld abheben/einzahlen *v.* to withdraw/deposit money (3) **2A**
Geldautomat, -en *m.* ATM (3) **2A**
Geldschein, -e *m.* bill (money) (3) **2A**
gemein *adj.* mean (1) **3B**
Gemüse, - *n.* vegetables (1) **4A**
genau *adv.* exactly
  genauso wie just as (2) **4A**
genießen *v.* to enjoy
geöffnet *adj.* open (3) **2A**
Gepäck *n.* luggage (2) **3B**
geradeaus *adv.* straight ahead (2) **4A**
gern *adv.* with pleasure (1) **2B**
  gern (+verb) to like to (+verb) (1) **2B**
  ich hätte gern... I would like... (1) **4A**
  Gern geschehen. My pleasure.; You're welcome. (1) **1A**
Geschäft, -e *n.* business (3) **3A**; store (1) **4A**
Geschäftsführer, - / Geschäftsführerin, -nen *m./f.* manager (3) **3A**
Geschäftsmann, ⸚er **/ Geschäftsfrau, -en** **(pl. Geschäftsleute)** *m./f.* businessman/businesswoman (1) **3B**
Geschenk, -e *n.* gift (2) **1A**
Geschichte, -n *f.* history (1) **2A**; story
geschieden *adj.* divorced (1) **3A**
Geschirr *n.* dishes (2) **2B**
  Geschirr spülen *v.* to do the dishes (2) **2B**
geschlossen *adj.* closed (3) **2A**
Geschmack, ⸚e *m.* flavor; taste (1) **4B**
Geschwister, - *n.* sibling (1) **3A**
Gesetz, -e *n.* law (3) **4B**
Gesicht, -er *n.* face (3) **1A**
gestern *adv.* yesterday (2) **1B**
gestreift *adj.* striped (2) **1B**
gesund *adj.* healthy (2) **4A**; (3) **1B**
  gesund werden *v.* to get better (3) **1B**
Gesundheit *f.* health (3) **1B**
geteilt durch divided by (1) **1B**
Getränk, -e *n.* beverage (1) **4B**
getrennt *adj.* separated (1) **3A**
gewaltfrei *adj.* nonviolent (3) **4B**
Gewerkschaft, -en *f.* labor union (3) **3B**
gewinnen *v.* to win (1) **2B**
Gewitter, - *n.* thunderstorm (2) **3A**
sich gewöhnen an *v.* to get used to (3) **1A**
gierig *adj.* greedy (1) **3B**
Giftmüll *m.* toxic waste (3) **4B**
Glas, ⸚er *n.* glass (1) **4B**
glatt *adj.* straight (1) **3A**
  glatte Haare *n. pl.* straight hair (1) **3A**

glauben *v.* to believe (2) **1A**
gleich *adj.* same
  ist gleich *v.* equals, is (1) **1B**
Glück *n.* happiness (2) **1A**
glücklich *adj.* happy (1) **3B**
Golf *n.* golf (1) **2B**
Grad *n.* degree (2) **3A**
  Es sind 18 Grad draußen. It's 18 degrees out. (2) **3A**
Gramm, -e *n.* gram (1) **4A**
Granit, -e *m.* granite (2) **2B**
Gras, ̈er *n.* grass (3) **4A**
gratulieren *v.* to congratulate (2) **1A**
grau *adj.* grey (2) **1B**
grausam *adj.* cruel
Grippe, -n *f.* flu (3) **1B**
groß *adj.* big; tall (1) **3A**
großartig *adj.* terrific (1) **3A**
Großeltern *pl.* grandparents (1) **1A**
Großmutter, ̈ *f.* grandmother (1) **3A**
Großvater, ̈ *m.* grandfather (1) **3A**
großzügig *adj.* generous (1) **3B**
grün *adj.* green (2) **1B**
  grüne Bohne (*pl.* die grünen Bohnen) *f.* green bean (1) **4A**
Gruß, ̈e *m.* greeting
  Mit freundlichen Grüßen Yours sincerely (1) **3B**
grüßen *v.* to greet (1) **2A**
günstig *adj.* cheap (2) **1B**
Gürtel, - *m.* belt (2) **1B**
gut *adj.* good; *adv.* well (1) **1A**
  gut aussehend *adj.* handsome (1) **3A**
  gut gekleidet *adj.* well-dressed (2) **1B**
  Gute Besserung! Get well! (2) **1A**
  Guten Appetit! Enjoy your meal! (1) **4B**
  Guten Abend! Good evening. (1) **1A**
  Guten Morgen! Good morning. (1) **1A**
  Gute Nacht! Good night. (1) **1A**
  Guten Tag! Hello. (1) **1A**

H

Haar, -e *n.* hair (1) **3A**, (3) **1A**
Haartrockner, - *m.* hair dryer (3) **1A**
haben *v.* to have (1) **1B**
Hagel *m.* hail (2) **3A**
Hähnchen, - *n.* chicken (1) **4A**
halb half; half an hour before (1) **2A**
Halbbruder, ̈ *m.* half brother (1) **3A**
Halbschwester, -n *f.* half sister (1) **3A**
halbtags *adj.* part-time (3) **3B**
Hallo! Hello. (1) **1A**
Hals, ̈e *m.* neck (3) **1A**
  Hals- und Beinbruch! Break a leg! (2) **1A**
Halskette, -n *f.* necklace (2) **1B**
Hand, ̈e *f.* hand (3) **1A**
handeln *v.* to act
  handeln von *v.* to be about; have to do with (2) **3A**
Handgelenk, -e *n.* wrist (3) **1B**
Handgepäck *n.* carry-on luggage (2) **3B**
Handschuh, -e *m.* glove (2) **1B**
Handtasche, -n *f.* purse (2) **1B**
Handtuch, ̈er *n.* towel (3) **1A**
Handy, -s *n.* cell phone (2) **4B**

hängen *v.* to hang (2) **1B**
Hase, -n *m.* hare (3) **4A**
hässlich *adj.* ugly (1) **3A**
Hauptspeise, -n *f.* main course (1) **4B**
Hauptstraße, -n *f.* main road (3) **2B**
Haus, ̈er *n.* house (2) **2A**
  nach Hause *adv.* home (2) **1B**
  zu Hause *adv.* at home (1) **4A**
Hausarbeit *f.* housework (2) **2B**
  Hausarbeit machen *v.* to do housework (2) **2B**
Hausaufgabe, -n *f.* homework (1) **1B**
Hausfrau, -en / Hausmann, ̈er *f./m.* homemaker (3) **3B**
hausgemacht *adj.* homemade (1) **4B**
Hausmeister, - / Hausmeisterin, -nen *m./f.* caretaker; custodian (3) **3B**
Hausschuh, -e *m.* slipper (3) **1A**
Haustier, -e *n.* pet (1) **3A**
Heft, -e *n.* notebook (1) **1B**
Hefter, - *m.* stapler (3) **3A**
heiraten *v.* to marry (1) **3A**
heiß *adj.* hot (2) **3A**
heißen *v.* to be named (1) **2A**
  Ich heiße... My name is... (1) **1A**
helfen *v.* to help (1) **2B**
  helfen bei *v.* to help with (2) **3A**
hell *adj.* light (1) **3A**; bright (2) **1B**
Hemd, -en *n.* shirt (2) **1B**
herauf *adv.* up; upwards (2) **2A**
heraus *adv.* out (2) **2A**
Herbst, -e *m.* fall, autumn (1) **2B**, (2) **3A**
Herd, -e *m.* stove (2) **2B**
Herr Mr. (1) **1A**
herunter *adv.* down; downwards (2) **2A**
heruntergehen *v.* to go down (3) **2B**
  die Treppe heruntergehen *v.* to go downstairs (3) **2B**
herunterladen *v.* to download (2) **4B**
Herz, -en *n.* heart
  Herzlichen Glückwunsch! Congratulations! (2) **1A**
heute *adv.* today (1) **2B**
  Heute ist der... Today is the... (1) **2A**
  Welcher Tag ist heute? What day is it today? (2) **3A**
  Der Wievielte ist heute? What is the date today? (1) **2A**
hier *adv.* here (1) **1A**
  Hier ist/sind... Here is/are... (1) **1B**
Himmel *m.* sky (3) **4A**
hin und zurück there and back (2) **3B**
sich hinlegen *v.* to lie down (3) **1A**
sich hinsetzen *v.* to sit down (3) **1A**
hinter *prep.* behind (2) **1B**
hinterlassen *v.* to leave (behind)
  eine Nachricht hinterlassen *v.* to leave a message (3) **3A**
Hobby, -s *n.* hobby (1) **2B**
hoch *adj.* high (2) **4A**
hochgehen *v.* to go up, climb up (3) **2B**
  die Treppe hochgehen *v.* to go upstairs (3) **2B**
Hochwasser, - *n.* flood (3) **4B**
Hochzeit, -en *f.* wedding (2) **1A**
Hockey *n.* hockey (1) **2B**
Höflichkeit, -en *f.* courtesy; polite expression (1) **1A**
Holz, ̈er *n.* wood (2) **2B**

hören *v.* to hear; listen to (1) **2A**
Hörer, - *m.* receiver (3) **3A**
Hörsaal (*pl.* Hörsäle) *m.* lecture hall (2) **2A**
Hose, -n *f.* pants (2) **1B**
  kurze Hose *f.* shorts (2) **1B**
Hotel, -s *n.* hotel (2) **3B**
  Fünf-Sterne-Hotel *n* five-star hotel. (2) **3B**
Hotelgast, ̈e *m.* hotel guest (2) **3B**
hübsch *adj.* pretty (1) **3A**
Hund, -e *m.* dog (1) **3A**
Hundewetter *n.* terrible weather (2) **3A**
husten *v.* to cough (3) **1B**
Hut, ̈e *m.* hat (2) **1B**
Hybridauto, -s *n.* hybrid car (3) **4B**

I

ich *pron.* I (1) **1A**
Idee, -n *f.* idea (1) **1A**
Ihr (*form., sing/pl.*) *poss. adj.* your (1) **3A**
ihr (*inf., pl.*) *pron.* you (1) **1A**; *poss. adj.* her, their (1) **3A**
immer *adv.* always (1) **4A**
Immobilienmakler, - / Immobilienmaklerin, -nen *m./f.* real estate agent (3) **3B**
in *prep.* in (2) **1B**
Inder, - / Inderin, -nen *m./f.* Indian (person) (3) **2B**
Indien *n.* India (3) **2B**
indisch *adj.* Indian (3) **2B**
Informatik *f.* computer science (1) **2A**
sich informieren (über) *v.* to find out (about) (3) **1A**
Ingenieur, -e / Ingenieurin, -nen *m./f.* engineer (1) **3B**
Innenstadt, ̈e *f.* city center; downtown (3) **2B**
innerhalb *prep.* inside of, within (2) **4B**
Insel, -n *f.* island (3) **4A**
intellektuell *adj.* intellectual (1) **3B**
intelligent *adj.* intelligent (1) **3B**
interessant *adj.* interesting (1) **2A**
sich interessieren (für) *v.* to be interested (in) (3) **1A**
Internet *n.* Web (2) **4B**
  im Internet surfen *v.* to surf the Web (2) **4B**
Internetcafé, -s *n.* internet café (3) **2A**
Italien *n.* Italy (3) **2B**
Italiener, - / Italienerin, -nen *m./f.* Italian (person) (3) **2B**
Italienisch *n.* Italian (language) (3) **2B**

J

ja yes (1) **1A**
Jacke, -n *f.* jacket (2) **1B**
Jahr, -e *n.* year (2) **3A**
  Ein gutes neues Jahr! Happy New Year! (2) **1A**
  Ich bin... Jahre alt. I am... years old (1) **1B**
Jahrestag, -e *m.* anniversary (2) **1A**
Jahreszeit, -en *f.* season (2) **3A**
Januar *m.* January (1) **2A**, (2) **3A**
Japan *n.* Japan (3) **2B**
Japaner, - / Japanerin, -nen *m./f.* Japanese (person) (3) **2B**
Japanisch *n.* Japanese (language) (3) **2B**
Jeans *f.* jeans (2) **1B**
jeder/jede/jedes *adj.* any, every, each (2) **4B**

jemand *pron.* someone (2) **3B**
jetzt *adv.* now (1) **4A**
joggen *v.* to jog (1) **2B**
Joghurt, -s *m.* yogurt (1) **4A**
Journalist, -en / Journalistin, -nen *m./f.* journalist (1) **3B**
Jugendherberge, -n *f.* youth hostel (2) **3B**
jugendlich *adj.* young; youthful (3) **2A**
Juli *m.* July (1) **2A**, (2) **3A**
jung *adj.* young (1) **3A**
Junge, -n *m.* boy (1) **1A**
Juni *m.* June (1) **2A**, (2) **3A**
Juweliergeschäft, -e *n.* jewelry store (3) **2A**

K

Kaffee, -s *m.* coffee (1) **4B**
Kaffeemaschine, -n *f.* coffeemaker (2) **2B**
Kalender, - *m.* calendar (1) **1B**
kalt *adj.* cold (2) **3A**
sich (die Haare) kämmen *v.* to comb (one's hair) (3) **1A**
Kanada *n.* Canada (3) **2B**
Kanadier, - / Kanadierin, -nen *m./f.* Canadian (3) **2B**
Kandidat, -en *m.* candidate (3) **3A**
Kaninchen, - *n.* rabbit (3) **4A**
Karotte, -n *f.* carrot (1) **4A**
Karriere, -n *f.* career (3) **3B**
Karte, -n *f.* map (1) **1B**, *f.* card (2) **2B**; (2) **1A**
eine Karte lesen *v.* to read a map (2) **3B**
mit der Karte bezahlen *v.* to pay by (credit) card (3) **2A**
Kartoffel, -n *f.* potato (1) **4A**
Käse, - *m.* cheese (1) **4A**
Katze, -n *f.* cat (1) **3A**
kaufen *v.* to buy (1) **2A**
Kaufhaus, ¨er *n.* department store (3) **2B**
Kaution, -en *f.* security deposit (2) **2A**
kein *adj.* no (1) **2B**
Keine Zufahrt. Do not enter. (1) **3B**
Keks, -e *m.* cookie (2) **1A**
Keller, - *m.* cellar (2) **2A**
Kellner, - / Kellnerin, -nen *m./f.* waiter/waitress (1) **3B**, (1) **4B**
kennen *v.* to know, be familiar with (2) **1B**
sich kennen *v.* to know each other (3) **1A**
(sich) kennen lernen *v.* to meet (one another) (1) **1A**
Keramik, -en *f.* ceramic (2) **2B**
Kernenergie *f.* nuclear energy (2) **1B**
Kernkraftwerk, -e *n.* nuclear power plant (3) **4B**
Kind, -er *n.* child (1) **1A**
Kino, -s *n.* movie theater (3) **2A**
Kiosk, -e *m.* newspaper kiosk (3) **2A**
Kirche, -n *f.* church (3) **2B**
Kissen, - *n.* pillow (2) **2B**
Klasse, -n *f.* class (1) **1B**
erste/zweite Klasse, -n first/second class (2) **4A**
Klassenkamerad, -en / Klassenkameradin, -nen *m./f.* (K-12) classmate (1) **1B**
Klassenzimmer, - *n.* classroom (1) **1B**
klassisch *adj.* classical (3) **2A**
Kleid, -er *n.* dress (2) **1B**

Kleidergröße, -n *f.* clothing size (2) **1B**
Kleidung *f. pl.* clothes (2) **1B**
klein *adj.* small; short (stature) (1) **3A**
Kleingeld *n.* change (money) (3) **2A**
Klempner, - / Klempnerin, -nen *m./f.* plumber (3) **3B**
klettern *v.* to climb (mountain) (1) **2B**
klingeln *v.* to ring (2) **4B**
Klippe, -n *f.* cliff (3) **4A**
Knie, - *n.* knee (3) **1A**
Knoblauch, -e *m.* garlic (1) **4A**
Koch, ¨e / Köchin, -nen *m./f.* cook, chef (1) **4B**
kochen *v.* to cook (1) **2B**
Koffer, - *m.* suitcase (2) **3B**
Kofferraum, ¨e *m.* trunk (2) **4A**
Kombi, -s *m.* station wagon (2) **4B**
Komma, -s *n.* comma (1) **1B**
kommen *v.* to come (1) **2A**
Kommilitone, -n / Kommilitonin, -nen *m./f.* (university) classmate (1) **1B**
Kommode, -n *f.* dresser (2) **2A**
kompliziert *adj.* complicated (3) **2A**
Konditorei, -en *f.* pastry shop (1) **4A**
können *v.* to be able, can (1) **3B**
Konto (*pl.* Konten) *n.* bank account (3) **2A**
Konzert, -e *n.* concert (2) **1B**
Kopf, ¨e *m.* head (3) **1A**
Kopfhörer, - *m.* headphones (2) **4B**
Kopfschmerzen *m. pl.* headache (3) **1B**
Korea *n.* Korea (3) **2B**
der Koreaner, - / die Koreanerin, -nen *m./f.* Korean (person) (3) **2B**
Koreanisch *n.* Korean (language) (3) **2B**
Körper, - *m.* body (3) **1A**
korrigieren *v.* to correct (1) **2A**
Kosmetiksalon, -s *m.* beauty salon (3) **2A**
kosten *v.* to cost (1) **2A**
Wie viel kostet das? *v.* How much is that? (1) **4A**
krank *adj.* sick (3) **1B**
krank werden *v.* to get sick (3) **1B**
Krankenhaus, ¨er *n.* hospital (3) **1B**
Krankenpfleger, - / Krankenschwester, -n *m./f.* nurse (3) **1B**
Krankenwagen, - *m.* ambulance (3) **1B**
Krawatte, -n *f.* tie (2) **1B**
Kreuzfahrt, -en *f.* cruise (2) **3B**
Kreuzung, -en *f.* intersection (3) **2B**
Küche, -n *f.* kitchen (2) **2A**
Kuchen, - *m.* cake; pie (1) **4A**
Kuh, ¨e *f.* cow (3) **4A**
kühl *adj.* cool (2) **3A**
Kühlschrank, ¨e *m.* refrigerator (2) **2B**
Kuli, -s *m.* (ball-point) pen (1) **1B**
Kunde, -n / Kundin, -nen *m./f.* customer (2) **1B**
kündigen *v.* to resign (3) **3B**
Kunst, ¨e *f.* art (1) **2A**
Kunststoff, -e *m.* plastic (2) **2B**
kurz *adj.* short (1) **3A**
kurze Haare *n. pl.* short hair (1) **3A**
kurze Hose *f.* shorts (2) **1B**
kurzärmlig *adj.* short-sleeved (2) **1B**
Kurzfilm, -e *m.* short film
Kuss, ¨e *m.* kiss (2) **1A**
küssen *v.* to kiss (1) **1A**
sich küssen *v.* to kiss (each other) (3) **1A**
Küste, -n *f.* coast (3) **4A**

L

lächeln *v.* to smile (1) **3B**
lachen *v.* to laugh (1) **3B**
Ladegerät, -e *n.* battery charger (2) **4B**
laden *v.* to charge; load (2) **4B**
Lage, -n *f.* location (2) **3B**
Laken, - *n.* sheet (2) **2B**
Lampe, -n *f.* lamp (2) **2A**
Land, ¨er *n.* country (2) **3B**
landen *v.* to land (2) **3B**
Landkarte, -n *f.* map (2) **3B**
Landschaft, -en *f.* landscape; countryside (3) **4A**
lang *adj.* long (1) **3A**
lange Haare *n. pl.* long hair (1) **3A**
langärmlig *adj.* long-sleeved (2) **1B**
langsam *adj.* slow (1) **3B**
Langsam fahren. Slow down. (1) **3B**
langweilig *adj.* boring (1) **2A**
Laptop, -s *m./n.* laptop (computer) (2) **4B**
lassen *v.* to let, allow (1) **2B**
laufen *v.* to run (1) **2B**
leben *v.* to live (1) **2A**
Lebenslauf, ¨e *m.* résumé; CV (3) **3A**
Lebensmittelgeschäft, -e *n.* grocery store (1) **4A**
lecker *adj.* delicious (1) **4B**
Leder, - *n.* leather (2) **1B**
ledig *adj.* single (1) **3A**
legen *v.* to lay (2) **1B**; *v.* to put; lay (3) **1A**
Lehrbuch, ¨er *n.* textbook (university) (1) **1B**
Lehrer, - / Lehrerin, -nen *m./f.* teacher (1) **1B**
leicht *adj.* light (1) **4B**; mild (3) **1B**
Leichtathletik *f.* track and field (1) **2B**
leider *adv.* unfortunately (1) **4A**
leiten *v.* to manage (3) **3B**
Lenkrad, ¨er *n.* steering wheel (2) **4A**
lernen *v.* to study; to learn (1) **2A**
lesen *v.* to read (1) **2B**
letzter/letzte/letztes *adj.* last (1) **2B**
Leute *pl.* people (1) **3B**
Licht, -er *n.* light (3) **4B**
Liebe, -n *f.* love (2) **1A**
Lieber/Liebe *m./f.* Dear (1) **3B**
lieben *v.* to love (1) **2A**
sich lieben *v.* to love each other (3) **1A**
lieber *adj.* rather (2) **4A**
liebevoll *adj.* loving (1) **3B**
Liebling, -e *m.* darling
Lieblings- favorite (1) **4B**
liegen *v.* to lie; to be located (2) **1B**
lila *adj.* purple (2) **1B**
Linie, -n *f.* line
Lippe, -n *f.* lip (3) **1A**
Lippenstift, -e *m.* lipstick (3) **1A**
Literatur, -en *f.* literature (1) **2A**
LKW, -s *m.* truck (2) **4A**
LKW-Fahrer, - / LKW-Fahrerin, -nen *m./f.* truck driver (3) **3B**
lockig *adj.* curly (1) **3A**
lockige Haare *n. pl.* curly hair (1) **3A**
Los! Start!; Go! (1) **2B**
löschen *v.* to delete (2) **4B**
Lösung, -en *f.* solution (3) **4B**

eine **Lösung vorschlagen** *v.* to propose a
solution (3) **4B**
Luft, ¨e *f.* air (3) **4A**
lügen *v.* to lie, tell a lie
Lust, ¨e *f.* desire
Lust haben *v.* to feel like (2) **3B**
lustig *adj.* funny (1) **3B**

M

machen *v.* to do; make (1) **2A**
Mach's gut! *v.* All the best! (1) **3B**
Mädchen, - *n.* girl (1) **1A**
Mahlzeit, -en *f.* meal (1) **4B**
Mai *m.* May (1) **2A**, (2) **3A**
Mal, -e *n.* time
das erste/letzte Mal the first/last time (2) **3B**
zum ersten/letzten Mal for the first/last time (2) **3B**
mal times (1) **1B**
Mama, -s *f.* mom (1) **3A**
man *pron.* one (2) **3B**
mancher/manche/manches *adj.* some (2) **4B**
manchmal *adv.* sometimes (2) **3B**
Mann, ¨er *m.* man (1) **1A**; *m.* husband (1) **3A**
Mannschaft, -en *f.* team (1) **2B**
Mantel, ¨ *m.* coat (2) **1B**
Markt, ¨e *m.* market (1) **4A**
Marmelade, -n *f.* jam (1) **4A**
Marmor *m.* marble (2) **2B**
März *m.* March (1) **2A**, (3) **3A**
Material, -ien *n.* material (2) **1B**
Mathematik *f.* mathematics (1) **2A**
Maus, ¨e *f.* mouse (2) **4B**
Mechaniker, - / Mechanikerin, -nen *m./f.*
mechanic (2) **4A**
Medikament, -e *n.* medicine (3) **1B**
Medizin *f.* medicine (1) **2A**
Meer, -e *n.* sea; ocean (3) **4A**
Meeresfrüchte *f. pl.* seafood (1) **4A**
mehr *adj.* more (2) **4A**
mein *poss. adj.* my (1) **3A**
meinen *v.* to mean; to believe; to
maintain (3) **4B**
Meisterschaft, -en *f.* championship (1) **2B**
Melone, -n *f.* melon (1) **4A**
Mensa (*pl.* Mensen) *f.* cafeteria (college/
university) (1) **1B**
Mensch, -en *m.* person
Messer, - *n.* knife (1) **4B**
Metzgerei, -en *f.* butcher shop (1) **4A**
Mexikaner, - / Mexikanerin, -nen *m./f.* Mexican
(person) (3) **2B**
mexikanisch *adj.* Mexican (3) **2B**
Mexiko *n.* Mexico (3) **2B**
Miete, -n *f.* rent (2) **2A**
mieten *v.* to rent (2) **2A**
Mikrofon, -e *n.* microphone (2) **4B**
Mikrowelle, -n *f.* microwave (2) **2B**
Milch *f.* milk (1) **4B**
Minderheit, -en *f.* minority (3) **4B**
Mineralwasser *n.* sparkling water (1) **4B**
minus minus (1) **1B**
mir *pron.* myself, me (2) **3A**

Mir geht's (sehr) gut. *v.* I am (very) well. (1) **1A**
Mir geht's nicht (so) gut. *v.* I am not (so) well. (1) **1A**
mit with (1) **4B**
Mitbewohner, - / Mitbewohnerin, -nen *m./f.*
roommate (1) **2A**
mitbringen *v.* to bring along (1) **4A**
mitkommen *v.* to come along (1) **4A**
mitmachen *v.* to participate (2) **4B**
mitnehmen *v.* to bring with (3) **2B**
jemanden mitnehmen *v.* to give someone a
ride (3) **2B**
Mittag, -e *m.* noon (1) **2A**
Mittagessen *n.* lunch (1) **4B**
Mitternacht *f.* midnight (1) **2A**
Mittwoch, -e *m.* Wednesday (1) **2A**
mittwochs *adv.* on Wednesdays (1) **2A**
Möbel, - *n.* furniture (2) **2A**
Möbelstück, -e *n.* piece of furniture (2) **2A**
möbliert *adj.* furnished (2) **2A**
modern *adj.* modern (3) **2A**
modisch *adj.* fashionable (2) **1B**
mögen *v.* to like (1) **4B**
Ich möchte... I would like... (1) **4B**
Monat, -e *m.* month (1) **2A**, (2) **3A**
Mond, -e *m.* moon (3) **4A**
Montag, -e *m.* Monday (1) **2A**
montags *adv.* on Mondays (1) **2A**
Morgen, - *m.* morning (1) **2B**
morgens *adv.* in the morning (1) **2A**
morgen *adv.* tomorrow (1) **2B**
morgen früh tomorrow morning (1) **2B**
Motor, -en *m.* engine (2) **4A**
Motorhaube, -n *f.* hood (of car) (2) **4A**
MP3-Player, - *m.* mp3 player (2) **4B**
müde *adj.* tired (1) **3B**
Müll *m.* trash (2) **2B**; *m.* waste (3) **4B**
den Müll rausbringen *v.* to take out the trash (2) **2B**
Müllwagen, - *m.* garbage truck (3) **4B**
Mund, ¨er *m.* mouth (3) **1A**
Münze, -n *f.* coin (3) **2A**
Musiker, - / Musikerin, -nen *m./f.* musician (1) **3B**
müssen *v.* to have to; must (1) **3B**
mutig *adj.* brave (1) **3B**
Mutter, ¨ *f.* mother (1) **1A**
Mütze, -n *f.* cap (2) **1B**

N

nach *prep.* after; to; according to (1) **4B**; *prep.*
past (time) (1) **2A**
nach rechts/links to the right/left (2) **2A**
nachdem *conj.* after (3) **2A**
nachmachen *v.* to imitate (2) **4B**
Nachmittag, -e *m.* afternoon (1) **2B**
nachmittags *adv.* in the afternoon (1) **2A**
Nachname, -n *m.* last name (1) **3A**
Nachricht, -en *f.* message (3) **3A**
eine Nachricht hinterlassen *v.* to leave a
message (3) **3A**
nächster/nächste/nächstes *adj.* next (1) **2B**
Nacht, ¨e *f.* night (1) **2B**
Nachtisch, -e *m.* dessert (1) **4B**
Nachttisch, -e *m.* night table (2) **2A**

nah(e) *adj.* near; nearby (3) **2B**
Nähe *f.* vicinity (3) **2B**
in der Nähe von *f.* close to (3) **2B**
naiv *adj.* naïve (1) **3B**
Nase, -n *f.* nose (3) **1A**
verstopfte Nase *f.* stuffy nose (3) **1A**
nass *adj.* wet (3) **4A**
Natur, *f.* nature (3) **4A**
Naturkatastrophe, -n *f.* natural disaster (3) **4A**
Naturwissenschaft, -en *f.* science (1) **2A**
Nebel, - *m.* fog; mist (2) **3A**
neben *prep.* next to (2) **1B**
Nebenkosten *pl.* additional charges (2) **2A**
Neffe, -n *m.* nephew (2) **4B**
nehmen *v.* to take (1) **2B**
nein no (1) **1A**
nennen *v.* to call (2) **1A**
nervös *adj.* nervous (1) **3B**
nett *adj.* nice (1) **3B**
neugierig *adj.* curious (1) **3B**
neun nine (1) **2A**
nicht *adv.* not (1) **2B**
nicht schlecht not bad (1) **1A**
nichts *pron.* nothing (2) **3B**
nie *adv.* never (1) **4A**
niedrig *adj.* low (3) **3A**
niemals *adv.* never (2) **3B**
niemand *pron.* no one (2) **3B**
niesen *v.* to sneeze (3) **1B**
noch *adv.* yet; still; in addition (1) **4A**
normalerweise *adv.* usually (3) **1B**
Notaufnahme, -n *f.* emergency room (3) **1B**
Note, -n *f.* grade (on an assignment) (1) **1B**
Notfall, ¨e *m.* emergency (3) **3B**
Notiz, -en *f.* note (1) **1B**
November *m.* November (1) **2A**, (2) **3A**
Nummernschild, -er *n.* license plate (2) **4A**
nur *adv.* only (1) **4A**
nützlich *adj.* useful (1) **2A**
nutzlos *adj.* useless (1) **2A**

O

ob *conj.* whether; if (3) **2A**
Obst *n.* fruit (1) **4A**
obwohl *conj.* even though (2) **2A**; *conj.* although
(3) **2A**
oder *conj.* or (1) **1B**
Ofen, ¨ *m.* oven (2) **2B**
öffentlich *adj.* public (2) **4A**
öffentliche Verkehrsmittel *n.* public
transportation (2) **4A**
öffnen *v.* to open (1) **2A**
oft *adv.* often (1) **4A**
ohne *prep.* without (1) **3B**
Ohr, -en *n.* ear (3) **1A**
Ökologie *f.* ecology (3) **4B**
ökologisch *adj.* ecological (3) **4B**
Oktober *m.* October (1) **2A**, (2) **3A**
Öl, -e *n.* oil (1) **4A**
Olivenöl, -e *n.* olive oil (1) **4A**
Oma, -s *f.* grandma (1) **3A**
online sein *v.* to be online (2) **4B**

Opa, -s *m.* grandpa (1) **3A**
orange *adj.* orange (2) **1B**
Orange, -n *f.* orange (1) **4A**
ordentlich *adj.* neat, tidy (2) **2B**
Ort, -e *m.* place (1) **1B**
Österreich *n.* Austria (3) **2B**
Österreicher, - / Österreicherin, -nen *m./f.* Austrian (person) (3) **2B**

P

Paar, -e *n.* couple (1) **3A**
packen *v.* to pack (2) **3B**
Paket, -e *n.* package (3) **2A**
Papa, -s *m.* dad (1) **3A**
Papier, -e *n.* paper
　Blatt Papier (*pl.* Blätter Papier) *n.* sheet of paper (1) **1B**
Papierkorb, ⁼e *m.* wastebasket (1) **1B**
Paprika, - *f.* pepper (1) **4A**
　grüne/rote Paprika *f.* green/red pepper (1) **4A**
Park, -s *m.* park (1) **1A**
parken *v.* to park (2) **4A**
　Parkverbot. No parking. (1) **3B**
Party, -s *f.* party (2) **1A**
　eine Party geben *v.* to throw a party (2) **1A**
Passagier, -e / Passagierin, -nen *m./f.* passenger (2) **3B**
passen *v.* to fit; to match (2) **1A**
passieren *v.* to happen (2) **1B**
Passkontrolle, -n *f.* passport control (2) **3B**
Passwort, ⁼er *n.* password (2) **4B**
Pasta *f.* pasta (1) **4A**
Patient, -en / Patientin, -nen *m./f.* patient (3) **1B**
Pause, -n *f.* break, recess (1) **1B**
Pension, -en *f.* guesthouse (2) **3B**
Person, -en *f.* person (1) **1A**
Personalausweis, -e *m.* ID card (2) **3B**
Personalchef, -s / die Personalchefin, -nen *m./f.* human resources manager (3) **3A**
persönlich *adj.* personal (1) **3B**
Pfanne, -n *f.* pan (2) **2B**
Pfeffer, - *m.* pepper (1) **4B**
Pferd, -e *n.* horse (1) **2B**
Pfirsich, -e *m.* peach (1) **4A**
Pflanze, -n *f.* plant (2) **2A**
Pfund, -e *n.* pound (1) **4A**
Physik *f.* physics (1) **2A**
Picknick, -s, *n.* picnic (3) **4A**
　ein Picknick machen *v.* to have a picnic (3) **4A**
Pilz, -e *m.* mushroom (1) **4A**
Pinnwand, ⁼e *f.* bulletin board (3) **3A**
Planet, -en *m.* planet (3) **4B**
　den Planeten retten *v.* to save the planet (3) **4B**
Platten, - *m.* flat tire (2) **4A**
　einen Platten haben *v.* to have a flat tire (2) **4A**
Platz, ⁼e *m.* court (1) **1A**
plus plus (1) **1B**
Politiker, - / Politikerin, -nen *m./f.* politician (3) **3B**
Polizeiwache, -n *f.* police station (3) **2A**
Polizist, -en / Polizistin, -nen *m./f.* police officer (2) **4A**
Post *f.* post office; mail (3) **2A**
　zur Post gehen *v.* to go to the post office (3) **2A**

Poster, - *n.* poster (1) **2A**
Postkarte, -n *f.* postcard (3) **2A**
Praktikum (*pl.* die Praktika) *n.* internship (3) **3A**
prima *adj.* great (1) **1A**
probieren *v.* to try (1) **3B**
　Probieren Sie mal! Give it a try!
Problem, -e *n.* problem (1) **1A**
Professor, -en / Professorin, -nen *m./f.* professor (1) **1B**
Programm, -e *n.* program (2) **4B**
Prost! Cheers! (1) **4B**
Prozent, -e *n.* percent (1) **1B**
Prüfung, -en *f.* exam, test (1) **1B**
Psychologe, -n / Psychologin, -nen *m./f.* psychologist (3) **3B**
Psychologie *f.* psychology (1) **2A**
Pullover, - *m.* sweater (2) **1B**
Punkt, -e *m.* period (1) **1B**
pünktlich *adj.* on time (2) **3B**
putzen *v.* to clean (2) **2B**
　sich die Zähne putzen *v.* to brush one's teeth (3) **1A**

Q

Querverweis, -e *m.* cross-reference

R

Radiergummi, -s *m.* eraser (1) **1B**
Rasen, - *m.* lawn, grass (1) **3B**
　Betreten des Rasens verboten. Keep off the grass. (1) **3B**
sich rasieren *v.* to shave (3) **1A**
Rasierer, - *m.* razor (3) **1A**
Rasierschaum, ⁼e *m.* shaving cream (3) **1A**
Rathaus, ⁼er *n.* town hall (3) **2A**
rauchen *v.* to smoke
　Rauchen verboten. No smoking. (1) **3B**
rausbringen *v.* to bring out (2) **2B**
　den Müll rausbringen *v.* to take out the trash (2) **2B**
realistisch *adj.* realistic (3) **2A**
Rechnung, -en *f.* check (1) **4B**
Rechtsanwalt, ⁼e / Rechtsanwältin, -nen *m./f.* lawyer (1) **3B**
Rechtschreibung *f.* spelling
recyceln *v.* to recycle (3) **4B**
reden *v.* to talk (2) **1A**
　reden über *v.* to talk about (2) **3A**
Referat, -e *n.* presentation (1) **2A**
Referenz, -en *f.* reference (3) **3A**
Regen *m.* rain (2) **3A**
Regenmantel, ⁼ *m.* raincoat (2) **3A**
Regenschirm, -e *m.* umbrella (2) **3A**
Regierung, -en *f.* government (3) **4B**
regnen *v.* to rain (1) **2A**, (2) **3A**
reich *adj.* rich (1) **3B**
Reis *m.* rice (1) **4A**
Reise, -n *f.* trip (2) **3B**
Reisebüro, -s *n.* travel agency (2) **3B**
reisen *v.* to travel (1) **2A**
Reisende, -n *m./f.* traveler (2) **3B**
Reiseziel, -e *n.* destination (2) **3B**
reiten *v.* to ride (1) **2B**

rennen *v.* to run (2) **1A**
Rente, -n *f.* pension
　in Rente gehen *v.* to retire (2) **1A**
Rentner, - / Rentnerin, -nen *m./f.* retiree (3) **3B**
reparieren *v.* to repair (2) **4A**
Restaurant, -s *n.* restaurant (1) **4B**
retten *v.* to save (3) **4B**
Rezept, -e *n.* recipe (1) **4A**; prescription (3) **1B**
Richter, - / Richterin, -nen *m./f.* judge (3) **3B**
Richtung, -en *f.* direction (3) **2B**
　in Richtung *f.* toward (3) **2B**
Rindfleisch *n.* beef (1) **4A**
Rock, ⁼e *m.* skirt (2) **1B**
rosa *adj.* pink (2) **1B**
rot *adj.* red (1) **3A**
rothaarig *adj.* red-haired (1) **3A**
Rücken, - *m.* back (3) **1A**
Rückenschmerzen *m. pl.* backache (3) **1B**
Rucksack, ⁼e *m.* backpack (1) **1B**
ruhig *adj.* calm (1) **3B**
Russe, -n / Russin, -nen *m./f.* Russian (person) (3) **2B**
Russisch *n.* Russian (language) (3) **2B**
Russland *n.* Russia (3) **2B**

S

Sache, -n *f.* thing (1) **1B**
Saft, ⁼e *m.* juice (1) **4B**
sagen *v.* to say (1) **2A**
Salat, -e *m.* lettuce; salad (1) **4A**
Salz, -e *n.* salt (1) **4B**
salzig *adj.* salty (1) **4B**
Samstag, -e *m.* Saturday (1) **2A**
　samstags *adv.* on Saturdays (1) **2A**
sauber *adj.* clean (2) **2B**
saurer Regen *m.* acid rain (3) **4B**
Saustall *n.* pigsty (2) **2B**
　Es ist ein Saustall! It's a pigsty! (2) **2B**
Schach *n.* chess (1) **2B**
Schaf, -e *n.* sheep (3) **4A**
Schaffner, - / Schaffnerin, -nen *m./f.* ticket collector (2) **4A**
Schal, -s *m.* scarf (2) **1B**
scharf *adj.* spicy (1) **4B**
schauen *v.* to look (2) **3A**
Scheibenwischer, - *m.* windshield wiper (2) **4A**
Scheinwerfer, - *m.* headlight (2) **4A**
scheitern *v.* to fail (3) **3B**
schenken *v.* to give (a gift) (2) **1A**
schicken *v.* to send (2) **4B**
Schiff, -e *n.* ship (2) **4A**
Schinken, - *m.* ham (1) **4A**
Schlafanzug, ⁼e *m.* pajamas (3) **1A**
schlafen *v.* to sleep (1) **2B**
Schlafzimmer, - *n.* bedroom (2) **2A**
Schlange, -n *f.* line (2) **3B**; *f.* snake (3) **4A**
　Schlange stehen *v.* to stand in line (2) **3B**
schlank *adj.* slim (1) **3A**
schlecht *adj.* bad (1) **3B**
　schlecht gekleidet *adj.* badly dressed (2) **1B**
schließlich *adv.* finally (2) **3B**
Schlüssel, - *m.* key (2) **3B**

schmecken *v.* to taste (1) **4B**
Schmerz, -en *m.* pain (3) **1B**
sich schminken *v.* to put on makeup (3) **1A**
schmutzig *adj.* dirty (2) **2B**
Schnee *m.* snow (2) **3A**
schneien *v.* to snow (2) **3A**
schnell *adj.* fast (1) **3B**
schon *adv.* already, yet (1) **4A**
schön *adj.* pretty; beautiful (1) **3A**
  Schön dich/Sie kennen zu lernen. Nice to meet you. (1) **1A**
  Schönen Tag noch! Have a nice day! (1) **1A**
  Es ist schön draußen. It's nice out. (2) **3A**
Schrank, ̈e *m.* cabinet; closet (2) **2A**
schreiben *v.* to write (1) **2A**
  schreiben an *v.* to write to (2) **3A**
  sich schreiben *v.* to write one another (3) **1A**
Schreibtisch, -e *m.* desk (1) **1B**
Schreibwarengeschäft, -e *n.* paper-goods store (3) **2A**
Schublade, -n *f.* drawer (2) **2A**
schüchtern *adj.* shy (1) **3B**
Schuh, -e *m.* shoe (2) **1B**
Schulbuch, ̈er *n.* textbook (K–12) (1) **1B**
Schule, -n *f.* school (1) **1B**
Schüler, - / Schülerin, -nen (K–12) *m./f.* student (1) **1B**
Schulleiter, - / Schulleiterin, -nen *m./f.* principal (1) **1B**
Schulter, -n *f.* shoulder (3) **1A**
Schüssel, -n *f.* bowl (1) **4B**
schützen *v.* to protect (3) **4B**
schwach *adj.* weak (1) **3B**
Schwager, ̈ *m.* brother-in-law (1) **3A**
Schwägerin, -nen *f.* sister-in-law (1) **3A**
schwanger *adj.* pregnant (3) **1B**
schwänzen *v.* to cut class (1) **1B**
schwarz *adj.* black (2) **1B**
schwarzhaarig *adj.* black-haired (1) **3A**
Schweinefleisch *n.* pork (1) **4A**
Schweiz (die) *f.* Switzerland (2) **3A**
Schweizer, - / Schweizerin, -nen *m./f.* Swiss (person) (3) **2B**
schwer *adj.* rich, heavy (1) **4B**; *adj.* serious, difficult (3) **1B**
Schwester, -n *f.* sister (1) **1A**
Schwiegermutter, ̈ *f.* mother-in-law (1) **3A**
Schwiegervater, ̈ *m.* father-in-law (1) **3A**
schwierig *adj.* difficult (1) **2A**
Schwimmbad, ̈er *n.* swimming pool (1) **2B**
schwimmen *v.* to swim (1) **2B**
schwindlig *adj.* dizzy (3) **1B**
sechs six (1) **2A**
See, -n *m.* lake (3) **4A**
sehen *v.* to see (1) **2B**
sehr *adv.* very (1) **3A**
Seide, -n *f.* silk (2) **1B**
Seife, -n *f.* soap (3) **1A**
sein *v.* to be (1) **1A**
  (gleich) sein *v.* to equal (1) **1B**
sein *poss. adj.* his, its (1) **3A**
seit since; for (1) **4B**
Sekt, -e *m.* champagne (2) **1A**
selten *adv.* rarely (1) **4A**

Seminar, -e *n.* seminar (1) **2A**
Seminarraum, -räume *m.* seminar room (1) **2A**
Sender, - *m.* channel (2) **4B**
September *m.* September (1) **2A**, (2) **3A**
Serviette, -n *f.* napkin (1) **4B**
Sessel, - *m.* armchair (2) **2A**
setzen *v.* to put, place (2) **1B**; *v.* to put, set (3) **1A**
Shampoo, -s *n.* shampoo (3) **1A**
sicher *adv.* probably (3) **2A**
Sicherheitsgurt, -e *m.* seatbelt (2) **4A**
sie *pron.* she/they (1) **1A**
Sie *pron.* (*form., sing./pl.*) you (1) **1A**
sieben seven (1) **2A**
Silvester *n.* New Year's Eve (2) **1A**
singen *v.* to sing (1) **2B**
sitzen *v.* to sit (2) **1B**
Ski fahren *v.* to ski (1) **2B**
Smartphone, -s *n.* smartphone (2) **4B**
SMS, - *f.* text message (2) **4B**
Snack, -s *m.* snack (1) **4B**
so *adv.* so (1) **4A**
Socke, -n *f.* sock (2) **1B**
Sofa, -s *n.* sofa; couch (2) **2A**
  Sofa surfen *v.* to couch surf (2) **3B**
Sohn, ̈e *m.* son (1) **3A**
solcher/solche/solches *pron.* such (2) **4B**
sollen *v.* to be supposed to (1) **3B**
Sommer, - *m.* summer (1) **2B**, (2) **3A**
sondern *conj.* but rather; instead (2) **2A**
Sonne, -n *f.* sun (3) **4A**
Sonnenaufgang, ̈e *m.* sunrise (3) **4A**
Sonnenbrand, ̈e *m.* sunburn (3) **1B**
Sonnenbrille, -n *f.* sunglasses (2) **1B**
Sonnenenergie *f.* solar energy (3) **4B**
Sonnenuntergang, ̈e *m.* sunset (3) **4A**
sonnig *adj.* sunny (2) **3A**
Sonntag, -e *m.* Sunday (1) **2A**
  sonntags *adv.* on Sundays (1) **2A**
Spanien *n.* Spain (3) **3B**
Spanier, - / Spanierin, -nen *m./f.* Spanish (person) (3) **2B**
Spanisch *n.* Spanish (language) (3) **2B**
spannend *adj.* exciting (3) **2A**
Spaß *m.* fun (1) **2B**
  Spaß haben/machen *v.* to have fun/to be fun (1) **2B**
  (keinen) Spaß haben *v.* to (not) have fun (2) **1A**
spät *adj.* late
  Wie spät ist es? What time is it? (1) **2A**
spazieren gehen *v.* to go for a walk (1) **2B**
Spaziergang, ̈e *m.* walk
speichern *v.* to save (2) **4B**
Speisekarte, -n *f.* menu (1) **4B**
Spiegel, - *m.* mirror (2) **2A**
Spiel, -e *n.* match, game (1)c**2B**
spielen *v.* to play (1) **2A**
Spieler, - / Spielerin, -nen *m./f.* player (1) **2B**
Spielfeld, -er *n.* field (1) **2B**
Spielkonsole, -n *f.* game console (2) **4B**
Spitze! *adj.* great! (1) **1A**
Sport *m.* sports (1) **2B**
  Sport treiben *v.* to exercise (3) **1B**
Sportart, -en *f.* sport; type of sport (1) **2B**
Sporthalle, - n *f.* gym (1) **2A**

sportlich *adj.* athletic (1) **3A**
sprechen *v.* to speak (1) **2B**
  sprechen über *v.* to speak about (2) **3A**
Spritze, -n *f.* shot (3) **1B**
  eine Spritze geben *v.* to give a shot (3) **1B**
Spüle, -n *f.* (kitchen) sink (2) **2B**
spülen *v.* to rinse (2) **2B**
  Geschirr spülen *v.* to do the dishes (2) **2B**
  Spülmaschine, -n *f.* dishwasher (2) **2B**
Stadion (*pl.* Stadien) *n.* stadium (1) **2B**
Stadt, ̈e *f.* city (2) **1B**; *f.* town (3) **2B**
Stadtplan, ̈e *m.* city map (2) **3B**
Stahl *m.* steel (2) **2B**
stark *adj.* strong (1) **3B**
starten *v.* to start (2) **4B**
statt *conj.* instead of
Statue, -n *f.* statue (3) **2B**
staubsaugen *v.* to vacuum (2) **2B**
Staubsauger, - *m.* vacuum cleaner (2) **2B**
stehen *v.* to stand (2) **1B**
  Schlange stehen *v.* to stand in line (2) **3B**
stehlen *v.* to steal (1) **2B**
steif *adj.* stiff (3) **1B**
steigen *v.* to climb (2) **1B**
Stein, -e *m.* rock (3) **4A**
Stelle, -n *f.* place, position (3) **2A**; job (3) **3A**
  an deiner/Ihrer Stelle *f.* if I were you (3) **2A**
  eine Stelle suchen *v.* to look for a job (3) **3A**
stellen *v.* to put, place (2) **1B**
Stellenangebot, -e *n.* job opening (3) **3A**
sterben *v.* to die (2) **1B**
Stereoanlage, -n *f.* stereo system (2) **4B**
Stern -e *m.* star (3) **4A**
Stiefel, - *m.* boot (2) **1B**
Stiefmutter, ̈ *f.* stepmother (1) **3A**
Stiefsohn, ̈e *m.* stepson (1) **3A**
Stieftochter, ̈ *f.* stepdaughter (1) **3A**
Stiefvater, ̈ *m.* stepfather (1) **3A**
Stift, -e *m.* pen (1) **1B**
Stil, -e *m.* style (2) **1B**
still *adj.* still (1) **4B**
  stilles Wasser *n.* still water (1) **4B**
Stipendium, (*pl.* Stipendien) *n.* scholarship, grant (1) **2A**
Stock, ̈e *m.* floor (2) **2A**
  erster/zweiter Stock first/second floor (2) **2A**
stolz *adj.* proud (1) **3B**
Stoppschild, -er *n.* stop sign (2) **4A**
Strand, ̈e *m.* beach (1) **2B**
Straße, -n *f.* street (2) **4A**
sich streiten *v.* to argue (3) **1A**
Strom, ̈e *m.* stream (3) **4A**
Student, -en / Studentin, -nen *m./f.* (college/university) student (1) **1A**
Studentenwohnheim, -e *n.* dormitory (1) **2A**
studieren *v.* to study; major in (1) **2A**
Studium (*pl.* Studien) *n.* studies (1) **2A**
Stuhl, ̈e *m.* chair (1) **1A**
Stunde, -n *f.* lesson (1) **1B**; hour (1) **2A**
Stundenplan, ̈e *m.* schedule (1) **2A**
Sturm, ̈e *m.* storm (2) **3A**
suchen *v.* to look for (1) **2A**
  eine Stelle suchen *v.* to look for a job (3) **3A**

Supermarkt, ⸚e *m.* supermarket (1) **4A**
Suppe, -n *f.* soup (1) **4B**
surfen *v.* to surf (2) **4B**
  im Internet surfen *v.* to surf the Web (2) **4B**
süß *adj.* sweet, cute (1) **3B**, (1) **4B**
Süßigkeit, -en *f.* candy (2) **1A**
Sweatshirt, -s *n.* sweatshirt (2) **1B**
Symptom, -e *n.* symptom (3) **1B**

T

Tablet, -s *n.* tablet (2) **4B**
Tablette, -n *f.* pill (3) **1B**
Tafel, -n *f.* board, black board (1) **1B**
Tag, -e *m.* day (1) **1A**, (2) **3A**
  Welcher Tag ist heute? What day is it today? (2) **3A**
täglich *adv.* every day; daily (1) **4A**
Tal, ⸚er *n.* valley (3) **4A**
tanken *v.* to fill up (2) **4A**
Tankstelle, -n *f.* gas station (2) **4A**
Tante, -n *f.* aunt (1) **3A**
tanzen *v.* to dance (1) **2B**
Taschenrechner, - *m.* calculator (1) **1B**
Taschentuch, ⸚er *n.* tissue (3) **1B**
Tasse, -n *f.* cup (1) **4B**
Tastatur, -en *f.* keyboard (2) **4B**
Taxi, -s *n.* taxi (2) **4A**
Taxifahrer, - / Taxifahrerin, -nen *m./f.* taxi driver (3) **3B**
Technik *f.* technology (2) **4B**
  Technik bedienen *v.* to use technology (2) **4B**
Tee, -s *m.* tea (1) **4B**
Teelöffel, - *m.* teaspoon (1) **4B**
Telefon, -e *n.* telephone (2) **4B**
  am Telefon on the telephone (3) **3A**
Telefonnummer, -n *f.* telephone number (3) **3A**
Telefonzelle, -n *f.* phone booth (3) **2B**
Teller, - *m.* plate (1) **4B**
Tennis *n.* tennis (1) **2B**
Teppich, -e *m.* rug (2) **2A**
Termin, -e *m.* appointment (3) **3A**
  einen Termin vereinbaren *v.* to make an appointment (3) **3A**
teuer *adj.* expensive (2) **1B**
Thermometer, - *n.* thermometer (1) **1B**
Thunfisch, -e *m.* tuna (1) **4A**
Tier, -e *n.* animal (3) **4A**
Tierarzt, ⸚e / Tierärztin, -nen *m./f.* veterinarian (3) **3B**
Tisch, -e *m.* table, desk (1) **1B**
  den Tisch decken *v.* to set the table (2) **2B**
Tischdecke, -n *f.* tablecloth (1) **4B**
Toaster, - *m.* toaster (2) **2B**
Tochter, ⸚ *f.* daughter (1) **3A**
Toilette, -n *f.* toilet (2) **2A**
Tomate, -n *f.* tomato (1) **4A**
Topf, ⸚e *m.* pot (2) **2B**
Tor, -e *n.* goal (in soccer, etc.) (1) **2B**
Tornado, -s *m.* tornado (3) **4A**
Torte, -n *f.* cake (2) **1A**
Touristenklasse *f.* economy class (2) **3B**
tragen *v.* to carry; wear (1) **2B**
Trägerhemd, -en *n.* tank top (1) **1B**

trainieren *v.* to practice (sports) (1) **2B**
Traube, -n *f.* grape (1) **4A**
träumen *v.* to dream (2) **3A**
traurig *adj.* sad (1) **3B**
treffen *v.* to meet; to hit (1) **2B**
  sich treffen *v.* to meet (each other) (3) **1A**
treiben *v.* to float; to push
  Sport treiben *v.* to exercise (3) **1B**
Treibsand *m.* quicksand (3) **4A**
sich trennen *v.* to separate, split up (3) **1A**
Treppe, -n *f.* stairway (2) **2A**
trinken *v.* to drink (1) **3B**
Trinkgeld, -er *n.* tip (1) **4B**
trocken *adj.* dry (3) **4A**
trotz *prep.* despite, in spite of (2) **4B**
Tschüss. Bye. (1) **1A**
T-Shirt, -s *n.* T-shirt (2) **1B**
  tun *v.* to do (3) **1B**
  Es tut mir leid. I'm sorry. (1) **1A**
  weh tun *v.* to hurt (3) **1B**
Tür, -en *f.* door (1) **1B**
  Türen schließen. Keep doors closed. (1) **3B**
Türkei (die) *f.* Turkey (3) **2B**
Türke, -n / die Türkin, -nen *m./f.* Turkish (person) (3) **2B**
Türkisch *n.* Turkish (language) (3) **2B**
Turnschuhe *m. pl.* sneakers (2) **1B**

U

U-Bahn, -en *f.* subway (2) **4A**
übel *adj.* nauseous (3) **1B**
über *prep.* over, above (2) **1B**
übernachten *v.* to spend the night (2) **3B**
überall *adv.* everywhere (1) **4A**
Überbevölkerung *f.* overpopulation (3) **4B**
überlegen *v.* to think over (1) **4A**
übermorgen *adv.* the day after tomorrow (1) **2B**
überqueren *v.* to cross (3) **2B**
überraschen *v.* to surprise (2) **1A**
Überraschung, -en *f.* surprise (2) **1A**
überzeugend *adj.* persuasive (3) **1B**
Übung, -en *f.* practice, exercise
Uhr, -en *f.* clock (1) **1B**
  um... Uhr at... o'clock (1) **2A**
  Wie viel Uhr ist es? *v.* What time is it? (1) **2A**
um *prep.* around; at (time) (3) **3B**
  um... zu in order to (2) **3B**
Umleitung, -en *f.* detour (2) **4A**
umtauschen *v.* to exchange (2) **2B**
Umwelt, -en *f.* environment (3) **4B**
umweltfreundlich *adj.* environmentally friendly (3) **4B**
Umweltschutz *m.* environmentalism (3) **4B**
umziehen *v.* to move (2) **2A**, (3) **1A**
  sich umziehen *v.* to change clothes (3) **1A**
unangenehm *adj.* unpleasant (1) **3B**
und *conj.* and (1) **1B**
Unfall, ⸚e *m.* accident (2) **4A**
  einen Unfall haben *v.* to have an accident (2) **4A**
Universität, -en *f.* university; college (1) **1B**
unmöbliert *adj.* unfurnished (2) **2A**
unser *poss. adj.* our (1) **3A**

unter *prep.* under, below (2) **1B**
untergehen *v.* to set (sun) (3) **4A**
sich unterhalten *v.* to chat, have a conversation (1) **1A**
Unterkunft, ⸚e *f.* accommodations (2) **3B**
Unterricht, -e *m.* class, instruction (1) **1B**
unterschreiben *v.* to sign (3) **2A**
Unterwäsche *f.* underwear (2) **1B**
Urgroßmutter, ⸚ *f.* great grandmother (1) **3A**
Urgroßvater, ⸚ *m.* great grandfather (1) **3A**
Urlaub, -e *m.* vacation (2) **3B**
  Urlaub machen *v.* to go on vacation (2) **3B**
  Urlaub nehmen *v.* to take time off (3) **3B**
USA (die) *pl.* USA (3) **2B**

V

Vase, -n *f.* vase (2) **2A**
Vater, ⸚ *m.* father (1) **3A**
Veranstaltung, -en *f.* class; course (1) **2A**
Verb, -en *n.* verb (3) **1A**
verbessern *v.* to improve (3) **4B**
verbringen *v.* to spend (1) **4A**
verdienen *v.* to earn (3) **3B**
Vereinigten Staaten (die) *pl.* United States (3) **2B**
Vergangenheit, -en *f.* past (3) **4A**
vergessen *v.* to forget (1) **2B**
verheiratet *adj.* married (1) **3A**
verkaufen *v.* to sell (1) **4A**
Verkäufer, - / Verkäuferin, -nen *m./f.* salesperson (2) **1B**
Verkehr *m.* traffic (2) **4A**
Verkehrsmittel *n.* transportation (2) **4A**
  öffentliche Verkehrsmittel *n. pl.* public transportation (2) **4A**
verkünden *v.* to announce (3) **4B**
sich verlaufen *v.* to get lost (3) **2B**
sich verletzen *v.* to hurt oneself (3) **1B**
Verletzung, -en *f.* injury (3) **1B**
sich verlieben (in) *v.* to fall in love (with) (3) **1A**
verlieren *v.* to lose (1) **2B**
verlobt *adj.* engaged (1) **3A**
Verlobte, -n *m./f.* fiancé(e) (1) **3A**
verschmutzen *v.* to pollute (3) **4B**
Verschmutzung *f.* pollution (3) **4B**
sich verspäten *v.* to be late (3) **1A**
Verspätung, -en *f.* delay (2) **3B**
Verständnis, -se *n.* comprehension
sich (das Handgelenk / den Fuß) verstauchen *v.* to sprain (one's wrist/ankle) (3) **1B**
verstehen *v.* to understand (1) **2A**
verstopfte Nase *f.* stuffy nose (3) **1B**
versuchen *v.* to try (3) **3B**
Vertrag, ⸚e *m.* contract (3) **3A**
verwandt *adj.* related (2) **2A**
Verwandte, -n *m.* relative (1) **3A**
viel *adv.* much, a lot (of) (1) **4A**
  Viel Glück! Good luck! (2) **1A**
  Vielen Dank. Thank you very much. (1) **1A**
vielleicht *adv.* maybe (1) **4A**
vier four (1) **2A**
Viertel, - *n.* quarter (1) **2A**; neighborhood (3) **2B**
  Viertel nach/vor quarter past/to (1) **2A**

Visum (*pl.* **Visa**) *n.* visa (2) **3B**
Vogel, ¨ *m.* bird (1) **3A**
voll *adj.* full (2) **3B**
   voll besetzt *adj.* fully occupied (2) **3B**
Volleyball *m.* volleyball (1) **2B**
von *prep.* from (1) **4B**
vor *prep.* in front of, before (2) **1B**; *prep.* to (1) **2A**
vorbei *adv.* over, past (2) **3A**
vorbereiten *v.* to prepare (1) **4A**
   sich vorbereiten (auf) *v.* to prepare oneself
     (for) (3) **1A**
   Vorbereitung, -en *f.* preparation
Vorhang, ¨e *m.* curtain (2) **2A**
Vorlesung, -en *f.* lecture (1) **2A**
vormachen *v.* to fool (2) **4B**
Vormittag, -e *m.* midmorning (1) **2B**
vormittags *adv.* before noon (1) **2A**
Vorspeise, -n *f.* appetizer (1) **4B**
vorstellen *v.* to introduce (3) **1A**
   sich vorstellen *v.* to introduce oneself (3) **1A**
   sich (etwas) vorstellen *v.* to imagine
     (something) (3) **1A**
Vorstellungsgespräch, -e *n.* job interview (3) **3A**
Vortrag, ¨e *m.* lecture (2) **2B**
Vulkan, -e *m.* volcano (3) **4A**

W

wachsen *v.* to grow (2) **1B**
während *prep.* during (2) **4B**
wahrscheinlich *adv.* probably (3) **2A**
Wald, ¨er *m.* forest (1) **2B**, (3) **4A**
Wand, ¨e *f.* wall (2) **1B**
wandern *v.* to hike (1) **2A**
wann *interr.* when (1) **2A**
   Wann hast du Geburtstag? When is your
     birthday? (1) **2B**
warm *adj.* warm (3) **2A**
warten *v.* to wait (for) (1) **2A**
   warten auf *v.* to wait for (2) **3A**
   in der Warteschleife sein *v.* to be on hold (3) **3B**
warum *interr.* why (1) **2A**
was *interr.* what (1) **2A**
   Was geht ab? What's up? (1) **1A**
   Was ist das? What is that? (1) **1B**
Wäsche *f.* laundry (2) **2B**
waschen *v.* to wash (1) **2B**
   sich waschen *v.* to wash (oneself) (3) **1A**
   Wäsche waschen *v.* to do laundry (2) **2B**
Wäschetrockner, - *m.* dryer (2) **2B**
Waschmaschine, -n *f.* washing machine (2) **2B**
Waschsalon, -s *m.* laundromat (3) **2A**
Wasser *n.* water (1) **4B**
Wasserfall, ¨e *m.* waterfall (3) **4A**
Wasserkrug, ¨e *m.* water pitcher (1) **4B**
Website, -s *f.* web site (2) **4B**
Weg, -e *m.* path (3) **4A**
wegen *prep.* because of (2) **4B**
wegräumen *v.* to put away (2) **2B**
wegwerfen *v.* to throw away (3) **4B**
weh tun *v.* to hurt (3) **1B**
Weihnachten, - *n.* Christmas (2) **1A**
weil *conj.* because (3) **2A**

Wein, -e *m.* wine (1) **4B**
weinen *v.* to cry (1) **3B**
weise *adj.* wise (1) **3B**
weiß *adj.* white (2) **1B**
weit *adj.* loose; big (2) **1B**; *adj.* far (3) **2B**
   weit von *adj.* far from (3) **2B**
   weiter geht's moving forward
welcher/welche/welches *interr.* which (1) **2A**
   Welcher Tag ist heute? What day is it today? (2) **3A**
Welt, -en *f.* world (3) **4B**
wem *interr.* whom (*dat.*) (1) **4B**
wen *interr.* whom (*acc.*) (1) **2A**
Wende, -n *f.* turning point (3) **4B**
wenig *adj.* little; not much (3) **2A**
wenn *conj.* when; whenever; if (3) **2A**
   wenn... dann if... then (3) **2A**
   wenn... nur if... only (3) **2A**
wer *interr.* who (1) **2A**
   Wer ist das? Who is it? (1) **1B**
   Wer spricht? Who's calling? (3) **3A**
werden *v.* to become (1) **2B**
werfen *v.* to throw (1) **2B**
Werkzeug, -e *n.* tool kit
wessen *interr.* whose (2) **4B**
Wetter *n.* weather (2) **3A**
   Wie ist das Wetter? What's the weather like? (2) **3A**
Wetterbericht, -e *m.* weather report (2) **3A**
wichtig *adj.* important (2) **3B**
wie *interr.* how (1) **2A**
   wie viel? *interr.* how much? (1) **1B**
   wie viele? *interr.* how many? (1) **1B**
   Wie alt bist du? How old are you? (1) **1B**
   Wie heißt du? (*inf.*) What's your name? (1) **1A**
wiederholen *v.* to repeat (1) **2A**
Wiederholung, -en *f.* repetition; revision
wiegen *v.* to weigh (2) **4B**
willkommen welcome (1) **1A**
   Herzlich willkommen! Welcome! (1) **1A**
Windenergie *f.* wind energy (3) **4B**
windig *adj.* windy (2) **3A**
Windschutzscheibe, -n *f.* windshield (2) **4A**
Winter, - *m.* winter (1) **2B**, (2) **3A**
wir *pron.* we (1) **1A**
wirklich *adv.* really (1) **4A**
Wirtschaft, -en *f.* business; economy (1) **2A**
wischen *v.* to wipe, mop (2) **2B**
wissen *v.* to know (information) (2) **1B**
Wissenschaftler, - / Wissenschaftlerin, -nen *m./f.*
   scientist (3) **3B**
Witwe, -n *f.* widow (1) **3A**
Witwer, - *m.* widower (1) **3A**
wo *interr.* where (1) **2A**
woanders *adv.* somewhere else (1) **4A**
Woche, -n *f.* week (1) **2A**
Wochenende, -n *n.* weekend (1) **2A**
woher *interr.* from where (1) **2A**; (2) **2A**
wohin *interr.* where to (1) **2A**
wohl *adv.* probably (3) **2A**
wohnen *v.* to live (somewhere) (1) **2A**
Wohnheim, -e *n.* dorm (2) **2A**
Wohnung, -en *f.* apartment (2) **2A**
Wohnzimmer, - *n.* living room (2) **2A**
Wolke, -n *f.* cloud (2) **3A**

wolkig *adj.* cloudy (2) **3A**
Wolle *f.* wool (2) **1B**
wollen *v.* to want (1) **3B**
Wörterbuch, ¨er *n.* dictionary (1) **1B**
Wortschatz, ¨e *m.* vocabulary
wünschen *v.* to wish (3) **1A**
   sich (etwas) wünschen *v.* to wish (for
     something) (3) **1A**
Würstchen, - *n.* (small) sausage (1) **4A**

Z

Zahn, ¨e *m.* tooth (3) **1A**
   sich die Zähne putzen *m.* to brush one's teeth (3) **1A**
Zahnarzt, ¨e **/ Zahnärztin, -nen** *m./f.* dentist (3) **1B**
Zahnbürste, -n *f.* toothbrush (3) **1A**
Zahnpasta (*pl.* **Zahnpasten**) *f.* toothpaste (3) **1A**
Zahnschmerzen *m. pl.* toothache (3) **1B**
Zapping *n.* channel surfing
Zebrastreifen, - *m.* crosswalk (3) **2B**
Zeh, -en *m.* toe (3) **1A**
zehn ten (1) **2A**
zeigen *v.* to show (1) **4B**
Zeit, -en *f.* time (1) **2A**
Zeitschrift, -en *f.* magazine (3) **2A**
Zeitung, -en *f.* newspaper (2) **3B**, (3) **2A**
Zelt, -e *n.* tent (2) **3B**
Zeltplatz, ¨e *m.* camping area (2) **3B**
Zeugnis, -se *n.* report card, grade report (1) **1B**
ziehen *v.* to pull (1) **3B**
ziemlich *adv.* quite (1) **4A**
   ziemlich gut pretty well (1) **1A**
Zimmer, - *n.* room (2) **1A**
   Zimmer frei vacancy (2) **2A**
Zimmerservice *m.* room service (2) **3B**
Zoll, ¨e *m.* customs (2) **3B**
zu *adv.* too (1) **4A**; *prep.* to; for; at (1) **4B**
   bis zu *prep.* until (3) **2B**
   um... zu (in order) to (2) **3B**
   Zum Wohl! Cheers! (1) **4B**
zubereiten *v.* to prepare (2) **3A**
zuerst *adv.* first (2) **3B**
Zug, ¨e *m.* train (2) **4A**
zumachen *v.* to close (2) **4B**
sich zurechtfinden *v.* to find one's way (3) **2B**
zurückkommen *v.* to come back (1) **4A**
zusammen *adv.* together (1) **3A**
zuschauen *v.* to watch (1) **4A**
Zutat, -en *m.* ingredient (1) **4A**
zuverlässig *adj.* reliable (3) **3B**
zwanzig twenty (1) **2A**
zwei two (1) **2A**
zweite *adj.* second (1) **2A**
Zwiebel, -n *f.* onion (1) **4A**
Zwilling, -e *m.* twin (1) **3A**
zwischen *prep.* between (2) **1B**
zwölf twelve (1) **2A**

Englisch-Deutsch

A

a ein/eine (1) **1A**
able: to be able to können *v.* (1) **3B**
about über *prep.* (2) **1B**
  to be about handeln von *v.* (2) **3A**
above über *prep.* (2) **1B**
abroad Ausland *n.* (2) **3B**
accident Unfall, ⸚e *m.* (2) **4A**
  to have an accident einen Unfall haben *v.* (2) **4A**
accommodation Unterkunft, ⸚e *f.* (2) **3B**
according to nach *prep.* (1) **4B**
accountant Buchhalter, - / Buchhalterin, -nen *m./f.* (3) **3B**
acid rain saurer Regen *m.* (3) **4B**
across (from) gegenüber (von) *prep.* (3) **2B**
address Adresse, -n *f.* (3) **2A**
adopt adoptieren *v.* (1) **3A**
afraid: to be afraid of Angst haben vor *v.* (2) **3A**
after nach *prep.* (1) **4B**; nachdem *conj.* (3) **2A**
afternoon Nachmittag, -e *m.* (1) **2B**
  in the afternoon nachmittags *adv.* (1) **2A**
against gegen *prep.* (1) **3B**
air Luft, ⸚e *f.* (3) **4A**
airplane Flugzeug, -e *n.* (2) **3B**
airport Flughafen, ⸚ *m.* (2) **3B**
all ganz *adj.* (2) **3B**; alle *pron.* (2) **3B**
allergic (to) allergisch (gegen) *adj.* (3) **1B**
allergy Allergie, -n *f.* (3) **1B**
allow lassen *v.* (1) **2B**
  to be allowed to dürfen *v.* (1) **3B**
almost fast *adv.* (1) **4A**
alone allein *adv.* (1) **4A**
along entlang *prep.* (1) **3B**
already schon (1) **4A**
alright: Are you alright? Alles klar? (1) **1A**
also auch *adv.* (1) **4A**
although obwohl *conj.* (3) **2A**
always immer *adv.* (1) **4A**
ambulance Krankenwagen, - *m.* (3) **1B**
America Amerika *n.* (3) **2B**
American amerikanisch *adj.* (3) **2B**; (person) Amerikaner, - / Amerikanerin, -nen *m./f.* (3) **2B**
  American football American Football *m.* (1) **2B**
and und *conj.* (1) **1B**
animal Tier, -e *n.* (3) **4A**
angry böse *adj.*
  to get angry (about) sich ärgern (über) *v.* (3) **1A**
anniversary Jahrestag, -e *m.* (2) **1A**
announce verkünden *v.* (3) **4B**
answer antworten *v.* (1) **2A**; beantworten *v.* (1) **4A**; Antwort, -en *f.*
  to answer the phone einen Anruf entgegennehmen *v.* (3) **3A**
anything: Anything else? Noch einen Wunsch? (1) **4B**; Sonst noch etwas? (1) **4A**
apartment Wohnung, -en *f.* (2) **2A**
appetizer Vorspeise, -n *f.* (1) **4B**
apple Apfel, ⸚ *m.* (1) **1A**
applicant Bewerber, - / Bewerberin, -nen *m./f.* (3) **3A**
apply sich bewerben *v.* (3) *3A*

appointment Termin, -e *m.* (3) **3A**
April April *m.* (1) **2A**
architect Architekt, -en / Architektin, -nen *m./f.* (1) **3B**
architecture Architektur, -en *f.* (1) **2A**
argue sich streiten *v.* (3) **1A**
arm Arm, -e *m.* (3) **1A**
armchair Sessel, - *m.* (2) **2A**
around um *prep.* (1) **3B**
arrival Ankunft, ⸚e *f.* (2) **3B**
arrive ankommen *v.* (1) **4A**
arrogant eingebildet *adj.* (1) **3B**
art Kunst, ⸚e *f.* (1) **2A**
artichoke Artischocke, -n *f.* (1) **4A**
as als *conj.* (2) **4A**
  as if als ob (3) **2A**
ask fragen *v.* (1) **2A**
  to ask about fragen nach *v.* (2) **3A**
assistant Assistent, -en / Assistentin, -nen *m./f.* (3) **3A**
at um *prep.* (1) **3B**; bei *prep.* (1) **4A**; an *prep.* (2) **1B**
  at...o'clock um...Uhr (1) **2A**
athletic sportlich *adj.* (1) **2B**
ATM Geldautomat, -en *m.* (3) **2A**
Attention! Achtung!
attic Dachboden, ⸚ *m.* (2) **2A**
August August *m.* (1) **2A**
aunt Tante, -n *f.* (1) **3A**
Austria Österreich *n.* (3) **2B**
Austrian österreichisch *adj.* (3) **2B**; (person) Österreicher, - / Österreicherin, -nen *m./f.* (3) **2B**
autumn Herbst, -e *m.* (1) **2B**
avenue Allee, -n *f.* (3) **2B**
awful furchtbar *adj.* (2) **3A**

B

baby Baby, -s *n.* (1) **3A**
back Rücken, - *m.* (3) **1A**
backache Rückenschmerzen *m. pl.* (3) **1B**
backpack Rucksack, ⸚e *m.* (1) **1B**
bad schlecht *adj.* (1) **3B**
  badly dressed schlecht gekleidet *adj.* (2) **1B**
baked goods Gebäck *n.* (2) **1A**
bakery Bäckerei, -en *f.* (1) **4A**
balcony Balkon, - *e m.* (2) **2A**
ball Ball, ⸚e *m.* (1) **2B**
balloon Ballon, -e *m.* (2) **1A**
ball-point pen Kuli, -s *m.* (1) **1B**
banana Banane, -n *f.* (1) **4A**
bank Bank, -en *f.* (3) **2A**
  at the bank auf der Bank *f.* (2) **2B**
bank account Konto (*pl.* Konten) *n.* (3) **2A**
bank employee Bankangestellte, -n *m./f.* (3) **3B**
baseball Baseball *m.* (1) **2B**
basketball Basketball *m.* (1) **2B**
bath: to take a bath sich baden *v.* (3) **1A**
bathing suit Badeanzug, ⸚e *m.* (2) **1B**
bathrobe Bademantel, ⸚ *m.* (3) **1A**
bathroom Badezimmer, - *n.* (3) **1A**
bathtub Badewanne, -n *f.* (2) **2A**
battery charger Ladegerät, -e *n.* (2) **4B**
be sein *v.* (1) **1A**
  Is/Are there... Ist/Sind hier…? *v.* (1) **1B**; Gibt es…? (1) **2B**

There is/are... Da ist/sind... *v.* (1) **1A**; Es gibt… (1) **2B**
beach Strand, ⸚e *m.* (1) **2B**
bean Bohne, -n *f.* (1) **4A**
beard Bart, ⸚e *m.* (3) **1A**
beautiful schön *adj.* (1) **3A**
beauty salon Kosmetiksalon, -s *m.* (3) **2A**
because denn *conj.* (2) **2A**; weil *conj.* (3) **2A**
  because of wegen *prep.* (2) **4B**
become werden *v.* (1) **2B**
bed Bett, -en *n.* (2) **2A**
  to go to bed ins Bett gehen *v.* (3) **1A**
  to make the bed das Bett machen *v.* (2) **2B**
bedroom Schlafzimmer, - *n.* (2) **2A**
beef Rindfleisch *n.* (1) **4A**
beer Bier, -e *n.* (1) **4B**
before vor *prep.* (2) **1B**; bevor *conj.* (2) **4A**
  before noon vormittags *adv.* (1) **2A**
begin anfangen *v.* (1) **4A**; beginnen *v.* (2) **4A**
behind hinter *prep.* (2) **1B**
believe glauben *v.* (2) **1A**; meinen *v.* (3) **4B**
belly Bauch, ⸚e *m.* (3) **1A**
belong gehören *v.* (1) **4B**
below unter *prep.* (2) **1B**
belt Gürtel, - *m.* (2) **1B**
bench Bank, ⸚e *f.* (3) **2B**
best beste/bester/bestes *adj.* (2) **4A**
All the best! Mach's gut! *v.* (1) **3B**; alles Gute (3) **2A**
better besser *adj.* (2) **4A**
  to get better gesund werden *v.* (3) **1B**
between zwischen *prep.* (2) **1B**
beverage Getränk, -e *n.* (1) **4B**
bicycle Fahrrad, ⸚er *n.* (1) **2B**
big groß, weit *adj.* (1) **3A**
bill (money) Geldschein, -e *m.* (3) **2A**
biology Biologie *f.* (1) **2A**
bird Vogel, ⸚ *m.* (1) **3A**
birth Geburt, -en *f.* (1) **1A**
birthday Geburtstag, -e *m.* (2) **1A**
  When is your birthday? Wann hast du Geburtstag? (1) **2B**
black schwarz *adj.* (2) **1B**
  black board Tafel, -n *f.* (1) **1B**
  black-haired schwarzhaarig *adj.* (1) **3A**
bland fade *adj.* (1) **4B**
blanket Decke, -n *f.* (2) **2B**
blond blond *adj.* (1) **3A**
  blond hair blonde Haare *n. pl.* (1) **3A**
blood pressure Blutdruck *m.* (3) **1B**
blouse Bluse, -n *f.* (2) **1B**
blue blau *adj.* (1) **3A**
board Tafel, -n *f.* (1) **1B**
boarding pass Bordkarte, -n *f.* (2) **3B**
boat Boot, -e *n.* (2) **4A**
body Körper, - *m.* (3) **1A**
book Buch, ⸚er *n.* (1) **1A**
bookshelf Bücherregal, -e *n.* (2) **2A**
boot Stiefel, - *m.* (2) **1B**
boring langweilig *adj.* (1) **2A**
boss Chef, -s / Chefin, -nen *m./f.* (3) **3B**
bottle Flasche, -n *f.* (1) **4B**
bowl Schüssel, -n *f.* (1) **4B**
boy Junge, -n *m.* (1) **1A**

brakes Bremse, -n *f.* (2) **4A**
brave mutig *adj.* (1) **3B**
bread Brot, -e *n.* (1) **4A**
break brechen *v.* (1) **2B**
  to break (an arm / a leg) sich (den Arm/Bein) brechen *v.* (3) **1B**
  Break a leg! Hals- und Beinbruch! (2) **1A**
breakfast Frühstück, -e *n.* (1) **4B**
bridge Brücke, -n *f.* (3) **2B**
bright hell *adj.* (2) **1B**
bring bringen *v.* (1) **2A**
  to bring along mitbringen *v.* (1) **4A**
  to bring out rausbringen (2) **2B**
  to bring with mitnehmen *v.* (3) **2B**
broom Besen, - *m.* (2) **2B**
brother Bruder, ⸚ *m.* (1) **1A**
brother-in-law Schwager, ⸚ *m.* (1) **3A**
brown braun *adj.* (2) **1B**
  brown-haired braunhaarig *adj.* (1) **3A**
bruise blauer Fleck, -e *m.* (3) **1B**
brush Bürste, -n *f.* (3) **1A**
  to brush one's hair sich die Haare bürsten *v.* (3) **1A**
  to brush one's teeth sich die Zähne putzen *v.* (3) **1A**
build bauen *v.* (1) **2A**
building Gebäude, - *n.* (3) **2A**
bulletin board Pinnwand, ⸚e *f.* (3) **3A**
burn brennen *v.* (2) **1A**
bus Bus, -se *m.* (2) **4A**
bus stop Bushaltestelle, -n *f.* (2) **4A**
bush Busch, ⸚e *m.* (3) **4A**
business Wirtschaft, -en *f.* (1) **2A**; Geschäft, -e *n.* (3) **4A**
  business class Businessklasse *f.* (2) **3B**
businessman / businesswoman Geschäftsmann, ⸚er / Geschäftsfrau, -en *m./f.* (*pl.* Geschäftsleute) (1) **3B**
but aber *conj.* (1) **1B**
  but rather sondern *conj.* (2) **2A**
butcher shop Metzgerei, -en *f.* (1) **4A**
butter Butter *f.* (1) **4A**
buy kaufen *v.* (1) **2A**
by an *prep.* (2) **1B**; bei; von (1) **4B**
Bye! Tschüss! (1) **1A**

C

cabinet Schrank, ⸚e *m.* (2) **2A**
café Café, -s *n.* (1) **2A**
cafeteria Cafeteria, (*pl.* Cafeterien) *f.*; **(college/university)** Mensa, Mensen *f.* (1) **1B**
cake Kuchen, - *m.* (1) **4A**; Torte, -n *f.* (2) **1A**
calculator Taschenrechner, - *m.* (1) **1B**
calendar Kalender, - *m.* (1) **1B**
call anrufen *v.* (1) **4A**; sich anrufen (3) **1A**; nennen *v.* (2) **1A**
  Who's calling? Wer spricht? (3) **3A**
calm ruhig *adj.* (1) **3B**
(to go) camping campen gehen *n.* (1) **2B**
camping area Zeltplatz, ⸚e *m.* (2) **3B**
can können *v.* (1) **3B**
Canada Kanada *n.* (3) **2B**
Canadian kanadisch *adj.* (3) **2B**; **(person)** Kanadier, - / Kanadierin, -nen *m./f.* (3) **2B**
cancel abbrechen, streichen *v.* (2) **3B**

candidate Kandidat, -en *m.* (3) **3A**
candy Süßigkeit, -en *f.* (2) **1A**
cap Mütze, -n *f.* (2) **1B**
car Auto, -s *n.* (1) **1A**
  to drive a car Auto fahren *v.* (2) **4A**
card Karte, -n *f.* (1) **2B**
career Karriere, -n *f.* (3) **3B**
caretaker Hausmeister, - / Hausmeisterin, -nen *m./f.* (3) **3B**
carpool Fahrgemeinschaft, -en *f.* (3) **4B**
carrot Karotte, -n *f.* (1) **4A**
carry tragen *v.* (1) **2B**
carry-on luggage Handgepäck *n.* (2) **3B**
cash bar *adj.* (3) **2A**; Bargeld *n.* (3) **2A**
  to pay in cash bar bezahlen *v.* (3) **2A**
cat Katze, -n *f.* (1) **3A**
catch fangen *v.* (1) **2B**
  to catch a cold sich erkälten *v.* (3) **1A**
celebrate feiern *v.* (2) **1A**
celebration Fest, -e *n.* (2) **1A**
cell phone Handy, -s *n.* (2) **4B**
cellar Keller, - *m.* (2) **2A**
ceramic Keramik, -en *f.* (2) **2B**
chair Stuhl, ⸚e *m.* (1) **1A**
champagne Sekt, -e *m.* (2) **1A**
championship Meisterschaft, -en *f.* (1) **2B**
change Kleingeld *n.* (3) **2A**
  to change clothes sich umziehen *v.* (3) **1A**
channel Sender, - *m.* (3) **4B**
  channel surfing Zapping *n.*
charge laden *v.* (2) **4B**
chat sich unterhalten *v.* (3) **1A**
cheap günstig *adj.* (2) **1B**
check Rechnung, -en *f.* (1) **4B**
Cheers! Prost! **4B**; Zum Wohl! (1) **4B**
cheese Käse, - *m.* (1) **4A**
chemistry Chemie *f.* (1) **2A**
chess Schach *n.* (1) **2B**
chicken Huhn, ⸚er *n.* (3) **4A**; **(food)** Hähnchen, - *n.* (1) **4A**
child Kind, -er *n.* (1) **1A**
China China *n.* (3) **2B**
Chinese (person) Chinese, -n / Chinesin, -nen *m./f.* (3) **2B**; **(language)** Chinesisch *n.* (3) **2B**
Christmas Weihnachten, - *n.* (2) **1A**
church Kirche, -n *f.* (3) **2B**
city Stadt, ⸚e *f.* (2) **1B**
  city center Innenstadt, ⸚e *f.* (3) **2B**
claim behaupten *v.* (3) **4B**
class Klasse, -n *f.* (1) **1B**; Unterricht *m.* (1) **1B**; Veranstaltung, -en *f.* (1) **2A**
  first/second class erste/zweite Klasse (2) **2A**
classical klassisch *adj.* (3) **2A**
classmate Kommilitone, -n / Kommilitonin, -nen; Klassenkamerad, -en / Klassenkameradin, -nen *m./f.* (1) **1B**
classroom Klassenzimmer, - *n.* (1) **1B**
clean sauber *adj.* (2) **2B**; putzen *v.* (2) **2B**
  to clean up aufräumen *v.* (2) **2B**
cliff Klippe, -n *f.* (3) **4A**
climb steigen *v.* (2) **1B**
  to climb (mountain) klettern *v.* (1) **2B**
  to climb (stairs) (die Treppe) hochgehen *v.* (3) **2B**
clock Uhr, -en *f.* (1) **1B**

at... o'clock um... Uhr (1) **2A**
close zumachen *v.* (2) **2B**; nah *adj.* (3) **2B**
  close to in der Nähe von *prep.* (3) **2B**
closed geschlossen *adj.* (3) **2A**
closet Schrank, ⸚e *m.* (2) **2A**
clothes Kleidung *f.* (2) **1B**
cloud Wolke, -n *f.* (2) **3A**
cloudy wolkig *adj.* (2) **3A**
coast Küste, -n *f.* (3) **4A**
coat Mantel, ⸚ *m.* (2) **1B**
coffee Kaffee, -s *m.* (1) **4B**
coffeemaker Kaffeemaschine, -n *f.* (2) **3B**
coin Münze, -n *f.* (3) **2A**
cold kalt *adj.* (2) **3A**; Erkältung, -en *f.* (3) **1B**
  to catch a cold sich erkälten *v.* (3) **1A**
college Universität, -en *f.* (1) **1B**
college instructor Dozent, -en / Dozentin, -nen *m./f.* (1) **2A**
color Farbe, -n *f.* (2) **1B**
  solid colored einfarbig *adj.* (2) **1B**
colorful bunt *adj.* (3) **2A**
comb Kamm, ⸚e *m.* (3) **1A**
  to comb (one's hair) sich (die Haare) kämmen *v.* (3) **1A**
come kommen *v.* (1) **2A**
  to come along mitkommen *v.* (1) **4A**
  to come back zurückkommen *v.* (1) **4A**
comma Komma, -s *f.* (1) **1B**
compact disc CD, -s *f.* (2) **4B**
company Firma (*pl.* die Firmen) *f.* (3) **3A**
complicated kompliziert *adj.* (3) **2A**
computer Computer, - *m.* (1) **1B**
computer science Informatik *f.* (1) **2A**
concert Konzert, -e *n.* (2) **1B**
congratulate gratulieren *v.* (2) **1A**
  Congratulations! Herzlichen Glückwunsch! (2) **1A**
construction zone Baustelle, -n *f.* (2) **4A**
contract Vertrag, ⸚e *m.* (3) **3A**
conversation: to have a conversation sich unterhalten *v.* (3) **1A**
cook kochen *v.* (1) **2B**; Koch, ⸚e / Köchin, -nen *m./f.* (1) **4B**
cookie Keks, -e *m.* (2) **1A**
cool kühl *adj.* (2) **3A**
corner Ecke, -n *f.* (3) **2B**
correct korrigieren *v.* (1) **2A**
cost kosten *v.* (1) **2A**
cotton Baumwolle *f.* (2) **1B**
couch Sofa, -s *n.* (2) **3B**
  to couch surf Sofa surfen *v.* (2) **3B**
cough husten *v.* (3) **1B**
country Land, ⸚er *n.* (2) **3B**
countryside Landschaft, -en *f.* (3) **4A**
couple Paar, -e *n.* (1) **3A**
courageous mutig *adj.*
course Veranstaltung, -en *f.* (1) **2B**; Gang, ⸚e *m.* (1) **4B**
  first/second course erster/zweiter Gang *m.* (1) **4B**
  main course Hauptspeise, -en *f.* (1) **4B**
court Platz, ⸚e *m.* (1) **1A**
cousin Cousin, -s / Cousine, -n *m./f.* (1) **3A**
cover decken *v.* (2) **2B**
cow Kuh, ⸚e *f.* (3) **4A**

cram (for a test) büffeln *v.* (1) **2A**
cross überqueren *v.* (3) **2B**
  to cross the street die Straße überqueren *v.* (3) **2B**
cross-reference Querverweis, -e *m.*
crosswalk Zebrastreifen, - *pl.* (3) **2B**
cruel grausam *adj.*; gemein *adj.* (1) **3B**
cruise Kreuzfahrt, -en *f.* (2) **3B**
cry weinen *v.* (1) **3B**
cup Tasse, -n *f.* (1) **4B**
curious neugierig *adj.* (1) **3B**
curly lockig *adj.* (1) **3A**
curtain Vorhang, ⸚e *m.* (2) **2A**
custodian Hausmeister, - / Hausmeisterin,
  -nen *m./f.* (3) **3B**
customer Kunde, -n /Kundin, -nen *m./f.* (2) **1B**
customs Zoll *m.* (2) **3B**
cut Schnitt, -e *m.* (2) **1B**
  to cut class schwänzen *v.* (1) **1B**
cute süß *adj.* (1) **3B**
CV Lebenslauf, ⸚e *m.* (3) **3A**

D

dad Papa, -s *m.* (1) **3A**
daily täglich *adv.* (1) **4A**
  daily routine Alltagsroutine *f.* (3) **1A**
dance tanzen *v.* (1) **2B**
danger Gefahr, -en *f.* (3) **4B**
dark dunkel *adj.* (1) **3A**
  dark-haired dunkelhaarig *adj.* (1) **3A**
darling Liebling, -e *m.*
date Datum (*pl.* Daten) *n.* (2) **3A**
  What is the date today? Der wievielte ist
  heute? (1) **2A**
daughter Tochter, ⸚ *f.* (1) **3A**
day Tag, -e *m.* (1) **1A**
  every day täglich *adv.* (1) **4A**
Dear Lieber/Liebe *m./f.* (1) **3B**
December Dezember *m.* (1) **2A**
decide sich entschließen *v.* (1) **4B**
definitely bestimmt *adv.* (1) **4A**
degree Abschluss, ⸚e *m.* (1) **2A**; Grad *n.* (2) **3A**
  It's 18 degrees out. Es sind 18 Grad
  draußen. (2) **3A**
delay Verspätung, -en *f.* (2) **3B**
delete löschen *v.* (2) **4B**
delicatessen Feinkostgeschäft, -e *n.* (1) **4A**
delicious lecker *adj.* (1) **4B**
demanding anspruchsvoll *adj.* (3) **3B**
dentist Zahnarzt, ⸚e / Zahnärztin, -nen *m./f.*
  (3) **1B**
department store Kaufhaus, ⸚er *n.* (3) **2B**
departure Abflug, ⸚e *m.* (2) **3B**
deposit (money) (Geld) einzahlen *v.* (3) **2A**
describe beschreiben *v.* (1) **2A**
description Beschreibung, -en *f.* (1) **3B**
desk Schreibtisch, -e *m.* (1) **1B**
despite trotz *prep.* (2) **4B**
dessert Nachtisch, -e, *m.* (1) **4B**
destination Reiseziel, -e *n.* (2) **3B**
detour Umleitung, -en *f.* (2) **4A**
develop entwickeln *v.* (3) **4B**
dictionary Wörterbuch, ⸚er *n.* (1) **1B**
die sterben *v.* (2) **1B**

diet Diät, -en *f.* (1) **4B**
  to be on a diet auf Diät sein *v.* (1) **4B**
difficult schwierig *adj.* (1) **2A**
digital camera Digitalkamera, -s *f.* (2) **4B**
dining room Esszimmer, - *n.* (2) **2A**
dinner Abendessen, - *n.* (1) **4B**
diploma Abschlusszeugnis, -se *n.* (1) **2A**; Diplom,
  -e *n.* (1) **2A**
direction Richtung, -en *f.* (3) **2B**
dirty schmutzig *adj.* (2) **2B**
discover entdecken *v.* (2) **2B**
discreet diskret *adj.* (1) **3B**
discuss besprechen *v.* (1) **4A**
dish Gericht, -e *n.* (1) **4B**
dishes Geschirr *n.* (2) **2B**
  to do the dishes Geschirr spülen (2) **2B**
dishwasher Spülmaschine, -n *f.* (2) **2B**
dislike nicht gern (+*verb*) (1) **3A**
divided by geteilt durch (1) **1B**
divorced geschieden *adj.* (1) **3A**
dizzy schwindlig *adj.* (3) **1B**
do machen *v.* (1) **2A**; tun *v.* (3) **1B**
  to do laundry Wäsche waschen *v.* (2) **2B**
  to do the dishes Geschirr spülen *v.* (2) **2B**
  to have to do with handeln von (2) **3A**
doctor Arzt, ⸚e / Ärztin, -nen *m./f.* (3) **1B**
  to go to the doctor zum Arzt gehen *v.* (3) **1B**
document Dokument, -e *n.* (2) **4B**
dog Hund, -e *m.* (1) **3A**
door Tür, -en *f.* (1) **1B**
dormitory (Studenten)wohnheim, -e *n.* (2) **2A**
down entlang *prep.* (1) **3B**; herunter *adv.* (2) **2A**
  to go down heruntergehen *v.* (3) **2B**
download herunterladen *v.* (2) **4B**
downtown Innenstadt, ⸚e *f.* (3) **2B**
dozen Dutzend, -e *n.* (1) **4A**
  a dozen eggs ein Dutzend Eier (1) **4A**
drawer Schublade, -n *f.* (2) **2A**
dream träumen *v.* (2) **3A**
dress Kleid, -er *n.* (2) **1B**
  to get dressed sich anziehen *v.* (3) **1A**
  to get undressed sich ausziehen *v.* (3) **1A**
dresser Kommode, -n *f.* (2) **2A**
drink trinken *v.* (1) **3B**
drive fahren *v.* (2) **4A**
  to drive a car Auto fahren *v.* (2) **4A**
driver Fahrer, - / Fahrerin, -nen *m./f.* (2) **4A**
drugstore Drogerie, -n *f.* (3) **2A**
dry trocken *adj.* (3) **4A**
  to dry oneself off sich abtrocknen *v.* (3) **1A**
dryer Wäschetrockner, - *m.* (2) **2B**
dumb dumm *adj.* (2) **4A**
during während *prep.* (2) **4B**
dust abstauben *v.* (2) **2B**
duvet Bettdecke, - n *f.* (2) **2B**
DVD DVD, -s *f.* (2) **4B**
DVD-player DVD-Player, - *m.* (2) **4B**
dye (one's hair) sich (die Haare) färben *v.* (3) **1A**

E

ear Ohr, -en *n.* (3) **1A**
early früh *adj.* (1) **2B**
earn verdienen *v.* (3) **3B**
earth Erde, -n *f.* (3) **4B**

earthquake Erdbeben, - *n.* (3) **4A**
easy einfach *adj.* (1) **2A**
eat essen *v.* (1) **2B**
  to eat out essen gehen *v.* (1) **2B**
ecological ökologisch *adj.* (3) **4B**
ecology Ökologie *f.* (3) **4B**
economy Wirtschaft, -en *f.* (1) **2A**
  economy class Touristenklasse *f.* (2) **3B**
education Ausbildung, -en *f.* (3) **3A**
egg Ei, -er *n.* (1) **4A**
eggplant Aubergine, -n *f.* (1) **4A**
eight acht (1) **2A**
elbow Ell(en)bogen, - *m.* (3) **1A**
electrician Elektriker, - / Elektrikerin,
  -nen *m./f.* (3) **3B**
elegant elegant *adj.* (2) **1B**
elevator Fahrstuhl, ⸚e *m.* (2) **3B**
eleven elf (1) **2A**
e-mail E-Mail, -s *f.* (2) **4B**
emergency Notfall, ⸚e *m.* (3) **3B**
emergency room Notaufnahme, -n *f.* (3) **1B**
employee Angestellte, -n *m./f.* (3) **3A**
endangered gefährdet *adj.* (3) **4B**
energy Energie, -n *f.* (3) **4B**
energy-efficient energiesparend *adj.* (2) **2B**
engaged verlobt *adj.* (1) **3A**
engine Motor, -en *m.* (2) **4A**
engineer Ingenieur, -e / Ingenieurin, -nen
  m./f. (1) **3B**
England England *n.* (3) **2B**
English (person) Engländer, - / Engländerin,
  -nen *m./f.* (3) **2B**; **(language)** Englisch *n.* (3) **2B**
enjoy genießen *v.*
  Enjoy your meal! Guten Appetit! (1) **4B**
envelope Briefumschlag, ⸚e *m.* (3) **2A**
environment Umwelt, -en *f.* (3) **4B**
  environmentally friendly umweltfreundlich
  adj. (2) **4B**
environmentalism Umweltschutz *m.* (3) **4B**
equal (gleich) sein *v.* (1) **1B**
eraser Radiergummi, -s *m.* (1) **1B**
errand Besorgung, -en *f.* (3) **2A**
  to run errands Besorgungen machen *v.* (3) **2A**
even though obwohl *conj.* (2) **2A**
evening Abend, -e *m.* (1) **2B**
  in the evening abends *adv.* (1) **2B**
every jeder/jede/jedes *adv.* (2) **4B**
everything alles *pron.* (2) **3B**
  Everything OK? Alles klar? (1) **1A**
everywhere überall *adv.* (1) **4A**
exam Prüfung, -en *f.* (1) **1B**
except (for) außer *prep.* (1) **4B**
exchange umtauschen *v.* (2) **2B**
exciting spannend *adj.* (3) **2A**; aufregend *adj.* (3) **4A**
Excuse me. Entschuldigung. (1) **1A**
exercise Sport treiben *v.* (3) **1B**
exit Ausgang, ⸚e *m.* (2) **1B**; Ausfahrt, -en *f.* (2) **4A**
expensive teuer *adj.* (2) **2B**
experience durchmachen *v.* (2) **4B**; Erfahrung,
  -en *f.* (3) **3A**
explain erklären *v.* (1) **4A**
explore erforschen *v.* (3) **4A**
expression Ausdruck, ⸚e *m.*

extinction Aussterben *n.* (3) **4B**
eye Auge, -n *n.* (1) **3A**
eyebrow Augenbraue, -n *f.* (3) **1A**

F

face Gesicht, -er *n.* (3) **1A**
factory Fabrik, -en *f.* (3) **4B**
factory worker Fabrikarbeiter, - / Fabrikarbeiterin,
-nen *m./f.* (3) **3B**
fail durchfallen *v.* (1) **1B**; scheitern *v.* (3) **3B**
fall fallen *v.* (1) **2B**; (season) Herbst, -e *m.* (1) **2B**
to fall in love (with) sich verlieben (in) *v.* (3) **1A**
familiar bekannt *adj.*
to be familiar with kennen *v.* (2) **1B**
family Familie, -n *f.* (1) **3A**
fan Fan, -s *m.* (1) **2B**
fantastic fantastisch *adj.* (3) **2A**
far weit *adj.* (3) **2B**
far from weit von *adj.* (3) **2B**
farm Bauernhof, ⸚e *m.* (3) **4A**
farmer Bauer, -n / Bäuerin, -nen *m./f.* (3) **3B**
fashionable modisch *adj.* (2) **1B**
fast schnell *adj.* (1) **3B**
fat dick *adj.* (1) **3A**
father Vater, ⸚ *m.* (1) **3A**
father-in-law Schwiegervater, ⸚ *m.* (1) **3A**
favorite Lieblings- (1) **4B**
fear Angst, ⸚e *f.* (2) **3A**
February Februar *m.* (1) **2A**
feel fühlen *v.* (1) **2A**; sich fühlen *v.* (3) **1A**
to feel like Lust haben *v.* (2) **3B**
to feel well sich wohl fühlen *v.* (3) **1A**
fever Fieber, - *n.* (3) **1B**
to have a fever Fieber haben *v.* (3) **1B**
fiancé(e) Verlobte, -n *m./f.* (1) **3A**
field Spielfeld, -er *n.* (1) **2B**; Feld, -er *n.* (3) **4A**
file Datei, -en *f.* (2) **4B**
fill füllen *v.*
to fill out ausfüllen *v.* (3) **2A**
to fill up tanken *v.* (2) **4A**
filthy dreckig *adj.* (2) **2B**
finally schließlich *adv.* (2) **3B**
find finden *v.* (1) **2A**
to find one's way sich zurechtfinden *v.* (3) **2B**
to find out (about) sich informieren (über) *v.* (3) **1A**
fine (monetary) Bußgeld, -er *n.* (2) **4A**
I'm fine. Mir geht's gut. (1) **1A**
finger Finger, - *m.* (3) **1A**
fire entlassen *v.* (3) **3B**; Feuer, - *n.*
firefighter Feuerwehrmann, ⸚er / Feuerwehrfrau,
-en (*pl.* Feuerwehrleute) *m./f.* (3) **3B**
firm Firma (*pl.* die Firmen) *f.* (3) **3A**
first erster/erste/erstes *adj.* (1) **2A**; zuerst *adv.* (2) **3B**
first course erster Gang *m.* (1) **4B**
first class erste Klasse *f.* (2) **4A**
fish Fisch, -e *m.* (1) **4A**
to go fishing angeln gehen *v.* (1) **2B**
fish store Fischgeschäft, -e *n.* (1) **4A**
fit passen *v.* (2) **1A**; fit *adj.* (1) **2B**
five fünf (1) **2A**
flat tire Platten, - *m.* (2) **4A**

to have a flat tire einen Platten haben *v.* (2) **4A**
flavor Geschmack, ⸚e *m.* (1) **4B**
flight Flug, ⸚e *m.* (2) **3B**
flood Hochwasser, - *n.* (3) **4B**
floor Stock, ⸚e *m.*; Boden, ⸚ *m.* (2) **2A**
first/second floor erster/zweiter Stock (2) **2A**
flower Blume, -n *f.* (1) **1A**
flower shop Blumengeschäft, -e *n.* (3) **2A**
flu Grippe, -n *f.* (3) **1B**
flunk durchfallen *v.* (1) **1B**
fly fliegen *v.* (2) **3B**
fog Nebel, - *m.* (3) **3A**
follow folgen *v.* (2) **1A**
food Essen, - *n.* (1) **4A**
foot Fuß, ⸚e *m.* (3) **1A**
football American Football *m.* (1) **2B**
for für *prep.* (1) **3B**; seit; zu *prep.* (1) **4B**
foreign language Fremdsprache, -n *f.* (1) **2A**
forest Wald, ⸚er *m.* (1) **2B**
forget vergessen *v.* (1) **2B**
fork Gabel, -n *f.* (1) **4B**
form Formular, -e *n.* (3) **2A**
to fill out a form ein Formular ausfüllen *v.* (3) **2A**
fountain Brunnen, - *m.* (3) **2B**
four vier (1) **2A**
France Frankreich *n.* (3) **2B**
French (person) Franzose, -n / Französin,
-nen *m./f.* (3) **2B**; (language) Französisch *n.* (3) **2B**
free time Freizeit, -en *f.* (1) **2B**
freezer Gefrierschrank, ⸚e *m.* (2) **2B**
Friday Freitag, -e *m.* (1) **2A**
on Fridays freitags *adv.* (1) **2A**
friend Freund, -e / Freundin, -nen *m./f.* (1) **1A**
friendly freundlich *adj.* (1) **3B**
friendship Freundschaft, -en *f.* (2) **1A**
from aus *prep.* (1) **4A**; von *prep.* (1) **4B**
where from woher *interr.* (1) **2A**
front: in front of vor *prep.* (2) **1B**
fruit Obst *n.* (1) **4A**
fry braten *v.* (1) **2B**
full voll *adj.* (3) **3B**
full-time ganztags *adj.* (3) **3B**
fully occupied voll besetzt *adj.* (2) **3B**
fun Spaß *m.* (1) **2B**
to be fun Spaß machen *v.* (1) **2B**
to (not) have fun (keinen) Spaß haben *v.* (2) **1A**
function funktionieren *v.* (2) **4B**
funny lustig *adj.* (1) **3B**
furnished möbliert *adj.* (2) **2A**
furniture Möbel, - *n.* (2) **2A**
piece of furniture Möbelstück, ,-e *n.* (2) **2A**

G

game Spiel, -e *n.* (1) **2B**
game console Spielkonsole, -en *f.* (2) **4B**
garage Garage, -n *f.* (2) **1B**
garbage truck Müllwagen, - *m.* (3) **4B**
gardener Gärtner, - / Gärtnerin, -nen *m./f.* (3) **3B**
garlic Knoblauch *m.* (1) **4A**
gas Benzin, -e *n.* (2) **4A**
gas station Tankstelle, -n *f.* (2) **4A**

generous großzügig *adj.* (1) **3B**
German (person) Deutsche *m./f.* (3) **2B**;
(language) Deutsch *n.* (3) **2B**
Germany Deutschland *n.* (1) **4A**
get bekommen *v.* (2) **1A**
to get up aufstehen *v.* (1) **4A**
to get sick/better krank/gesund werden *v.* (3) **1B**
gift Geschenk, -e *n.* (2) **1A**
girl Mädchen, - *n.* (1) **1A**
give geben *v.* (1) **2B**
to give (a gift) schenken *v.* (2) **1A**
glass Glas, ⸚er *n.* (1) **4B**
glasses Brille, -n *f.* (2) **1B**
global warming Erderwärmung *f.* (2) **4B**
glove Handschuh, -e *m.* (2) **1B**
go gehen *v.* (1) **2A**; fahren *v.* (1) **2B**
to go out ausgehen *v.* (1) **4A**
Go! Los! (1) **2B**
goal (in soccer) Tor, -e *n.* (1) **2B**
golf Golf *n.* (1) **2B**
good gut *adj.*; nett *adj.* (1) **1A**
Good evening. Guten Abend! (1) **1A**
Good morning. Guten Morgen! (1) **1A**
Good night. Gute Nacht! (1) **1A**
Good-bye. Auf Wiedersehen! (1) **1A**
Good luck! Viel Glück! (2) **1A**
government Regierung, -en *f.* (3) **4B**
grade Note, -n *f.* (1) **1B**
grade report Zeugnis, -se *n.* (1) **1B**
graduate Abschluss machen, ⸚e *v.* (1) **1A**
graduation Abschluss, ⸚e *m.* (1) **1B**
gram Gramm, -e *n.* (1) **4A**
100 grams of cheese 100 Gramm Käse (1) **4A**
granddaughter Enkeltochter, ⸚ *f.* (1) **3A**
grandson Enkelsohn, ⸚e *m.* (1) **3A**
grandchild Enkel, - *m.* (1) **3A**; Enkelkind, -er *n.* (1) **3A**
grandfather Großvater, ⸚ *m.* (1) **3A**
grandma Oma, -s *f.* (1) **3A**
grandmother Großmutter, ⸚ *f.* (1) **3A**
grandpa Opa, -s *m.* (1) **3A**
grandparents Großeltern *pl.* (1) **1A**
grape Traube, -n *f.* (1) **4A**
grass Gras, ⸚er *n.* (3) **4A**
gray grau *adj.* (2) **1B**
great toll *adj.* (1) **3B**; prima *adj.*; spitze *adj.* (1) **1A**
great grandfather Urgroßvater, ⸚ *m.* (1) **3A**
great grandmother Urgroßmutter, ⸚ *f.* (1) **3A**
greedy gierig *adj.* (1) **3B**
green grün *adj.* (2) **1B**
green bean grüne Bohne (*pl.* die grünen
Bohnen) *f.* (1) **4A**
greet grüßen *v.* (1) **2A**
greeting Begrüßung, -en *f.* (1) **1A**; Gruß, ⸚e *m.*
(1) **1A**
grocery store Lebensmittelgeschäft, -e *n.* (1) **4A**
ground floor Erdgeschoss, -e *n.* (2) **2A**
grow wachsen *v.* (2) **1B**
grown-up erwachsen *adj.* (3) **2A**
guest Gast, ⸚e *m.* (2) **1A**
hotel guest Hotelgast, ⸚e *m.* (2) **3B**
guesthouse Pension, -en *f.* (2) **3B**
gym Sporthalle, -n *f.* (1) **2A**

H

hail Hagel *m.* (2) **3A**
hair Haar, -e *n.* (1) **3A**
hair dryer Haartrockner, - *m.* (3) **1A**
hairdresser Friseur, -e / Friseurin, -nen *m./f.* (1) **3B**
half halb *adj.* (1) **2A**
half brother Halbbruder, ⸚ *m.* (1) **3A**
half sister Halbschwester, -n *f.* (1) **3A**
hall Flur, -e *m.* (2) **2A**
ham Schinken, - *m.* (1) **4A**
hand Hand, ⸚e *f.* (3) **1A**
handsome gut aussehend *adj.* (1) **3A**
hang hängen *v.* (2) **1B**
 to hang up auflegen *v.* (3) **3A**
happen passieren *v.* (2) **1B**
happiness Glück *n.* (2) **1A**
happy glücklich *adj.* (1) **3B** froh *adj.* (1) (1) **3B**
 Happy birthday! Alles Gute zum Geburtstag! (2) **1A**
 Happy Easter! Frohe Ostern! (2) **1A**
 Happy New Year! Ein gutes neues Jahr! (2) **1A**
 to be happy (about) sich freuen (über) *v.* (3) **1A**
hard schwer *adj.* (3) **1B**
hard drive Festplatte, -en *f.* (2) **4B**
hard-working fleißig *adj.* (1) **3B**
hare Hase, -n *m.* (3) **4A**
hat Hut, ⸚e *m.* (2) **1B**
have haben *v.* (1) **1B**
 Have a nice day! Schönen Tag noch! (1) **1A**
 to have to müssen *v.* (3) **3B**
he er *pron.* (1) **1A**
head Kopf, ⸚e *m.* (3) **1A**
headache Kopfschmerzen *m. pl.* (3) **1B**
headlight Scheinwerfer, -e *m.* (2) **4A**
headphones Kopfhörer, - *m.* (2) **4B**
health Gesundheit *f.* (3) **1B**
health-food store Bioladen, ⸚ *m.* (3) **1B**
healthy gesund *adj.* (2) **4A**
hear hören *v.* (1) **2A**
heat stroke Hitzschlag, ⸚e *m.* (3) **1B**
heavy schwer *adj.* (1) **4B**
hello Guten Tag!; Hallo! (1) **1A**
help helfen *v.* (1) **2B**
 to help with helfen bei *v.* (2) **3A**
her ihr *poss. adj.* (1) **3A**
here hier *adv.* (1) **1A**
 Here is/are... Hier ist/sind... (1) **1B**
high hoch *adj.* (2) **4A**
highway Autobahn, -en *f.* (2) **4A**
hike wandern *v.* (1) **2A**
his sein *poss. adj.* (1) **3A**
history Geschichte, -en *f.* (1) **2A**
hit treffen *v.* (1) **2B**
hobby Hobby, -s *n.* (1) **2B**
hockey Hockey *n.* (1) **2B**
hold: to be on hold in der Warteschleife sein *v.* (3) **3B**
 Please hold. Bleiben Sie bitte am Apparat! (3) **3A**
holiday Feiertag, -e *m.* (2) **1A**
home Haus, ⸚er *adv.* (2) **1B**
 at home zu Hause *adv.* (1) **4A**
home office Arbeitszimmer, - *n.* (2) **2A**
homemade hausgemacht *adj.* (1) **4B**
homemaker Hausfrau, -en / Hausmann, ⸚er *f./m.* (3) **3B**

homework Hausaufgabe, -n *f.* (1) **1B**
hood Motorhaube, -en *f.* (2) **4A**
horse Pferd, -e *n.* (1) **2B**
hospital Krankenhaus, ⸚er *n.* (3) **1B**
host / hostess Gastgeber, - / Gastgeberin, -nen *m./f.* (2) **1A**
host family Gastfamilie, -n *f.* (3) **4B**
hot heiß *adj.* (2) **3A**
hotel Hotel, -s *n.* (2) **3B**
 five-star hotel Fünf-Sterne-Hotel *n.* (2) **3B**
hour Stunde,-n *f.* (1) **2A**
house Haus, ⸚er *n.* (2) **2A**
housework Hausarbeit *f.* (2) **2B**
 to do housework Hausarbeit machen *v.* (2) **2B**
how wie *interr.* (1) **2A**
 How are you? (form.) Wie geht es Ihnen? (1) **1A**
 How are you? (inf.) Wie geht's (dir)? (1) **1A**
 how many wie viele *interr.* (1) **1B**
 how much wie viel *interr.* (1) **1B**
human resources manager Personalchef, -s / die Personalchefin, -nen *m./f.* (3) **3A**
humble bescheiden *adj.*
hurry sich beeilen *v.* (3) **1A**
hurt weh tun *v.* (3) **1B**
 to hurt oneself sich verletzen *v.* (3) **1B**
husband Ehemann, ⸚er *m.* (1) **3A**
hybrid car Hybridauto, -s *n.* (3) **4B**

I

I ich *pron.* (1) **1A**
ice cream Eis *n.* (2) **1A**
ice cream shop Eisdiele, -n *f.* (1) **4A**
ice cube Eiswürfel, - *m.* (2) **1A**
ice hockey Eishockey *n.* (1) **2B**
ID card Personalausweis, -e *m.* (2) **3B**
idea Idee, -n *f.* (1) **1A**
if wenn *conj.;* ob *conj.* (3) **2A**
 as if als ob (3) **2A**
 if I were you an deiner/Ihrer Stelle *f.* (3) **2A**
 if... only wenn... nur (3) **2A**
 if... then wenn... dann (3) **2A**
imagine sich (etwas) vorstellen *v.* (3) **1A**
imitate nachmachen *v.* (2) **4B**
important wichtig *adj.* (2) **3B**; bedeutend *adj.* (3) **4A**
improve verbessern *v.* (3) **4B**
in in *prep.* (2) **1B**
 in the afternoon nachmittags *adv.* (1) **2A**
 in the evening abends *adv.* (1) **2A**
 in the morning morgens *adv.* (1) **2A**
 in spite of trotz *prep.* (2) **4B**
India Indien *n.* (3) **2B**
Indian indisch *adj.* (3) **2B**; **(person)** Inder, - / Inderin, -nen *m./f.* (3) **2B**
ingredient Zutat, -en *f.* (1) **4A**
injury Verletzung, -en *f.* (3) **1B**
inside (of) innerhalb *prep.* (3) **4B**
instead sondern *conj.* (2) **2A**
 instead of statt *prep.;* anstatt *prep.* (2) **4B**
intellectual intellektuell *adj.* (1) **3B**
intelligent intelligent *adj.* (1) **3B**
interested: to be interested (in) sich interessieren (für) *v.* (3) **1A**
interesting interessant *adj.* (1) **2A**

internet café Internetcafé, -s *n.* (3) **2A**
internship Praktikum (*pl.* die Praktika) *n.* (3) **3A**
intersection Kreuzung, -en *f.* (3) **2B**
introduce: to introduce (oneself) (sich) vorstellen *v.* (3) **1A**
invent erfinden *v.* (2) **3A**
invite einladen *v.* (2) **1A**
iron Bügeleisen, - *n.* (2) **2B**; bügeln *v.* (2) **2B**
ironing board Bügelbrett, -er *n.* (2) **2B**
island Insel, -n *f.* (3) **4A**
it es *pron.* (1) **1A**
Italian (person) Italiener, - / Italienerin, -nen *m./f.* (3) **2B**; **(language)** Italienisch *n.* (3) **2B**
Italy Italien *n.* (3) **2B**
its sein *poss. adj.* (1) **3A**

J

jacket Jacke, -n *f.* (2) **1B**
jam Marmelade, -n *f.* (1) **4A**
January Januar *m.* (1) **2A**
Japan Japan *n.* (3) **2B**
Japanese (person) Japaner, - / Japanerin, -nen *m./f.* (3) **2B**; **(language)** Japanisch *n.* (3) **2B**
jealous eifersüchtig *adj.* (1) **3B**
jeans Jeans, - *f.* (2) **1B**
jewelry store Juweliergeschäft, -e *n.* (3) **2A**
job Beruf, -e *m.* (3) **3B**; Stelle, -n *f.* (3) **3A**
 to find a job Arbeit finden *v.* (3) **3A**
job interview Vorstellungsgespräch, -e *n.* (3) **3A**
job opening Stellenangebot, -e *n.* (3) **3A**
jog joggen *v.* (1) **2B**
journalist Journalist, -en / Journalistin, -nen *m./f.* (1) **3B**
judge Richter, - / Richterin, -nen *m./f.* (3) **3B**
juice Saft, ⸚e *m.* (1) **4B**
July Juli *m.* (1) **2A**
June Juni *m.* (1) **2A**
just as genauso wie (2) **4A**

K

key Schlüssel, - *m.* (2) **3B**
keyboard Tastatur, -en *f.* (2) **4B**
kind nett *adj.*
kiosk Kiosk, -e *m.* (3) **2A**
kiss Kuss, ⸚e *m.* (2) **1A**; küssen *v.* (2) **1A**
 to kiss (each other) sich küssen *v.* (3) **1A**
kitchen Küche, -n *f.* (2) **2A**
knee Knie, - *n.* (3) **1A**
knife Messer, - *n.* (1) **4B**
know kennen *v.* (2) **1B**; wissen *v.* (2) **1B**
 to know each other sich kennen *v.* (3) **1A**
know-it-all Besserwisser, - / Besserwisserin -nen *m./f.* (1) **2A**
Korea Korea *n.* (3) **2B**
Korean (person) Koreaner, - / Koreanerin, -nen *m./f.* (3) **2B**; **(language)** Koreanisch *n.* (3) **2B**

L

labor union Gewerkschaft, -en *f.* (3) **3B**
lake See, -n *m.* (3) **4A**
lamp Lampe, -n *f.* (2) **2A**

land landen *v.* (2) **3B**; Land, ⸚er *n.* (2) **3B**
landscape Landschaft, -en *f.* (3) **4A**
laptop (computer) Laptop, -s *m./n.* (2) **4B**
last letzter/letzte/letztes *adj.* (1) **2B**
last name Nachname, -n *m.* (1) **3A**
late spät *adj.* (1) **2A**
  to be late sich verspäten *v.* (3) **1A**
laugh lachen *v.* (1) **2A**
laundromat Waschsalon, -s *m.* (3) **4A**
laundry Wäsche *f.* (2) **2B**
  to do laundry Wäsche waschen *v.* (2) **2B**
law Gesetz, -e *n.* (3) **4B**
lawyer Rechtsanwalt, ⸚e / Rechtsanwältin, -nen *m./f.* (1) **3B**
lay legen *v.* (2) **1B**
lazy faul *adj.* (1) **3B**
leaf Blatt, ⸚er *n.* (3) **4A**
learn lernen *v.* (1) **2A**
leather Leder, - *n.* (2) **1B**
leave abfahren *v.* (2) **4A**
lecture Vorlesung, -en *f.* (1) **2A**; Vortrag, ⸚e *m.* (2) **2B**
lecture hall Hörsaal (*pl.* Hörsäle) *m.* (1) **2A**
leg Bein, -e *n.* (3) **1A**
leisure Freizeit *f.* (1) **2B**
lesson Stunde, -n *f.* (1) **1B**
let lassen *v.* (1) **2B**
letter Brief, -e *m.* (3) **2A**
  to mail a letter einen Brief abschicken *v.* (3) **2A**
  letter of recommendation Empfehlungsschreiben, - *n.* (3) **3A**
lettuce Salat, -e *m.* (1) **4A**
library Bibliothek, -en *f.* (1) **1B**
license plate Nummernschild, -er *n.* (2) **4A**
lie liegen *v.* (2) **1B**
  to lie down sich (hin)legen *v.* (3) **1A**
  to tell a lie lügen *v.*
light hell *adj.* (3) **3A**; leicht *adj.* (1) **4B**; Licht, -er *n.* (3) **4B**
lightning Blitz, -e *m.* (2) **3A**
like mögen *v.* **4B**; gern (+*verb*) *v.* (1) **2B**; gefallen *v.* (2) **1A**
  I would like... ich hätte gern... (1) **4A**; Ich möchte... (1) **4B**
line Schlange, -n *f.* (2) (1) **3B**; Linie, -n *f.*
  to stand in line Schlange stehen *v.* (2) **3B**
lip Lippe, -n *f.* (3) **1A**
lipstick Lippenstift, -e *m.* (3) **1A**
listen (to) hören *v.* (1) **2A**
literature Literatur, -en *f.* (1) **2A**
little klein *adj.* (1) **3A**; wenig *adj.* (3) **2A**
live wohnen *v.* (1) **2A**; leben *v.* (1) **2A**
living room Wohnzimmer, - *n.* (2) **2A**
load laden *v.* (2) **4B**
location Lage, -n *f.* (2) **3B**
long lang *adj.* (1) **3A**
  long-sleeved langärmlig *adj.* (2) **1B**
look schauen *v.* (2) **3A**
  to look at anschauen *v.* (2) **3A**
  to look for suchen *v.* (1) **2A**
  to look forward to sich freuen auf *v.* (3) **1A**
loose weit *adj.* (2) **1B**
lose verlieren *v.* (1) **2B**
  to get lost sich verlaufen *v.* (3) **2B**

love lieben *v.* (1) **2A**; Liebe *f.* (2) **1A**
  to fall in love (with) sich verlieben (in) *v.* (3) **1A**
  to love each other sich lieben *v.* (3) **1A**
loving liebevoll *adj.* (1) **3B**
low niedrig *adj.* (3) **3A**
luggage Gepäck *n.* (2) **3B**
lunch Mittagessen, - *n.* (1) **4B**

magazine Zeitschrift, -en *f.* (3) **2A**
mail Post *f.* (3) **2A**
  to mail a letter einen Brief abschicken *v.* (3) **2A**
mail carrier Briefträger, - / Briefträgerin, -nen *m.* (3) **2A**
mailbox Briefkasten, ⸚ *m.* (3) **2A**
main course Hauptspeise, -n *f.* (3) **4B**
main road Hauptstraße, -n *f.* (3) **2B**
major: to major in studieren *v.* (1) **2A**
make machen *v.* (1) **2A**
makeup: to put on makeup sich schminken *v.* (3) **1A**
mall Einkaufszentrum (*pl.* Einkaufszentren) *n.* (3) **2B**
man Mann, ⸚er *m.* (1) **1A**
manage leiten *v.* (3) **4B**
manager Geschäftsführer, - / die Geschäftsführerin, -nen *m./f.* (3) **3A**
map Karte, -n *f.* (1) **1B**; Landkarte, -n *f.* (2) **3B**
  city map Stadtplan, ⸚e *m.* (2) **3B**
  to read a map eine Karte lesen *v.* (2) **3B**
marble Marmor *m.* (2) **2B**
March März *m.* (1) **2A**
marital status Familienstand, ⸚e *m.* (1) **3A**
market Markt, ⸚e *m.* (1) **4A**
marriage Ehe, -n *f.* (2) **1A**
married verheiratet *adj.* (1) **3A**
marry heiraten *v.* (1) **3A**
match Spiel, -e *n.* (1) **2B**; passen *v.* (2) **1A**
material Material, -ien *n.* (2) **1B**
mathematics Mathematik *f.* (1) **2A**
May Mai *m.* (1) **2A**
may dürfen *v.* (1) **3B**
maybe vielleicht *adv.* (1) **4A**
mayor Bürgermeister, - / Bürgermeisterin, -nen *m./f.* (3) **2B**
meal Mahlzeit, -en *f.* (1) **4B**
mean bedeuten *v.* (1) **2A**; meinen *v.* (3) **4B**; gemein *adj.* (1) **3B**
meat Fleisch *n.* (1) **4A**
mechanic Mechaniker, - / Mechanikerin, -nen *m./f.* (2) **4A**
medicine Medizin *f.* (1) **2A**; Medikament, -e *n.* (3) **1B**
meet (sich) treffen *v.* (1) **2B**; **(for the first time)** (sich) kennen lernen *v.* (3) **1A**
  Pleased to meet you. Schön dich/Sie kennen zu lernen! (1) **1A**
meeting Besprechung, -en *f.* (3) **3A**
melon Melone, -n *f.* (1) **4A**
menu Speisekarte, -n *f.* (1) **4B**
Merry Christmas! Frohe Weihnachten! (2) **1A**
message Nachricht, -en *f.* (3) **3A**
Mexico Mexiko *n.* (3) **2B**
Mexican mexikanisch *adj.* (3) **2B**; **(person)** Mexikaner, - / Mexikanerin, -nen *m./f.* (3) **2B**
microphone Mikrofon, -e *n.* (2) **4B**

microwave Mikrowelle, -n *f.* (2) **2B**
midmorning Vormittag, -e *m.* (1) **2B**
midnight Mitternacht *f.* (1) **2A**
mild leicht *adj.* (3) **1B**
milk Milch *f.* (1) **4B**
minority Minderheit, -en *f.* (3) **4B**
minus minus (1) **1B**
mirror Spiegel, - *m.* (2) **2A**
mist Nebel, - *m.* (2) **3A**
modern modern *adj.* (3) **2A**
modest bescheiden *adj.* (1) **3B**
mom Mama, -s *f.* (1) **3A**
Monday Montag, -e *m.* (1) **2A**
  on Mondays montags *adv.* (1) **2A**
money Geld, -er *n.* (3) **2A**
month Monat, -e *m.* (1) **2A**
moon Mond, -e *m.* (3) **4A**
mop wischen *v.* (2) **2B**
more mehr *adj.* (2) **4A**
morning Morgen, - *m.* (1) **2B**
  in the morning vormittags (1) **2A**
  tomorrow morning morgen früh (1) **2B**
mother Mutter, ⸚ *f.* (1) **1A**
mother-in-law Schwiegermutter, ⸚ *f.* (1) **3A**
mountain Berg, -e *m.* (1) **2B**; (3) **4A**
mouse Maus, ⸚e *f.* (2) **4B**
mouth Mund, ⸚er *m.* (3) **1A**
move umziehen *v.* (2) **2A**; sich bewegen *v.*
movie Film, -e *m.*
movie theater Kino, -s *n.* (3) **2A**
mp3 player MP3-Player, - *m.* (2) **4B**
Mr. Herr (1) **1A**
Mrs. Frau (1) **1A**
Ms. Frau (1) **1A**
much viel *adv.* (1) **4A**
mushroom Pilz, -e *m.* (1) **4A**
musician Musiker, - / Musikerin, -nen *m./f.* (1) **3B**
must müssen *v.* (1) **3B**
my mein *poss. adj.* (1) **3A**
myself mich *pron.*; mir *pron.* (3) **1A**

naïve naiv *adj.* (1) **3B**
name Name, -n *m.* (1) **1A**
  to be named heißen *v.* (1) **2A**
  What's your name? Wie heißen Sie? (form.) / Wie heißt du? (inf.) *v.* (1) **1A**
napkin Serviette, -n *f.* (1) **4B**
natural disaster Naturkatastrophe, -n *f.* (3) **4A**
nature Natur, -en *f.* (3) **4A**
nauseous übel *adj.* (3) **1B**
near bei *prep.* (1) **4B**; nah *adj.* (3) **2B**
neat ordentlich *adj.* (2) **2B**
neck Hals, ⸚e *m.* (3) **1A**
necklace Halskette, -n *f.* (2) **1B**
need brauchen *v.* (1) **2A**
  to need to müssen *v.* (1) **3B**
neighborhood Viertel, - *n.* (3) **2B**
nephew Neffe, -n *m.* (2) **4B**
nervous nervös *adj.* (1) **3B**
never nie *adv.* **4A**; niemals *adv.* (2) **3 B**
New Year's Eve Silvester *n.* (2) **1A**

newlywed Frischvermählte, -n *m./f.* (2) **1A**
newspaper Zeitung, -en *f.* (2) **3B**
next nächster/nächste/nächstes *adj.* (1) **2B**
  next to neben *prep.* (2) **1B**
nice nett *adj.* (1) **3B**
  It's nice out. Es ist schön draußen. (2) **3A**
  Nice to meet you. Schön dich/Sie kennen zu
    lernen! (1) **1A**
  The weather is nice. Das Wetter ist gut. (2) **3A**
night Nacht, ¨e *f.* (1) **2B**
  to spend the night übernachten *f.* (2) **3B**
night table Nachttisch, -e *m.* (2) **2A**
nine neun (1) **2A**
no nein (1) **1A**; kein *adj.* (1) **2B**
no one niemand *pron.* (2) **3B**
nonviolent gewaltfrei *adj.* (3) **4B**
noon Mittag, -e *m.* (1) **2A**
nose Nase, -n *f.* (3) **1A**
not nicht *adv.* (1) **2B**
  Do not enter. Keine Zufahrt. (1) **3B**
  not bad nicht schlecht (1) **1A**
  not much wenig *adj.* (3) **2A**
note Notiz, -en *f.* (1) **1B**
notebook Heft, -e *n.* (1) **1B**
nothing nichts *pron.* (2) **3B**
November November *m.* (1) **2A**
now jetzt *adv.* (1) **4A**
nuclear energy Kernenergie *f.* (3) **4B**
nuclear power plant Kernkraftwerk, -e *n.* (3) **4B**
nurse Krankenpfleger, - / Krankenschwester,
  -n *m./f.* (3) **1B**

O

ocean Meer, -e *n.* (3) **4A**
occasion Anlass, ¨e *m.* (2) **1A**
  special occasions besondere Anlässe *m. pl.* (2) **1A**
October Oktober *m.* (1) **2A**
offer Angebot, -e *n.* (2) **1B**; bieten *v.* (3) **1B**;
  anbieten *v.* (3) **4B**
office Büro, -s *n.* (3) **3B**
office supplies Büromaterial, -ien *n.* (3) **3A**
often oft *adv.* (1) **4A**
oil Öl, -e *n.* (1) **4A**
old alt *adj.* (1) **3A**
  How old are you? Wie alt bist du? (1) **1B**
  I am... years old. Ich bin... Jahre alt. (1) **1B**
olive oil Olivenöl, -e *n.* (1) **4A**
on an *prep.*; auf *prep.* (2) **1B**
once einmal *adv.* (2) **3B**
one eins (1) **2A**; man *pron.* (2) **3B**
  by oneself allein *adv.* (1) **4A**
one-way street Einbahnstraße, -n *f.* (2) **4A**
onion Zwiebel, -n *f.* (1) **4A**
online: to be online online sein *v.* (2) **4B**
only nur *adv.* (1) **4A**
  only child Einzelkind, -er *n.* (1) **3A**
on-time pünktlich *adj.* (2) **3B**
onto auf *prep.* (2) **1B**
open öffnen *v.* (1) **2A**; aufmachen *v.* (2) **4B**;
  geöffnet *adj.* (3) **2A**
or oder *conj.* (1) **1B**
orange Orange, -n *f.* (1) **4A**; orange *adj.* (2) **1B**

order bestellen *v.* (1) **4A**
organic biologisch *adj.* (3) **4B**
our unser *poss. adj.* (1) **3A**
out draußen *adv.* (2) **3A**; heraus *adv.* (2) **2A**
  It's nice out. Es ist schön draußen. (2) **3A**
  to go out ausgehen *v.* (1) **4A**
  to bring out rausbringen (2) **2B**
outside draußen *prep.* (2) **3A**
  outside of außerhalb *prep.* (2) **4B**
oven Ofen, ¨ *m.* (2) **2B**
over über *prep.* (2) **1B**; vorbei *adv.* (2) **3A**
  over there drüben *adv.* (1) **4A**
overpopulation Überbevölkerung *f.* (3) **4B**
owner Besitzer, - / Besitzerin, -nen *m./f.* (1) **3B**

P

pack packen *v.* (2) **3B**
package Paket, -e *n.* (3) **2A**
pain Schmerz, -en *m.* (3) **1B**
pajamas Schlafanzug, ¨e *m.* (3) **1A**
pan Pfanne, -n *f.* (2) **2B**
pants Hose, -n *f.* (2) **1B**
paper Papier, -e *n.* (1) **1B**
  sheet of paper Blatt Papier (*pl.* Blätter)
    Papier *n.* (1) **1B**
paperclip Büroklammer, -n *f.* (3) **3A**
paper-goods store Schreibwarengeschäft, -e *n.* (3) **2A**
paragraph Absatz, ¨e *m.* (2) **1B**
parents Eltern *pl.* (1) **3A**
park Park, -s *m.* (1) **1A**; parken *v.* (2) **4A**
  No parking. Parkverbot. (1) **3B**
participate mitmachen *v.* (2) **4B**
part-time halbtags *adj.* (3) **3B**
party Party, -s *f.* (2) **1A**
  to go to a party auf eine Party gehen *prep.* (3) **2B**
  to throw a party eine Party geben *v.* (2) **1A**
pass (a test) bestehen *v.* (1) **1B**
passenger Passagier, -e *m.* (2) **3B**
passport control Passkontrolle, -n *f.* (3) **3B**
password Passwort, ¨er *n.* (2) **4B**
past Vergangenheit, -en *f.* (3) **4A**; nach *prep.* (1) **2A**
pasta Pasta *f.* (1) **4A**
pastries Gebäck *n.* (2) **1A**
pastry shop Konditorei, -en *f.* (1) **4A**
path Weg, -e *m.* (3) **4A**
patient geduldig *adj.* (1) **3B**; Patient, -en /
  Patientin, -nen *m./f.* (3) **1B**
pay (for) bezahlen *v.* (1) **4A**
  to pay by (credit) card mit der Karte
    bezahlen *v.* (3) **2A**
  to pay in cash bar bezahlen *v.* (3) **2A**
peach Pfirsich, -e *m.* (1) **4A**
pear Birne, -n *f.* (1) **4A**
pedestrian Fußgänger, - / Fußgängerin,
  -nen *m./f.* (3) **2B**
pen Kuli, -s *m.* (1) **1B**
pencil Bleistift, -e *m.* (1) **1B**
people Leute *pl.* (1) **3B**; Menschen *pl.*
pepper Paprika, - *f.* (1) **4A**; Pfeffer, - *m.* (1) **4B**
percent Prozent, -e *n.* (1) **1B**
period Punkt, -e *m.* (1) **1B**
person Person, -en *f.* (1) **1A**; Mensch, -en *m.*

personal persönlich *adj.* (1) **3B**
pet Haustier, -e *n.* (1) **3A**
pharmacy Apotheke, -n *f.* (3) **1B**
phone booth Telefonzelle, -n *f.* (3) **2B**
photo Foto, -s *n.* (1) **1B**
physics Physik *f.* (1) **2A**
picnic Picknick, -s *n.* (3) **4A**
  to have a picnic ein Picknick machen *v.* (3) **4A**
picture Foto, -s *n.* (1) **1B**; Bild, -er *n.* (2) **2A**
pie Kuchen, - *m.* (1) **4A**
pigsty Saustall, ¨e *n.* (2) **2B**
  It's a pigsty! Es ist ein Saustall! (2) **2B**
pill Tablette, -n *f.* (3) **1B**
pillow Kissen, - *n.* (2) **1B**
pineapple Ananas, - *f.* (1) **4A**
pink rosa *adj.* (2) **1B**
place Ort, -e *m.* (1) **1B**; Lage, -n *f.* (2) **3B**;
  setzen *v.* (2) **2B**
  in your place an deiner/Ihrer Stelle *f.* (3) **2A**
plant Pflanze, -n *f.* (2) **2A**
plastic Kunststoff, -e *m.* (2) **2B**
plate Teller, - *m.* (1) **4B**
platform Bahnsteig, -e *m.* (2) **4A**
play spielen *v.* (1) **2A**
player Spieler, - / Spielerin, -nen *m./f.* (1) **2B**
pleasant angenehm *adj.* (1) **3B**
please bitte **1A**; gefallen *v.* (2) **1A**
  Pleased to meet you. Freut mich! (1) **1A**
plumber Klempner, - / Klempnerin, -nen *m./f.* (3) **3B**
plus plus (1) **1B**
police officer Polizist, -en / Polizistin,
  -nen *m./f.* (2) **4A**
police station Polizeiwache, -n *f.* (3) **2A**
politician Politiker, - / Politikerin, -nen *m./f.* (3) **3B**
pollute verschmutzen *v.* (3) **4B**
pollution Verschmutzung *f.* (3) **4B**
poor arm *adj.* (1) **3B**
pork Schweinefleisch *n.* (1) **4A**
position Stelle, -n *f.* (3) **3A**
post office Post, - *f.* (3) **2A**
  to go to the post office zur Post gehen *v.* (3) **2A**
postcard Postkarte, -n *f.* (3) **2A**
poster Poster, - *n.* (2) **2A**
pot Topf, ¨e *m.* (2) **2B**
potato Kartoffel, -n *f.* (1) **4A**
pound Pfund, -e *n.* (1) **4A**
  a pound of potatoes ein Pfund Kartoffeln (1) **4A**
practice (sports) trainieren *v.* (1) **2B**; Übung, -en *f.*
pregnant schwanger *adj.* (3) **1B**
preparation Vorbereitung, -en *f.*
prepare vorbereiten *v.* (1) **4A**; zubereiten *v.* (2) **3A**
  to prepare oneself (for) sich vorbereiten
    (auf) *v.* (3) **1A**
prescription Rezept, -e *n.* (3) **1B**
presentation Referat, -e *n.* (1) **2A**
preserve erhalten *v.* (3) **4B**
president Präsident, - / Präsidentin, -nen *m./f.* (2) **4B**
  federal president Bundespräsident, - /
    Bundespräsidentin, -nen *m./f.* (2) **4B**
pretty hübsch *adj.* (1) **3A**
  pretty well ziemlich gut *adv.* (1) **1A**
principal Schulleiter, - *m.* / Schulleiterin, -nen
  f. (1) **1B**

print drucken *v.* (2) **4B**
printer Drucker, - *m.* (2) **4B**
probably wohl ; wahrscheinlich *adv.*(3) **2A**; sicher *adv.* (3) **2A**
problem Problem, -e *n.* (1) **1A**
profession Beruf, -e *m.* (1) **3B**
professional training Berufsausbildung, -en *f.* (3) **3A**
professor Professor, -en / Professorin, -nen *m./f.* (1) **1B**
program Programm, -e *n.* (2) **4B**
promotion Beförderung, -en *f.* (3) **3B**
pronunciation Aussprache *f.*
propose vorschlagen *v.* (3) **4B**
protect schützen *v.* (3) **4B**
proud stolz *adj.* (1) **3B**
psychologist Psychologe, -n / Psychologin, -nen *m./f.* (3) **3B**
psychology Psychologie *f.* (1) **2A**
public öffentlich *adj.* (2) **4A**
　public transportation öffentliche Verkehrsmittel *n. pl.* (2) **4A**
pull ziehen *v.* (1) **3B**
purple lila *adj.* (2) **1B**
purse Handtasche, -n *f.* (2) **1B**
push drücken *v.* (1) **3B**
put stellen *v.* (2) **1B**; legen *v.* (3) **1A**; setzen *v.* (3) **1A**
　to put away wegräumen *v.* (2) **2B**
　to put on anziehen *v.* (2) **1B**

Q

quarter Viertel, - *n.* (1) **2A**
　quarter past/to Viertel nach/vor (1) **2A**
question Frage, -n *f.* (1) **1B**
quicksand Treibsand *m.* (3) **4A**
quite ziemlich *adv.* (1) **4A**

R

rabbit Kaninchen, - *n.* (3) **4A**
rain Regen *m.* (2) **3A**; regnen *v.* (1) **2A**
raincoat Regenmantel, ⸚ *m.* (2) **3A**
raise Gehaltserhöhung, -en *f.* (3) **3B**
rarely selten *adv.* (1) **4A**
rather lieber *adj.* (2) **4A**
rating Bewertung, -en *f.* (2) **3B**
razor Rasierer, - *m.* (3) **4A**
read lesen *v.* (1) **2B**
ready fertig *adj.* (3) **3B**
real estate agent Immobilienmakler, - / Immobilienmaklerin, -nen *m./f.* (3) **3B**
realistic realistisch *adj.* (3) **2A**
really wirklich *adv.* (1) **4A**
receive bekommen *v.* (2) **1A**
receiver Hörer, - *m.* (3) **3A**
recess Pause, -n *f.* (1) **1B**
recipe Rezept, -e *n.* (1) **4A**
recognize erkennen *v.* (2) **3A**
recommend empfehlen *v.* (1) **2B**
record aufnehmen *v.* (2) **4B**
recycle recyceln *v.* (3) **4B**
red rot *adj.* (1) **3A**
　red-haired rothaarig *adj.* (3) **3A**
reference Referenz, -en *f.* (3) **3A**

refrigerator Kühlschrank, ⸚e *m.* (2) **2B**
related verwandt *adj.* (3) **2A**
relative Verwandte, -n *m.* (1) **3A**
relax sich entspannen *v.* (3) **1A**
reliable zuverlässig *adj.* (1) **3B**
remember sich erinnern (an) *v.* (3) **1A**
remote control Fernbedienung, -en *f.* (2) **4B**
remove entfernen *v.* (2) **2B**
renewable energy erneuerbare Energie, -en *f.* (3) **4B**
rent Miete, -n *f.* (2) **2A**; mieten *v.* (2) **2A**
repair reparieren *v.* (2) **4A**
repeat wiederholen *v.* (1) **2A**
repetition Wiederholung, -en *f.*
report berichten *v.* (3) **4B**
report card Zeugnis, -se *n.* (1) **1B**
reservation: to make a (hotel) reservation buchen *v.* (2) **3B**
resign kündigen *v.* (3) **3B**
rest sich ausruhen *v.* (3) **1A**
restaurant Restaurant, -s *n.* (1) **4B**
result Ergebnis, -se *n.* (1) **1B**
résumé Lebenslauf, ⸚e *m.* (3) **3A**
retire in Rente gehen *v.* (2) **1A**
retiree Rentner, - / Rentnerin, -nen *m./f.* (3) **3B**
review Besprechung, -en *f.* (2) **4B**
rice Reis *m.* (1) **4A**
rich reich *adj.* (1) **3B**
ride fahren *v.* (1) **2B**; reiten *v.* (1) **2B**
　to give (someone) a ride (jemanden) mitnehmen *v.* (3) **2B**
　to ride a bicycle Fahrrad fahren *v.* (1) **2B**
ring klingeln *v.* (2) **4B**
rinse spülen *v.* (2) **2B**
rise (sun) aufgehen *v.* (3) **4A**
river Fluss, ⸚e *m.* (1) **3B**
rock Stein, -e *m.* (3) **4A**
roll Brötchen, - *n.* (1) **4A**
room Zimmer, - *n.* (2) **1A**
room service Zimmerservice *m.* (2) **3B**
roommate Mitbewohner, - / Mitbewohnerin, -nen *m./f.* (1) **2A**
rug Teppich, -e *m.* (2) **2A**
run laufen *v.* (1) **2B**; rennen *v.* (2) **1A**
Russia Russland *n.* (3) **2B**
Russian (person) Russe, -n / Russin, -nen *m./f.* (3) **2B**; **(language)** Russisch *n.* (3) **2B**

S

sad traurig *adj.* (1) **3B**
salad Salat, -e *m.* (1) **4A**
salary Gehalt, ⸚er *n.* (3) **3A**
　high/low salary hohes/niedriges Gehalt, ⸚er *n.* (3) **3A**
sale Verkauf, ⸚e *m.*
　on sale im Angebot (2) **1B**
salesperson Verkäufer, - / Verkäuferin, -nen *m./f.* (2) **1B**
salt Salz, -e *n.* (1) **4B**
salty salzig *adj.* (1) **4B**
same gleich *adj.*
Saturday Samstag, -e *m.* (1) **2A**
　on Saturdays samstags *adv.* (1) **2A**
sausage Würstchen, - *n.* (1) **4A**

save speichern *v.* (2) **4B**; retten *v.* (3) **4B**
　to save the planet den Planeten retten *v.* (3) **4B**
say sagen *v.* (1) **2A**
scarf Schal, -s *m.* (2) **1B**
schedule Stundenplan, ⸚e *m.* (1) **2A**; Fahrplan, ⸚e *m.* (2) **4A**
scholarship Stipendium (*pl.* Stipendien) *n.* (1) **2A**
school Schule, -n *f.* (1) **1B**
science Naturwissenschaft, -en *f.* (1) **2A**
scientist Wissenschaftler, - / Wissenschaftlerin, -nen *m./f.* (3) **3B**
score Ergebnis, -se *n.* (1) **1B**
screen Bildschirm, -e *m.* (2) **4B**
screen name Benutzername, -n *m.* (2) **4B**
sea Meer, -e *n.* (3) **4A**
seafood Meeresfrüchte *f. pl.* (1) **4A**
season Jahreszeit, -en *f.* (2) **3A**
seatbelt Sicherheitsgurt, -e *m.* (2) **4A**
second zweite *adj.* (1) **2A**
　second-hand clothing Altkleider *pl.* (3) **4B**
see sehen *v.* (1) **2B**
　See you later. Bis später! (1) **1A**
　See you soon. Bis gleich! / Bis bald. (1) **1A**
　See you tomorrow. Bis morgen! (1) **1A**
selfish egoistisch *adj.* (1) **3B**
sell verkaufen *v.* (1) **4A**
seminar Seminar, -e *n.* (1) **2A**
seminar room Seminarraum (*pl.* Seminarräume) *m.* (1) **2A**
send schicken *v.* (2) **4B**; abschicken *v.* (3) **3B**
separate (sich) trennen *v.* (3) **1A**
separated getrennt *adj.* (1) **3A**
September September *m.* (1) **2A**
serious ernst *adj.* (3) **3B**; schwer *adj.* (3) **1B**
set setzen *v.* (3) **1A**; (sun) untergehen *v.* (3) **4A**
　to set the table den Tisch decken *v.* (3) **4B**
seven sieben (1) **2A**
shampoo Shampoo, -s *n.* (3) **1A**
shape Form, -en *f.* (3) **1B**
　in good shape fit *adj.* (1) **2B**
　to be in/out of shape in guter/schlechter Form sein *v.* (3) **1B**
shave sich rasieren *v.* (3) **1A**
shaving cream Rasierschaum, ⸚e *m.* (3) **1A**
she sie *pron.* (1) **1A**
sheep Schaf, -e *n.* (3) **4A**
sheet Laken, - *n.* (2) **2B**
　sheet of paper Blatt Papier (*pl.* Blätter) Papier *n.* (1) **1B**
ship Schiff, -e *n.* (2) **4A**
shirt Hemd, -en *n.* (2) **1B**
shoe Schuh, -e *m.* (2) **1B**
shop einkaufen *v.* (1) **4A**; Geschäft, -e *n.* (1) **4A**
　to go shopping einkaufen gehen *v.* (1) **4A**
shopping Einkaufen *n.* (2) **1B**
shopping center Einkaufszentrum, -(*pl.* Einkaufszentren) *n.* (3) **2B**
short kurz *adj.* (1) **3A**; (stature) klein *adj.* (1) **3A**
　short film Kurzfilm, -e *m.* (3) **2A**
　short-sleeved kurzärmlig *adj.* (2) **1B**
shorts kurze Hose, -n *f.* (2) **1B**
shot Spritze, -n *f.* (3) **1B**
　to give a shot eine Spritze geben *v.* (3) **1B**
shoulder Schulter, -n *f.* (3) **1A**

show zeigen *v.* (1) **4B**
shower: to take a shower (sich) duschen *v.* (3) **1A**
shrimp Garnele, -n *f.* (1) **4A**
shy schüchtern *adj.* (1) **3B**
sibling Geschwister, - *n.* (1) **3A**
sick krank *adj.* (3) **1B**
  to get sick krank werden *v.* (3) **1B**
side dish Beilage, -n *f.* (1) **4B**
sidewalk Bürgersteig, -e *m.* (3) **2B**
sign unterschreiben *v.* (3) **2A**; Schild, -er *n.*
silk Seide, -n *f.* (2) **1B**
silverware Besteck *n.* (1) **4B**
since seit (1) **4B**
sincere aufrichtig *adj.* (1) **3B**
  Yours sincerely Gruß, ⸚e (1) **3B**
sing singen *v.* (1) **2B**
single ledig *adj.* (1) **3A**
sink Spüle, -n *f.* (2) **2B**
sister Schwester, -n *f.* (1) **1A**
sister-in-law Schwägerin, -nen *f.* (1) **3A**
sit sitzen *v.* (2) **1B**
  to sit down sich (hin)setzen *v.* (3) **1A**
six sechs (1) **2A**
size Kleidergröße, -n *f.* (2) **1B**
ski Ski fahren *v.* (1) **2B**
skirt Rock, ⸚e *m.* (2) **1B**
sky Himmel *m.* (3) **4A**
sleep schlafen *v.* (1) **2B**
  to go to sleep einschlafen *v.* (1) **4A**
slim schlank *adj.* (1) **3A**
slipper Hausschuh, -e *m.* (3) **1A**
slow langsam *adj.* (1) **3B**
  Please speak more slowly. Sprechen Sie bitte langsamer! (1) **3B**
  Slow down. Langsam fahren. (1) **3B**
small klein *adj.* (1) **3A**
smartphone Smartphone, -s *n.* (2) **4B**
smile lächeln *v.* (2) **1A**
smoke rauchen *v.*
  No smoking. Rauchen verboten. (1) **3B**
snack Snack, -s *m.* (1) **4B**
snake Schlange, -n *f.* (3) **4A**
sneakers Turnschuhe *m. pl.* (2) **1B**
sneeze niesen *v.* (3) **1B**
snow Schnee *m.* (2) **3A**; schneien *v.* (2) **3A**
so so *adv.* (1) **4A**
  so far, so good so weit, so gut (1) **1A**
  so that damit *conj.* (3) **2A**
soap Seife, -n *f.* (3) **1A**
soccer Fußball *m.* (1) **2B**
sock Socke, -n *f.* (2) **1B**
sofa Sofa, -s *n.* (2) **2A**
soil verschmutzen *v.* (2) **2B**
solar energy Sonnenenergie *f.* (3) **4B**
solid colored einfarbig *adj.* (2) **1B**
solution Lösung, -en *f.* (3) **4B**
some mancher/manche/manches *pron.* (2) **4B**
someone jemand *pron.* (2) **3B**
something etwas *pron.* (2) **3B**
  something else etwas anderes *n.* (3) **2A**
sometimes manchmal *adv.* (2) **3B**
somewhere else woanders *adv.* (1) **4A**
son Sohn, ⸚e *m.* (1) **3A**

soon bald (1) **1A**
  See you soon. Bis bald.; Bis gleich. (1) **1A**
sorry: I'm sorry. Es tut mir leid. (1) **1A**
so-so (I'm so-so) Es geht. (1) **1A**
soup Suppe, -n *f.* (4) **4B**
soup spoon Esslöffel, - *m.* (1) **4B**
Spain Spanien *n.* (3) **2B**
Spanish (person) Spanier, - / Spanierin, -nen *m./f.* (3) **2B**; **(language)** Spanisch *n.* (3) **2B**
sparkling water Mineralwasser *n.* (1) **4B**
speak sprechen *v.* (1) **2B**
  to speak about sprechen über; reden über *v.* (2) **3A**
special besonderes *adj.* (3) **2A**
  nothing special nichts Besonderes *adj.* (3) **2A**
species Art, -en *f.* (3) **4B**
spelling Rechtschreibung *f.*
spend verbringen *v.* (1) **4A**
spicy scharf *adj.* (1) **4B**
split up sich trennen *v.* (3) **1A**
spoon Löffel, - *m.* (1) **4B**
sport Sport *m.* (2) **2B**; Sportart, -en *f.* (1) **2B**
sprain (one's wrist/ankle) sich (das Handgelenk / den Fuß) verstauchen *v.* (3) **1B**
spring Frühling, -e *m.* (1) **2B**
squirrel Eichhörnchen, - *n.* (3) **4A**
stadium Stadion (*pl.* Stadien) *n.* (1) **2B**
stairs Treppe, -n *f.* (2) **2A**
  to go up/down stairs die Treppe hochgehen/ heruntergehen *v.* (3) **2B**
stamp Briefmarke, -n *f.* (3) **2A**
stand stehen *v.* (2) **1B**
  to stand in line Schlange stehen *v.* (2) **3B**
stapler Hefter, - *m.* (3) **3A**
star Stern, -e *m.* (3) **4A**
start starten *v.* (2) **4B**; anfangen *v.* (1) **4A**; beginnen *v.* (2) **2A**
station wagon Kombi, -s *m.* (2) **4B**
statue Statue, -n *f.* (3) **2B**
stay bleiben *v.* (2) **1B**
steal stehlen *v.* (1) **2B**
steering wheel Lenkrad, ⸚er *n.* (2) **4A**
stepbrother Halbbruder, ⸚ *m.* (1) **3A**
stepdaughter Stieftochter, ⸚ *f.* (3) **3A**
stepfather Stiefvater, -s⸚ *m.* (1) **3A**
stepmother Stiefmutter, ⸚ *f.* (1) **3A**
stepsister Halbschwester, -n *f.* (1) **3A**
stepson Stiefsohn, ⸚ *m.* (3) **3A**
stereo system Stereoanlage, -n *f.* (2) **4B**
still noch *adv.* (1) **4A**; still *adj.* (1) **4B**
  still water stilles Wasser *n.* (1) **4B**
stomachache Bauchschmerzen *m. pl.* (3) **1B**
stop sign Stoppschild, -er *n.* (2) **4A**
store Geschäft, -e *n.* (1) **4A**
storm Sturm, ⸚e *m.* (2) **3A**
stove Herd, -e *m.* (2) **2B**
straight glatt *adj.* (1) **3A**
  straight hair glatte Haare *n. pl.* (3) **3A**
  straight ahead geradeaus *adv.* (2) **4A**
strawberry Erdbeere, -n *f.* (1) **4A**
stream Strom, ⸚e *m.* (3) **4A**
street Straße, -n *f.* (2) **4A**
  to cross the street die Straße überqueren *v.* (3) **2B**
striped gestreift *adj.* (2) **1B**

strong stark *adj.* (1) **3B**
student Schüler, - / Schülerin, -nen *m./f.* (1) **1B**; **(college/university)** Student, -en / Studentin, -nen *m./f.* (1) **1A**
studies Studium (*pl.* Studien) *n.* (1) **2A**
study lernen *v.* (1) **2A**
stuffy nose verstopfte Nase *f.* (3) **1B**
style Stil, -e *m.* (2) **1B**
subject Fach, ⸚er *n.* (1) **2A**
subway U-Bahn, -en *f.* (2) **4A**
success Erfolg, -e *m.* (3) **3B**
such solcher/solche/solches *pron.* (2) **4B**
suit Anzug, ⸚e *m.* (2) **1B**
suitcase Koffer, - *m.* (2) **3B**
summer Sommer, - *m.* (1) **2B**
sun Sonne, -n *f.* (3) **4A**
sunburn Sonnenbrand, ⸚e *m.* (3) **1B**
Sunday Sonntag, -e *m.* (1) **2A**
  on Sundays sonntags *adv.* (1) **2A**
sunglasses Sonnenbrille, -n *f.* (2) **1B**
sunny sonnig *adj.* (2) **3A**
sunrise Sonnenaufgang, ⸚e *m.* (3) **4A**
sunset Sonnenuntergang, ⸚e *m.* (3) **4A**
supermarket Supermarkt, ⸚e *m.* (1) **4A**
supposed: to be supposed to sollen *v.* (1) **3B**
surf surfen *v.* (2) **4B**
  to surf the Web im Internet surfen *v.* (2) **4B**
surprise überraschen *v.* (2) **1A**; Überraschung, -en *f.* (1) **1A**
sweater Pullover, - *m.* (2) **1B**
sweatshirt Sweatshirt, -s *n.* (2) **1B**
sweep fegen *v.* (2) **2B**
sweet süß *adj.* (1) **3B**
swim schwimmen *v.* (1) **2B**
swimming pool Schwimmbad, ⸚er *n.* (1) **2B**
Switzerland die Schweiz *f.* (2) **3A**
Swiss schweizerisch, Schweizer *adj.* (3) **2B**; **(person)** Schweizer, - / Schweizerin, -nen *m./f.* (3) **2B**
symptom Symptom, -e *n.* (3) **1B**

<table>
<tr><td>T</td></tr>
</table>

table Tisch, -e *m.* (1) **1B**
  to set the table den Tisch decken (2) **2B**
tablecloth Tischdecke, -n *f.* (1) **4B**
tablet Tablet, -s *n.* (2) **4B**
take nehmen *v.* (1) **2B**
  to take (a class) belegen *v.* (1) **2A**
  to take out the trash den Müll rausbringen (2) **2B**
  to take a shower (sich) duschen *v.* (3) **1A**
  to take off abfliegen *v.* (2) **3B**
talk reden *v.* (2) **1A**
  to talk about erzählen von; sprechen/reden über *v.* (3) **3A**
tall groß *adj.* (1) **3A**
tank top Trägerhemd, -en *n.* (2) **1B**
taste schmecken *v.* (1) **4B**; Geschmack, ⸚e *m.* (1) **4B**
taxi Taxi, -s *n.* (2) **4A**
taxi driver Taxifahrer, - / Taxifahrerin, -nen *m./f.* (3) **3B**
tea Tee, -s *m.* (1) **4B**
teacher Lehrer, - / Lehrerin, -nen *m./f.* (1) **1B**
team Mannschaft, -en *f.* (1) **2B**

teaspoon Teelöffel, - *m.* (1) **4B**
technology Technik *f.* (2) **4B**
  to use technology Technik bedienen *v.* (2) **4B**
telephone Telefon, -e *n.* (2) **4B**
  on the telephone am Telefon (3) **3A**
telephone number Telefonnummer, -n *f.* (3) **3A**
television Fernsehen *n.*
  television (set) Fernseher -*m.* (2) **4B**
tell erzählen *v.* (2) **3A**
  to tell a story about erzählen von *v.* (2) **3A**
temperature Temperatur, -en *f.*
  What's the temperature? Wie warm/kalt ist
    es? (2) **3A**
tennis Tennis *n.* (1) **2B**
tent Zelt, -e *n.* (2) **3B**
ten zehn (1) **2A**
terrific großartig *adj.* (1) **3A**
test Prüfung, -en *f.* (1) **1B**
text message SMS, - *f.* (2) **4B**
textbook Lehrbuch, ¨er *n.*; Schulbuch, ¨er *n.* (1) **1B**
thank danken *v.* (1) **2A**
  Thank you. Danke! (1) **1A**
  Thank you very much. Vielen Dank! (1) **1A**
that das **1A**; dass *conj.* (3) **2A**
the das/der/die (1) **1A**
their ihr *poss. adj.* (1) **3A**
then dann *adv.* (2) **3B**
there da (1) **1A**
  Is/Are there...? Ist/Sind hier...? (1) **1B**;
    Gibt es...? (1) **2B**
  There is/are... Da ist/sind... (1) **1A**; Es
    gibt... (1) **2B**
  there and back hin und zurück (2) **3B**
  over there drüben *adv.* (1) **4A**
therefore also; deshalb *conj.* (3) **1B**
thermometer Thermometer, - *n.* (3) **1B**
these diese *pron.* (2) **4B**
  These are... Das sind... (1) **1A**
they sie *pron.* (1) **1A**
thick dick *adj.* (1) **3A**
thin dünn *adj.* (1) **3A**
thing Sache, -n *f.* (1) **1B**; Ding, -e *n.*
think denken *v.* (2) **1A**
  to think about denken an *v.* (2) **3A**
  to think over überlegen *v.* (1) **4A**
third dritter/dritte/drittes *adj.* (1) **2A**
this das **1A**; dieser/diese/dieses *pron.* (2) **4B**
  This is... Das ist... (1) **1A**
three drei (1) **2A**
through durch *prep.* (1) **3B**
throw werfen *v.* (1) **2B**
  to throw away wegwerfen *v.* (3) **4B**
thunder Donner, - *m.* (2) **3A**
thunderstorm Gewitter, - *n.* (2) **3A**
Thursday Donnerstag, -e *m.* (1) **2A**
  on Thursdays donnerstags *adv.* (1) **2A**
ticket Flugticket, -s *n.* (2) **3B**; Fahrkarte, -n *f.* (2) **4A**
ticket collector Schaffner, - / Schaffnerin,
  -nen *m./f.* (2) **4A**
ticket office Fahrkartenschalter, - *m.* (2) **4A**
tidy ordentlich *adj.* (2) **2B**
tie Krawatte, -n *f.* (2) **1B**
tight eng *adj.* (2) **1B**

time Zeit, -en *f.* (1) **2A**; Mal, -e *n.* (2) **3B**
  for the first/last time zum ersten/letzten
    Mal (2) **3B**
  the first/last time das erste/letzte Mal (2) **3B**
  this time diesmal *adv.* (2) **3B**
  What time is it? Wie spät ist es?; Wie viel Uhr
    ist es? (1) **2A**
times mal (1) **1B**
tip Trinkgeld, -er *n.* (1) **4B**
tired müde *adj.* (1) **3B**
tissue Taschentuch, ¨er *n.* (3) **1B**
to vor *prep.* (1) **2A**; nach; zu *prep.* (1) **4B**; auf,
  an *prep.* (2) **1B**
  (in order) to um...zu (2) **3B**
  to the right/left nach rechts/links (2) **2A**
toast anstoßen *v.* (2) **1A**
toaster Toaster, - *m.* (2) **2B**
today heute *adv.* (1) **2B**
  Today is... Heute ist der... (1) **2A**
  What day is it today? Welcher Tag ist heute? (3) **3A**
toe Zeh, -en *m.* (3) **1A**
together zusammen *adv.* (1) **3A**
toilet Toilette, -n *f.* (2) **2A**
tomato Tomate, -n *f.* (1) **4A**
tomorrow morgen *adv.* (1) **2B**
  the day after tomorrow übermorgen *adv.* (1) **2B**
  tomorrow morning morgen früh (1) **2B**
too zu *adv.* (1) **4A**; auch *adv.* (1) **1A**
tool kit Werkzeug, -e *n.*
tooth Zahn, ¨e *m.* (3) **1A**
toothache Zahnschmerzen *m. pl.* (3) **1B**
toothbrush Zahnbürste, -n *f.* (3) **1A**
toothpaste Zahnpasta (*pl.* Zahnpasten) *f.* (3) **1A**
tornado Tornado, -s *m.* (3) **4A**
toward in Richtung *f.* (3) **2B**
towel Handtuch, ¨er *n.* (3) **1A**
town Stadt, ¨e *f.* (3) **2B**
town hall Rathaus, ¨er *n.* (3) **2A**
toxic waste Giftmüll *m.* (3) **4B**
track Bahnsteig, -e *m.* (2) **4A**
track and field Leichtathletik *f.* (1) **2B**
traffic Verkehr *m.* (2) **4A**
traffic light Ampel, -n *f.* (3) **2B**
train Zug, ¨e *m.* (2) **4A**
transportation Verkehrsmittel, - *n.* (2) **4A**
  public transportation öffentliche
    Verkehrsmittel *n. pl.* (2) **4A**
trash Müll *m.* (2) **2B**
  to take out the trash den Müll rausbringen (2) **2B**
travel reisen *v.* (1) **2A**
travel agency Reisebüro, -s *n.* (2) **3B**
traveler Reisende, -n *m./f.* (2) **3B**
tree Baum, ¨e *m.* (3) **4A**
trendy angesagt *adj.* (2) **1B**
trip Reise, -n *f.* (2) **3B**
truck LKW, -s *m.* (2) **4A**
truck driver LKW-Fahrer, - / LKW-Fahrerin,
  -nen *m./f.* (3) **3B**
trunk Kofferraum, ¨e *m.* (2) **4A**
try probieren *v.* (1) **3B**; versuchen *v.* (2) **3B**
  Give it a try! Probieren Sie mal!
T-shirt T-Shirt, -s *n.* (2) **1B**
Tuesday Dienstag, -e *m.* (1) **2A**
  on Tuesdays dienstags *adv.* (1) **2A**

tuition fee Studiengebühr, -en *f.* (1) **2A**
tuna Thunfisch, -e *m.* (1) **4A**
Turkey die Türkei *f.* (3) **2B**
Turkish (person) Türke, -n / Türkin, -nen *m./f.*
  (3) **2B**; **Turkish (language)** Türkisch *n.* (3) **2B**
turn abbiegen *v.* (3) **2B**
  to turn right/left rechts/links abbiegen *v.* (2) **4A**
  to turn off ausmachen *v.* (2) **4B**; einschalten *v.*
    (3) **4B**
  to turn on anmachen *v.* (2) **4B**; auschalten *v.* (3) **4B**
turning point Wende, -n *f.* (3) **4B**
twelve zwölf (1) **2A**
twenty zwanzig (1) **2A**
twin Zwilling, -e *m.* (1) **3A**
two zwei (1) **2A**

ugly hässlich *adj.* (1) **3A**
umbrella Regenschirm, -e *m.* (2) **3A**
under unter *prep.* (2) **1B**
understand verstehen *v.* (1) **2A**
underwear Unterwäsche *f.* (2) **1B**
undressed: to get undressed sich ausziehen *v.* (3) **1A**
unemployed arbeitslos *adj.* (3) **2A**
unfortunate arm *adj.* (1) **3B**
unfortunately leider *adv.* (1) **4A**
unfurnished unmöbliert *adj.* (2) **2A**
university Universität, -en *f.* (1) **1B**
unpleasant unangenehm *adj.* (1) **3B**
until bis *prep.* (1) **3B**; bis zu *prep.* (3) **2B**
up herauf *adv.* (2) **2A**
  to get up aufstehen *v.* (1) **4A**
  to go up hochgehen *v.* (3) **2B**
USA die USA *pl.*; die Vereinigten Staaten *pl.* (3) **2B**
use benutzen *v.* (2) **4A**; bedienen *v.* (2) **4B**
  to get used to sich gewöhnen an *v.* (3) **1A**
useful nützlich *adj.* (1) **2A**
useless nutzlos *adj.* (1) **2A**

vacancy Zimmer frei *f.* (2) **2A**
vacation Ferien *pl.*; Urlaub, -e *m.* (2) **3B**
  to go on vacation Urlaub machen *v.* (2) **3B**
vacuum staubsaugen *v.* (2) **2B**
vacuum cleaner Staubsauger, - *m.* (2) **2B**
validate entwerten *v.* (2) **4A**
  to validate a ticket eine Fahrkarte
    entwerten *v.* (2) **4A**
valley Tal, ¨er *n.* (3) **4A**
vase Vase, -n *f.* (2) **2A**
vegetables Gemüse *n.* (1) **4A**
verb Verb, -en *n.* (3) **1A**
very sehr *adv.* (1) **3A**
  very well sehr gut (1) **1A**
veterinarian Tierarzt, ¨e / Tierärztin, -nen *m./f.*
  (3) **3B**
visa Visum (*pl.* Visa) *n.* (2) **3B**
visit besuchen *v.* (1) **4A**
vocabulary Wortschatz, ¨e *m.*
volcano Vulkan, -e *m.* (3) **4A**
volleyball Volleyball *m.* (1) **2B**

W

wait warten *v.* (1) **2A**
  to wait for warten auf *v.* (2) **3A**
waiter / waitress Kellner, - / Kellnerin,
  -nen *m./f.* (1) **3B**
  Waiter! Herr Ober! (1) **4B**
wake up aufwachen *v.* (3) **1A**
walk Spaziergang, ⸚e *m.*
  to go for a walk spazieren gehen *v.* (1) **2B**
wall Wand, ⸚e *f.* (2) **1B**
want wollen *v.* (1) **3B**
warm warm *adj.* (3) **2A**
wash waschen *v.* (1) **2B**
  to wash (oneself) sich waschen *v.* (3) **1A**
washing machine Waschmaschine, -n *f.* (2) **2B**
waste Müll *m.* (3) **4B**; Abfall, ⸚e *m.* (3) **4B**
wastebasket Papierkorb, ⸚e *m.* (1) **1B**
watch zuschauen *v.* (1) **4A**; anschauen *v.* (2) **3A**
  to watch television fernsehen *v.* (2) **4B**
water Wasser *n.*
  sparkling water Mineralwasser *n.* (1) **4B**
  still water stilles Wasser *n.* (1) **4B**
water pitcher Wasserkrug, ⸚e *m.* (1) **4B**
waterfall Wasserfall, ⸚e *m.* (3) **4A**
we wir *pron.* (1) **1A**
weak schwach *adj.* (1) **3B**
wear tragen *v.* (1) **2B**
weather Wetter *n.* (2) **3A**
  What's the weather like? Wie ist das Wetter? (2) **3A**
weather report Wetterbericht, -e *m.* (2) **3A**
Web Internet *n.* (2) **4B**
  to surf the Web im Internet surfen *v.* (2) **4B**
Web site Website, -s *f.* (2) **4B**
wedding Hochzeit, -en *f.* (2) **1A**
Wednesday Mittwoch, -e *m.* (1) **2A**
  on Wednesdays mittwochs *adv.* (1) **2A**
week Woche, -n *f.* (1) **2A**
weekend Wochenende, -n *n.* (1) **2A**
weigh wiegen *v.* (2) **4B**
welcome (herzlich) willkommen (1) **1A**
  You're welcome. Gern geschehen! (1) **1A**
well gut *adv.*
  I am (very) well. Mir geht's (sehr) gut. (1) **1A**
  I am not (so) well. Mir geht's nicht (so) gut. (1) **1A**
  Get well! Gute Besserung! (2) **1A**
well-dressed gut gekleidet *adj.* (2) **1B**
well-known bekannt *adj.* (3) **2A**
wet nass *adj.* (3) **4A**
what was *interr.* (1) **2A**
  What is that? Was ist das? (1) **1B**
  What's up? Was geht ab? (1) **1A**
when wann *interr.* (1) **2A**
whenever wenn *conj.* (3) **2A**
where wo *interr.* (1) **2A**
  where from woher *interr.* (1) **2A**
  where to wohin *interr.* (1) **2A**
whether ob *conj.* (3) **2A**
which welcher/welche/welches *interr.* (1) **2A**
white weiß *adj.* (2) **1B**
who wer *interr.* (1) **2A**
  Who is it? Wer ist das? (1) **1B**
whom wen *acc. interr.* (1) **2A**; wem *dat. interr.* (1) **4B**

whose wessen *interr.* (2) **4B**
why warum *interr.* (1) **2A**
widow Witwe, -n *f.* (1) **3A**
widower Witwer, - *m.* (1) **3A**
wife Ehefrau, -en *f.* (1) **3A**
win gewinnen *v.* (1) **2B**
wind energy Windenergie *f.* (3) **4B**
window Fenster, - *n.* (1) **1A**
windshield Windschutzscheibe, -n *f.* (2) **4A**
windshield wiper Scheibenwischer, - *m.* (2) **4A**
windy windig *adj.* (2) **3A**
wine Wein, -e *m.* (1) **4B**
winter Winter, - *m.* (1) **2B**
wipe wischen *v.* (2) **2B**
wise weise *adj.* (1) **3B**
wish wünschen *v.* (3) **1A**
  to wish (for something) sich (etwas)
    wünschen *v.* (3) **1A**
with mit (1) **4B**
withdraw (money) (Geld) abheben *v.* (3) **2A**
within innerhalb *prep.* (2) **4B**
without ohne *prep.* (1) **3B**
woman Frau, -en *f.* (1) **1A**
wonder sich fragen *v.* (3) **1A**
wood Holz *n.* (2) **2B**
wool Wolle *f.* (2) **1B**
work Arbeit, -en *f.* (3) **4B**; arbeiten *v.* (1) **2A**;
  funktionieren *v.* (2) **4B**
  at work auf der Arbeit (3) **3B**
  to work on arbeiten an *v.* (2) **3A**
world Welt, -en *f.* (3) **4B**
worried besorgt *adj.* (1) **3B**
write schreiben *v.* (1) **2A**
  to write to schreiben an *v.* (2) **3A**
  to write to one another sich schreiben *v.* (3) **1A**

Y

year Jahr, -e *n.* (2) **3A**
yellow gelb *adj.* (2) **1B**
yes ja **1A**; (contradicting) doch *adv.* (1) **2B**
yesterday gestern *adv.* (2) **1B**
yet noch *adv.* (1) **4A**
yogurt Joghurt, -s *m.* (1) **4A**
you du/ihr/Sie *pron.* (1) **1A**
young jung *adj.* (1) **3A**; jugendlich *adj.* (3) **2A**
your euer/Ihr *poss. adj.* (1) **3A**
youth hostel Jugendherberge, -n *f.* (2) **3B**

Index

Understanding the Index references

The numbers following each entry can be understood as follows:

(2A) **51** = (Chapter, Lesson) **page**

So, the entry above would be found in Chapter 2, Lesson A, page 51.

About the Authors

Christine Anton, a native of Germany, is Associate Professor of German and Director of the Language Resource Center at Berry College. She received her B.A. in English and German from the Universität Erlangen and her graduate degrees in Germanic Languages and Literatures from the University of North Carolina at Chapel Hill. She has published two books on German realism and German cultural memory of National Socialism, and a number of articles on 19th and 20th century German and Austrian literature, as well as on second language acquisition. Dr. Anton has received several awards for excellence in teaching and was honored by the American Association of Teachers of German with the Duden Award for her "outstanding efforts and achievement in the teaching of German." Dr. Anton previously taught at the State University of New York and the University of North Carolina, Chapel Hill.

Tobias Barske, a native of Bavaria, is an Associate Professor of German and Applied Linguistics at the University of Wisconsin-Stevens Point. He has a Ph.D. in German Applied Linguistics from the University of Illinois at Urbana-Champaign with emphases on language and social interaction as well as language pedagogy. He has also studied at the Universität Regensburg in Germany. Tobias has over 10 years of experience teaching undergraduate and graduate courses at the university level and has earned numerous awards for excellence in teaching.

Megan McKinstry has an M.A. in Germanics from the University of Washington. She is an Assistant Teaching Professor of German Studies and Co-Coordinator for Elementary German at the University of Missouri, where she received the University's "Purple Chalk" teaching award and an award for "Best Online Course." Ms. McKinstry has been teaching for over fifteen years.

Acknowledgments

On behalf of its authors and editors, Vista Higher Learning expresses its sincere appreciation to the teachers nationwide who reviewed materials from **Mosaik**. Their input and suggestions were vitally helpful in forming and shaping the program in its final, published form. Philippe Radelet from Benjamin Franklin High School, Baton Rouge, Louisiana provided a thorough accuracy check.

We also extend a special thank you to the contributing writers of **Mosaik** whose hard work was central to the publication.

Credits

Every effort has been made to trace the copyright holders of the works published herein. If proper copyright acknowledgment has not been made, please contact the publisher and we will correct the information in future printings.

Photography and Art Credits

All images © Vista Higher Learning unless otherwise noted. All Fotoroman photos provided by Xavier Roy.

Cover: Thorsten Frisch/500px.

Front Matter (SE): xiii: (l) Digital Vision/Getty Images; (r) Andres Rodriguez/Big Stock Photo; **xiv:** Johannes Simon/Getty Images; **xv:** (l) Konstantin Chagin/123RF; (r) Tyler Olson/Shutterstock; **xvi:** PH3/Patrick Hoffmann/WENN/Newscom.

Front Matter (TE): T11: Jean Glueck/Media Bakery; **T29:** Monkey Business Images/Bigstock; **T30:** Simmi Simons/iStockphoto; **T31:** Getty RF.

Chapter 1: Xavier Roy; **3:** 36clicks/iStockphoto; **4:** Paula Diez; **8:** Laurence Mouton/Media Bakery; **9:** (l) Michaeljung/iStockphoto; (tr) Sashagala/Shutterstock; (br) Imac/Alamy; **13:** (tl) Anne Loubet; (tm) Igor Tarasov/Fotolia; (tr) Jack Hollingsworth/Corbis; (ml) Gualtiero Boffi/Shutterstock; (mml) Tupungato/Shutterstock; (mmr) Nicole Winchell; (mr) Tabitha Patrick/iStockphoto; (b) Eugenio Marongiu/Shutterstock; **15:** (tl) Lazar Mihai-Bogdan/Shutterstock; (tr) Vanessa Bertozzi; (ml) Nicole Winchell; (mm) Anne Loubet; (mr) Nicole Winchell; (bl) Gudrun Hommel; (bm) Nicole Winchell; (br) Paula Diez; **16:** Auremar/Fotolia; **20:** Richard Foreman/iStockphoto; **28:** Woodapple/Fotolia; **29:** (l) ChristArt/Fotolia; (tr) Arnd Wiegmann/RTR/Newscom; (br) Kyle Monk/Blend Images/Getty Images; **36:** (all) Nicole Winchell; **38:** Sarah2/Shutterstock; **39:** Monkey Business Images/Shutterstock **40:** (t) Shishic/iStockphoto; (m) PeterSVETphoto/Shutterstock; (b) Hollandse Hoogte/Redux; **41:** (tl),Vaclav Volrab/Shutterstock; (tr) Steve Raymer/Corbis; (m) CrazyD/iStockphoto; (b) Horst Galuschka/DPA/Corbis; **44:** Chris Schmidt/iStockphoto; **45:** StockLite/Shutterstock.

Chapter 2: 47: Xavier Roy; **50:** Chris Schmidt/iStockphoto; **54:** Sabine Lubenow/AGE Fotostock; **55:** (l) Heinz-Peter Bader/Reuters/Newscom; (tr) Ingolf Pompe/AGE Fotostock; (br) Laviana/Shutterstock; **56:** (l) Nicole Winchell; (r) Martin Bernetti; **58:** Nicole Winchell; **66:** (left col: t) IDP Manchester Airport Collection/Alamy; (left col: ml) Javier Larrea/AGE Fotostock; (left col: mm) Noam/Fotolia; (left col: mr) Martín Bernetti; (left col: bl) Ana Cabezas Martín; (left col: bm) Tetra Images/Alamy; (left col: br) Jacob Wackerhausen/iStockphoto; (right col) Martinap/Shutterstock; **74:** Roland Syba/Shutterstock; **75:** (tl) Imagebroker.net/SuperStock; (tr) Imago Sportfotodienst/Imago/Moritz Müller/Newscom; (m) Daniel Karmann/Picture-Alliance/DPA/AP Images; (b) Allan Grosskrueger/Shutterstock; **78:** (t) Nicole Winchell; (ml) Polka Dot Images/JupiterImages; (mm) Martín Bernetti; (mr) Robert Michael/Media Bakery; (bl) Losevsky Photo and Video/Shutterstock; (bm) Gudrun Hommel; (br) Nicole Winchell; **83:** Janne Hämäläinen/Shutterstock; **84:** Auremar/Shutterstock; **85:** (tl) Ilyashenko Oleksiy/Shutterstock; (tm) Martín Bernetti; (tr) Carlos Gaudier; (bl) Karens4/Big Stock Photo; (bml) Val Thoermer/Big Stock Photo; (bmr) Ben Blankenburg/Corbis; (br) Danny Warren/iStockphoto; **86:** (l) Neustockimages/iStockphoto; (r) JupiterImages; **87:** (tl) Martín Bernetti; (tm) Monkey Business/Fotolia; (tr) Katie Wade; (bl) Brand X Pictures/Fotosearch; (bml) Ana Cabezas Martín; (bmr) Anne Loubet; (br) Harry Neave/Fotolia; **88:** (tl) Gudrun Hommel; (tr) Noppasinw/Fotolia; (ml) Nicole Winchell; (mr) VVO/Shutterstock; (b) Bettmann/Corbis; **89:** (tl) Riccardo Sala/Alamy; (tr) Lexan/123RF; (m) Akg-images/Newscom; (b) Philip Lange/Shutterstock; **90–91:** Jorg Greuel/Getty Images; **92:** Jack Hollingsworth/Cardinal/Corbis; **93:** (t) Paylessimages/123RF; (b) Nadezda Verbenko/Shutterstock.

Chapter 3: 95: Xavier Roy; **102:** Westend61/Getty Images; **103:** (tl) John Dowland/Getty Images; (tr) Michael Gottschalk/AFP/Getty Images; (b) Wrangler/Shutterstock; **105:** George Olsson/iStockphoto; **106:** (tl) Martín Bernetti; (tm) Ray Levesque; (tr) Martín Bernetti; (bl) Martín Bernetti; (bml) David N. Madden/Shutterstock; (bmr) Martín Bernetti; (br) Prism68/Shutterstock; **112:** (t) Aspen Stock/AGE Fotostock; (ml) Martín Bernetti; (mm) Carlos Gaudier; (mr) Alexander Rochau/Fotolia; (bl) Imag'In Pyrénées/Fotolia; (bm) Pixtal/AGE Fotostock; (br) Raberry/Big Stock Photo; **116:** (top row: tl) José Blanco; (top row: tm) Michael Jung/iStockphoto; (top row: tr) Anne Loubet; (top row: bl) Rasmus Rasmussen/iStockphoto (top row: bml) Ana Cabezas Martín; (top row: bmr) Javier Larrea/AGE Fotostock; (top row: br) Martín Bernetti; (bottom row: l) Vanessa Nel/Shutterstock; (bottom row: r) Photoinjection/Shutterstock; **120:** OneInchPunch/Shutterstock; **121:** (l) Tatiana Lebedeva/Shutterstock; (r) David Fernandez/EPA/Newscom; (b) Sonya Etchison/Shutterstock; **123:** Anne Loubet; **125:** Minerva Studio /Shutterstock; **131:** Nicole Winchell; **132:** (left col: tl) Lichtmeister/Shutterstock; (left col: tr) Gudrun Hommel; (left col: bl) Martín Bernetti; (left col: br) Gudrun Hommel; (right col) Anne Loubet; **134:** (tl) Andre Jenny/Alamy; (tr) ShyMan/iStockphoto; (m) RosaIreneBetancourt 3/Alamy; (b) Frymire Archive/Alamy; **135:** (tl) Aspen Rock/

Shutterstock; (tr) Ruggles Susan/AGE Fotostock; (m) MWaits/Shutterstock; (b) Sergey Peterman/Shutterstock; **136:** Aleksandar Mijatovic/ Shutterstock; **137:** Serg64/Shutterstock; **138:** Gudrun Hommel; **139:** Gudrun Hommel.

Chapter 4: 141: Xavier Roy; **143:** (tl) VHL; (tr) Smit/Shutterstock; (bl) Susan Schmitz/Shutterstock; (bml) Smileus/Shutterstock; (bmr) Vanessa Bertozzi; (br) Vanessa Bertozzi; **144:** (tl) Nancy Camley; (tr) Vanessa Bertozzi; (bl) Vanessa Bertozzi; (bml) Nicole Winchell; (bmr) Monkey Business Images/Shutterstock; (br) Martín Bernetti; **148:** Ernst Wrba/Image Broker/Newscom; **149:** (l) Karandaev/ Fotolia; (r) Ted Soqui/Corbis; (b) StockPixstore/Fotolia; **151:** Tyler Olson/Shutterstock; **153:** (tl) Rafael Rios; (tr) Steve Debenport/ iStockphoto; (bl) Nicole Winchell; (bml) Oscar Artavia Solano; (bmr) Anne Loubet; (br) MAEWJPHO/Shutterstock; **155:** (tl) Moori/Big Stock Photo; (tr) Alexey Tkachenko/iStockphoto; (bl) Martín Bernetti; (bml) Pixtal/AGE Fotostock; (bmr) Martín Bernetti; (br) Gudrun Hommel; **157:** Javier Larrea/AGE Fotostock; **158:** (tl) Pixart/Big Stock Photo; (tm) Pictrough/Big Stock Photo; (tr) Monkey Business Images/Shutterstock; (bl) PhotoAlto/Alamy; (bml) Nicole Winchell; (bmr) Janet Dracksdorf; (br) Sonyae/Big Stock Photo; **159:** Haveseen/Shutterstock; **163:** (hot dog) Sapik/Shutterstock; (bread) Kheng Guan Toh/Shutterstock; (pie) Notkoo/Shutterstock; **164:** (tl) Katie Wade; (tm) Katie Wade; (tr) Stocksnapp/Big Stock Photo; (bl) Barry Gregg/Corbis; (bml) Carlos Hernandez/Media Bakery; (bmr) Jack Puccio/iStockphoto; (br) Ruth Black/Shutterstock; **168:** Jean-Pierre Lescourret/Corbis; **169:** (tl) Mimmo Lobefaro/Alamy; (tr) Stefan Liewehr; (b) Norbert Enker/Laif/Redux; **175:** (tl) Alistair Scott/Alamy; (bl) Paula Díez; (bml) Photo courtesy of www.Tahiti-Tourisme.com; (bmr) Gudrun Hommel; (br) Andersen Ross/Blend Images/Corbis; **176:** (t) Gudrun Hommel; (ml) Subbotina Anna/ Big Stock Photo; (mm) Willmetts/Big Stock Photo; (mr) LepasR/Big Stock Photo; (bl) Jacek Chabraszewski/Fotolia; (bm) Karandaev/ Fotolia; (br) Nicole Winchell; **177:** YinYang/iStockphoto; **178:** (t) Tupungato/123RF; (ml) Michal Durinik/Shutterstock; (mr) Phil Emmerson/Shutterstock; (b) Catherine Lane/iStockphoto; **179:** (tl) Mac99/iStockphoto; (tr) Nikonaft/Crestock/Masterfile; (m) Bettmann/ Corbis; (b) Brian Kersey/UPI/Newscom; **180:** OPIS Zagreb/Shutterstock; **181:** PavleMarjanovic/Shutterstock; **182:** Webphotographeer/ iStockphoto; **183:** Wavebreakmedia/Shutterstock.

Television Credits

21: Courtesy of Deutsche Bahn AG.

67: Courtesy of Technische Universität Berlin. First broadcast 2008. Technische Universität Berlin disclaims all liability for any information appearing herein that may be outdated or incorrect. Please view Technische Universität Berlin's website for the most current information.

113: Courtesy of Privatmolkerei Bauer GmbH & Co. KG.

161: Mit Filmproduktion und ggfs. sonstigen Dritten abzustimmen, die Rechte haben, z.B.: Agency: Jung von Matt, Film production: Film Deluxe GmbH.